Lecture Notes in Computer Science 1474

Edited by G. Goos, J. Hartmanis and J. van Leeuwen

Springer

Berlin
Heidelberg
New York
Barcelona
Budapest
Hong Kong
London
Milan
Paris
Singapore
Tokyo

Frank Mueller   Azer Bestavros (Eds.)

Languages, Compilers, and Tools for Embedded Systems

ACM SIGPLAN Workshop LCTES'98
Montreal, Canada, June 19-20, 1998
Proceedings

Springer

Series Editors

Gerhard Goos, Karlsruhe University, Germany
Juris Hartmanis, Cornell University, NY, USA
Jan van Leeuwen, Utrecht University, The Netherlands

Volume Editors

Frank Mueller
Humboldt Universität Berlin, Institut für Informatik
Unter den Linden 6, D-10099 Berlin, Germany
E-mail: mueller@informatik.hu-berlin.de

Azer Bestavros
Boston University, Department of Computer Science
111 Cummington Street, Boston, MA 02215, USA
E-mail: best@bu.edu

Cataloging-in-Publication data applied for

Die Deutsche Bibliothek - CIP-Einheitsaufnahme

Languages, compilers, and tools for embedded systems :
proceedings / ACM SIGPLAN Workshop LCTES '98, Montreal,
Canada, June 19 - 20, 1998. Frank Mueller ; Azer Bestavros (ed.). -
Berlin ; Heidelberg ; New York ; Barcelona ; Budapest ; Hong Kong
; London ; Milan ; Paris ; Singapore ; Tokyo : Springer, 1998
    (Lecture notes in computer science ; Vol. 1474)
    ISBN 3-540-65075-X

CR Subject Classification (1991): D.4.7, C.3, D.3, D.2

ISSN 0302-9743
ISBN 3-540-65075-X Springer-Verlag Berlin Heidelberg New York

Typesetting: Camera-ready by author
SPIN 10638685   06/3142 – 5 4 3 2 1 0   Printed on acid-free paper

Preface

From 19th to the 20th of June the ACM SIGPLAN 1998 Workshop on Languages, Compilers, and Tools for Embedded Systems (LCTES'98) was held in Montreal, Canada. LCTES'98 is a reincarnation of the Workshop on Languages, Compilers, and Tools for Real-Time Systems, which was held three times in previous years. The change of focus from real-time systems to embedded systems came as a response to the growing importance of embedded systems. Embedded systems research is rapidly growing since the number of embedded processors (and thereby installed systems) already exceeds the number of general-purpose processors (personal computers and workstations) today. The shift of focus from real-time systems to embedded systems also reflects the more general nature of embedded systems, which encompasses a multitude of aspects in addition to real-time systems. These aspects include embedded languages, memory restrictions, special-purpose processors and peripheral devices, and power consumption, just to name a few.

In the past, custom kernels, non-standard languages, vendor-specific device interfaces and custom hardware were often employed for building embedded systems. Today, there is an emerging trend to exploit off-the-shelf hardware and to enhance standard software to meet embedded requirements, ranging from real-time extensions of common programming languages and operating systems to appropriate tools for embedded programmers.

For both real-time and embedded systems, electrical engineers and computer scientists are active in addressing many similar problems, but with different backgrounds and approaches. LCTES is intended to expose researchers and developers from the areas of embedded systems and real-time systems to relevant work and interesting problems in the other area and provide a forum where they can interact. The range of topics covered by LCTES reaches from experimental work over commercial systems to applied theory.

LCTES'98 featured two invited talks and presentations of seven long and twelve short refereed papers. The papers were selected out of 54 submissions. Twelve referees prepared written multiple reviews for each submission. The recommendations of the referees determined an initial set of papers selected for acceptance. The members of the program committee were then given the option to resolve differences in opinion for the papers they refereed based on the written reviews. After the resolution process, the 19 papers included in the workshop proceedings were selected for presentation and publication.

Summary of the Papers

The accurate estimation of Worst Case Execution Time (WCET) plays an important role in the design of correct and efficient embedded software. WCET is typically overestimated because of insufficient compiler path analysis and timing analysis. Existing methods require annotations or static path analysis, which establish upper bounds on loop iterations and identify some infeasible paths. Static timing analysis are too simple; fixed penalties are usually charged by cache misses and pipeline hazards. In their paper entitled "Integrating path and timing analysis using instruction-level simulation techniques", Thomas Lundqvist and Per Stenström of Chalmers University of Technology, Sweden, propose a new method to estimate WCET on contemporary processors with complex pipelines and multilevel hierarchies. The new method integrates path analysis and timing analysis based on an instruction level simulator, which handles unknown data values. The simulator automatically performs path analysis while simulating the program. For some classes of programs, this approach has specific advantages compared to other approaches as it naturally integrates path and timing analysis. The WCET predictions can be very precise.

Another important functionality of compilers targeted at embedded software systems is the prediction of cache performance. In their paper entitled "On predicting data cache behavior for real-time systems", Christian Ferdinand and Reinhard Wilhelm of the University of the Saarland, Germany, present analysis techniques for determining memory locations within a cache that do not get replaced during the program's execution. This gives an upper bound on the number of cache misses. The technique used is similar to dataflow analysis to determine the fixed point state of the cache. This state is analyzed to provide the memory blocks that would never get replaced. To do this, the authors present representations for the components of the cache and transfer functions that map cache states based on memory references.

In their paper entitled "Automatic accurate time-bound analysis for high-level languages", Yanhong A. Liu and Gustavo Gomez of Indiana University, USA, present an approach to automate timing analysis and tuning of embedded programs. This involves initially transforming the program functions to add timing functions at the source level. These are optimized symbolically with respect to specific values of the input parameters. There are some further transformations proposed to improve accuracy, in the presence of conditionals. An implementation has been carried out for a subset of the Scheme language and a comparison of calculated and measured execution times for some programs is presented.

The construction of execution environments, in which real-time and non-real-time application components coexist is important. In their paper "Extending RT-Linux to support flexible hard real-time systems with optional components", A. Terrasa, A. Espinosa and A. Garcia-Fornes, of the Universidad Politecnica de Valencia, Spain, present their RT-Linux solution to this problem, which is based on the well-known partitioning of a task into an initial part, an optional part, and a final part.

Another aspect of cache behavior that impacts real-time embedded software systems is cache reloading. In their paper entitled "Limited preemptible scheduling to embrace cache memory in real-time systems", Sheayun Lee et. al. of Seoul National University, Korea, propose a technique that allows preemption only at certain points in tasks scheduled using fixed priority preemptive scheduling. By analyzing cache behavior, these preemption points are chosen to minimize cache reload times when resuming the preempted process. In order to determine the useful cache blocks in a program, all tasks are considered in isolation. However, due to periodic tasks or due to shared code, there may be cache blocks which are useful for other tasks or other incarnations of the same task.

Distributed systems are entering the stage of real-time systems. In "A uniform reliable multicast protocol with guaranteed response times", Laurent George and Pascale Minet from INRIA, France, extend a well-known broadcast algorithm to a multicast protocol in a distributed environment. Their goal includes tolerating failures of nodes and omissions of messages while still guaranteeing end-to-end response times. The work assumes a variant of multiprocessor earliest-deadline-first scheduling under a number of restrictions.

An important functionality for embedded software designers is the ability to fine-tune the timing behavior of their programs. In their paper entitled "A tool to assist in fine-tuning and debugging embedded real-time systems", Gaurav Arora and David B. Stewart of the University of Maryland, USA, present a tool that can be used late in the development cycle of embedded software to adjust the system to meet its timing requirements. The tool takes data sampled from actual executions (via some monitor tool) and correlates it with the specification and/or the modeled behavior. The tool enables adjustments in the code/timing parameters to be specified and effects thereof to be predicted.

The use of distributed architectures for embedded systems has been hampered by the unavailability of appropriate programming environments for such architectures. In their paper entitled "Debugging distributed implementations of modal process systems", Ken Hines and Gaetano Borriello of the University of Washington in Seattle, USA, discuss some of the debugging techniques enabled by the modal process model of Chou and Borriello. This modal process model enables the use of distributed architectures for embedded systems because it alleviates the problem of additional costs in their design, implementation, and maintenance.

The advent of the Java Virtual Machine promises many benefits to embedded software development. In their paper entitled "Using Inferno to run Java on small devices", C. F. Yurkoski, L. R. Rau, and B. K. Ellis, of Bell Labs, USA, present an implementation of Java on the Inferno operating system. Inferno is similar to Java in that it uses a virtual machine for its basic program execution engine. However, the Inferno VM is superior to the Java VM from a performance viewpoint – and thus more suitable for embedded systems. In this paper, the authors discuss a variety of approaches that were considered for supporting Java on Dis (the Inferno VM). The approach finally taken was to translate Java bytecode to Dis instructions.

The work of Michael Weiss et. al. of the Open Group Research Institute, USA, takes an alternative approach to Java bytecode compilation, ensuring compatibility and the possibility of dynamic class loading. In their paper entitled "TurboJ, a Java bytecode-to-native compiler", the authors present a bytecode to native code compiler for Java (JVM code). Their approach is to coexist with the JVM, allowing JVM bytecode and native code to be executed. They translate class files into C files and new versions of class files, thereby performing a variety of optimizations. The C files are compiled and linked into a shared library to be used by the JVM at run time.

Another approach to minimizing the timing unpredictability caused by cache systems is presented in a paper entitled "Cache-sensitive pre-runtime scheduling", by Daniel Kästner and Stephan Thesing of the University of the Saarland, Germany. The paper presents an interesting technique that attempts to avoid switching between tasks that have incompatible cache contents. The paper presents an integration of cache-behavior prediction into a pre-runtime scheduling schema. Tasks are split into segments. The static cache-analysis predicts (interprets) the cache behavior of every segment which is used in the defined scheduling algorithm.

Recently, dynamic reactive systems have been studied where tasks are only triggered by external events. The work titled "Priority assignment for embedded reactive real-time systems" by Felice Balarin from Cadence Berkeley Labs, USA, presents a theoretical framework to assign priorities to precedence-related tasks. It extends an existing optimal priority assignment algorithm to limit the number of possible priority orderings examined for an optimal solution – the limit is reduced from an exponential function in the number of tasks, to a quadratic.

Scheduling and schedulability analysis are key issues for real-time, embedded computing systems, especially when the deadlines imposed on processes are hard. In their paper entitled "Mapping an embedded hard real-time systems SDL specification to an analyzable task network – A case study", Thomas Kolloch and Georg Färber of TU München, Germany, present a method to transform an SDL specification of a system into a precedence graph that can be analyzed for real-time schedulability. It presents a mine-control system as a case study to illustrate the process.

The deadlines imposed on embedded system processes are often specified to guarantee specific end-to-end delays. In their paper entitled "End-to-end optimization in heterogeneous distributed real-time systems", Seonho Choi of Bowie State University, USA, describes a method to merge a bunch of scheduling tests for local systems (CPUs and networks) into a big end-to-end schedulability test in such a way that a linear programming optimization algorithm can be used to find some optimal local/intermediate deadlines.

Compilers and tools developed for engineering embedded systems must rely on a canonical description of the underlying machinery to be able to provide meaningful analysis (*e.g.*, timing and schedulability analysis). Toward that goal, the paper entitled "Machine descriptions to build tools for embedded systems", by Norman Ramsey and Jack W. Davidson of the University of Virginia Charlottesville, USA, presents techniques for specifying descriptions of machines that can be used by a variety of tools. These tools include compilers, simulators, assemblers, linkers, debuggers, and profilers. The authors describe in detail the notation used for representing machine instructions, registers, memory, etc.

Compiler optimizations for embedded systems often aim at goals that differ from those for general-purpose architectures. In "Non-local instruction scheduling with limited code growth" by Keith D. Cooper and Philip J. Schielke from Rice University, USA, two techniques for global instruction scheduling without increasing the code size are presented. One technique is novel, the other is an extension of earlier work (with a counterexample for the previous method). The methods are applied (via simulation) to VLIW architectures to show that 6–7% execution time can be saved and the code size can be reduced by 11%.

Embedded systems are typically subjected to stringent constraints on memory size. Thus, techniques and tools that assist in the partitioning and overlaying of data structures to minimize memory needs are pivotal for such limited-memory systems. In their paper entitled "An efficient data partitioning method for limited memory embedded systems", Anantharaman Sundaram and Santosh Pande of the University of Cincinnati, USA, propose a framework for efficient data partitioning of arrays on limited memory embedded systems based on the concept of footprint, which is associated with array references in programs. The idea behind footprinting is to partition arrays into local and remote sections of memory. The main goal is to place the data that is referenced most frequently in the local memory to minimize the number of remote references.

In their paper entitled "A design environment for counterflow pipeline synthesis", Bruce R. Childers and Jack W. Davidson of the University of Virginia, USA, outline a hardware/software codesign approach for special purpose embedded architectures. First, the kernel (*i.e.*, the part associated with high execution frequency) of an application is identified, then a search in the design space of the pipeline is performed to determine the number/functionality of stages. The intent is to optimize the timing of the pipeline for this piece of code given timings for each functional unit. Heuristics are used to guide the search by taking data dependencies and timings into account. Results show a 1.3 to 2 times speedup over comparable general-purpose designs.

Embedded systems use special-purpose operating systems, *e.g.*, micro kernels with limited, application-specific functionality and fast response to events. The paper titled "Efficient user-level I/O in the ARX real-time operating system" by Yangmin Seo, Jungkeun Park, and Seongsoo Hong from Seoul National University, Korea, discusses a variation on the implementation of UNIX signals in the ARX real-time operating system. The focus is on propagating kernel-level interrupts to user space efficiently.

Workshop History and Future

LCTES was preceded by three workshops on Languages, Compilers, and Tools for Real-Time Systems (LCT-RTS). The proceedings of the previous workshops are available online. In addition, the final program with links to the authors of the current workshop (LCTES'98) is also online. Finally, the next LCTES workshop is currently being planned for 1999, and online information will be made available during the Fall of 1998.

http://www.cs.indiana.edu/~liu/lctes99/
    LCTES 1999 Call for Papers (Atlanta, Georgia, USA)

http://www.informatik.hu-berlin.de/~mueller/lctes98
    LCTES 1998 Program (Montreal, Quebec, Canada)

http://www.cs.pitt.edu/~gupta/lct-rts97.html
    LCT-RTS 1997 Online Proceedings (Las Vegas, Nevada, USA)

http://www.cs.umd.edu/projects/TimeWare/sigplan95
    LCT-RTS 1995 Online Proceedings (La Jolla, California, USA)

http://www.cs.umd.edu/users/pugh/sigplan_realtime_workshop/lct-rts94
    LCT-RTS 1994 Online Proceedings (Orlando, Florida, USA)

LCTES Program Committee

- Gul Agha, University of Illinois, USA

- Azer Bestavros, Boston University, USA

- Rajiv Gupta, University of Pittsburgh, USA

- John Gough, Queensland University of Technology, Australia

- Wolfgang Halang, University of Hagen, Germany

- Annie Liu, Indiana University, USA

- Thomas Marlowe, Seton Hall University, USA

- Frank Mueller, Humboldt University Berlin, Germany

- Manas Saksena, Concordia University, Canada

- Andy Wellings, University of York, UK

- David Whalley, Florida State University, USA

- Reinhard Wilhelm, University of the Saarland, Germany

Acknowledgments

The workshop chairs would like to acknowledge the following people:

- the invited speakers, Bran Selic and Marc Campbell, for their voluntary contributions to the workshop;

- Manas Saksena for his local support;

- Richard Gerber and Manas Saksena for their support of the workshop program;

- Alfred Hofmann for his work as a contact person to Springer LNCS;

- Thomas Ball for his programs to facilitate the review process;

- Jack Davidson and the ACM crew, Donna Baglio, Carole Mann, Judy Osteller, and David Mann, for their organizational support;

- the ACM SIGPLAN executive committee for their endorsement of LCTES;

- and last but not least the eager members of the program committee and the anonymous external reviewers.

The Co-Chairs,

June 1998   Frank Mueller and Azer Bestavros

Table of Contents

Refereed Papers

Integrating Path and Timing Analysis Using Instruction-Level Simulation
Techniques 1
Thomas Lundqvist and Per Stenström

On Predicting Data Cache Behavior for Real-Time Systems 16
Christian Ferdinand and Reinhard Wilhelm

Automatic Accurate Time-Bound Analysis for High-Level Languages 31
Yanhong A. Liu and Gustavo Gomez

Extending RT-Linux to Support Flexible Hard Real-Time Systems with Optional
Components 41
A. Terrasa, A. Espinosa and A. García-Fornes

Limited Preemptible Scheduling to Embrace Cache Memory in Real-Time Systems 51
Sheayun Lee, Chang-Gun Lee, Minsuk Lee, Sang Lyul Min and Chong Sang Kim

A Uniform Reliable Multicast Protocol with Guaranteed Response Times 65
Laurent George and Pascale Minet

A Tool to Assist in Fine-Tuning and Debugging Embedded Real-Time Systems . 83
Gaurav Arora and David B. Stewart

Debugging Distributed Implementations of Modal Process Systems 98
Ken Hines and Gaetano Borriello

Using Inferno™ to Execute Java™ on small devices 108
C. F. Yurkoski, L. R. Rau and B. K. Ellis

TurboJ, a Java Bytecode-to-Native Compiler 119
Michael Weiss, François de Ferrière, Bertrand Delsart, Christian Fabre,
Frederick Hirsch, E. Andrew Johnson, Vania Joloboff, Fridtjof Siebert and
Xavier Spengler

Cache-Sensitive Pre-runtime Scheduling 131
Daniel Kästner and Stephan Thesing

Priority Assignment for Embedded Reactive Real-Time Systems 146
Felice Balarin

Mapping an Embedded Hard Real-Time Systems SDL Specification to an
Analyzable Task Network - A Case Study 156
Thomas Kolloch and Georg Färber

Efficient User-Level I/O in the ARX Real-Time Operating System 166
Yangmin Seo, Jungkeun Park and Seongsoo Hong

Machine Descriptions to Build Tools for Embedded Systems 176
Norman Ramsey and Jack W. Davidson

Non-local Instruction Scheduling with Limited Code Growth 193
Keith D. Cooper and Philip J. Schielke

An Efficient Data Partitioning Method for Limited Memory Embedded Systems . 208
Sundaram Anantharaman and Santosh Pande

A Design Environment for Counterflow Pipeline Synthesis 223
Bruce R. Childers and Jack W. Davidson

End-to-End Optimization in Heterogeneous Distributed Real-Time Systems . . . 235
Seonho Choi

Invited Talks

Using UML for Modeling Complex Real-Time Systems 250
Bran Selic

Evaluating ASIC, DSP, and RISC Architectures for Embedded Applications . . . 261
Marc Campbell

Integrating Path and Timing Analysis Using Instruction-Level Simulation Techniques

Thomas Lundqvist and Per Stenström

Department of Computer Engineering
Chalmers University of Technology
SE–412 96 Göteborg, Sweden
{thomasl,pers}@ce.chalmers.se

Abstract. Previously published methods for estimation of the worst-case execution time on contemporary processors with complex pipelines and multi-level memory hierarchies result in overestimations owing to insufficient path and/or timing analysis. This paper presents a new method that integrates path and timing analysis to address these limitations. First, it is based on instruction-level architecture simulation techniques and thus has a potential to perform arbitrarily detailed timing analysis of hardware platforms. Second, by extending the simulation technique with the capability of handling unknown input data values, it is possible to exclude infeasible (or false) program paths in many cases, and also calculate path information, such as bounds on number of loop iterations, without the need for annotating the programs. Finally, in order to keep the number of program paths to be analyzed at a manageable level, we have extended the simulator with a path-merging strategy. This paper presents the method and particularly evaluates its capability to exclude infeasible paths based on seven benchmark programs.

1   Introduction

Static estimation of the worst-case execution time (WCET) has been identified as an important problem in the design of systems for time-critical applications. One reason is that most task scheduling techniques assume that such estimations are known before run-time to schedule the application tasks so that imposed timing constraints, e.g. deadlines, are met at run-time.

The WCET of a program is defined by the program path that takes the longest time to execute regardless of input data and initial system state. Ideally, a WCET estimation method should take as input a program and estimate a tight upper-bound on the actual WCET for a given hardware platform. There are two important sources to overestimations of the WCET. First, the estimation technique may encounter program paths that can never be executed regardless of the input data, usually referred to as *infeasible* (or false) program paths. Second, the timing model of the hardware platform may introduce pessimism because of simplifying timing assumptions.

The first problem can be addressed by requiring that the programmer provides path annotations [14] which clearly is both time-consuming and error-prone. A more attractive method is to automatically detect infeasible paths through static *path analysis methods* [1, 3]. As for the second problem, several *timing analysis* approaches have been proposed that statically estimate the execution time of a given path by taking into account the effects of, e.g., pipeline stalls and cache misses [5, 7–10, 13, 16]. Unfortunately, since these timing analysis approaches typically charge fixed penalties caused by cache misses and pipeline hazards, they have difficulties to take into account the timing effect of dynamic interactions such as resource contention in the hardware platforms caused by buffering of instructions and memory requests. More seriously, no study has shown how timing analysis methods can be integrated with path analysis methods to relieve the programmer from the burden of identifying and excluding infeasible paths from the analysis.

In this paper we present a new approach to WCET estimation that integrates path analysis with accurate timing analysis. Our WCET estimation method achieves this goal by (1) using instruction-level simulation techniques [12, 17] that conceptually simulate *all* feasible paths on arbitrarily detailed timing models of the hardware platform; (2) by reducing the number of infeasible paths by extending architectural simulation techniques to handle unknown input data; and (3) by calculating, e.g., bounds on number of loop iterations with no need for making annotations for statically known bounds.

A practical limitation of the method in its basic form is that the number of paths to simulate can easily be prohibitive, especially in loop constructs. We have therefore extended the architecture simulation method with a path-merging approach that manages to bound the number of simulated paths in a loop to just a few paths. This merging strategy reduces the number of simulated paths drastically and makes the approach useful for realistically sized programs. We outline how the method can be applied to pipelined processors with instruction and data caches and present how the merging strategy is implemented to encounter the worst-case effects of these features.

The next three sections are devoted to describing our method focusing on the basic simulation approach in Section 2, the WCET algorithm in Section 3 and how detailed timing models of architectural features are integrated into the method in Section 4. An evaluation of the method focusing on the path analysis of seven test programs is presented in Section 5. In Section 6, we discuss the potential of the method along with its weaknesses in the context of previous work in this area before we conclude in Section 7.

2 The Approach

Consider programs for which the WCET is statically decidable; i.e., all possible execution paths in the program are finite in length. For example, bounds on number of iterations in loops are known before run-time, although they might be difficult to determine due to limitations in compiler analysis methods. Second, for the time being, we will consider processors with fixed instruction execution times although our method is applicable to arbitrary complex processor architectures with associated memory hierarchies which we show in Section 4. Given these assumptions, WCET could be conceptually determined by identifying the feasible path through the program with the longest execution time.

Instruction-level architectural simulation techniques have now matured so that the execution time of a program run on complex processor architectures can be accurately determined with a reasonable simulation efficiency [12, 17]. The advantages of using architectural simulation techniques are twofold. First, it is possible to make arbitrarily accurate estimations of the execution time of a program, given a combination of input data. Second, and presumably more importantly, when a given path through the program has been simulated, all input data independent dependencies will be resolved.

We first describe how we have extended traditional instruction-level simulation to automate the path analysis in Section 2.1. Then, in Section 2.2 we discuss some performance issues with the basic approach and how they are addressed.

2.1 Path analysis using instruction-level simulation techniques

Instruction-level simulation techniques assume that input data is known and therefore only analyze a single path through the program associated with this input data. To find the WCET of a program using this approach, however, the program would have to be run with all possible combinations of input data which is clearly not feasible. Our approach is instead to simulate all paths through the program and in this process exclude the paths that are not possible regardless of input data. To do this, we have extended traditional instruction-level simulation techniques with the capability to handle unknown data, using an element denoted *unknown*. Then the semantics for each data-manipulating instruction is extended to correctly perform arithmetics with the unknown data values. Examples of the extended semantics for some common instruction types can be seen in Table 1.

The load and stores need special treatment, since the reference address used may be *unknown*. For loads, this results in an *unknown* being loaded into a register. For stores, however, an unknown address can modify an arbitrary memory location. Therefore, the correct action would be to assign the value *unknown* to all memory locations to capture the worst-case situation. This is of course a major limitation. For the time being, we will assume that all addresses are statically known. However, we will discuss efficient solutions to overcome this limitation later in Section 2.2.

The semantics for a conditional branch is also special. When a conditional branch whose branch condition is *unknown* is encountered, both paths must be simulated. To understand how this is used to automate path analysis, consider the program in Figure 1 which sums values in the upper-right triangle of matrix *b*. In the beginning of the simulation, the data values in matrix *b* are treated as unknown input and all elements are assigned the value *unknown*. The boolean values in matrix *m* are considered known.

Table 1. Extended semantics of instructions.

Instruction type	Example	Semantics
ALU	ADD T,A,B	$T \leftarrow \begin{cases} unknown & \text{if } A = unknown \lor B = unknown \\ A + B & \text{otherwise} \end{cases}$
Compare	CMP A,B	$A - B$ and update the condition code (cc) register. May set bits in the cc-register to *unknown*.
Conditional branch	BEQ L1	Test bit in cc-register to see if we should branch. If bit is *unknown* simulate both paths.
Load	LD R,A	Copy data from memory at address A to register R (the data can be *unknown*). If address is *unknown*, set R to *unknown*.
Store	ST R,A	Copy data from register R to memory at address A (the data can be *unknown*). If address is *unknown*, all memory locations are assigned *unknown* (a more efficient solution is discussed in Section 2.2).

```
1    for (i = 0 ; i < 4 ; i++)
2      if (b[i][i] > 0)
3        for (j = i+1 ; j < 4 ; j++)
4          if (m[i][j])
5            sum += b[i][j];
```

Fig. 1. Example program.

When simulating this program, the conditional branch on line 2 will be the only branch depending on unknown values and the total number of simulated (and feasible) paths will be $2^4 = 16$. The infeasible paths that the conditional branch on line 4 could create are automatically eliminated since the branch condition is known when simulating. Also, no loop bound is needed for the inner loop since the iteration count only depends on variable i which is known during the simulation. Thus, we see that an important advantage of the instruction-level simulation approach is that all conditions that depend on data values that are known statically will be computed during the simulation. This eliminates, in this example, the need for program annotations.

2.2 Discussion

Ideally, for each combination of input data, the goal is to eliminate all infeasible program paths. The domain of values we use, however, makes it sometimes impossible to correctly analyze mutually exclusive paths. Consider for example the statements below where b is *unknown*.

```
if (b < 100) fun1()
if (b > 200) fun2()
```

Variable b will be *unknown* in both conditions, forcing the simulation of four paths even if fun1() and fun2() are mutually exclusive and the number of feasible paths are three. The effect of this will be a potential overestimation of the WCET which is caused by the fact that we only distinguish between known and unknown values. However, there is nothing in the approach that would hinder us from extending the domain of values to, e.g., ranges of values. By doing this, it would be possible to handle cases like the one above. The simulation technique we have implemented, and which we evaluate later in the paper, uses the simpler domain. However, we will discuss the implications of using ranges in Section 6.

As mentioned above, store instructions with an unknown reference address need special treatment. To efficiently handle these accesses, we identify all data structures that are accessed with unknown store instructions as *unpredictable data structures*. These are mapped by the linker into a memory area which can only respond with unknown values. This means that stores to this area can be ignored and loads will always return *unknown* as a result, thus assuring us of a correct estimation of the WCET with no added cost in simulation time.

We identify the unpredictable data structures by letting the simulator output a list of all unknown stores it encounters. With the help of a source-code debugger, it is possible to connect each store instruction to a data structure which is marked as unpredictable. Eventually, the linking phase is redone to properly map the marked data structures to the 'unknown' area of memory. After this step, a correct estimation may be done. The approach mentioned above can be used for statically allocated data structures only. For unpredictable dynamically allocated data structures we do not yet have any solution.

A key problem with the simulation approach in this section is the explosion in number of paths to be simulated. If a loop iteration has n feasible paths and the number of loop iterations is k, the number of paths to simulate is n^k. Fortunately, good heuristics exist to drastically reduce the number of paths we need to simulate. We have used a path merging strategy, which forms the basis of our WCET method to be presented in the next section.

3 The WCET Method

To reduce the number of paths that have to be explored in the path analysis, we apply a path-merge strategy. This reduces the number of paths to be explored from n^k down to n for a loop containing n feasible paths in each iteration and doing k iterations. In each loop iteration, all n paths are explored but in the beginning of the next iteration all these n paths are merged into one. Thus, the number of simulated paths are less than or equal to n. We first describe how the merging operation is performed in Section 3.1. This operation is used in the WCET algorithm which we present in Section 3.2. Finally, in Section 3.3 we discuss how we have implemented the method with a reasonable time complexity.

3.1 Merging algorithm

In order to understand how the merging of two paths is done, consider again the example program in Figure 1. In the second iteration of the outer loop, when the simulator encounters the unknown conditional branch on line 2, two paths can be merged. When merging, the long path (the one with the highest WCET) is kept and the short path is discarded. However, to make a valid estimation of the worst-case execution path throughout the program execution, the impact of the short path on the total WCET must be taken into account. For example, variable sum can be assigned different values in the two paths. Therefore, all variables whose values differ, must be assigned the value *unknown* in the resulting path of the merge operation.

Formally, the algorithm views a path, p_A, as consisting of a WCET for the path, $p_A.wcet$, and the system state at the end of the path, $p_A.state$. The state of a path is the partial result of the execution including, e.g., the content of all memory locations, registers, and status bits that can affect the WCET in the future. In order to compute the state of the path resulting from the merging of several paths, the states of the merged paths are compared and *unknown* values are assigned to locations whose values differ. We denote this operation as the *union* operation of path states.

The merging algorithm is described in Algorithm 1. It creates a new path p_C from two paths p_A and p_B. The program counter, which must not differ in the two paths merged, is copied to the new path. The new WCET is the maximum of the WCET of the two original paths. Finally, states of the merged paths are unioned. The union operation between values is defined as:

$$a \cup b \Leftrightarrow \begin{cases} unknown \text{ if } a = unknown \vee b = unknown \\ unknown \text{ if } a \neq b \\ a \qquad \text{otherwise} \end{cases}$$

Algorithm 1 Merging two paths p_A and p_B creating p_C.

{PCT = program counter, CC = condition code}
Require: $p_A.state.PCT = p_B.state.PCT$
$p_C.state.PCT \leftarrow p_A.state.PCT$

$p_C.wcet \leftarrow \max(p_A.wcet, p_B.wcet)$

$p_C.state.CC \leftarrow p_A.state.CC \cup p_B.state.CC$
for all registers i **do**
$\quad p_C.state.R[i] \leftarrow p_A.state.R[i] \cup p_B.state.R[i]$
end for
for all memory positions a **do**
$\quad p_C.state.MEM[a] \leftarrow p_A.state.MEM[a] \cup p_B.state.MEM[a]$
end for

3.2 WCET algorithm

In order to implement the WCET simulation technique and the merging algorithm, one important issue is in which order paths should be simulated. Consider a loop with two feasible paths in each iteration. In order to merge these two paths, they must have been simulated the same number of iterations. To accomplish this, the WCET algorithm uses loop information from the control flow graph of the program.

The algorithm (see Algorithm 2) starts the simulation from the beginning of the program. Whenever an unknown conditional branch is found, the simulation is stopped and the algorithm selects, as the next path to simulate, the path that has made the least progress, *a minimum progress path*, in terms of loop iterations. If this path is not unique, all paths that have made the same progress and are at the same position in the program, *equal progress paths*, are merged into one before simulation is continued.

By always selecting the path that has made least progress, the algorithm makes it certain that all paths in a loop iteration is simulated before a new iteration begins. In fact, merging will occur every time two paths that have made equal progress meet at the same position in the program. This makes an exponential growth of the number of paths impossible.

3.3 Performance considerations

The performance of this method depends on how many paths we need to simulate, how often merging is done and how fast the actual merge operation is. How often the merging should be done is a complex question. If we merge often, it is likely that we will have fewer paths to simulate. However, when doing a merge we can lose information in a way that makes us fail to eliminate infeasible paths. Thus, merging too often can also create more infeasible paths and in the end lead to a larger number of simulated paths.

The algorithm we have evaluated merges as often as possible. This makes an exponential growth of the number of paths impossible, e.g. in loops. Typically, each unknown branch found during the simulation would lead to the creation of yet another path, which later would result in an additional merge operation. The total number of paths simulated, as well as the number of merge operations, can in some cases grow in proportion to the number of loop iterations done in the program. One example is a loop with one unknown exit condition. The simulation of this loop would produce one new path (the exit path) to simulate each iteration. All these paths would, unless they reach the end of the program, be merged resulting in an equal number of merge operations.

For each merge operation, one must union the content of all registers and memory locations. This might be a quite slow process if the amount of memory is large. We can speed up this operation considerably by utilizing the fact that paths that are to be merged, often shared a long history of execution before they got split up. By only recording changes made to the system state since the time where the two paths were created, we can quickly identify the parts of memory

---

Algorithm 2 WCET algorithm handling merge.

{A is set of active paths, C completed paths, $\emptyset$ = empty set, $\backslash$ = set minus}
$A \leftarrow \emptyset, C \leftarrow \emptyset$

$p \leftarrow$ starting null path
Simulate(p)
if p reached end of program **then**
   $C \leftarrow C \cup \{p\}$
else {p reached an unknown conditional branch}
   $A \leftarrow A \cup \{p\}$
end if

while A not empty **do**
   $p \leftarrow$ minimal progress path in A
   $A \leftarrow A \backslash \{p\}$
   for all paths q with equal progress as p **do**
     $A \leftarrow A \backslash \{q\}$
     $p \leftarrow \text{merge}(p, q)$
   end for
   {Path p ends with a branch forcing a split}
   for each possible branch target i **do**
     $p_i \leftarrow$ copy of p
     Simulate(p_i) along target i
     if p_i reached end of program **then**
       $C \leftarrow C \cup \{p_i\}$
     else {p_i reached an unknown conditional branch}
       $A \leftarrow A \cup \{p_i\}$
     end if
   end for
end while

$wcet \leftarrow \max_{p \in C} p.wcet$

---

where the two system states differ. As an example, suppose that the system we model contains 1 Mbyte of main memory. Then one can divide this memory into small fixed size pages (say 512 bytes each) and each path only keeps the accessed pages in its system state. In this way, only a few pages of memory need to be compared during merging.

4 Timing Analysis

The WCET algorithm in the previous section can estimate WCET for hardware platforms with fixed instruction execution times. In this section, we extend it to model the timing of pipelined processors with caches. To demonstrate the approach, we particularly focus on systems with separate, direct-mapped instruction and data caches and a single-issue pipelined execution unit. However, the approach extends to more sophisticated architectures.

In order to update the WCET properly during simulation, the simulator must of course be extended to model the timing of caches and pipelines. In the context of caches, the simulator must model the impact of cache misses on the execution time. And in the context of pipelines, the simulator must account for the impact of structural, data, and control hazards [6] on the execution time. With this capability, it is possible to make a safe estimation of the execution time of a given path through the program.

A critical issue is how to carry out a merge operation. To do this, one must be able to estimate the impact of the system state on the future execution time. Such state information is exemplified by the content of the tag memory in the caches (which affects future misses) and resources occupied by an instruction, such as data-path components and registers (which affect future structural, data and control hazards). The merging operation introduced in Section 3 must be extended to handle such state information, which we will refer to as *timing state*.

To merge the timing state, we could use the same general principle as used when merging the content of memory locations; for all locations where the timing state differs we assert a pessimistic value, such as *unknown* in the merged timing state. For example, in the case of most caches *unknown* means that a cache block is invalid, and the unioning of two cache timing states makes all cache blocks whose tags differ invalid. We call this method the *pessimistic merge*, since it can incur a severe pessimism in the estimation.

Fortunately, it is possible to reduce the pessimism when merging. If it was known in advance which path belongs to the worst case path through the program, one could update the worst-case execution time with the execution time of that path and also choose the timing state of that path when merging and discard the timing state of the other path. Then, no pessimism would be incurred on a merge operation. While it is not possible to know in advance which of the two paths belongs to the worst-case path, a good guess would be that the longer of the two belongs to the worst-case path. If we also estimate how big effect the timing state of the shorter path has on the future execution time, we can make sure whether it is correct to use the WCET of the longer path along with its timing state when merging two paths. This approach is formulated in the following algorithm where we assume that the worst-case execution times of the long and the short paths are $WCET_L$ and $WCET_S$, respectively.

1. Estimate the *worst-case penalty* ($WCET_P$) that the short path would incur on the future execution time that will not be incurred by the long execution path.
2. If $WCET_L \geq WCET_S + WCET_P$ then use the timing state and WCET of the long path in the merge operation and discard the timing state of the short path.
3. Otherwise, the pessimistic merge approach must be used.

In order to make this algorithm useful, we must clearly define what we mean with timing state and worst-case penalty, and how to perform the pessimistic merge. This is done in the next two sections in the context of caches and pipelining.

4.1 Instruction and data cache analysis

Both instruction and data caches can be described and treated using the same principles. Therefore, we make no distinction between them. Consider the timing state of two caches, C_L and C_S, belonging to the long and short path, respectively. The timing state of a cache is represented by an array of tags showing how blocks are currently mapped in the cache. To calculate the worst-case penalty, we must consider all cases where C_S may lead to a greater number of future cache misses than C_L would. The worst case is found if we imagine that all cache blocks resident in C_L but not found in C_S will be needed in the future. We would then lose all these potential misses if we discard C_S. To find the worst-case penalty, we go through all cache blocks and compare the tag in C_S with the tag in C_L and sum up the cache miss penalties caused by all differences found.

While pessimistic merging might be needed if it is not possible to discard C_S, it is not always necessary to invalidate all blocks found different. By invalidating a block in C_L we make it impossible for C_S to cause any additional misses in the future. Thus, for each block we invalidate in C_L we reduce the worst-case penalty. Eventually, it may became small enough to proceed and actually discard C_S.

4.2 Pipeline analysis

A timing model of a pipeline must keep track of the resources (pipeline stages and registers) an instruction uses and when each resource is released in order to resolve structural, data and control hazards. The time when each resource is last released influences the future instructions and the worst-case penalty. Consider the timing state of two pipelines, P_L and P_S, belonging to the long and short path, respectively. We want to estimate the possible future effect on the execution time that P_S may lead to compared to P_L, and must in this case consider all future hazards that P_S can lead to, which P_L cannot lead to. For each resource we determine when it is last released and whether it is released later in P_S compared to P_L. The worst-case penalty is the maximum difference in release time found among all resources.

If we are not allowed to discard P_S, we must do the pessimistic merge instead. However, this can sometimes be avoided using the same principle as for the caches; we change P_L in a way that reduces the possible future effect on the execution time that P_S may lead to compared to P_L. For each possible structural or data hazard resulting from P_S but not from P_L, we can change P_L so that resources are released later. In this way we can gradually reduce the worst-case penalty, until at last, we are allowed to discard P_S.

5 Experimental Results

We have estimated the WCET of seven benchmark programs, running on an idealized architecture with no caches, and where all instructions execute in one clock cycle. Thus, the evaluation focuses on the path analysis aspects of the method.

5.1   Methodology

A WCET simulator has been constructed by extending an existing instruction-level simulator, PSIM [2], which simulates the POWERPC instruction set. The original simulator has been extended with the capability of handling unknown values. Also, the WCET algorithm described in Section 3.2 has been added to control the path exploration and merging. No cache and pipeline simulation was enabled and the execution time is equal to the simulated instruction count.

   The GNU compiler (gcc 2.7.2.2) and linker has been used to compile and link the benchmarks. No optimization was enabled. The simulated run-time environment contains no operating system; consequently, we disabled all calls to system functions such as I/O in the benchmarks.

Benchmarks and metrics   An overview of the seven benchmark programs can be seen in Table 2. There are four small programs: *matmult*, *bsort*, *isort*, and *fib*, and three larger programs: *DES*, *jfdctint*, and *compress*.

   The two benchmarks *fib* and *compress* both contain a loop where the exit condition depends on unknown input data. In order to bound the number of iterations, we need to add manual annotations. This is not supported in our implementation. Instead, we have added an extra exit condition in the loops. In *fib* we have added the condition: $i \leq 30$ because we know that input data is always in this range. In *compress* we bound an inner loop whose iteration variable is j, using the current iteration count, i, of the outer loop: $j \leq i$. This is a safe but very pessimistic bound, but we found it difficult to prove that a tighter bound could be used.

   The true WCETs of all programs have been measured by running the programs in the simulator with the worst-case input data. This works fine for all programs except *compress*, where the worst case input data is hard to find. Instead, a random sequence of 50 bytes has been used as input.

   Besides the estimated WCET from the extended simulator, we also did a manual estimate of the structural WCET, i.e., the execution time of the longest structural path in the control flow graph of the program and using fixed bounds on the number of iterations of all loops. This figure would represent a WCET estimation method that eliminates no infeasible paths and uses fixed iteration bounds for loops. The purpose of doing this is to analyze the capability of the method to eliminate infeasible paths.

5.2   Estimation results

Table 2 compares the measured true WCET with the estimated WCET from the simulator and the manually derived structural estimation for the benchmark programs. (WCET is expressed in clock cycles, ratio is the WCET relative to the measured, true WCET.)

   For all benchmarks, except *compress*, we find that the method succeeds in finding the true WCET. In *compress*, the overestimation is caused by the inner

Table 2. The estimated and true WCET of benchmark programs.

Program	Description	Measured true WCET	Estimated WCET	Ratio	Estimated structural WCET	Ratio
matmult	Multiplies 2 10x10 matrices	7063912	7063912	1	7063912	1
bsort	Bubblesort of 100 integers	292026	292026	1	572920	1.96
isort	Insertsort of 10 integers	2594	2594	1	4430	1.71
fib	Calculate n:th element of the Fibonacci sequence	697	697	1	697	1
DES	Encrypts 64-bit data	118675	118675	1	119877	1.01
jfdctint	Discrete cosine transform of an 8x8 image	6010	6010	1	6010	1
compress	Compresses 50 bytes of data	9380	49046	5.2	161161	17.2

loop. As mentioned previously, we bound this loop using the very pessimistic condition $j \leq i$, but when measuring the true WCET, we found that this inner loop is actually only doing one single iteration. For *compress*, we do not know if the measured WCET is actually the true WCET. The true WCET is probably higher than the measured one.

Two of the benchmarks, *matmult* and *jfdctint*, have no infeasible paths at all, and only one path was simulated. In *DES*, however, there exist infeasible paths caused by data dependencies between different functions. These infeasible paths were eliminated and only one path was simulated. In *bsort* and *isort*, all infeasible paths were not eliminated. Still, this did not lead to any over-estimation, since all simulated infeasible paths were shorter than the worst-case path found.

If we take a look at the estimated structural WCET of the programs, we see that the WCET is grossly over-estimated for *bsort*, *isort*, and *compress*. In *bsort* and *isort* it depends entirely on using a fixed iteration count for an inner loop which is normally bounded by the outer loops current iteration count. This leads to an over-estimation of a factor of two for the loop and influences *bsort* more than *isort* because of the greater number of iterations done in *bsort*. In *compress* there is a similar inner loop which is forced to have a fixed iteration bound again causing an over-estimation of a factor of two. In addition, there exists a very long infeasible path that extends the structural estimate. This path is eliminated when estimating with our simulation method. The tiny over-estimation in *DES* results from infeasible paths that are not possible to eliminate.

One strength of doing the analysis on the instruction level can be seen when looking at *DES*. In the source code, one can find several conditional expressions which should indicate several possible feasible paths through the program. However, the compiler (gcc with no optimization enabled) automatically generates code without any branches for these conditional expressions and the resulting program has only a single feasible path. In summary, the method in this paper appears promising in eliminating infeasible paths.

6 Discussion and Related Work

As the results indicate, to get a tight estimation of the WCET of a program, it is crucial to eliminate infeasible paths, especially in the presence of loops with dynamic bounds. Of equal importance is an accurate timing analysis. This has not been evaluated in this study, but the potential can be seen when looking at *DES*, *matmult*, and *jfdctint*, where the simulator only needs to simulate one path through the program. This path can be simulated with an arbitrary detailed timing model and will always give us the tightest possible WCET. Thus, by eliminating infeasible paths we can concentrate on the feasible ones, and make a more accurate timing analysis.

A big advantage of integrating the path and timing analysis can be seen when comparing with solutions where the path and timing analyses are kept separated. If the path analysis is done first, we would need a way to represent the path information generated from the path analysis, and the timing analysis phase must be able to utilize this information. On the other hand, if the timing analysis is done first, we would be forced to work with fixed WCETs for blocks of statements when doing the path and WCET calculation. These problems are not present in our method, which does the path and timing analysis simultaneously.

Our method is related to the *path analysis* methods presented in [1, 3]. The method of Ermedahl and Gustafsson operate on the source-program level. It establishes upper bounds on the number of loop iterations and also identifies infeasible paths, but makes no timing analysis. Altenbernd's method uses precalculated execution times on each basic code block. These times are used to prune paths during the path exploration. However, in some cases, the method suffers from complexity problems. We use a path-merging strategy instead, which guarantees a manageable number of paths, and also makes it possible to integrate it with a detailed timing analysis. In [15], Stappert and Altenbernd present a new method which handles caches and pipelines by first making a timing analysis for each basic block and then searching for the longest feasible path. The method only handles programs without loops. In [4], a way to automatically derive loop bounds by means of a syntactical analysis has been proposed. They successfully use this technique together with timing analysis in order to reduce the work for the user, but they do no general path analysis in order to identify infeasible paths. In a recent work, Liu and Gomez [11] construct time-bound functions for high-level languages, using a technique related to ours. However, no concern is made for doing accurate low-level timing analysis.

In our method, the simulator uses a very simple domain where values can be either known or unknown. This domain performs quite well compared to a more complex domain, e.g., based on intervals of values which is used in [1, 3]. However, as we saw in Section 2.2, overestimations may sometimes arise for mutually exclusive paths. There is no inherent problem in extending our method to a more powerful domain. The result would be a slower simulator needing more memory. Our choice of domain results in an additional 1 bit of memory for each 32-bit word of memory to hold the known/unknown status. An interval representation would need 2 extra words for each word of memory. Also, a more complex semantics would be needed, which would result in a slower execution of each instruction. On the other hand, the more complex domain might be preferable for some applications, if it manages to cut more infeasible paths and thereby gain speed and accuracy compared to our simple domain.

A more serious problem with our simple domain is that if all exit conditions of a loop is input data dependent, we get a completely unknown upper bound on the number of iterations in the loop, and our WCET algorithm will not terminate. This can be detected by using some heuristic or by user interaction. For cases like this, we must add a manual annotation or add a known exit condition by modifying the loop condition in the program. For example, the loop in the program below, where b is unknown input data, will never do more than 100 iterations regardless of b. This fact cannot be represented with our simple domain, and during the simulation the loop will get a completely unknown exit condition, forcing us to add annotations or modify the program.

```
if (b < 100)
  for (i = 0 ; i < b ; i++)
    sum = sum + i;
```

In the example above the simple domain was causing the problem. A similar problem can also arise when merging. The union operation used when merging may cause information needed to bound a loop to be lost. If this happens, we are also forced to annotate or change the program.

7   Conclusions

In this paper we have presented a new method for estimating the WCET of a program. This method integrates path and timing analysis and thereby has the potential to do tight estimations by eliminating infeasible paths and concentrating the timing analysis on the feasible ones. A study of seven benchmark programs, focusing on the path analysis aspects, show that many infeasible paths were indeed eliminated by the method, and the true WCET was found for almost all programs. However, it remains to be shown how well the method performs when considering the timing analysis as well. This is the topic of our current and future work.

Acknowledgments

We are deeply indebted to Dr. Jan Jonsson of Chalmers for his constructive comments on previous versions of this manuscript. This research is supported by a grant from Swedish Research Council on Engineering Science under contract number 221-96-214.

References

1. P. Altenbernd. On the false path problem in hard real-time programs. In *Proceedings of the 8th Euromicro Workshop on Real-Time Systems*, pages 102–107, June 1996.

2. A. Cagney. PSIM, POWERPC simulator. ftp://ftp.ci.com.au/pub/psim/index.html

3. A. Ermedahl and J. Gustafsson. Deriving annotations for tight calculation of execution time. In *Proceedings of EUROPAR'97*, pages 1298–1307, August 1997.

4. C. Healy, M. Sjödin, V. Rustagi, and D. Whalley. Bounding Loop Iterations for Timing Analysis. In *Proceedings of the 4th IEEE Real-Time Technology and Applications Symposium*, June 1998. To appear.

5. C. A. Healy, D. B. Whalley, and M. G. Harmon. Integrating the timing analysis of pipelining and instruction caching. In *Proceedings of the 16th IEEE Real-Time Systems Symposium*, pages 288–297, December 1995.

6. J. L. Hennessy and D. A. Patterson. *Computer Architecture: A Quantitative Approach, 2ed*. Morgan Kaufmann, 1996.

7. S.-K. Kim, S. L. Min, and R. Ha. Efficient worst case timing analysis of data caching. In *Proceedings of the 2nd IEEE Real-Time Technology and Applications Symposium*, pages 230–240, June 1996.

8. Y.-T. S. Li, S. Malik, and A. Wolfe. Efficient microarchitecture modeling and path analysis for real-time software. In *Proceedings of the 16th IEEE Real-Time Systems Symposium*, pages 298–307, December 1995.

9. Y.-T. S. Li, S. Malik, and A. Wolfe. Cache modeling for real-time software: Beyond direct mapped instruction caches. In *Proceedings of the 17th IEEE Real-Time Systems Symposium*, pages 254–263, December 1996.

10. S.-S. Lim, Y. H. Bae, G. T. Jang, B.-D. Rhee, S. L. Min, C. Y. Park, H. Shin, K. Park, and C. S. Kim. An accurate worst case timing analysis technique for RISC processors. In *Proceedings of the 15th IEEE Real-Time Systems Symposium*, pages 97–108, December 1994.

11. Y. A. Liu and G. Gomez. Automatic Accurate Time-Bound Analysis for High-Level Languages. *Dept. of Computer Science, Indiana University, Technical Report TR-508*, April 1998.

12. P. Magnusson, F. Dahlgren, H. Grahn, M. Karlsson, F. Larsson, A. Moestedt, J. Nilsson, P. Stenström, and B. Werner. Simics/sun4m: A virtual workstation. In *Proceedings of USENIX98*, 1998. To appear.

13. G. Ottosson and M. Sjödin. Worst-case execution time analysis for modern hardware architectures. In *Proceedings of ACM SIGPLAN Workshop on Language, Compiler, and Tool Support for Real-Time Systems*, June 1997.

14. P. Puschner and C. Koza. Calculating the maximum execution time of real-time programs. *The Journal of Real-Time Systems*, pages 159–176, 1989.

15. F. Stappert and P. Altenbernd. Complete Worst-Case Execution Time Analysis of Straight-line Hard Real-Time Programs. *C-LAB Report 27/97*, Paderborn, Germany, December 1997.

16. R. T. White, F. Mueller, C. A. Healy, D. B. Whalley, and M. G. Harmon. Timing analysis for data caches and set-associative caches. In *Proceedings of the 3nd IEEE Real-Time Technology and Applications Symposium*, pages 192–202, June 1997.

17. E. Witchel and M. Rosenblum. Embra: Fast and flexible machine simulation. In *Proceedings of ACM SIGMETRICS '96*, pages 68–79, 1996.

On Predicting Data Cache Behavior for Real-Time Systems

Christian Ferdinand* Reinhard Wilhelm**

Universität des Saarlandes / Fachbereich Informatik
Postfach 15 11 50 / D-66041 Saarbrücken / Germany

Abstract. In the presence of data or combined data/instruction caches there can be memory references that may access multiple memory locations such as those used to implement array references in loops. We examine how data dependence analysis and program restructuring methods to increase data locality can be used to determine worst case bounds on cache misses. To complement these methods we present a persistence analysis on sets of possibly referenced memory locations (e.g., arrays). This analysis determines memory locations that survive in the cache thus providing effective and efficient means to compute an upper bound on the number of possible cache misses.

1 Introduction

Caches are used to improve the access times of fast microprocessors to relatively slow main memories. They can reduce the number of cycles a processor is waiting for data by providing faster access to recently referenced regions of memory. Caching is more or less used for all general purpose processors, and, with increasing application sizes it becomes more and more relevant and used for high performance microcontrollers and DSPs (Digital Signal Processors).

Programs with hard real-time constraints have to be subjected to a schedulability analysis. This should determine whether all timing constraints can be satisfied. WCET (Worst Case Execution Time) estimations for processes have to be used for this. The degree of success of such a timing validation depends on sharp WCET estimations.

For hardware with caches, the worst case assumption is that all accesses miss the cache. This is an overly pessimistic assumption which leads to a waste of hardware resources.

In previous work [7, 1, 6, 5], abstract interpretation has been applied to the problem of predicting the cache behavior of programs. Abstract interpretation is a technique for the static detection of dynamic properties of programs. It is semantics based, i.e., it computes approximative properties of the semantics of programs. On this basis, it supports correctness proofs of analyses. It replaces commonly used ad hoc techniques by systematic, provable ones, and it allows for the automatic generation of analyzers from specifications by existing tools (e.g. PAG, the program analyzer generator [2]).

Starting from a program semantics that reflects only memory accesses (to fixed addresses) and its effects on cache memories, analyses were developed that

---

* Supported by the Deutsche Forschungsgemeinschaft (DFG).
** {ferdi,wilhelm}@cs.uni-sb.de   http://www.cs.uni-sb.de/~{ferdi,wilhelm}

approximate the "collecting" semantics. The collecting semantics associate with each program point the set of all cache states that can occur when program control reaches that point. The set of all cache states can be very large. Therefore, *abstract cache states* have been used to efficiently describe the sets of possible concrete cache states. A *must analysis* has been presented that computes for all program points sets of memory blocks that will be definitely in the cache whenever control reaches this point and a *may analysis* that computes sets of memory blocks that may be in the cache. These analyses can be used to determine memory references that under all circumstances will result in a *cache hit*, and memory references that under all circumstances will result in a *cache miss*.

In this paper, we present an analysis that is able to handle sets of possibly referenced memory blocks.

2 Overview

In the following Section we briefly sketch the necessary extensions of the cache analyses to handle scalar variables. Section 4 describes how data dependence analysis and program restructuring methods to increase data locality can be used to determine worst case bounds on cache misses.

To complement these methods, Section 5 presents a persistence analysis that allows to determine memory locations that survive in the cache. First, in Section 5.5 the analysis is introduced for single memory locations. Then, Section 5.5 presents the extension to sets of possibly referenced memory locations (e.g. arrays). Section 6 describes related work from the area of WCET estimation for real-time systems and Section 7 concludes.

3 Scalar Variables

Must and may analyses can be used to predict the behavior of data caches or combined instruction/data caches, if the addresses of referenced data can be statically computed.

The determination of addresses can be partitioned into the following steps:

- Local variables and procedure parameters that are allocated on the stack are usually addressed relatively to the stack pointer or frame pointer, i.e., a register that points to a known address within the procedure frame on the execution stack. For programs without recursive procedures, it is possible to determine all values of the stack or frame pointers for all procedures for the distinguished execution contexts of the cache behavior analysis.
- The values of the stack pointer or frame pointer can then be used in a data flow analysis [11, 24] to determine the absolute addresses of the referenced memory blocks.

4 Arrays

Data cache analysis is more difficult than instruction cache analysis because different executions of an instructions may access different data addresses. This is usually the case if a program handles arrays.

To determine if an array element is in the cache when it is referenced, it is necessary to know the last time it was used. In general, it is impossible to determine exactly the cache behavior of each reference. Different sets of input data to the same program can result in a very different cache behavior. Even if the input data set is known, it is generally undecidable to determine whether array accesses by arbitrary functions access the same memory location. If it is impossible to determine whether one data reference uses the same memory location as another, then it is also impossible to determine whether the reference will result in a cache hit.

Nevertheless, for many real programs the access functions for arrays are very simple. This is taken advantage of in the area of program vectorization and parallelization where data dependence analysis of arrays is usually restricted to access functions that are affine in the loop control variables of FORTRAN DO-loop like loops, i.e., have the form $a_0 + a_1 * i_1 + \ldots + a_k * i_k$, where i_j is a loop control variable and a_j is constant. Under these restrictions, a system of linear equations can be constructed that describes the references to each set of a cache and allows to determine the cache behavior. Solving the equation system exactly can be very expensive.

In Section 4.1 we show how data dependence analysis can be used for some restricted classes of programs to predict lower bounds for cache misses. In Section 5.5 we present a persistence analyses that handles sets of possibly referenced memory blocks. The persistence analysis can detect that all memory blocks referenced in a program fragment fit into the cache. This is not restricted to a limited class of access functions and can be used to determine an upper bound on the number of cache misses.

4.1 Data Dependence Analysis of Arrays

A data dependence corresponds to a possible reuse of a value. A reuse is a prerequisite for a cache hit. Classical data dependence analysis as used in compilers for supercomputers constructs a dependence graph that represents a super set of dependences that *may* exist. To bound the number of cache misses definite reuses of data, i.e., *must* dependences, have to be considered.

In [8], Gannon, Jalby, and Gallivan describe program transformations to improve the handling of arrays in nested loops. Their strategy is to use the fast local memory available in some supercomputers to store array elements between reuses. They consider a special form of must dependences, the "uniformly" generated dependences that lead to definite reuses. The different executions of a statement in a loop nest are described by a vector where each vector element describes the iteration count of one surrounding loop. A distance vector [28] relates different references to the same memory location. It describes the number of iterations of each loop between two executions of the statement. The distance vector for uniformly generated references can be determined exactly and consists only of constants. For such dependences the minimum set of elements of an array X necessary to maximize reuse in a loop nest (called the "reference window") can be directly determined. By keeping a selected set of reference windows in local memory, the "local memory hit ratio" can be calculated by counting the number of references inside the reference windows and the number of different locations accessed by the references. The hit ratio is then the number of references minus the number of different locations divided by the number of references.

Example 1 (Uniformly generated dependencies).

```
            for i := m to n
S₁    ...:= x[i]
S₂    ...:= x[i-3]
            end
```

The loop has an input dependence between S_1 and S_2. The distance vector is (3). The reference window at the beginning of the loop body is: {x[i-3],x[i-2],x[i-1]}.

The method of Gannon, Jalby, and Gallivan to determine the hit ratio of local memories can be transfered to cache memories, if one can show that the reference windows will survive in the cache (or are removed from the cache a bounded number of times).

Porterfield [22] has given an algorithm for estimating the hit ratio of a fully associative cache with LRU replacement strategy. The algorithm considers only uniformly generated dependences. Porterfield argues that nonuniformly generated dependences usually contribute only rarely to reuses and the effect of ignoring them is marginal. The basic idea is to find the "overflow iteration" of a loop, i.e., the maximum number of iterations of that loop that can surely hold all of the data accessed by the loop in the cache. The determination of the "overflow iteration" was used to estimate the benefit of program transformations on the cache performance.

The "overflow iteration" can be used to find reuses of array elements that are definitely still in the cache for fully associative caches. This determines a lower bound on the number of cache hits which can be used in a WCET estimation. The method is not transferable to other cache organizations to compute deterministic lower bounds, as the effects of interference of data in the cache is ignored.

Wolf and Lam [26, 27] have developed a loop transformation theory to improve locality of references in loop nests. The basic idea is to work only on small parts of the arrays (blocks). This limits intervening iterations executed from innermost loops so that cache data is reused before it is replaced. By considering possible reuses of array elements within loops described by dependences, their algorithm automatically transforms a loop nest and uses heuristics to determine appropriate "blocking" factors.

Example 2 (Blocking of matrix multiplication.). The classical and most studied example of a blocked algorithm is the N × N matrix multiplication.

```
                              for kk := 1 to N step B do
for i := 1 to N do              for jj := 1 to N step B do
  for k := 1 to N do              for i := 1 to N do
    r := X[i,k];          ⟹        for k := kk to min(kk+B-1,N) do
    for j:=1 to N do                 r := X[i,k];
      Z[i,j] += r * Y[k,j];          for j:=jj to min(jj+B-1,N) do
                                       Z[i,j] += r * Y[k,j];
```

The blocking factor B should be chosen so that the B × B submatrix of Y and a row of length B of Z fit in the cache.

The performance of blocked code can fluctuate dramatically with the size of the arrays due to cache interference misses[1] [12]. To predict the amount of cache misses due to interference, Lam, Rothberg, and Wolf [12] have developed a model for some classes of access patterns. The model makes some probabilistic assumptions about the referenced locations to estimate the number of cross interferences. In the absence of cross interferences, the model can be used to bound the number of cache misses for a WCET estimation.

In [23], Schreiber and Dongarra describe methods to automatically perform blocking of nested loops. Their work includes a method to determine the data reuse for (blocked) algorithms on matrices. Their approach is limited to loop nests with only uniformly generated dependences and cache interferences are not taken into consideration. In the absence of interferences, their methods can be used to precisely determine the reuse and thereby the number of cache misses for some restricted classes of loop nests.

In [9], Ghosh, Martonosi, and Malik present an analysis to compute an equation system (called cache miss equations CMEs) that describes the number of data cache misses produced by the array references of *one* loop nest with perfectly nested loops and affinely addressed arrays for direct mapped caches. In contrast to the above mentioned approaches, the CMEs describe the number of misses precisely. While the effort to compute the CMEs for a loop nest seems to be moderate, the effort to evaluate the CMEs seems to be very high.

However, for many algorithms on matrices (like matrix multiplication), whose cache behavior could be predicted by the methods described above, the execution path is not input data dependent. This means, that for the purpose of WCET estimation in a real time setting the cache behavior can be directly measured or computed by a simple simulation.

5 Cache Behavior Prediction by Abstract Interpretation

5.1 Program Analysis

The program analyzer generator PAG [2] offers the possibility to generate a program analyzer from a description of the abstract domain and of the abstract semantic functions in two high level languages, one for the domains and the other for the semantic functions. Domains can be constructed inductively starting from simple domains using operators like constructing power sets and function domains. The semantic functions are described in a functional language which combines high expressiveness with efficient implementation. Additionally the user has to supply a join function combining two domain values into one. This function is applied whenever a point in the program has two (or more) possible execution predecessors.

---

[1] These are also called conflict misses or collision misses.

5.2 Cache Memories

A cache can be characterized by three major parameters:
- *capacity* is the number of bytes it may contain.
- *line size* (also called block size) is the number of contiguous bytes that are transferred from memory on a cache miss. The cache can hold at most $n = capacity/line size$ blocks.
- *associativity* is the number of cache locations where a particular block may reside. $n/associativity$ is the number of *sets* of a cache.

If a block can reside in any cache location, then the cache is called *fully associative*. If a block can reside in exactly one location, then it is called *direct mapped*. If a block can reside in exactly A locations, then the cache is called *A-way set associative*. The fully associative and the direct mapped caches are special cases of the A-way set associative cache where $A = n$ and $A = 1$, rsp.

In the case of an associative cache, a cache line has to be selected for replacement when the cache is full and the processor requests further data. This is done according to a replacement strategy. Common strategies are *LRU* (Least Recently Used), *FIFO* (First In First Out), and *random*.

5.3 Cache Semantics

We restrict our description to the semantics of A-way set associative caches with LRU replacement strategy.

In the following, we consider an A-way set associative cache as a sequence of (fully associative) sets $F = \langle f_1, \ldots, f_{n/A} \rangle$ where $n = capacity/line size$, a set f_i as a sequence of set lines $L = \langle l_1, \ldots, l_A \rangle$, and the store as a set of memory blocks $M = \{m_1, \ldots, m_s\}$.

The function $adr : M \to \mathbb{N}_0$ gives the address of each memory block. The function $set : M \to F$ determines the set where a memory block would be stored (% denotes the modulo division):

$$set(m) = f_i; \text{ where } i = adr(m)\%(n/A) + 1$$

To indicate the absence of any memory block in a set line, we introduce a new element I; $M' = M \cup \{I\}$.

Our cache semantics separates two key aspects:
- The set where a memory block is stored: This can be statically determined as it depends only on the address of the memory block. The dynamic allocation of memory blocks to sets is modeled by the *cache states*.
- The aspect of associativity and the replacement strategy within one set of the cache: Here, the history of memory reference is relevant. This is modeled by the *set states*.

Definition 1 (concrete set state). A *(concrete) set state* is a function $s : L \to M'$. S denotes the set of all concrete set states.

Definition 2 (concrete cache state). A *(concrete) cache state* is a function $c : F \to S$. C denotes the set of all concrete cache states.

If $s(l_x) = m$ for a concrete set state s, then x describes the relative age of the memory block according to the LRU replacement strategy and not the physical position in the cache hardware.

The *update* function describes the side effects on the set (cache) of referencing the memory:

- The set where a memory block may reside in the cache is uniquely determined by the address of the memory block, i.e., the behavior of the sets is independent of each other.
- The LRU replacement strategy is modeled by using the positions of memory blocks within a set to indicate their relative age. The order of the memory blocks reflects the "history" of memory references[2].
  The most recently referenced memory block is put in the first position l_1 of the set. If the referenced memory block m is in the set already, then all memory blocks in the set that have been more recently used than m are shifted by one position to the next set line, i.e., they increase their relative age by one. If the memory block m is not yet in the set, then all memory blocks in the cache are shifted and the 'oldest', i.e., least recently used memory block is removed from the set.

Definition 3 (set update). A set update function $\mathcal{U}_S : S \times M \to S$ describes the new set state for a given set state and a referenced memory block.

Definition 4 (cache update). A cache update function $\mathcal{U}_C : C \times M \to C$ describes the new cache state for a given cache state and a referenced memory block.

Updates of fully associative sets with LRU replacement strategy are modeled in the following way:

$$\mathcal{U}_S(s,m) = \begin{cases} [l_1 \mapsto m, \\ \quad l_i \mapsto s(l_{i-1}) \mid i = 2 \ldots h, \\ \quad l_i \mapsto s(l_i) \mid i = h+1 \ldots A]; & \text{if } \exists l_h : s(l_h) = m \\ \\ [l_1 \mapsto m, \\ \quad l_i \mapsto s(l_{i-1}) \text{ for } i = 2 \ldots A]; & \text{otherwise} \end{cases}$$

Notation: $[y \mapsto z]$ denotes a function that maps y to z. $f[y \mapsto z]$ denotes a function that maps y to z and all $x \neq y$ to $f(x)$.

Updates of A-way set associative caches are modeled in the following way:

$$\mathcal{U}_C(c,m) = c[set(m) \mapsto \mathcal{U}_S(c(set(m)),m)]$$

5.4 Control Flow Representation

We represent programs by control flow graphs consisting of nodes and typed edges. The nodes represent *basic blocks*[3]. For each basic block, the sequence of

---

[2] Our semantics describes the *observable* behavior of cache memories. We do not intend to mimic the physical cache implementation.

[3] A basic block is a sequence (of fragments) of instructions in which control flow enters at the beginning and leaves at the end without halt or possibility of branching except at the end.

references to memory is known[4], i.e., there exists a mapping from control flow nodes to sequences of memory blocks: $\mathcal{L} : V \to M^*$.

We can describe the working of a cache with the help of the update function $\mathcal{U}_C$. Therefore, we extend $\mathcal{U}_C$ to sequences of memory references:

$$\mathcal{U}_C(c, \langle m_1, \ldots, m_y \rangle) = \mathcal{U}_C(\ldots \mathcal{U}_C(c, m_1) \ldots, m_y)$$

The cache state for a path $(k_1, \ldots, k_p)$ in the control flow graph is given by applying $\mathcal{U}_C$ to the initial cache state c_I that maps all set lines in all sets to I and the concatenation of all sequences of memory references along the path: $\mathcal{U}_C(c_I, \mathcal{L}(k_1) \ldots \mathcal{L}(k_p))$.

5.5 Abstract Semantics

In order to generate an analyzer, the program analyzer generator PAG requires the specification of a domain (this will be the domain of abstract cache states), a transfer function (this will be the abstract cache update function), and a join function that is used to combine two elements of the domain from two different paths in the control flow graph.

The domain for our abstract interpretation consists of *abstract cache states* that are constructed from *abstract set states*. In order to keep track of memory blocks that have already been replaced in the cache, i.e., are relatively older than all memory blocks in the corresponding set, we introduce additional set lines $l_\top$ in which we will collect the possibly replaced memory blocks, $L' = L \cup l_\top$.

Definition 5 (abstract set state). An *abstract set state* $\hat{s} : L' \to 2^{M'}$ maps set lines to sets of memory blocks. $\hat{S}$ denotes the set of all abstract set states.

Definition 6 (abstract cache state). An *abstract cache state* $\hat{c} : F \to \hat{S}$ maps sets to abstract set states. $\hat{C}$ denotes the set of all abstract cache states.

The abstract semantic functions describe the effect of a memory reference on an element of the abstract domain. The **abstract set (cache) update** function $\hat{\mathcal{U}}$ for abstract set (cache) states is an extension of the set (cache) update function $\mathcal{U}$ to abstract set (cache) states.

On control flow nodes with at least two[5] predecessors, *join*-functions are used to combine the abstract cache states.

Definition 7 (join function). A *join function* $\hat{\mathcal{J}} : \hat{C} \times \hat{C} \mapsto \hat{C}$ combines two abstract cache states.

In the next section we will present the *persistence analysis*. It determines memory blocks that are *persistent* in the cache, i.e., stay in the cache after they have been initially loaded into the cache. A memory reference to a memory block that can be determined to be *persistent* can produce at most one cache miss for repeated executions. This information can be used to predict the cache behavior of programs.

---

[4] This is appropriate for instruction caches and can be too restrictive for data caches and combined caches. See Chapter 5.5 for weaker restrictions.

[5] Our join functions are associative. On nodes with more than two predecessors, the join function is used iteratively.

Persistence Analysis Our goal is to determine the *persistence* of a memory block, i.e., the *absence* of the possibility that a memory block m is removed from the cache. If there is no possibility to remove m from the cache, then the first reference to m may result in a cache miss, but *all* further references to m cannot result in cache misses.

This is achieved as follows: The *maximal* position (relative age) for all memory blocks that *may* be in the cache is computed. This means, the position (the relative *age*) of a memory block in the abstract set state $\hat{s}$ is an upper bound of the positions (the relative *ages*) of the memory block in the concrete set states that $\hat{s}$ represents. In order to keep track of memory blocks that have already been replaced in the cache, i.e., are relatively older than all memory blocks in the corresponding set, we introduce additional set lines $l_\top$ in which we collect the possibly replaced memory blocks with the update and join function.

Let $m_a \in \hat{s}(l_x)$. The position (relative age) x of a memory block m_a in a set can only be changed by references to memory blocks m_b with $set(m_a) = set(m_b)$, i.e., by memory references that go into the same set. Other memory references do not change the position of m_a. The position is also not changed by references to memory blocks $m_b \in \hat{s}(l_y)$ where $y \leq x$, i.e., memory blocks that are already in the cache and are "younger" or the same age as m_a. m_a can stay in the cache at least for the next $A - x$ references that go to the same set and are not yet in the cache or are *older* than m_a.

The meaning of an abstract cache state is given by a *concretization function* $conc_{\hat{C}} : \hat{C} \to 2^C$. For the memory blocks that are collected in the additional set lines $l_\top$ during the analysis, our analysis cannot determine the persistence. This does not mean that these memory blocks are never in the cache during program execution. Accordingly, the concretization function makes no assertion with respect to these memory blocks. The concretization function for the persistence analysis $conc_{\hat{C}}$ is given by:

$$conc_{\hat{C}}(\hat{c}) = \{c \mid \forall 1 \leq i \leq n/A : c(f_i) \in conc_{\hat{s}}(\hat{c}(f_i))\}$$
$$conc_{\hat{s}}(\hat{s}) = \{s \mid \forall 1 \leq a \leq A : \exists b \in \{1, ..., \top\} : s(l_a) \in \hat{s}(l_b) \text{ and } a \leq b\}$$

We use the following abstract set update function:

$$\hat{\mathcal{U}}_{\hat{s}}(\hat{s}, m) = \begin{cases} \begin{aligned} &[l_1 \mapsto \{m\}, \\ &l_i \mapsto \hat{s}(l_{i-1}) \mid i = 2 \ldots h-1, \\ &l_h \mapsto \hat{s}(l_{h-1}) \cup (\hat{s}(l_h) - \{m\}), \\ &l_i \mapsto \hat{s}(l_i) \mid i = h+1 \ldots A, \\ &l_\top \mapsto \hat{s}(l_\top)]; \end{aligned} & \text{if } \exists h \in \{1, ..., A\} : m \in \hat{s}(l_h) \\ \\ \begin{aligned} &[l_1 \mapsto \{m\}, \\ &l_i \mapsto \hat{s}(l_{i-1}) \text{ for } i = 2 \ldots A, \\ &l_\top \mapsto (\hat{s}(l_\top) - \{m\}) \cup \hat{s}(l_A)]; \end{aligned} & \text{otherwise} \end{cases}$$

Example 3 ($\hat{\mathcal{U}}_{\hat{s}}$).

	l_1	l_2	l_3	l_4	$l_\top$
$\hat{s}$	$\{m_a\}$	$\{\}$	$\{m_b, m_c\}$	$\{m_d\}$	$\{m_e\}$
$\hat{\mathcal{U}}_{\hat{s}}(\hat{s}, m_f)$	$\{m_f\}$	$\{m_a\}$	$\{\}$	$\{m_b, m_c\}$	$\{m_d, m_e\}$

The address of a memory block determines the set in which it is stored. This is reflected in the abstract cache update function in the following way:

$$\hat{\mathcal{U}}_{\hat{C}}(\hat{c}, m) = \hat{c}[set(m) \mapsto \hat{\mathcal{U}}_{\hat{S}}(\hat{c}(set(m)), m)]$$

The join function is similar to set *union*, except that if a memory block s has two different ages in two abstract cache states then the join function takes the oldest age.

$$\hat{\mathcal{J}}_{\hat{S}}(\hat{s}_1, \hat{s}_2) = \hat{s}, \text{ where:}$$

$$\hat{s}(l_x) = \{m \mid \exists l_a, l_b \text{ with } m \in \hat{s}_1(l_a), m \in \hat{s}_2(l_b) \text{ and } x = max(a, b)\}$$
$$\cup \{m \mid m \in \hat{s}_1(l_x) \text{ and } \not\exists l_a \text{ with } m \in \hat{s}_2(l_a)\}$$
$$\cup \{m \mid m \in \hat{s}_2(l_x) \text{ and } \not\exists l_a \text{ with } m \in \hat{s}_1(l_a)\}$$

This includes $\hat{s}(l_\top) = \hat{s}_1(l_\top) \cup \hat{s}_2(l_\top)$.

Example 4 $(\hat{\mathcal{J}}_{\hat{S}})$.

	l_1	l_2	l_3	l_4	$l_\top$
$\hat{s}_1$	$\{m_e\}$	$\{m_b\}$	$\{m_c\}$	$\{m_d\}$	$\{m_a\}$
$\hat{s}_2$	$\{m_c\}$	$\{m_e, m_f\}$	$\{m_a\}$	$\{m_d\}$	$\{m_b\}$
$\hat{\mathcal{J}}_{\hat{S}}(\hat{s}_1, \hat{s}_2)$	$\{\}$	$\{m_e, m_f\}$	$\{m_c\}$	$\{m_d\}$	$\{m_a, m_b\}$

The join function for abstract cache states applies the join function for abstract set states to all its abstract set states:

$$\hat{\mathcal{J}}_{\hat{C}}(\hat{c}_1, \hat{c}_2) = [f_i \mapsto \hat{\mathcal{J}}_{\hat{S}}(\hat{c}_1(f_i), \hat{c}_2(f_i)) \mid \text{ for all } 1 \le i \le n/A]$$

In order to solve the persistence analysis for a program, one can construct a system of recursive equations from its control flow graph (in classical dataflow analysis and in the program analyzer generator **PAG** this is only done implicitly). The variables in the equation system stand for abstract cache states for program points. For every control flow node[6] k, with $\mathcal{L}(k) = \langle m_1, ..., m_y \rangle$ there is an equation $\hat{c}_k = \hat{\mathcal{U}}_{\hat{C}}(...\hat{\mathcal{U}}_{\hat{C}}(pred(k), m_1)..., m_y)$. If k has only one direct predecessor k', then $pred(k) = \hat{c}_{k'}$. If k has more than one direct predecessor $k_1, ..., k_x$, then there is an equation $\hat{c}_{k'} = \hat{\mathcal{J}}_{\hat{C}}(\hat{c}_{k_1}, ...\hat{\mathcal{J}}_{\hat{C}}(\hat{c}_{k_{x-1}}, \hat{c}_{k_x})...)$, and $pred(k) = \hat{c}_{k'}$. The least fixpoint of the equation system is computed by iteration. The iteration starts with the abstract cache state of the start node set to an abstract cache state $\hat{c}_I$ that describes the cache when the program execution starts and all other variables $\hat{c}_k$ set to the least element $\perp_{\hat{C}}$.

An abstract cache state $\hat{c}$ at a control flow node k that references a memory block m is interpreted in the following way: Let $\hat{s} = \hat{c}(set(m))$. If $m \in \hat{s}(l_y)$ for $y \in \{1, ..., A\}$, then the maximal relative age of m is less or equal to y provided that m is in the cache. From this follows that m cannot be replaced in the cache after an initial load. m is *persistent*. This means that all (repeated) executions of the reference to m can produce *at most one* cache miss.

---

[6] For our cache analysis, it is most convenient to have one memory reference per control flow node. Therefore, our nodes may represent the different fragments of machine instructions that access memory.

Extension to Sets of Memory Locations So far, the update function $\hat{\mathcal{U}}$ describes the effect of *one* memory reference on abstract cache states. To support the analysis of programs for which not all addresses of the memory references can be precisely determined, the $\hat{\mathcal{U}}$ functions are extended to handle sets of possibly referenced memory locations. References to an array X can either be treated conservatively by using a reference to the set $\{m_1, ..., m_x\}$ of all memory blocks of X or by using an interval analysis to determine the address range more precisely [3, 24].

The persistence analysis computes the *maximal* relative age of all memory blocks. The update function $\hat{\mathcal{U}}_{\hat{C}}$ applied to a set $\{m_1, ..., m_x\}$ of possible memory locations and an abstract cache state $\hat{c}$ distributes all elements of $\{m_1, ..., m_x\}$ into their corresponding sets.

$$\hat{\mathcal{U}}_{\hat{C}}(\hat{c}, \{m_1, ..., m_x\}) = \hat{c}[f_i \mapsto \hat{\mathcal{U}}_{\hat{S}}(\hat{c}(f_i), X_{f_i})\text{for all } f_i \in \{set(m_1), ..., set(m_x)\}]$$
$$\text{where } X_{f_i} = \{m_y \mid m_y \in \{m_1, ..., m_x\} \text{ and } set(m_y) = f_i\}$$

The basic idea of the persistence analysis is to simulate what would happen to a memory block, if it had indeed been referenced. The additional set lines l_T are used to collect memory blocks that may have been removed from the cache. There are two components in the update function $\hat{\mathcal{U}}_{\hat{S}}$ for a set of possibly referenced memory blocks:

- References to memory blocks that are not yet in the abstract set state. Such memory blocks are inserted into the abstract set states by the function $\mathcal{I}_{\hat{S}}$.
- References to memory blocks that are in the abstract set state, i.e., have possibly been referenced before. Since it is not definitely known which memory block has been referenced, we are not allowed to decrease the relative age of any possibly referenced memory block. Nevertheless, we have to consider the effect of the memory references on the ages of the other memory blocks in the abstract set. This is described by the application of $\mathcal{A}_{\hat{S}}$ for all possibly referenced memory blocks that are possibly in the cache.

$$\hat{\mathcal{U}}_{\hat{S}}(\hat{s}, \{m_1, ..., m_x\}) = \mathcal{A}_{\hat{S}}(... \mathcal{A}_{\hat{S}}(\mathcal{I}_{\hat{S}}(\hat{s}, \{m_y, ..., m_z\}), m_a) ..., m_b)$$
$$\text{where } \{m_a, ..., m_b\} = \{m_1, ..., m_x\} \cap (\hat{s}(l_1) \cup ... \cup \hat{s}(l_T))$$
$$\text{and } \{m_y, ..., m_z\} = \{m_1, ..., m_x\} - (\hat{s}(l_1) \cup ... \cup \hat{s}(l_T))$$

$$\mathcal{I}_{\hat{S}}(\hat{s}, \{m_1, ..., m_x\}) = \begin{cases} [l_i \mapsto \{\} \mid i = 1 ... z - 1, \\ \quad l_z \mapsto \{m_1, ..., m_x\}, \\ \quad l_i \mapsto \hat{s}(l_{i-z}) \mid i = z + 1 ... A, \\ \quad l_T \mapsto (\hat{s}(l_{A-z+1}) \cup ... \cup \hat{s}(l_A) \cup \hat{s}(l_T))] \\ \quad \text{where } z = |\{m_1, ..., m_x\}| \qquad\qquad \text{if } z \leq A \\[2ex] [l_i \mapsto \{\} \mid i = 1 ... A, \\ \quad l_T \mapsto (\hat{s}(l_1) \cup ... \cup \hat{s}(l_A) \cup \hat{s}(l_T) \\ \qquad\qquad \cup \{m_1, ..., m_x\})] \qquad\qquad \text{otherwise} \end{cases}$$

$$
\mathcal{A}_{\hat{s}}(\hat{s}, m) = \begin{cases} \hat{s} & \text{if } m \in \hat{s}(l_1) \\[2ex] \begin{aligned} & [l_1 \mapsto \{\}, \\ & l_i \mapsto \hat{s}(l_{i-1}) \mid i = 2 \ldots h-1, \\ & l_h \mapsto \hat{s}(l_{h-1}) \cup \hat{s}(l_h), \\ & l_i \mapsto \hat{s}(l_i) \mid i = h+1 \ldots A, \\ & l_\top \mapsto \hat{s}(l_\top)]; \end{aligned} & \text{if } \exists h \in \{2, ..., A\} : m \in \hat{s}(l_h) \\[2ex] \begin{aligned} & [l_1 \mapsto \{\}, \\ & l_i \mapsto \hat{s}(l_{i-1}) \text{ for } i = 2 \ldots A, \\ & l_\top \mapsto \hat{s}(l_\top) \cup \hat{s}(l_A)]; \end{aligned} & \text{otherwise} \end{cases}
$$

Let us consider the set $\hat{L}$ of all abstract cache states of the solution of the persistence analysis of a program fragment l (instruction, loop, loop nest, procedure, program) of a program, and a set of memory blocks $X = \{m_1, ..., m_x\}$. All memory blocks that may have been removed from the cache are in the following set:

$$
R = \bigcup_{\hat{c} \in \hat{L}} \bigcup_{i=1}^{n/A} \hat{c}(f_i)(l_\top)
$$

If $X \cap R = \emptyset$, then the memory blocks of X will not be removed from the cache after they have been referenced for the first time. There will be at most $|X|$ cache misses for all references to memory blocks in X within the program fragment l.

6 Related Work

The work of Arnold, Mueller, Whalley, and Harmon has been one of the starting points of our work. [19, 17] describe a data flow analysis for the prediction of instruction cache behavior of programs for direct mapped caches. Their approach does not analyze executables but requires specific extensions to the compiler. In contrast to our method that derives semantics based categorizations of memory references only from the results of our analyses, an additional bottom-up algorithm over the control flow graph is used to compute a classification of the instructions for each loop level. A very "complex" extension to set associative instruction caches has later been given in [18]. Possibilities to handle data caching are mentioned in [25], but this article does not allow for a comparison to our approach.

In [13, 14] Yau-Tsun Steven Li, Sharad Malik, and Andrew Wolfe describe an integrated method to determine the worst case execution path of a program and to model architecture features like instruction caches and/or pipelines. The problem of finding an accurate worst case execution time bound is formulated as an integer linear program that must be solved. Solving integer linear programs is known to be NP-hard. This approach has been implemented in the cinderella tool[7]. Unlike the method described in [19] or our method that rely only on the

---

[7] See http://www.ee.princeton.edu/~yauli/cinderella-3.0/

control flow graph to determine the cache behavior of a memory reference, user provided *functionality constraints* can be used to describe the control flow more precisely. For direct mapped instruction caches and programs whose execution path is well defined and not very input dependent the predictions can be computed fast and are very accurate [14]. Increasing levels of associativity where the cache behavior of one memory reference depends on more (other) references and less defined execution paths lead to prohibitively high analysis times.

Widely based on [14], Greger Ottoson and Mikael Sjödin [20] have tried to develop a framework to estimate WCETs for architectures with pipelines, instruction and data caches. Unlike the approach of Li, Malik, and Wolfe, they are not restricted to linear constraints but use logical constraints (formulas) to model microarchitectural properties. Nevertheless, they experience the same problems. In an experiment to predict the cache behavior of a very small program they report analysis times of several hours.

In [15], Lim et al. describe a general framework for the computation of WCETs of programs in the presence of pipelines and cache memories based on the timing schema approach of Park and Shaw [21]. Unlike our method that is based on well explored theories and tools for abstract interpretation, the set of timing equations must be explicitly solved. An approximation to the solution for the set of timing equations has been proposed. Experimental results are reported for three small programs, but they cannot be easily compared with our experiments.

The approach of Lim et al. has also been applied to data caches. In [10], Hur et al. treat references to unknown addresses as two cache misses. The reported results are worse than the ones without data cache analysis where one assumes one cache miss for every data reference. But the authors expect that the results improve with better methods to resolve addresses of data references. For loops that reference only data that fit entirely into the cache, Kim et al. [11] have improved the approach based on the *pigeonhole principle*. Applied to the cache analysis, the pigeonhole principle says: If we have n memory reference to m memory locations and $n > m$ and all referenced memory blocks fit into the cache, then there must inevitably be some cache hits.

In [16], Liu and Lee present a worst case execution time analysis restricted to direct mapped instruction caches. The problem of finding the worst case execution time is formulated as finding the longest path in their *cache contents graphs*. They show that the problem is NP-hard and propose an exact and an approximative solution. In the worst case the exact solution corresponds to an exhaustive search over all (input dependent) execution paths of the program. The approximative solution can be given a parameter k saying that the WCET of the first k iterations of a loop should be computed exactly. For the remaining iterations they use a save WCET estimation based on the exact WCET of the previous iterations. There are experimental results for a binary search program and two small "program structures" reported. The approximative solution can require relative high values of k to give tight WCET estimations. This can lead to high analysis times even for the small examples.

7 Conclusion and Future Work

We have given an overview on how data dependence analysis and program restructuring methods to increase data locality can be used to determine worst case bounds on cache misses for very restricted classes of programs. To complement these methods we have presented the persistence analysis. This analysis determines memory locations that survive in the cache thus providing effective and efficient means to compute an upper bound on the number of possible cache misses for general programs.

Practical experiments to evaluate the applicability of the persistence analysis for instruction caches show promising results (see [4]). Future work will include practical experiments with the persistence analysis for sets of memory locations.

References

1. M. Alt, C. Ferdinand, F. Martin, and R. Wilhelm. Cache Behavior Prediction by Abstract Interpretation. In *Proceedings of SAS'96, Static Analysis Symposium*, LNCS 1145, pages 52–66. Springer, Sept. 1996.
2. M. Alt and F. Martin. Generation of Efficient Interprocedural Analyzers with PAG. In *Proceedings of SAS'95, Static Analysis Symposium*, LNCS 983, pages 33–50. Springer, Sept. 1995.
3. P. Cousot and R. Cousot. Static Determination of Dynamic Properties of Programs. In *Proceedings of the Second International Symposium on Programming*, pages 106–130, Dunod, Paris, France, 1976.
4. C. Ferdinand. A Fast and Efficient Cache Persistence Analysis. Technical Report 10/97, Universität des Saarlandes, Sonderforschungsbereich 124, Aug. 1997.
5. C. Ferdinand. Cache Behavior Prediction for Real-Time Systems. Dissertation, Universität des Saarlandes, Sept. 1997.
6. C. Ferdinand, F. Martin, and R. Wilhelm. Applying Compiler Techniques to Cache Behavior Prediction. In *Proceedings of the ACM SIGPLAN Workshop on Language, Compiler and Tool Support for Real-Time Systems*, pages 37–46, June 1997.
7. C. Ferdinand, F. Martin, and R. Wilhelm. Cache Behavior Prediction by Abstract Interpretation. *Science of Computer Programming*, 1998. Selected for SAS'96 special issue.
8. D. Gannon, W. Jalby, and K. Gallivan. Strategies for Cache and Local Memory Management by Global Program Transformation. In *Proceedings of the First International Conference on Supercomputing*, June 1987.
9. S. Ghosh, M. Martonosi, and S. Malik. Cache Miss Equations: An Analytical Representation of Cache Misses. In *Proceedings of the Eleventh ACM International Conference on Supercomputing*, July 1997.
10. Y. Hur, Y. H. Bea, S.-S. Lim, B.-D. Rhee, S. L. Min, Y. C. Park, M. Lee, H. Shin, and C. S. Kim. Worst Case Timing Analysis of RISC Processors: R3000/R3010 Case Study. In *Proceedings of the IEEE Real-Time Systems Symposium*, pages 308–319, Dec. 1995.
11. S. Kim, S. Min, and R. Ha. Efficient Worst Case Timing Analysis of Data Caching. In *Proceedings of the 1996 IEEE Real-Time Technology and Applications Symposium*, pages 230–240, June 1996.

12. M. S. Lam, E. E. Rothberg, and M. E. Wolf. The Cache Performance and Optimization of Blocked Algorithms. In *Proceedings of the Sixth International Conference on Architectural Support for Programming Languages and Operating Systems*, Apr. 1991.

13. Y.-T. S. Li, S. Malik, and A. Wolfe. Efficient Microarchitecture Modeling and Path Analysis for Real-Time Software. In *Proceedings of the IEEE Real-Time Systems Symposium*, pages 298–307, Dec. 1995.

14. Y.-T. S. Li, S. Malik, and A. Wolfe. Cache Modeling for Real-Time Software: Beyond Direct Mapped Instruction Caches. In *Proceedings of the IEEE Real-Time Systems Symposium*, Dec. 1996.

15. S.-S. Lim, Y. H. Bae, G. T. Jang, B.-D. Rhee, S. L. Min, C. Y. Park, H. Shin, K. Park, S.-M. Moon, and C. S. Kim. An Accurate Worst Case Timing Analysis for RISC Processors. *IEEE Transactions on Software Engineering*, 21(7):593–604, July 1995.

16. J.-C. Liu and H.-J. Lee. Deterministic Upperbounds of the Worst-Case Execution Time of Cached Programs. In *Proceedings of the IEEE Real-Time Systems Symposium*, pages 182–191, Dec. 1994.

17. F. Mueller. Static Cache Simulation and its Applications. PhD Thesis, Florida State University, July 1994.

18. F. Mueller. Generalizing Timing Predictions to Set-Associative Caches. Technical Report TR 96-66, Institut für Informatik, Humboldt-University, July 1996.

19. F. Mueller, D. B. Whalley, and M. Harmon. Predicting Instruction Cache Behavior. In *Proceedings of the ACM SIGPLAN Workshop on Language, Compiler and Tool Support for Real-Time Systems*, 1994.

20. G. Ottoson and M. Sjödin. Worst-Case Execution Time Analysis for Modern Hardware Architectures. In *Proceedings of the ACM SIGPLAN Workshop on Language, Compiler and Tool Support for Real-Time Systems*, pages 47–55, June 1997.

21. C. Y. Park and A. C. Shaw. Experiments with a Program Timing Tool Based on Source-Level Timing Schema. *IEEE Computer*, 24(5):48–57, May 1991.

22. A. K. Porterfield. Software Methods for Improvement of Cache Performance on Supercomputer Applications. PhD Thesis, Rice University, May 1989.

23. R. Schreiber and J. J. Dongarra. Automatic Blocking of Nested Loops. RIACS Technical Report 90.38, Research Institute for Advanced Computer Science, NASA Ames Research Center, Moffett Field, CA 94035, Aug. 1990.

24. M. Sicks. Adreßbestimmung zur Vorhersage des Verhaltens von Daten-Caches. Diplomarbeit, Universität des Saarlandes, 1997.

25. R. White, F. Mueller, C. A. Healy, D. B. Whalley, and M. Harmon. Timing Analysis for Data Caches and Set-Associative Caches. In *Proceedings of the Real-Time Technology and Applications Symposium*, pages 192–202, June 1997.

26. M. E. Wolf and M. S. Lam. A Data Locality Optimizing Algorithm. In *Proceedings of the ACM SIGPLAN Conference on Programming Language Design and Implementation*, pages 30–44, June 1991.

27. M. E. Wolf and M. S. Lam. A Loop Transformation Theory and an Algorithm to Maximize Parallelism. *IEEE Transactions on Parallel and Distributed Systems*, July 1991.

28. M. Wolfe. Optimizing Supercompilers for Supercomputers. PhD Thesis, University of Illinois at Urbana-Champaign, 1982.

Automatic Accurate Time-Bound Analysis for High-Level Languages

Yanhong A. Liu* and Gustavo Gomez*

Computer Science Department, Indiana University, Bloomington, IN 47405
{liu,ggomezes}@cs.indiana.edu

Abstract. This paper describes a general approach for automatic and accurate time-bound analysis. The approach consists of transformations for building time-bound functions in the presence of partially known input structures, symbolic evaluation of the time-bound function based on input parameters, optimizations to make the overall analysis efficient as well as accurate, and measurements of primitive parameters, all at the source-language level. We have implemented this approach and performed a number of experiments for analyzing Scheme programs. The measured worst-case times are closely bounded by the calculated bounds.

1 Introduction

Analysis of program running time is important for real-time systems, interactive environments, compiler optimizations, performance evaluation, and many other computer applications. It has been extensively studied in many fields of computer science: algorithms [11, 8], programming languages [25, 12, 20, 22], and systems [23, 19, 21]. It is particularly important for many applications, such as real-time systems, to be able to predict accurate time bounds automatically and efficiently, and it is particularly desirable to be able to do so for high-level languages [23, 19].

Since Shaw proposed timing schema for analyzing system running time based on high-level languages [23], a number of people have extended it for analysis in the presence of compiler optimizations [5], pipelining [13], cache memory [13, 7], etc. However, there remains an obvious and serious limitation of the timing schema, even in the absence of low-level complications. This is the inability to provide loop bounds, recursion depths, or execution paths automatically and accurately for the analysis [18, 1]. For example, the inaccurate loop bounds cause the calculated worst-case time to be as much as 67% higher than the measured worst-case time in [19], while the manual way of providing such information is potentially an even larger source of error, in addition to its inconvenience [18]. Various program analysis methods have been proposed to provide loop bounds or execution paths [1, 6, 9]. They ameliorate the problem but can not completely solve it, because they apply only to some classes of programs or use approximations that are too crude for the analysis, and because separating the loop and path information from the rest of the analysis is in general less accurate than an integrated analysis [17].

This paper describes a general approach for automatic and accurate time-bound analysis. The approach combines methods and techniques studied in theory, languages, and systems. We call it a *language-based* approach, because it primarily exploits methods and techniques for static program analysis and transformation.

* This work was partially supported by NSF under Grant CCR-9711253.

The approach consists of transformations for building time-bound functions in the presence of partially known input structures, symbolic evaluation of the time-bound function based on input parameters, optimizations to make overall the analysis efficient as well as accurate, and measurements of primitive parameters, all at the source-language level. We describe analysis and transformation algorithms and explain how they work. We have implemented this approach and performed a large number of experiments analyzing Scheme programs. The measured worst-case times are closely bounded by the calculated bounds. We describe our prototype system, ALPA, as well as the analysis and measurement results.

This approach is general in the sense that it works for other kinds of cost analysis as well, such as space analysis and output-size analysis. The basic ideas also apply to other programming languages. Furthermore, the implementation is independent of the underlying systems (compilers, operating systems, and hardware).

2 Language-based approach

Language-based time-bound analysis starts with a given program written in a high-level language, such as C or Lisp. The first step is to build a *timing function* that (takes the same input as the original program but) returns the running time in place of (or in addition to) the original return value. This is done easily by associating a parameter with each program construct representing its running time and by summing these parameters based on the semantics of the constructs [25, 23]. We call parameters that describe the running times of program constructs *primitive parameters*.

Since the goal is to calculate running time without being given particular inputs, the calculation must be based on certain assumptions about inputs. Thus, the first problem is to characterize the input data and reflect them in the timing function. In general, due to imperfect knowledge about the input, the timing function is transformed into a *time-bound function*.

In programming-language area, Rosendahl proposed the use of *partially known input structures* to characterize input data [20]. For example, instead of replacing an input list l with its length n, as done in algorithm analysis, or annotating loops with numbers related to n, as done in systems, we simply use as input a list of n unknown elements. We call parameters for describing partially known input structures *input parameters*. The timing function is then transformed automatically into a time-bound function: at control points where decisions depend on unknown values, the maximum time of all possible branches is computed; otherwise, the time of the chosen branch is computed. Rosendahl concentrated on proving the correctness of this transformation. He assumed constant 1 for primitive parameters and relied on optimizations to obtain closed forms in terms of input parameters, but closed forms can not be obtained for all time-bound functions.

Combining results from theory to systems, we have studied a general approach for computing time bounds automatically, efficiently, and more accurately. The approach analyzes programs written in a functional subset of scheme. Functional programming languages, together with features like automatic garbage collection, have become increasingly widely used, yet work for calculating actual running time of functional programs has been lacking. Analyses and transformations developed for functional language can be applied to improve analyses of imperative languages as well [26].

Language. We use a first-order, call-by-value functional language that has structured data, primitive arithmetic, Boolean, and comparison operations, conditionals, bindings, and mutually recursive function calls. For example, the program below selects the least element in a non-empty list.

$$least(x) = \textbf{if } null(cdr(x)) \textbf{ then } car(x)$$
$$\textbf{else } \textbf{let } s = least(cdr(x))$$
$$\textbf{in } \textbf{if } car(x) \leq s \textbf{ then } car(x) \textbf{ else } s \textbf{ end}$$

To present various analysis results, we use the following examples: insertion sort, selection sort (which uses *least*), mergesort, set union, list reversal (the standard linear-time version), and reversal with append (the standard quadratic-time version).

Even though this language is small, it is sufficiently powerful and convenient to write sophisticated programs. Structured data is essentially records in Pascal and C. We can also see that time analysis in the presence of arrays and pointers is not fundamentally harder [19], because the running times of the program constructs for them can be measured in the same way as times of other constructs. Note that side effects caused by these features often cause other analysis to be difficult [4]. For pure functional languages, higher-order functions and lazy evaluations are important. Time-bound functions that accommodate these features have been studied [24, 22]. The symbolic evaluation and optimizations we describe apply to them as well.

3 Constructing time-bound functions

Constructing timing functions. We first transform the original program to construct a timing function, which takes the original input and primitive parameters as arguments and returns the running time. This is straightforward based on the semantics of the program constructs.

Given an original program, we add a set of timing functions, one for each original function, which simply count the time while the original program executes. The algorithm, given below, is presented as a transformation $\mathcal{T}$ on the original program, which calls a transformation $\mathcal{T}_e$ to recursively transform subexpressions. For example, a variable reference is transformed into a symbol T_{varref} representing the running time of a variable reference; a conditional statement is transformed into the time of the test plus, if the condition is true, the time of the true branch, otherwise, the time of the false branch, and plus the time for the transfers of control.

$$\text{program: } \mathcal{T} \left[\!\left[\begin{array}{l} f_1(v_1, ..., v_{n_1}) = e_1; \\ ... \\ f_m(v_1, ..., v_{n_m}) = e_m; \end{array} \right]\!\right] = \begin{array}{ll} f_1(v_1, ..., v_{n_1}) = e_1; & tf_1(v_1, ..., v_{n_1}) = \mathcal{T}_e[e_1]; \\ ... & ... \\ f_m(v_1, ..., v_{n_m}) = e_m; & tf_m(v_1, ..., v_{n_m}) = \mathcal{T}_e[e_m]; \end{array}$$

variable reference:	$\mathcal{T}_e[v]$	$= T_{varref}$
data construction:	$\mathcal{T}_e[c(e_1, ..., e_n)]$	$= add(T_c, \mathcal{T}_e[e_1], ..., \mathcal{T}_e[e_n])$
primitive operation:	$\mathcal{T}_e[p(e_1, ..., e_n)]$	$= add(T_p, \mathcal{T}_e[e_1], ..., \mathcal{T}_e[e_n])$
conditional:	$\mathcal{T}_e[\textbf{if } e_1 \textbf{ then } e_2 \textbf{ else } e_3]$	$= add(T_{if}, \mathcal{T}_e[e_1], \textbf{if } e_1 \textbf{ then } \mathcal{T}_e[e_2] \textbf{ else } \mathcal{T}_e[e_3])$
binding:	$\mathcal{T}_e[\textbf{let } v = e_1 \textbf{ in } e_2 \textbf{ end}]$	$= add(T_{let}, \mathcal{T}_e[e_1], \textbf{let } v{=}e_1 \textbf{ in } \mathcal{T}_e[e_2] \textbf{ end})$
function call:	$\mathcal{T}_e[f(e_1, ..., e_n)]$	$= add(T_{call}, \mathcal{T}_e[e_1], ..., \mathcal{T}_e[e_n], tf(e_1, ..., e_n))$

This transformation is similar to the local cost assignment [25], step-counting function [20], cost function [22], etc. in other work. Our transformation handles bindings and makes all primitive parameters explicit at the source-language level. For example, each primitive operation p is given a different symbol T_p, and each constructor c is given a different symbol T_c. Note that the timing function terminates with the appropriate sum of primitive parameters if the original program terminates, and it runs forever to sum to infinity if the original program does not terminate, which is the desired meaning of a timing function.

Constructing time-bound functions. Characterizing program inputs and capturing them in the timing function are difficult to automate [25, 12, 23]. However, partially known input structures provide a natural means [20]. A special value *unknown* represents unknown values. For example, to capture all input lists of length n, the following partially known input structure can be used.

$$list(n) = \textbf{if } n = 0 \textbf{ then } nil$$
$$\textbf{else } cons(unknown, list(n-1))$$

Similar structures can be used to describe an array of n elements, etc.

Since partially known input structures give incomplete knowledge about inputs, the original functions need to be transformed to handle the special value *unknown*. In particular, for each primitive function p, we define a new function f_p such that $f_p(v_1, ..., v_n)$ returns *unknown* if any v_i is *unknown* and returns $p(v_1, ..., v_n)$ as usual otherwise. We also define a new function lub that takes two values and returns the most precise partially known structure that both values conform with.

$$f_p(v_1, ..., v_n) = \textbf{if } v_1 = unknown \qquad lub(v_1, v_2) = \textbf{if } v_1 \textit{ is } c_1(x_1, ..., x_i) \wedge$$
$$\vee ... \vee \qquad\qquad\qquad v_2 \textit{ is } c_2(y_1, ..., y_j) \wedge$$
$$v_n = unknown \qquad\qquad\qquad c_1 = c_2 \wedge i = j$$
$$\textbf{then } unknown \qquad\qquad \textbf{then } c_1(lub(x_1, y_1), ..., lub(x_i, y_i))$$
$$\textbf{else } p(v_1, ..., v_n) \qquad\qquad \textbf{else } unknown$$

Also, the timing functions need to be transformed to compute an upper bound of the running time: if the truth value of a conditional test is known, then the time of the chosen branch is computed normally, otherwise, the maximum of the times of both branches is computed. Transformation C embodies these algorithms, where C_e transforms an expression in the original functions, and C_t transforms an expression in the timing functions.

$$\text{prog: } C \left[\left[\begin{array}{ll} f_1(v_1, ..., v_{n_1}) = e_1; & tf_1(v_1, ..., v_{n_1}) = e_1'; \\ ... & ... \\ f_m(v_1, ..., v_{n_m}) = e_m; & tf_m(v_1, ..., v_{n_m}) = e_m'; \end{array} \right] \right]$$

$$= \begin{array}{lll} f_1(v_1, ..., v_{n_1}) = C_e\,[e_1]; & tf_1(v_1, ..., v_{n_1}) = C_t\,[e_1']; & f_p(v_1, ..., v_n) = ... \text{ as above} \\ ... & & \\ f_m(v_1, ..., v_{n_m}) = C_e\,[e_m]; & tf_m(v_1, ..., v_{n_m}) = C_t\,[e_m']; & lub(v_1, v_2) = ... \text{ as above} \end{array}$$

variable ref.:	$C_e\,[v]$	$= v$
data const.:	$C_e\,[c(e_1, ..., e_n)]$	$= c(C_e\,[e_1], ..., C_e\,[e_n])$
primitive op.:	$C_e\,[p(e_1, ..., e_n)]$	$= f_p(C_e\,[e_1], ..., C_e\,[e_n])$
conditional:	$C_e\,[\textbf{if } e_1 \textbf{ then } e_2 \textbf{ else } e_3]$	$= \textbf{let } v = C_e\,[e_1]$
		$\quad\textbf{in if } v = unknown \textbf{ then } lub(C_e\,[e_2], C_e\,[e_3])$
		$\quad\textbf{else if } v \textbf{ then } C_e\,[e_2] \textbf{ else } C_e\,[e_3] \textbf{ end}$
binding:	$C_e\,[\textbf{let } v = e_1 \textbf{ in } e_2 \textbf{ end}]$	$= \textbf{let } v = C_e\,[e_1] \textbf{ in } C_e\,[e_2] \textbf{ end}$
function call:	$C_e\,[f(e_1, ..., e_n)]$	$= f(C_e\,[e_1], ..., C_e\,[e_n])$
primitive parameter:	$C_t\,[T]$	$= T$
summation:	$C_t\,[add(e_1, ..., e_n)]$	$= add(C_t\,[e_1], ..., C_t\,[e_n])$
conditional:	$C_t\,[\textbf{if } e_1 \textbf{ then } e_2 \textbf{ else } e_3]$	$= \textbf{let } v = C_e\,[e_1]$
		$\quad\textbf{in if } v = unknown \textbf{ then } max(C_t\,[e_2], C_t\,[e_3])$
		$\quad\textbf{else if } v \textbf{ then } C_t\,[e_2] \textbf{ else } C_t\,[e_3] \textbf{ end}$
binding:	$C_t\,[\textbf{let } v = e_1 \textbf{ in } e_2 \textbf{ end}]$	$= \textbf{let } v = C_t\,[e_1] \textbf{ in } C_t\,[e_2] \textbf{ end}$
function call:	$C_t\,[tf(e_1, ..., e_n)]$	$= tf(C_t\,[e_1], ..., C_t\,[e_n])$

The resulting time-bound function takes as arguments partially known input structures, such as $list(n)$, which take as arguments input parameters, such as n. Therefore, we can obtain a resulting function that takes as arguments input parameters and primitive parameters and computes the most accurate time bound possible.

Both transformations $\mathcal{T}$ and $\mathcal{C}$ take linear time in terms of the size of the program, so they are extremely efficient, as also seen in our prototype system ALPA. Note that the resulting time-bound function may not terminate, but this occurs only if the recursive structure of the original program depends on unknown parts in the partially known input structure. As a trivial example, if partially known input structure given is *unknown*, then the corresponding time-bound function for any recursive function does not terminate.

4 Optimizing time-bound functions

This section describes symbolic evaluation and optimizations that make computation of time bounds more efficient. The transformations consist of partial evaluation, realized as global inlining, and incremental computation, realized as local optimization. In the worst case, evaluation of the time-bound functions takes exponential time in terms of the input parameters, since it essentially searches for the worst-case execution path for all inputs satisfying the partially known input structures.

Partial evaluation of time-bound functions. In practice, values of input parameters are given for almost all applications. While in general it is not possible to obtain explicit loop bounds automatically and accurately, we can implicitly achieve the desired effect by evaluating the time-bound function symbolically in terms of primitive parameters given specific values of input parameters.

The evaluation simply follows the structures of time-bound functions. Specifically, the control structures determine conditional branches and make recursive function calls as usual, and the only primitive operations are sums of primitive parameters and maximums among alternative sums, which can easily be done symbolically. Thus, the transformation simply inlines all function calls, sums all primitive parameters symbolically, determines conditional branches if it can, and takes maximum sums among all possible branches if it can not.

The symbolic evaluation $\mathcal{E}$ defined below performs the transformations. It takes as arguments an expression e and an environment ρ of variable bindings and returns as result a symbolic value that contains the primitive parameters. The evaluation starts with the application of the program to be analyzed to a partially unknown input structure, e.g., $mergesort(list(250))$, and it starts with an empty environment. Assume $symbAdd$ is a function that symbolically sums its arguments, and $symbMax$ is a function that symbolically takes the maximum of its arguments.

variable ref.:	$\mathcal{E}[\![v]\!]\rho$	$= \rho(v)$ look up binding in environment
primitive parameter:	$\mathcal{E}[\![T]\!]\rho$	$= T$
data constr.:	$\mathcal{E}[\![c(e_1,...,e_n)]\!]\rho$	$= c(\mathcal{E}[\![e_1]\!]\rho,...,\mathcal{E}[\![e_n]\!]\rho)$
primitive op.:	$\mathcal{E}[\![p(e_1,...,e_n)]\!]\rho$	$= p(\mathcal{E}[\![e_1]\!]\rho,...,\mathcal{E}[\![e_n]\!]\rho)$
summation:	$\mathcal{E}[\![add(e_1,...,e_n)]\!]\rho$	$= symbAdd(\mathcal{E}[\![e_1]\!]\rho,...,\mathcal{E}[\![e_n]\!]\rho)$
maximum:	$\mathcal{E}[\![max(e_1,...,e_n)]\!]\rho$	$= symbMax(\mathcal{E}[\![e_1]\!]\rho,...,\mathcal{E}[\![e_n]\!]\rho)$
conditional:	$\mathcal{E}[\![\text{if } e_1 \text{ then } e_2 \text{ else } e_3]\!]\rho$	$= \mathcal{E}[\![e_2]\!]\rho$ if $\mathcal{E}[\![e_1]\!]\rho = true$
		$\quad\ \ \mathcal{E}[\![e_3]\!]\rho$ if $\mathcal{E}[\![e_1]\!]\rho = false$
binding:	$\mathcal{E}[\![\text{let } v = e_1 \text{ in } e_2 \text{ end}]\!]\rho$	$= \mathcal{E}[\![e_2]\!]\rho[v \mapsto \mathcal{E}[\![e_1]\!]\rho]$ bind v in environment
function call:	$\mathcal{E}[\![f(e_1,...,e_n)]\!]\rho$	$= e[v_1 \mapsto \mathcal{E}[\![e_1]\!]\rho,...,v_n \mapsto \mathcal{E}[\![e_n]\!]\rho]$
		$\quad$ where f is defined by $f(v_1,...,v_n) = e$

This symbolic evaluation is exactly a specialized partial evaluation. It is fully automatic and computes the most accurate time bound possible with respect to the given program structure. It always terminates as long as the time-bound function terminates.

Avoiding repeated summations over recursions. The symbolic evaluation above is a global optimization over all time-bound functions involved. During the evaluation, summations of symbolic primitive parameters within each function definition are performed repeatedly while the computation recurses. Thus, we can speed up the symbolic evaluation by first performing such summations in a pre-processing step. Specifically, we create a vector and let each element correspond to a primitive parameter. The transformation S performs this optimization.

program: $S \begin{bmatrix} tf_1(v_1, ..., v_{n_1}) = e_1''; \\ ... \\ tf_m(v_1, ..., v_{n_m}) = e_m''; \end{bmatrix} = \begin{array}{l} tf_1(v_1, ..., v_{n_1}) = S_t[e_1']; \\ ... \\ tf_m(v_1, ..., v_{n_m}) = S_t[e_m']; \end{array}$

primitive parameter: $S_t[T]$ = create a vector of 0's except with the component corresponding to T set to 1

summation: $S_t[add(e_1, ..., e_n)]$ = component-wise summation of all the vectors among $S_t[e_1], ..., S_t[e_n]$

maximum: $S_t[max(e_1, ..., e_n)]$ = component-wise maximum of all the vectors among $S_t[e_1], ..., S_t[e_n]$

all other: $S_t[e]$ = e

This incrementalizes the computation in each recursion to avoid repeated summation. Again, this is fully automatic and takes time linear in terms of the size of the cost-bound function.

The result of this optimization is dramatic. For example, optimized symbolic evaluation of the same quadratic-time reverse takes only 2.55 milliseconds, while direct evaluation takes 0.96 milliseconds, resulting in less than 3 times slowdown.

5   Making time-bound functions accurate

While loops and recursions affect time bounds most, the accuracy of the time bounds calculated also depends on the handling of the conditionals in the original program, which is reflected in the time-bound function. For conditionals whose test results are known to be true or false at the symbolic-evaluation time, the appropriate branch is chosen; so other branches, which may even take longer, are not considered for the worst-case time. This is a major source of accuracy for our worst-case bound.

For conditionals whose test results are not known at symbolic-evaluation time, we need to take the maximum time among all alternatives. The only case in which this would produce inaccurate time bound is when the test in a conditional in one subcomputation implies the test in a conditional in another subcomputation. For example, consider an expression e_0 whose value is *unknown* and

$e_1 =$ **if** e_0 **then** 1 **else** $Fibonacci(1000)$
$e_2 =$ **if** e_0 **then** $Fibonacci(2000)$ **else** 2

If we compute time bound for $e_1 + e_2$ directly, it is at least $tFibonacci(1000) + tFibonacci(2000)$. However, if we consider only the two realizable execution paths, we know that the worst case is $tFibonacci(2000)$ plus some small constants. This is known as the false-path elimination problem [1].

Two transformations, *lifting conditions* and *simplifying conditionals*, allow us to achieve the accurate analysis results above. In each function definition, the former lifts conditions to the outmost scope that the test does not depend on, and the latter simplifies conditionals according to the lifted condition. These transformations are not needed for the examples in this paper. They are discussed further in [14].

6 Implementation and experimentation

We have implemented the analysis approach in a prototype system, ALPA (Automatic Language-based Performance Analyzer). The implementation is for a subset of Scheme. The measurements and analyses are performed for source programs compiled with Chez Scheme compiler [3]. The particular numbers below are taken on a Sun Ultra 1 with 167MHz UltraSPARC CPU and 64MB main memory, but we have also performed the analysis for several other kinds of SPARC stations, and the results are similar.

We tried to avoid compiler optimizations by setting the optimization level to 0. To handle garbage-collection time, we performed two sets of experiments: one set excludes garbage-collection times in both calculations and measurements, while the other includes them in both.

Since the minimum running time of a program construct is about 0.1 microseconds, and the precision of the timing function is 10 milliseconds, we use control/test loops that iterate 10,000,000 times, keeping measurement error under 1%. Such a loop is repeated 100 times, and the average value is taken to compute the primitive parameter for the tested construct (the variance is less than 10% in most cases). The calculation of the time bound is done by plugging these measured parameters into the optimized time-bound function. We then run each example program an appropriate number of times to measure its running time with less than 1% error.

Figure 1 shows the calculated and measured worst-case times for six example programs on inputs of size 10 to 2000. For the set union example, we used inputs where both arguments were of the given sizes. These times do not include garbage-collection times. The item me/ca is the measured time expressed as a percentage of the calculated time. In general, all measured times are closely bounded by the calculated times (with about 90-95% accuracy) except when inputs are extremely small (10 or 20, in 1 case) or extremely large (2000, in 3 cases), which is analyzed below.

For measurements that include garbage-collection times, the results are similar, except that the percentages are consistently higher and underestimates occur for a few more inputs and start on inputs of size 1000 instead of 200. We believe that this is the effect of garbage collection, which we have not analyzed specifically.

Examples such as sorting are classified as complex examples in previous study [19, 13], where calculated time is as much as 67% higher than measured time, and where only the result for one sorting program on a single input (of size 10 [19] or 20 [13]) is reported in each experiment.

We found that when inputs are extremely small, the measured time is occasionally above the calculated time for some examples. Also, when inputs are large, the measured times for some examples are above the calculated time. We attribute these to cache memory effects, and this is further confirmed by measuring programs, such as Cartesian product, that use extremely large amount of space even on small inputs (50-200). While this shows that cache effects need to be considered for larger applications, it also helps validate that our calculated results are accurate relative to our current model.

size	insertion sort			selection sort			mergesort		
	calculated	measured	me/ca	calculated	measured	me/ca	calculated	measured	me/ca
10	0.06751	0.06500	96.3	0.13517	0.12551	92.9	0.11584	0.11013	95.1
20	0.25653	0.25726	100.3	0.52945	0.47750	90.2	0.29186	0.27546	94.4
50	1.55379	1.48250	95.4	3.26815	3.01125	92.1	0.92702	0.85700	92.4
100	6.14990	5.86500	95.4	13.0187	11.9650	91.9	2.15224	1.98812	92.4
200	24.4696	24.3187	99.4	51.9678	47.4750	91.4	4.90017	4.57200	93.3
300	54.9593	53.8714	98.0	116.847	107.250	91.8	7.86231	7.55600	96.1
500	152.448	147.562	96.8	324.398	304.250	93.8	14.1198	12.9800	91.9
1000	609.146	606.000	99.5	1297.06	1177.50	90.8	31.2153	28.5781	91.6
2000	2435.29	3081.25	126.5	5187.17	5482.75	105.7	68.3816	65.3750	95.6

size	set union			list reversal			reversal w/app.		
	calculated	measured	me/ca	calculated	measured	me/ca	calculated	measured	me/ca
10	0.10302	0.09812	95.2	0.00918	0.00908	98.8	0.05232	0.04779	91.3
20	0.38196	0.36156	94.7	0.01798	0.01661	92.4	0.19240	0.17250	89.7
50	2.27555	2.11500	92.9	0.04436	0.04193	94.5	1.14035	1.01050	88.6
100	8.95400	8.33250	93.1	0.08834	0.08106	91.8	4.47924	3.93600	87.9
200	35.5201	33.4330	94.1	0.17629	0.16368	92.9	17.7531	15.8458	89.3
300	79.6987	75.1000	94.2	0.26424	0.24437	92.5	39.8220	35.6328	89.5
500	220.892	208.305	94.3	0.44013	0.40720	92.5	110.344	102.775	93.1
1000	882.094	839.780	95.2	0.87988	0.82280	93.5	440.561	399.700	90.7
2000	3525.42	3385.31	96.0	1.75937	1.65700	94.2	1760.61	2235.75	127.0

Fig. 1. Calculated and measured worst-case times (in milliseconds), without garbage collection.

Among fifteen programs we analyzed using ALPA, two of the time-bound functions did not terminate. One is quicksort, and the other is a contrived variation of sorting; both diverge because the recursive structure for splitting a list depends on the values of unknown list elements. We have found a different symbolic-evaluation strategy that uses a kind of incremental path selection, and the evaluation would terminate for both examples, as well as all other examples, giving accurate worst-case bounds. We are implementing that algorithm. We also noticed that static analysis can be exploited to identify sources of nontermination.

7   Related work and conclusion

Compared to work in algorithm analysis and program complexity analysis [12, 22], this work consistently pushes through symbolic primitive parameters, so it allows us to calculate actual time bounds and validate the results with experimental measurements. Compared to work in systems [23, 19, 18, 13], this work explores program analysis and transformation techniques to overcome the difficulties caused by the inability to obtain loop bounds, recursion depths, or execution paths automatically and precisely. There is also work for measuring primitive parameters of Fortran programs for the purpose of general performance prediction [21], not worst-case analysis.

A number of techniques have been studied for obtaining loop bounds or execution paths [18, 1, 6, 9]. Manual annotations [18, 13] are inconvenient and error-prone [1]. Automatic analysis of such information has two main problems. First, separating the loop and path information from the rest of the analysis [6] is in general less accurate than an integrated analysis [17]. Second, approximations for merging paths from loops, or recursions, very often lead to nontermination of the time analysis, not just looser bounds [6, 17]. Some new methods, while powerful, apply only to certain classes of programs [9]. In contrast, our method allows recursions, or loops, to be considered naturally in the overall execution-time analysis based on partially known input structures.

The most recent work by Lundqvist and Stenstrom [17] is based on essentially the same ideas as ours. They apply the ideas at machine instruction level and can more accurately take into account the effects of instruction pipelining and data caching, but their method for merging paths for loops would lead to nonterminating analysis for many programs, e.g., a program that computes the union of two lists with no repeated elements. Our experiments show that we can calculate more accurate time bound and for many more programs than merging paths, and the calculation is still efficient.

The idea of using partially known input structures originates from Rosendahl [20]. We have extended it to manipulate primitive parameters. We also handle binding constructs, which is simple but necessary for efficient computation. An innovation in our method is to optimize the time-bound function using partial evaluation [2,10], incremental computation [16,15], and transformations of conditionals to make the analysis more efficient and more accurate.

We are starting to explore a suite of new language-based techniques for timing analysis, in particular, analyses and optimizations for further speeding up the evaluation of the time-bound function. To make the analysis even more accurate and efficient, we can automatically generate measurement programs for all maximum subexpressions that do not include transfers of control; this corresponds to the large atomic-blocks method [19]. We also believe that the lower-bound analysis is entirely symmetric to the upper-bound analysis, by replacing maximum with minimum at all conditional points. Finally, we plan to accommodate more lower-level dynamic factors for timing at the source-language level [13,7]. In particular, we plan to apply our general approach to analyze space consumption and hence to help predict garbage-collection and caching behavior.

References

1. P. Altenbernd. On the false path problem in hard real-time programs. In *Proceedings of the 8th EuroMicro Workshop on Real-Time Systems*, pages 102–107, L'Aquila, June 1996.
2. B. Bjørner, A. P. Ershov, and N. D. Jones, editors. *Partial Evaluation and Mixed Computation*. North-Holland, Amsterdam, 1988.
3. Cadence Research Systems. *Chez Scheme System Manual*. Cadence Research Systems, Bloomington, Indiana, revision 2.4 edition, July 1994.
4. D. R. Chase, M. Wegman, and F. K. Zadeck. Analysis of pointers and structures. In *Proceedings of the ACM SIGPLAN '90 Conference on Programming Language Design and Implementation*, pages 296–310. ACM, New York, June 1990.
5. J. Engblom, P. Altenbernd, and A. Ermedahl. Facilitating worst-case execution time analysis for optimized code. In *Proceedings of the 10th EuroMicro Workshop on Real-Time Systems*, Berlin, Germany, June 1998.
6. A. Ermedahl and J. Gustafsson. Deriving annotations for tight calculation of execution time. In *In Proceedings of Euro-Par'97*, volume 1300 of *Lecture Notes in Computer Science*, pages 1298–1307. Springer-Verlag, Berlin, Aug. 1997.
7. C. Ferdinand, F. Martin, and R. Wilhelm. Applying compiler techniques to cache behavior prediction. In *Proceedings of the ACM SIGPLAN 1997 Workshop on Languages, Compilers, and Tools for Real-Time Systems*, pages 37–46, 1997.
8. P. Flajolet, B. Salvy, and P. Zimmermann. Automatic average-case analysis of algorithms. *Theoretical Computer Science, Series A*, 79(1):37–109, Feb. 1991.
9. C. Healy, M. Sjödin, V. Rustagi, and D. Whalley. Bounding loop iterations for timing analysis. In *Proceedings of the IEEE Real-Time Applications Symposium*. IEEE CS Press, Los Alamitos, Calif., June 1998.
10. N. D. Jones, C. K. Gomard, and P. Sestoft. *Partial Evaluation and Automatic Program Generation*. Prentice-Hall, Englewood Cliffs, N.J., 1993.
11. D. E. Knuth. *The Art of Computer Programming*, volume 1. Addison-Wesley, Reading, Mass., 1968.
12. D. Le Métayer. Ace: An automatic complexity evaluator. *ACM Trans. Program. Lang. Syst.*, 10(2):248–266, Apr. 1988.

13. S.-S. Lim, Y. H. Bae, G. T. Jang, B.-D. Rhee, S. L. Min, C. Y. Park, H. Shin, K. Park, S.-M. Moon, and C.-S. Kim. An accurate worst case timing analysis for RISC processors. *IEEE Trans. Softw. Eng.*, 21(7):593–604, July 1995.

14. Y. A. Liu and G. Gomezes. Automatic accurate time-bound analysis for high-level languages. Technical Report TR 508, Computer Science Department, Indiana University, Bloomington, Indiana, Apr. 1998.

15. Y. A. Liu, S. D. Stoller, and T. Teitelbaum. Static caching for incremental computation. *ACM Trans. Program. Lang. Syst.*, 20(3), May 1998.

16. Y. A. Liu and T. Teitelbaum. Systematic derivation of incremental programs. *Sci. Comput. Program.*, 24(1):1–39, Feb. 1995.

17. T. Lundqvist and P. Stenström. Integrating path and timing analysis using instruction-level simulation techniques. Technical Report No. 98-3, Department of Computer Engineering, Chalmers University of Technology, Göteborg, Sweden, 1998.

18. C. Y. Park. Predicting program execution times by analyzing static and dynamic program paths. *Real-Time Systems*, 5:31–62, 1993.

19. C. Y. Park and A. C. Shaw. Experiments with a program timing tool based on source-level timing schema. *IEEE Computer*, 24(5):48–57, 1991.

20. M. Rosendahl. Automatic complexity analysis. In *Proceedings of the 4th International Conference on Functional Programming Languages and Computer Architecture*, pages 144–156. ACM, New York, Sept. 1989.

21. R. H. Saavedra and A. J. Smith. Analysis of benchmark characterization and benchmark performance prediction. *ACM Transactions on Computer Systems*, 14(4):344–384, Nov. 1996.

22. D. Sands. Complexity analysis for a lazy higher-order language. In *Proceedings of the 3rd European Symposium on Programming*, volume 432 of *Lecture Notes in Computer Science*, pages 361–376. Springer-Verlag, Berlin, May 1990.

23. A. Shaw. Reasoning about time in higher level language software. *IEEE Trans. Softw. Eng.*, 15(7):875–889, July 1989.

24. P. Wadler. Strictness analysis aids time analysis. In *Conference Record of the 15th Annual ACM Symposium on Principles of Programming Languages*. ACM, New York, Jan. 1988.

25. B. Wegbreit. Mechanical program analysis. *Commun. ACM*, 18(9):528–538, Sept. 1975.

26. D. Weise, R. F. Crew, M. Ernst, and B. Steensgaard. Value dependence graphs: Representation without taxation. In *Conference Record of the 21st Annual ACM Symposium on Principles of Programming Languages*. ACM, New York, Jan. 1994.

Extending RT-Linux to Support Flexible Hard Real-Time Systems with Optional Components

A. Terrasa, A. Espinosa and A. García-Fornes

Departamento de Sistemas Informáticos y Computación,
Universidad Politécnica de Valencia,
Camino de Vera, 46022 Valencia, Spain.
{aterrasa, aespinos, agarcia}@dsic.upv.es

Abstract. This paper describes a framework that provides a task programming model with optional components and the appropriate operating system mechanisms for supporting it. The approach provides 100% guarantees to hard real-time tasks using fixed priority pre-emptive scheduling. Optional components, which increase the utility of the guaranteed tasks, are executed when spare processor capacity is available. The framework has been developed extending the existing RT-Linux capabilities. Furthermore, the design of these kernel extensions have been proved to be predictable, in such a way that it is possible to perform a schedulability analysis of the entire system, including kernel overheads.

1   Introduction

Hard real-time systems are characterized by the fact that severe consequences will result if logical as well as timing correctness properties of the system are not satisfied. Conventionally, real-time systems were configured at design time to perform a given set of tasks and could not easily adapt to dynamic situations.

In hard real-time systems, the focus is on ensuring that in a set of tasks each task completes within its deadline. A hard real-time application is then formed by a number of critical periodic tasks, each of which is characterized by its period, its deadline and its worst-case execution time. These tasks must be guaranteed by an off-line schedulability test in order to prove that all tasks always meet their deadlines. This test assumes a particular scheduling policy at run time. Fixed priority pre-emptive scheduling and associated feasibility theory [Aud95] is becoming a standard in developing hard real-time systems.

On the other hand, the requirement to support flexible, adaptive and intelligent behavior whilst also providing the 100% guarantees needed by hard real-time services has been identified as one of the key challenges presented by the next generation of real-time systems [Sta93]. The imprecise and approximate computation techniques [Nat95], and in particular, the concept of *optional components* have emerged as the basis of new approaches for dealing with these issues. Optional components are not provided with off-line guarantees, but they may be executed at run-time if sufficient resources are available.

These techniques can be utilized in a wide variety of application areas. In particular we are developing a tool for building process control applications which require both hard real-time services and intelligent behavior [Gar96b]. The intelligent behavior is provided via the incorporation of optional components into processes with hard deadlines. This paper describes the operating system mechanisms needed for supporting such a task model and their implementation extending RT-Linux within the context of fixed priority pre-emptive scheduling.

Furthermore, the related feasibility test must include all kernel overheads in order to be useful in real applications. In this way, our studies have proven that the extensions introduced to RT-Linux are predictable, in order to be able to perform a schedulability analysis as discussed in [Gar97].

The following section outlines the task model, the software organization and the assumptions used. The remainder of the paper is organized as follows: section 3 describes the original RT-Linux capabilities. Section 4 discusses the main real-time techniques added to RT-Linux. Section 5 describes how the task model has been implemented in RT-Linux, and finally section 6 presents the conclusions and future lines of work.

2   The Framework

2.1   The Task Model and Assumptions

We consider that a real-time system comprises a fixed set of hard periodic tasks. Each periodic task has a period, a worst case execution time (*wcet*), and a deadline and is assigned a unique priority. Furthermore, each task is made up of three parts: the first one is the *initial part*, which is mandatory and reads information from sensors and computes a primary solution for these values. The second one is the *optional part*, which refines the solution computed by the initial part, but only executes if spare capacity is available when the initial part ends. The third one is the *final part*, which is mandatory and is in charge of accessing the environment to write the outcomes computed by either the optional or the initial part. Communication between the different parts is accomplished by means of a shared data area.

Both the initial and final parts have bounded computation requirements with known *wcet*. The optional part can have unbounded computation; however, if it exhausts the assigned time for its execution, it is then terminated.

The hard periodic task set is supposed to be schedulable according to an exact feasibility test [Aud95], which assumes a fixed priority pre-emptive dispatching following the deadline monotonic priority ordering. We compute the sum of its initial and final *wcets* as the task *wcet*. Tasks deadlines are assumed to be less than or equal to their periods. Mandatory components can communicate with each other via shared memory, by locking and unlocking semaphores according to the Priority Ceiling Protocol [Sha90]. Sharing memory between tasks is a common requirement in many real-time applications.

2.2 The Software Architecture

The software architecture (shown in Fig. 1) separates the execution of the mandatory components from the execution of the optional components. All the mandatory components are executed by a fixed priority pre-emptive scheduler. Optional components are always executed when spare capacity is available and they are selected by a second-level scheduler.

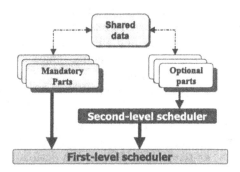

Fig. 1. The software organization

A set of scheduling techniques has been developed to efficiently determine the processor spare capacity at run time. In particular, slack-stealing algorithms [Dav93] are used to determine the amount of time the critical tasks can be delayed without losing their timing constraints. This time is known as *slack time*. The task model presented here uses the Approximate Dynamic Slack Stealing Algorithm (DASS) [Dav94] to compute the available slack time at run time. Within this technique, some different ways of using the slack time have been tested in previous works [Gar96a], in order to improve flexibility in the optional component scheduling. The reason for using slack time techniques in order to schedule optional components is that it naturally fits the presented task model: the precedence relationship among the three parts of each task is directly maintained, and the dynamic nature of the algorithm permits making good use of the processor spare capacity just when it is needed (at the end of each task's initial part).

Furthermore, a main goal in the framework presented here is to develop a generic set of functions that permits the designer to build a customized second-level scheduler. Then, a specific best-effort scheduling policy can be implemented depending on the particular application characteristics.

3 An Overview of Real-Time Linux

Real-Time Linux [Bar96] is a small and efficient piece of code that transforms Linux into a real-time operating system while preserving all its features such as driver management, X window system, network accessibility, etc. It is based on an idea which is quite simple: to put a real-time executive *underneath* the Linux kernel, that is, between the hardware and the kernel. This executive basically provides a support for running real-time tasks at the kernel level, and turns the entire Linux into one of these tasks. By this *Linux task* we denote the Linux kernel and all the Linux processes running above it. Thus, a real-time application can be defined as a collection of real-time tasks, and Linux would be the one with the lowest priority, running when no other task wants to run.

In this way, RT-Linux exhibits two independent levels of computation: the real-time tasks and Linux. The real-time tasks run at the kernel level with kernel privileges. On the other hand, Linux and all its user processes run whenever no real-time task is ready to execute. Furthermore, Linux is preempted whenever a higher priority task activates (normally as a response to a timer interrupt), despite being run at user or kernel level. In order to avoid unpredictable interrupt dispatch latencies, RT-Linux has changed the original functions enabling and disabling interrupts (cli, sti, and iret) by emulating macros. This mechanism is called *soft interrupts*, and it will permit interrupts to still be available for the real-time tasks, even when the kernel of Linux has disable them.

The original real-time support implemented in RT-Linux includes the RT_TASK and RTIME data types, and the set of functions shown in Fig. 2. The RT_TASK structure hides all the information the scheduler stores about each real-time task, such as its priority, its period, etc. On the other hand, RT-Linux has introduced a different way to represent the system. This new representation of time (the RTIME type) measures the time in tics. In addition, RT-Linux exploits the PC's Intel 8354 timer chip to its maximum resolution, leading to an approximate precision of one tic per microsecond. The system time can be consulted by calling the rt_get_time function. This function has been added as a built-in function in the kernel of RT-Linux.

```
RTIME rt_get_time(void);
int   rt_task_init(RT_TASK *task, void (*fn)(int data),
                   int data, int stack_size, int priority);
int   rt_task_make_periodic(RT_TASK *task, RTIME start_time,
                   RTIME period);
int   rt_task_wait(void);
int   rt_task_suspend(RT_TASK *task);
int   rt_task_wakeup(RT_TASK *task);
int   rt_task_delete(RT_TASK *task);
```

Fig. 2. The original RT-Linux functions to manage real-time tasks

The rest of the functions in Fig. 2 are defined in the RT-Linux's scheduler, which is a kernel-compiled, loadable module, called rt_prio_sched.o. This introduces another key idea of RT-Linux: it is possible to take advantage of the

Linux's dynamic loading of kernel modules to load and unload some RT-Linux modules without having to recompile the kernel or even reboot the computer. In this way, the support for RT-FIFOs (described below), the RT-Linux's scheduler and the user real-time application are compiled as kernel modules. These modules can be started and stopped just by typing the appropriate commands in a Linux shell.

In particular, the module corresponding to the user application creates the real-time tasks by calling the rt_task_init function. The entry arguments of this function are the function name that the task must run (as well as its initial data), the size of the stack for this task, and its priority; then the task is created and a task pointer is returned. If this task is intended to be periodic, an extra call to rt_task_make_periodic must be done, indicating the period of the task, and the (absolute) time the task must start for the first time. In RT-Linux, a periodic task must be an endless loop which contains the task's code plus a call to rt_task_wait. This call stops the execution of the task until its next release (according to its period). It is also possible to suspend and wake up a task within the code of this (or another) task, by calling rt_task_suspend and rt_task_wakeup respectively. A call to rt_task_delete simply destroys the task.

In the original support offered by RT-Linux, there is also a form of interprocess communication: The RT-FIFOs. This mechanism provides a set of buffers (allocated in kernel address space) to allow bidirectional communication between Linux processes and real-time tasks. From the real-time tasks' point of view, FIFOs are identified by integer numbers, and are accessed by calling some reading and writing functions (rt_fifo_get and rt_fifo_put). These functions are atomic and non blocking. From the Linux processes' point of view, RT-FIFOs are accessed like traditional UNIX character devices (called /dev/rtf0, /dev/rtf1, etc.).

4 Features Added to Real-Time Linux

Three main features have been added to the original version of RT-Linux: mutexes (binary semaphores) following the Priority Ceiling Protocol (PCP) as synchronization primitives, a technique to calculate the slack and gain times from real-time tasks and use it to schedule optional components, and some mechanisms to share memory within the real-time tasks and the traditional Linux processes.

The PCP-mutexes provided in this new version of RT-Linux have been introduced as a new data type called RT_MUTEX, and they are only usable from real-time tasks. The set of functions available to manage these mutexes are summarized in the Fig. 3. All the mutexes to be used in a real-time application must be created before real-time tasks are released for the first time. This is done by calling the rt_mutex_init function, which has the priority ceiling of the mutex being created as an entry parameter, and returns a pointer of this new mutex as an output parameter. The real-time tasks will use the mutexes as a way to synchronize themselves, by calling the functions rt_mutex_lock and rt_mutex_unlock, which will attempt to lock the mutex and release the mutex, respectively. The rt_mutex_destroy function simply removes the mutex.

```
int rt_mutex_init(RT_MUTEX *new_mutex, int mutex_ceiling);
int rt_mutex_lock(RT_MUTEX mutex);
int rt_mutex_unlock(RT_MUTEX mutex);
int rt_mutex_destroy(RT_MUTEX mutex);
```

Fig. 3. Interface for the PCP-mutexes

The DASS algorithm is a method used in real-time systems at run time (in particular, by the system's scheduler) to determine whether hard real-time tasks have slack time available or not. The slack time available is computed at each priority level, and all these *slack counters* must be updated at run time. When a non-critical task (e.g. an optional part of a hard task) wants to be executed then the scheduler calculates the actual slack available. If the calculated value is greater than zero, then the non-critical task may start running immediately, and keep running for an interval equal to this value. This technique has been introduced in RT-Linux by adding two internal (private) functions to the RT-Linux's scheduler: the rt_calculate_slack function accepts a priority level as an entry argument, and returns the current slack time available at this level. The second function, rt_slack_available, examines the available slack time at each priority level from the level passed as an argument to the lowest level and returns the minimum of all those values. This second function is used by the scheduler to determine the amount of time it can run an optional part.

The mechanism implemented to provide shared memory must take into consideration the fact that real-time tasks run in kernel space and any Linux process runs in its own virtual space. RT-Linux users achieve both spaces to be visible from each other by using Linux features such as mapping files in memory space (the mmap system call) and accessing the special file /dev/mem, which represents the entire physical memory of the system. We have encapsulated this mechanism in a module called Map_Ram, which offers two functions: the Map_Ram function maps a certain amount of physical memory into the user level process space, and the Unmap_Ram function unmaps this space.

This basic mechanism has been extended by providing a *storage manager*, which has been implemented in a module called Storage (Fig. 4). This manager offers the programmer a set of very efficient functions to allocate and deallocate entities in the shared space. The storage must be initialized by using the Storage_Create function, either by a real-time task or by a user level process. Once created, it may be used by any other application component, by using the Storage_Bind function. The manager allows three different types of entities to be created (allocate) in the storage space: objects, pools and items. An *object* is allocated by means of calling the Storage_Create_Object function and it is intended to represent a single variable which cannot be deallocated. A *pool* is allocated by the Storage_Create_Pool function and it represents a collection of potential *items*, all of which are identical in size. The pool is initially empty of items. Finally, *items* are allocated and deallocated within their pool by using the Storage_Create_Item and the Storage_Destroy_Item functions. All these functions are carefully designed to be very efficient. In fact, the computational cost of all of them is O(1), except the Storage_Create_Pool function, which has a computational cost of O(N), with N being the number of items to pre-allocate in the pool.

```
int    Storage_Create(void *Start_Address,
                        Entity_Size_T Total_Size);
int    Storage_Bind(void *Start_Address);
void *Storage_Create_Object( Entity_Size_T Size_Of_Object);
void *Storage_Create_Item(Pool_Handler_T In_Pool);
int    Storage_Destroy_Item(Pool_Handler_T In_Pool);
Pool_Handler_T Storage_Create_Pool(Entity_Size_T Item_Size,
                        unsigned int How_Many_Items);
```

Fig. 4. The Storage module functions

5   Implementing the Task Model

The new real-time techniques added to RT-Linux (which were presented in the previous section) are the basis of implementing the task model described above. Some changes have been introduced to the RT_TASK structure, and mainly to the RT-Linux scheduler. The new set of functions to manage real-time tasks are listed in Fig. 5. Note that some functions have been removed from the original set (shown in Fig. 2). This is because the implemented task model offers the programmer a more guided way to implement his/her application, and then some original functions (as rt_task_sleep or rt_task_wakeup) are not necessary (nor are they supported by the underlying feasibility analysis theory).

Each hard periodic task mentioned in the task model is implemented by a RT-Linux's real-time task. Since a task in our task model is somehow more sophisticated, some information must be added to the RT_TASK structure: the two functions it must run (for the initial and final parts), the wcet of both parts, the absolute deadline[1], its initial priority, the slack counter associated with the task's priority level, and an internal task identifier. The new rt_task_init function specifies the name of both functions corresponding to the initial and final parts of a given task, as well as the initial data passed to each. The other added argument, id, is a task identification number used in the communication between the first level scheduler and the second level scheduler. The redefinition

---
[1] The next absolute instant at which its deadline will be reached.

of the rt_task_make_periodic function specifies some other timing attributes to the task (the deadline and the initial and final wcet), which are needed by the slack algorithm. On the other hand, when all tasks have been created the rt_start_application function is invoked to inform the scheduler that the application can start. This is also necessary because the slack algorithm must calculate an initial value of the slack time available at each priority level before starting the tasks for the first time.

```
int rt_task_init(RT_TASK *task, void (*initial) (int ini_data),
                 int ini_data, void (*final) (int fin_data),
                 int fin_data,int stack_size, int priority, int id);
int rt_task_make_periodic(RT_TASK *task, RTIME start_time,
                 RTIME period, RTIME deadline, RTIME ini_wcet,
                 RTIME fin_wcet);
int rt_start_application( void );
int rt_task_delete( void );
```

Fig. 5. New functions to manage real-time tasks

By using this new set of functions, the programmer is not in charge of coding each task as an endless loop with a call to a specific function. On the contrary, the programmer only indicates two functions (coded without restrictions), and the scheduler will transform them into a periodic task with two mandatory parts. In particular, the threads of all real-time task execute the same internal function, named rt_task_runner, which executes each part of the task. The code of this function is shown in Fig. 6.

```
static int rt_task_runner(RT_TASK *task)
{
  while(1) {
    (task->initial)(task->initial_data);
    rt_task_wait();
    (task->final)(task->final_data);
    rt_task_wait();
  }
  return 0;
}
```

Fig. 6. Code of the rt_task_runner function

At the end of the initial part, the rt_task_runner function calls rt_task_wait. At this moment, the scheduler invokes its internal function rt_slack_available in order to determine whether the task's optional part can be executed. If no slack is available, the call to rt_task_wait ends and the task automatically resumes the execution (of its final part). However, if there is some slack time, then the execution of the task is temporally suspended, and the second level scheduler (described below) is invoked to execute that part. When the slack time has been exhausted, the final part resumes execution. At the end of the final part, the rt_task_wait function is called again, this time to inform the scheduler that the current invocation of the task has ended. Then, the scheduler calls the rt_calculate_slack function in order to compute the slack time available at the task's priority level.

Optional parts execute at the user level of Linux. In particular, the second level scheduler plus the code of all tasks' optional parts are implemented as *one* multi-threaded, user-level Linux process. This is a special process, running at Linux's highest priority. In other words, real-time applications will have two different running components (the real-time tasks and a Linux process containing all optional parts), which must be compiled and started separately and which execute in different address spaces. However, both components run as a whole application in a synchronized manner: whenever an optional part of a task can be executed, and there is slack available, the RT-Linux (first level) scheduler informs the second-level scheduler about it. In particular, the identification number of the task and the amount of slack time are passed via a message through a dedicated RT-FIFO. Once the message is sent, the first level scheduler lets the Linux task continue for an interval of time equal to the slack available. During this interval, as the second level scheduler runs in the Linux's highest priority process, it starts running immediately and gets the message from the FIFO. It then uses the information about the optional part that is ready to run and executes it. It is possible for more than one optional part to be ready in certain *slack intervals*. In such an interval, the second level scheduler will apply a best-effort scheduling policy to determine the best way to execute all of them within the interval.

6 Conclusions and Future Work

In this work, RT-Linux has been extended with the basic features needed to implement a task model and an architecture which allow for the construction of flexible hard real-time systems. The choice of using RT-Linux is due to the fact that this operating system offers an appropriate environment to develop hard real-time applications. In particular, its original support has been an excellent starting point in developing our framework.

Furthermore, as opposed to using a custom kernel, non-standard languages or ad-hoc schedulability analyses, the RT-Linux extensions have been designed within the context of fixed priority pre-emptive scheduling. Fixed priority pre-emptive scheduling and associated feasibility theory is becoming a standard in developing hard real-time systems.

It must be noted that the new services have been carefully designed in order to satisfy the need for the system's predictable behavior. This requirement is needed to completely guarantee the hard deadlines of the application tasks. In that way, it is possible to perform a schedulability analysis with kernel overheads.

Finally, the approach allows the designer to incorporate the most appropriate second level scheduling policy (to execute optional components) to a particular application. This feature provides the framework with enough flexibility so as to be an appropriate engineering approach for constructing flexible hard real-time systems.

Future work includes the development of a graphical tool in order to make the development of a real-time application within RT-Linux easier. On the other hand, further work is needed in order to measure the computation costs (wcet) of each kernel component, especially the scheduling overheads. This allows for the performance of a schedulability analysis for a given hardware architecture. Another line of research is to develop a library of functions containing a set of standard second level (best-effort) scheduling policies.

References

[Aud95]   Audsley, N.C., Burns, A., Davis, R., Tindell, K., and Wellings, J. (1995). "Fixed priority pre-emptive scheduling: an historical perspective". *Real-Time Systems*, **Volume 8**, 173–198.

[Bar96]   Barabanov, M. and Yodaiken, V. (1996). "Real-Time Linux". New Mexico Institute of Mining and Technology.

[Dav93]   Davis, R.I., Tindell, K.W., and Burns, A. (1993). "Scheduling Slack Time in Fixed Priority Preemptive Systems". *Proc. Real-Time Systems Symposium*, Raleigh-Durham, North Carolina, December 1–3, pp. 222–231, IEEE Computer Society Press.

[Dav94]   Davis, R.I. (1994). "Approximate Slack Stealing Algorithms for Fixed Priority Pre-emptive Systems".Real-Time Systems Research Group. Department of Computer Science. University of York, UK. Report number YCS-93-217.

[Gar96a] Garcia-Fornes, A., Hassan, H., and Crespo, A. (1996). "Strategies for scheduling optional tasks in intelligent real-time environments". *Journal of Systems Architecture*,**Volume 42**, pp.391-407.

[Gar96b] Garcia-Fornes, A., Terrasa, A., and Botti, V. (1996). "Engineering a tool for building hard predictable real-time artificial intelligent systems". *Proc. of the 21th IFAC/IFIP Workshop on Real-Time Programming*, Gramado, Brazil.

[Gar97]   Garcia-Fornes, A., Terrasa, A., Botti, V., and Crespo, A. (1997). "Analyzing the schedulability of hard real-time artificial intelligence systems". *Engineering Applications of Artificial Intelligence*,**Volume 10, n0. 4**, pp.369-377.

[Nat95]   Natarajan, S.(editor) (1995). "Imprecise and Approximate Computation". Kluwer Academic Publishers. ISBN 0-7923-9579-4.

[Sha90]   Sha, L., Rajkumar, R., and Lehoczky, J.P. (1990). "Priority inheritance protocols: An approach to Real-Time Synchronization". *IEEE Transactions on Computers*, **Volume 39 no. 9**, pp. 1175-1185.

[Sta93]   Stankovic, J. and Ramamritham, K. (1993). "Advances in Real-Time Systems". IEEE Computer Society Press. ISBN 0-8186-3792-7.

Limited Preemptible Scheduling to Embrace Cache Memory in Real-Time Systems

Sheayun Lee[1], Chang-Gun Lee[1], Minsuk Lee[2],
Sang Lyul Min[1], and Chong Sang Kim[1]

[1] Dept. of Computer Engineering,
Seoul National University, Seoul 151-742, Korea
{sylee,cglee,symin,cskim}@archi.snu.ac.kr
[2] Dept. of Computer Engineering,
Hansung University, Seoul 136-792, Korea
mslee@ice.hansung.ac.kr

Abstract. In multi-tasking real-time systems, inter-task cache interference due to preemptions degrades system performance and predictability, complicating system design and analysis. To address this problem, we propose a novel scheduling scheme, called LPS (Limited Preemptible Scheduling), that limits preemptions to predetermined points with small cache-related preemption costs. We also give an accompanying analysis method that determines the schedulability of a given task set under LPS. By limiting preemption points, the proposed LPS scheme reduces preemption costs and thus increases the system throughput. Experimental results show that LPS can increase schedulable utilization by more than 10 % and save processor time by up to 44 % as compared with a traditional fully preemptible scheduling scheme.

1 Introduction

Cache memory is used in almost all computer systems today to bridge the ever increasing speed gap between the processor and main memory. However, if cache memory is to be used in real-time systems, special attention must be paid since cache memory introduces unpredictability to the system. For example, in a multi-tasking real-time system, when a task is preempted by a higher priority task, the preempted task's memory blocks in the cache are replaced by the preempting higher priority task's memory blocks. Later, when the preempted task resumes its execution, a considerable amount of delay occurs to reload the previously replaced memory blocks into the cache. When preemptions are frequent, the sum of such cache reloading delays takes a significant portion of task execution time. Moreover, the portion gets even larger as the speed gap between the processor and main memory increases.

The cache reloading costs due to preemptions have largely been ignored in real-time scheduling. Without a suitable analysis method, we have to conservatively assume that each preemption causes one cache miss for each cache block used by the preempted task. This will result in a severe overestimation of the cache reloading time.

In this paper, we propose a novel scheduling scheme, called LPS (Limited Preemptible Scheduling), that allows preemptions only at predetermined execution points with small cache reloading costs. The selection of preemptible points is based on the number of *useful cache blocks* [6]. A useful cache block at an execution point contains a memory block that *may* be re-referenced before being replaced by another memory block of the same task. The number of useful cache blocks at a given execution point in a task can be calculated by using a data-flow analysis technique explained in [6] and it gives an upper bound on the number of cache blocks that need to be reloaded when preemption occurs at that execution point. By limiting preemptible points to those with a small number of useful cache blocks, the cache-related preemption delay can be significantly reduced.

Although limiting preemptible points can significantly reduce the cache-related preemption delay, it increases the *blocking time* suffered by higher priority tasks. For example, if the processor is executing a nonpreemptible code section of a lower priority task when a higher priority task arrives, the higher priority task cannot begin its execution until the lower priority task exits the nonpreemptible code section. This blocks the execution of the higher priority task and can potentially make it miss its deadline. Fortunately, such blocking delay is bounded and we give a method for analyzing the worst case blocking delay based on the *extended timing schema* approach [8]. The method determines the worst case blocking time of a lower priority task by estimating the WCET (worst case execution time) of the longest nonpreemptible code section.

For the proposed LPS scheduling scheme, we give an analysis method that can determine whether a given task set is schedulable. The schedulability analysis compares each task's deadline with its WCRT (worst case response time) that is computed by augmenting the response time equation explained in [4, 10] to take into account both the cache-related preemption delay and the blocking delay.

The reduction of the cache-related preemption delay by LPS reduces the WCRTs of lower priority tasks. However, the accompanying increase of the blocking delay increases the WCRTs of higher priority tasks. Thus, LPS can improve or degrade the schedulability of a task set depending on the characteristics of the task set. However, since lower priority tasks constrain the schedulability of the task set in many cases, the improvement of lower priority tasks' WCRT by LPS usually enhances the schedulability. Furthermore, assuming that a given task set is schedulable, LPS significantly reduces the cache reloading time and the resulting savings in processor time can be used to perform other useful jobs.

We performed a set of experiments to assess the impact of LPS on schedulability and system utilization. The results show that the LPS can improve a task set's schedulability when lower priority tasks constrain the schedulability of the whole task set. The results also show that the LPS can save processor time by up to 44 % when compared with a traditional fully preemptible scheduling scheme.

The rest of this paper is organized as follows: In Section 2, we survey the related work. Section 3 details the proposed LPS scheme and the accompanying schedulability analysis method. Section 4 gives the results from our experiments. We conclude this paper in Section 5.

2 Related Work

Although caches are used in almost all computer systems today, they have not been widely used in real-time systems due to their unpredictable worst case performance. The unpredictable performance results from two sources: intra-task interference and inter-task interference. Intra-task interference, which occurs when more than one memory block of the same task are mapped to the same cache block, has been extensively studied in [1-3,7,8]. In this paper, we focus on inter-task interference of caches caused by task preemptions.

There have been two approaches to address the unpredictability resulting from the inter-task cache interference. The first is to eliminate the inter-task cache interference by using a cache partitioning technique where cache memory is divided into mutually disjoint partitions and one or more partitions are dedicated to each task [5,11]. Although cache partitioning eliminates cache interferences due to preemptions, it has a number of drawbacks. One drawback is that the size of the cache seen by each task is significantly reduced, since a task can access only its own partitions. Another drawback is that the technique requires modification of existing hardware and/or software.

The second approach to address the unpredictability resulting from inter-task cache interference is to take into account the effect of cache interference in schedulability analysis. In [6], Lee et al. propose such an analysis technique based on the worst case response time equation [4,10]. In this technique, the original response time equation is augmented to include the cache-related preemption delay as follows (assuming that task τ_i has a higher priority than task τ_j if $i < j$):

$$R_i = C_i + \sum_{j=1}^{i-1} \lceil \frac{R_i}{T_j} \rceil C_j + PC_i(R_i) , \tag{1}$$

where R_i, C_i, and T_i denote the response time, the WCET, and the period of task τ_i, respectively. The cache-related preemption delay is included in the equation in the additional term $PC_i(R_i)$. The term $PC_i(R_i)$ is computed by an integer linear programming technique that takes as its input the worst case cache reloading cost of each task. The calculation of the worst case cache reloading cost considers only the useful cache blocks, which significantly improves the accuracy of the WCRT prediction [6].

The cache-related preemption delay takes a significant portion of a task's response time. Its impact becomes more significant as the cache refill time increases. Simonson shows in his PhD thesis [9] that cache misses caused by preemptions can be significantly reduced by limiting preemptions to predetermined points called *preferred preemption points*. The preferred preemption points are determined by analyzing a given task's execution trace and selecting points that incur small preemption costs. One limitation of this approach is that the preferred preemption points cannot be determined from the program code since the approach is based on trace driven analysis. Thus, the approach cannot be applied during the design phase of a real-time system. Furthermore, the approach does not offer any schedulability analysis technique.

In this paper, we propose a technique that can determine preemption points with small cache reloading costs from the program code. We also give a schedulability analysis technique that considers not only the cache-related preemption delay but also the blocking delay resulting from limiting preemptible points.

3 Limited Preemptible Scheduling

In this section, we first explain how to determine preemptible points with small cache reloading costs. Then, we explain the technique to calculate the blocking time caused by limiting preemptible points. Finally, we explain the schedulability analysis that takes into account the cache-related preemption delay and the blocking delay.

3.1 Determining Preemptible Points

Since the number of useful cache blocks at an execution point gives an upper bound on the cache reloading cost at that point, a preemption at an execution point with a small number of useful cache blocks incurs a low preemption cost.

We divide the set of execution points of a given task into *preemptible execution points* and *nonpreemptible execution points* depending on the number of useful cache blocks. Specifically, if an execution point has more than M useful cache blocks, it is a nonpreemptible execution point; otherwise, it is a preemptible execution point. Here, M is a threshold value that controls the upper bound on the cache reloading cost.

When a task is executing within a nonpreemptible code section, preemption is not allowed even when there is a pending higher priority task. One possible way to implement the preemption control is to insert extra instructions to the execution points that correspond to entry points or exit points of nonpreemptible code sections. The inserted instructions modify a boolean variable that indicates whether the execution of the program is within a nonpreemptible code section or not. When the scheduler is invoked by an arrival of a task (in event-driven scheduling) or by a clock tick (in tick scheduling), the boolean variable is checked by the scheduler to determine whether it should perform a context switch.

3.2 Bounding Blocking Time

As we mentioned earlier, limiting preemptible code sections causes blocking of high priority tasks that arrive while a lower priority task is executing within a nonpreemptible code section. We call the amount of time that a lower priority task blocks a higher priority task's execution the *blocking time* of the lower priority task. To guarantee the worst case performance of the system, we need to bound the blocking time in the worst case, which we call the WCBT (worst case blocking time).

The tighter the WCBT bounds of tasks, the more accurate the prediction of the worst case performance of the system. In the following, we explain a technique that computes a tight bound of the WCBT based on the *extended timing schema* [8], which was originally proposed to compute the WCET of a program.

In the extended timing schema, the syntax tree of the given program is hierarchically analyzed, recursively applying a set of timing formulas to each program construct. The timing formulas are defined with two types of basic operations on the timing abstraction called PA (path abstraction); the concatenation ($\oplus$) operation models the sequential execution of two execution paths, and the set union ($\cup$) operation reflects the possibility of more than one execution path in a program construct.

To calculate the WCBT of a given task from its program code, we associate a data structure called WCBTA (worst case blocking time abstraction) with each program construct. The WCBTA maintains timing information of *blocking paths* that *might* have the largest execution time in the corresponding program construct. A blocking path is a partial execution path that consists only of nonpreemptible code sections, and thus preemption is not allowed when the execution of the program is on such a path. Since it is not possible to determine which blocking path in a program construct will give the largest execution time until the preceding/succeeding program constructs are analyzed, the WCBTA needs to maintain timing information for more than one blocking path. Thus, the WCBTA of a program construct has a set of abstractions, called BPAs (blocking path abstractions), for the blocking paths in the program construct. In addition to the timing information maintained in a PA of the extended timing schema, each BPA maintains information about whether the entry point and/or exit point of the corresponding path is preemptible or not. This information is needed when the concatenation operation is performed between two BPAs to determine whether the two paths lead to a longer blocking path.

When the hierarchical analysis reaches the top level, the WCETs of all the blocking paths in the program are calculated, among which the maximum value is chosen as the program's WCBT.

3.3 Schedulability Analysis

The schedulability analysis for the LPS scheme is based on the response time equation [4, 10]. To take into account the cache-related preemption delay and the blocking delay, the response time equation is augmented as follows:

$$R_i = C_i + \sum_{j=1}^{i-1} \lceil \frac{R_i}{T_j} \rceil C_j + PC_i(R_i) + B_i \, , \tag{2}$$

where R_i, C_i, and T_i denote the response time, the WCET, and the period of τ_i, respectively. The augmented response time equation includes both the cache-related preemption delay $PC_i(R_i)$ and the blocking delay B_i. The cache-related preemption delay is estimated using Lee et al.'s linear programming method. Since smaller preemption costs are used in LPS, the cache-related preemption delay is smaller than in a fully preemptible scheduling scheme.

The blocking delay B_i is the amount of time that task τ_i is blocked by a lower priority task in the worst case. The worst case is when task τ_i arrives immediately after the lower priority task with the largest WCBT begins executing its longest blocking path. Therefore, the worst case blocking delay B_i is equal to the WCBT of the task with the largest WCBT among the lower priority tasks. This is given by

$$B_i = \max_{j>i}(Z_j) \ , \tag{3}$$

where Z_j is the WCBT of task τ_j.

In estimating the WCRTs of the lower priority tasks, the cache-related preemption delay is significantly reduced since it includes the delay caused by preemptions of not only the task itself but also all the higher priority tasks. Therefore, in general, when the lower priority tasks in a given task set have relatively tight deadlines, LPS enhances the schedulability of the task set. On the other hand, LPS increases the blocking time of the higher priority tasks. In the case where the higher priority tasks have tight deadlines, the increased blocking delay may degrade the schedulability of the system. In other words, whether LPS leads to better schedulability depends on the characteristics of the task set. However, once LPS guarantees the schedulability of a given task set, a significant amount of processor time is saved due to reduced cache reloading costs. This saved processor time can be used for other useful jobs in the system, achieving a higher system throughput.

4 Experimental Results

To assess the effectiveness of the proposed LPS scheme, we performed three kinds of experiments. First, the WCBTs of several benchmark programs are analyzed, and the results are presented in Section 4.1. Second, experimental results showing the impact of the LPS scheme on schedulability are given in Sections 4.2 and 4.3. Finally, we present in Section 4.4 results that show how much processor time can be saved by LPS.

4.1 Per-Task Analysis for WCBTs

Our WCBT analysis assumes the MIPS R3000 RISC processor as the target machine. The processor has a direct mapped cache of 16 KB with a block size of 4 bytes. The cache refill time is assumed to be 16 machine cycles.

We set the M value (the maximum allowable number of useful cache blocks at preemptible execution points) of all the tasks to zero. In other words, preemption is allowed only at execution points with zero cache reloading costs.

Five simple benchmark programs were chosen: *matmul*, *jfdctint*, *fft*, *ludcmp*, and *fir*. The *matmul* benchmark performs multiplication on two 5 × 5 floating-point matrices. The *jfdctint* benchmark implements an integer discrete cosine transformation for the JPEG algorithm. The *fft* benchmark performs the FFT and inverse FFT operations on an array of 10 floating-point numbers, and *ludcmp* solves 10 simultaneous linear equations by the LU decomposition method. Finally, *fir* implements the FIR (Finite Impulse Response) filter.

Table 1. WCBTs of five benchmarks

Name	WCET	WCBT	$\frac{\text{WCBT}}{\text{WCET}}$
matmul	10795	10044	93.0 %
jfdctint	11932	3964	33.2 %
fft	24698	22647	91.7 %
ludcmp	37009	27133	73.3 %
fir	71298	71201	99.9 %

(unit: cycles)

The WCBTs and WCETs of the five benchmarks are shown in Table 1. The ratio WCBT/WCET varies depending on the characteristics of the benchmark program. It is affected mainly by the structure of loop statements in the program. Specifically, the *fir* benchmark consists of several nested loops and the outermost loop occupies most of the program code. In such a case, all the execution points inside the outermost loop have the same maximum number of useful cache blocks, and the whole loop becomes a single nonpreemptible code section. The *fir* program spends most of its execution time in this loop and, thus, its WCBT is very close to the WCET of the benchmark. On the other hand, in the *jfdctint* benchmark, there are three outermost loops that have nearly equal execution times. Thus, the WCBT is about 1/3 of the WCET.

4.2 Schedulability: A Good Case

We predicted the WCRTs of the tasks in a sample task set to see how LPS affects the schedulability of the task set as a whole. For this experiment, we used the task set given in Table 2. In the table, the frequency of a task is the number of invocations of the task within the system period (hyperperiod) of the task set.

The workload factor W of the task set is calculated by

$$W = \frac{\sum F_i \cdot C_i}{system\ period} ,\qquad (4)$$

Table 2. Task Set 1

Task	Name	Frequency
τ_1	matmul	32
τ_2	jfdctint	24
τ_3	fft	18
τ_4	ludcmp	12
τ_5	fir	9

where F_i denotes the number of invocations of τ_i in the system period and C_i the WCET of τ_i. The workload factor gives the system's pure workload that excludes the time for cache reloading due to preemptions. We performed schedulability analysis as we increased the workload factor by gradually decreasing the system period. The deadline of each task, which is assumed to be equal to the period of the task, was adjusted accordingly as we decreased the system period.

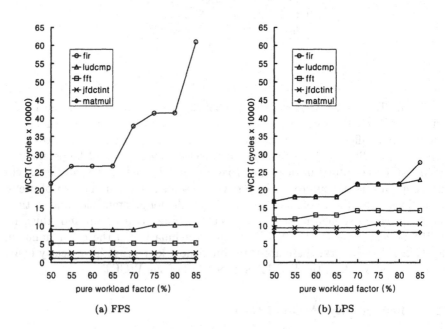

Fig. 1. WCRT predictions for Task Set 1

Figure 1 depicts the WCRT predictions for both the traditional fully pre-emptible scheduling (denoted by FPS) and LPS. The x-axis of the graphs is the system's workload factor W whereas the y-axis is the WCRTs of tasks (in machine cycles).

Figure 1(a) shows the results when FPS is used. In FPS, the WCRT of the highest priority task τ_1 (*matmul*) is equal to its WCET since it begins its execution immediately after release and is never preempted. The WCRTs of the intermediate priority tasks (i.e., τ_2, τ_3, and τ_4) do not increase much even when the workload factor is as high as 85 %. However, the WCRT of the lowest priority task τ_5 (*fir*) increases rapidly as the workload factor increases. This results from a rapid increase of the cache-related preemption delay that includes the cache reloading costs of not only itself but also all the higher priority tasks.

Figure 1(b) shows the results when LPS is used. As compared with FPS, the WCRTs of $\tau_1, \cdots, \tau_4$ become slightly larger because the WCRTs now include the blocking delay, which is equal to the WCBT of τ_5 (*fir*). However, the WCRT of the lowest priority task *fir* becomes much smaller than in the FPS case and does not increase as rapidly. This results from the fact that the cache-related preemption delay is zero in the LPS case since preemptions can occur only at execution points with no useful cache blocks.

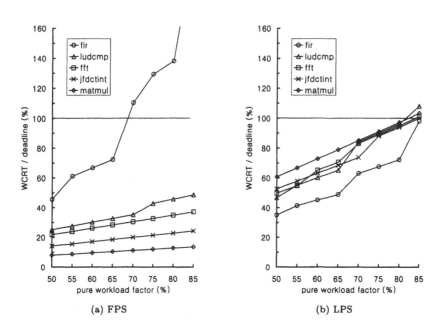

Fig. 2. WCRT/deadline for Task Set 1

Figure 2 depicts the ratio of the WCRT to the deadline assuming that each task's deadline is equal to its period. The results show that in the FPS case the lowest priority task *fir* is the one that limits the schedulability of the whole task set. Thus, the reduction of the WCRT of *fir* in the LPS case by reducing the cache-related preemption delay proves to be helpful in improving the schedulability of the given task set as we can see in Figure 2(b). The graphs show that the breakdown utilization of the task set is about 81 % for LPS, which is more than 10 % higher than the FPS's 68 %.

4.3 Schedulability: A Bad Case

We performed another experiment that was intended to show potential problems of LPS. Table 3 gives the sample task set used for this purpose. The task set consists of four tasks: *matmul*, *jfdctint*, *fft*, and *ludcmp*. For this task set, the ratio of the frequency of the highest priority task *matmul* to those of the other tasks is much higher than in the previous task set. This gives a much tighter deadline to the highest priority task as compared with the deadlines of the other tasks.

Table 3. Task Set 2

Task	Name	Frequency
τ_1	matmul	20
τ_2	jfdctint	5
τ_3	fft	4
τ_4	ludcmp	2

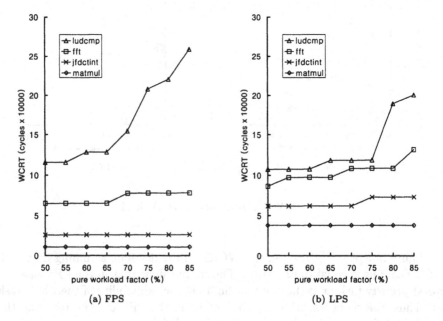

Fig. 3. WCRT predictions for Task Set 2

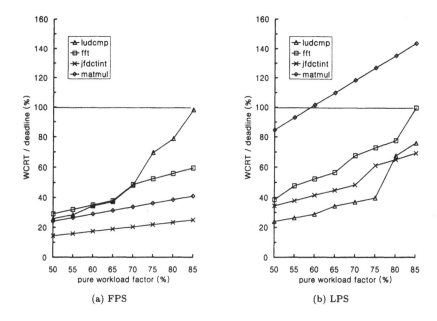

Fig. 4. WCRT/deadline for Task Set 2

Figures 3 and 4 show the WCRT and the ratio of the WCRT to the deadline, respectively, for the new task set. LPS now fails to schedule the task set when the workload factor is about 59 % whereas FPS can still schedule the task set even when the workload factor is over 85 %. This results from the fact that the highest priority task has a much tighter deadline than the other tasks and, thus, even a small amount of blocking delay can make it miss the deadline.

The blocking delay can be reduced by transforming the source code of tasks. For example, a task's WCBT can be reduced by unrolling loops in the program of the task. In this case, a single loop is transformed into a number of equivalent loops. This helps reduce the WCBT of the task since most of the useful cache blocks are due to loop statements. This transformation places preemptible execution points between the resulting unrolled loops, thus reducing the WCBT. If a loop is transformed into n loops, the WCBT due to the loop becomes approximately $1/n$ of the WCBT of the loop before the loop unrolling.

However, the loop unrolling decreases temporal locality of instruction references and increases the code size. Thus, this technique trades increased WCET (due to increased cache misses) and code size for reduction in the WCBT.

Loop unrolling was applied to the tasks *fft* and *ludcmp*. After the loop unrolling, the ratios of the WCBT to the WCET of the two tasks are reduced from 91.7 % to 19.1 % and from 73.3 % to 6.3 %, respectively. Figures 5(a) and (b) give the WCRT and the ratio of the WCRT to the deadline of each task, respectively, for the LPS case after the loop unrolling is applied. As expected, the WCRT of higher priority tasks (most notably the highest priority task *matmul*)

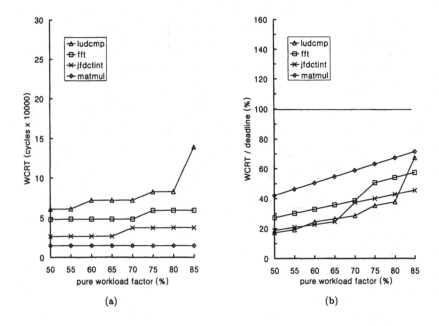

Fig. 5. Results of source code transformation

is reduced significantly due to the reduction of the WCBTs of the *fft* and *ludcmp* tasks. This improves the schedulability of the whole task set.

4.4 System Utilization

Figure 6 gives the processor time gain obtained by using LPS for the two previous task sets. The x-axis is the cache refill time, and the y-axis is the percentage of processor time saved by LPS. The results were obtained by averaging the processor time over 100 different simulation runs with random phasing between tasks. The results show that as the cache refill time increases, the percentage of the saved processor time increases too (up to 44 %). The percentage gain is greater for Task Set 1 than for Task Set 2 since the number of preemptions in Task Set 1 is larger than that in Task Set 2 and so are the savings.

5 Conclusion

We have proposed a novel scheduling scheme called LPS (Limited Preemptible Scheduling) that allows preemptions only at execution points with small cache reloading costs. We have also given a schedulability analysis technique that considers not only the reduction of the cache-related preemption delay by LPS but also the increase in the blocking delay resulting from nonpreemptible code sections. The worst case blocking delay resulting from nonpreemptible code sections

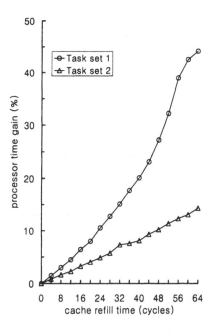

Fig. 6. Processor time gain

of a lower priority task was estimated by augmenting a method for estimating the worst case execution time explained in [8].

We assessed the impact of the LPS scheme on schedulability and system utilization through a set of experiments. The results showed that LPS can enhance the schedulability of a task set when the task set suffers from tight deadlines for lower priority tasks. The results also show that LPS saves a significant amount of processor time (by up to 44 %) and that the percentage of saved processor time increases as the cache refill time increases.

We are currently working on an optimization technique that assigns M values to tasks in such a way that maximizes the schedulability of the given task set. This technique uses information about how the WCBT of a task changes as the M value increases, which is obtained by a per-task analysis. The technique identifies the task that limits the schedulability of the task set and changes the M values of tasks accordingly.

References

1. R. Arnold, F. Mueller, D. B. Whalley, and M. Harmon. Bounding worst-case instruction cache performance. In *Proceedings of the 15th Real-Time Systems Symposium*, pages 172–181, Dec. 1994.
2. C. A. Healy, D. B. Whalley, and M. Harmon. Integrating the timing analysis of pipelining and instruction caching. In *Proceedings of the 16th Real-Time Systems Symposium*, pages 288–297, Dec. 1994.

3. Y. Hur, Y. H. Bae, S.-S. Lim, S.-K. Kim, B.-D. Rhee, S. L. Min, C. Y. Park, H. Shin, and C. S. Kim. Worst case timing analysis of RISC processors: R3000/R3010 case study. In *Proceedings of the 16th Real-Time Systems Symposium*, pages 308–321, Dec. 1995.

4. M. Joseph and P. Pandya. Finding response times in a real-time system. *The BCS Computer Journal*, 29(5):390–395, Oct. 1986.

5. D. B. Kirk. SMART (strategic memory allocation for real-time) cache design. In *Proceedings of the 10th Real-Time Systems Symposium*, pages 229–237, Dec. 1989.

6. C.-G. Lee, J. Hahn, Y.-M. Seo, S. L. Min, R. Ha, S. Hong, C. Y. Park, M. Lee, and C. S. Kim. Analysis of cache-related preemption delay in fixed-priority preemptive scheduling. In *Proceedings of the Seventeenth Real-Time Systems Symposium*, pages 264–274, Dec. 1996.

7. Y. T. S. Li, S. Malik, and A. Wolfe. Efficient microarchitecture modeling and path analysis for real-time software. In *Proceedings of the 16th Real-Time Systems Symposium*, pages 298–307, Dec. 1995.

8. S.-S. Lim, Y. H. Bae, G. T. Jang, B.-D. Rhee, S. L. Min, C. Y. Park, H. Shin, K. Park, S.-M. Moon, and C. S. Kim. An accurate worst case timing analysis for RISC processors. *IEEE Transactions on Software Engineering*, 21(7):593–604, Jul. 1995.

9. J. Simonson. *Cache Memory Management in Real-Time Systems*. PhD thesis, University of Illinois at Urbana-Champaign, Sep. 1996.

10. K. Tindell, A. Burns, and A. Wellings. An extendible approach for analyzing fixed priority hard real-time tasks. *The Journal of Real-Time Systems*, 6(2):133–151, Mar. 1994.

11. A. Wolfe. Software-based cache partitioning for real-time applications. In *Proceedings of the 3rd International Workshop on Responsive Computer Systems*, Sep. 1993.

A Uniform Reliable Multicast Protocol with Guaranteed Response Times

Laurent George[1] and Pascale Minet[2]

[1] ESIGETEL, Département Télécom, 1 rue du port Valvins, 77210 Avon, France
`george@esigetel.fr`
[2] INRIA Rocquencourt, Projet Reflecs, 78153 Le Chesnay Cedex, France
`pascale.minet@inria.fr`

Abstract. Uniform reliable multicast protocols with a guaranteed response time are of concern in numerous distributed real-time systems (e.g. distributed transactional systems, high available systems). We focus on uniform reliable multicast protocols in processors groups. The source of a message can belong or not to the destination group. A bounded number of processors crashes and network omissions is tolerated. The uniform reliable multicast protocol, designed and proved in this paper, works with Earliest Deadline First (EDF) scheduling, proved optimal in the uniprocessor context. A worst-case response time analysis for sporadic tasks subject to release jitter is given for non-preemptive EDF on a uniprocessor and extended to the distributed case using the holistic scheduling approach.

1 Introduction

Contrary to a broadcast that is targeted to the set of all the processors in the system, a multicast is targeted to a subset of processors. In the following such a subset is called a group. Informally, a reliable multicast service ensures that for any message m_i, all the correct processors (i.e. processors that do not crash) in the destination group agree either to deliver m_i or not to deliver m_i. Notice the distinction between *deliver* and *receive*: a message is received from the network (lower interface of the reliable multicast module). A message is delivered in the user queue (upper interface of the reliable multicast module).

We can notice that only the behavior of correct processors in the destination group is specified. Just before crashing, a processor in the destination group can deliver messages which are not delivered by correct processors in that group. Such a behavior is prevented by the following requirement: all messages delivered by a processor, whether correct or not, in the destination group, are delivered by all the correct processors in that group. That requirement is captured by the uniform reliable multicast.

The paper is organized as follows: in section 2 the problem to solve is specified: the assumptions made and the properties to be achieved are described. Section 3 contrasts our approach with related work. In section 4, the reliable multicast algorithm is given. Section 5 is concerned with the real-time dimension. A worst case analysis based on EDF scheduling [11], is given that enables to establish the worst case end-to-end response time for the reliable multicast of a message.

2 The problem: Assumption and required properties

According to the TRDF (Real-Time, Distribution and Fault-Tolerance) method, a method for designing and dimensioning critical complex computing systems [12], a problem is specified by a pair $< assumptions, properties >$. The assumptions are given by five models defined hereafter.

2.1 Assumptions

a) The structural model
The structural model consists of K network controllers $NC_1, NC_2, .., NC_K$ interconnected by means of a communication network. Each network controller is connected to all the others. The network controllers provide the uniform reliable multicast service. The network controllers are organized in groups, in which messages are multicast. A network controller can belong to one or several groups. For a sake of simplicity, groups are assumed to be static (i.e. no voluntary departure, no join). Each network controller has a local clock used to timestamp the messages it multicasts.

b) The computational model
The computational model defines the assumptions made concerning the transmission delays and the processing delays. In this study, the computational model taken is the synchronous one. The network transmission delay has a known upper bound *Max* and a known lower bound *Min*. The controller processing delay has a known upper bound. Moreover the controllers clocks are assumed to be ε-synchronized: the maximum difference between two clocks of non-crashed controllers is not higher than the precision ε.

c) The processing model
We now focus on the network controllers. Any network controller only knows to which groups it belongs, but it does not know the other controllers in these groups: it does not know the membership of these groups. With each message m_i is associated a relative deadline D_i: the maximum response time acceptable for the reliable multicast of message m_i in the destination group $dest(m_i)$. The timestamp of message m_i, denoted $ts(m_i)$, is the time, given by the network controller clock, when the reliable multicast of message m_i is requested by the host. Consequently, the absolute deadline of message m_i, denoted $d(m_i)$, is equal to $ts(m_i) + D_i$. At their upper interface, the network controllers offer two primitives (see figure 1):

- $R\_Multicast\ (m_i,\ dest(m_i),\ src(m_i),\ ts(m_i),\ d(m_i))$: where the network controller $src(m_i)$ performs the reliable multicast of message m_i in the network controllers group $dest(m_i)$, the message m_i having $ts(m_i)$

for timestamp and $d(m_i)$ for absolute deadline. Notice that there is no constraint on $dest(m_i)$ and $src(m_i)$: $src(m_i)$ can belong to $dest(m_i)$ or not.

- *R_Deliver (mi, dest(mi), src(mi), ts(mi), d(mi))*: where a network controller in $dest(m_i)$ notifies its host of the reliable delivery of message m_i, the message m_i having $src(m_i)$ for source, $ts(m_i)$ for timestamp and $d(m_i)$ for absolute deadline.

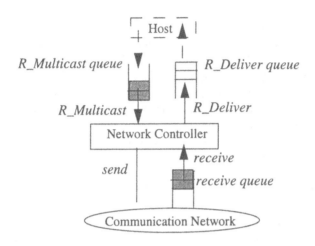

Fig. 1. The primitives provided / used by the uniform reliable multicast service.

At their lower interface (the communication network), the network controllers use two basic primitives (see figure 1):

- *send (mᵢ, dest(mᵢ), src(mᵢ), ts(mᵢ), d(mᵢ))*: where a network controller requests the network to send the message m_i, originated from $src(m_i)$, to all network controllers in $dest(m_i)$ except itself; the message m_i being timestamped with $ts(m_i)$ and having $d(m_i)$ for absolute deadline. Notice that a network controller does not send a message m_i to itself, even if it belongs to $dest(m_i)$. The primitive *send()* returns only when the message has been sent by the network.

- *receive (mᵢ, dest(mᵢ), src(mᵢ), ts(mᵢ), d(mᵢ))*: where a network controller in $dest(m_i)$, receives from the network a message m_i, originated from $src(m_i)$, timestamped with $ts(m_i)$ and having $d(m_i)$ for absolute deadline.

d) The failure model

The failures model defines, for each system component, the possible failures:

- A controller can fail by crash. The execution of a reliable multicast must tolerate up to f_c controller crashes.

- The network can fail by omission. More precisely the network can omit to put a message in one receive queue. The execution of a reliable multicast must tolerate up to f_o network omissions.

- The clocks of non-crashed controllers are assumed to be monotonically increasing (see for instance [14]) and their drift rate is assumed to be bounded by a constant.

e) The events model

The events model defines the events originated from the system environment and triggering a processing by the system. In our case such an event is the insertion of the *R_Multicast* request of an occurrence of a message m_i, in the *R_Multicast* queue. In the following, "the message m_i" stands for "the occurrence of message m_i whose *R_Multicast* is requested at time $ts(m_i)$". Events are assumed to occur according to a sporadic law: T_i is the minimum interarrival time between two successive *R_Multicast* requests of message m_i. In the following, T_i is called the period.

2.2 Required properties

Before defining the properties that must be achieved by the uniform reliable multicast service, we first define the notion of correct network controller. A controller that does not crash is said *correct*, otherwise it is said faulty. A controller is said non-crashed if it has not yet crashed. The properties given here are the ones defined in [8], adapted to our context. Properties (P1) to (P3) specify a uniform reliable multicast in any destination group. Notice that according to our processing model, property (P1) does not require that the source of the message belongs to the destination group.

- **(P1) Validity**: if a correct controller R_Multicasts a message m_i, then some correct controller in *dest(m_i)* eventually R_Delivers m_i.

- **(P2) Uniform Agreement**: if a controller, whether correct or not, R_Delivers a message m_i, then all correct controllers in *dest(m_i)* eventually R_Deliver m_i.

- **(P3) Uniform Integrity**: for any message m_i, every controller NC_j, whether correct or not, R_Delivers m_i at most once and only if NC_j is in *dest(m_i)* and m_i was previously R_Multicast by the network controller *src(m_i)*.

- **(P4) Uniform Timeliness**: no message m_i, whose R_Multicast has been requested at real time t, is R_Delivered after its absolute deadline $t+D_i$.

3 Related work

Our Uniform Reliable Multicast protocol relies on the concept of relays. The relays are introduced to mask the source crash and the network omissions: the relays are in charge of repeating the messages initially sent by the source. That is the main difference with the protocol given in [8] where all controllers relay any message received for the first time. The relays limit the number of messages generated by the algorithm. Another difference is that the choice of the message to be processed is specified: the one with the earliest absolute deadline. Earliest Deadline First scheduling has been proved optimal in the uniprocessor non-preemptive context [9], when the release times of tasks are not known in advance. The worst case response time analysis of EDF is done before implementation, based on the identification of worse case scenarios.

In [3], the network omissions are masked by redundant channels. Our protocol does not need redundant channels. As defined in [6], our protocol is a genuine multicast protocol: the execution of the algorithm implementing the reliable multicast of a message m_i to a destination group $dest(m_i)$ involves only the source processor and the processors in $dest(m_i)$. It does not use group membership services. However contrary to [8] and [1], our reliable multicast protocol works only in synchronous systems.

End-to-end delay guarantee has been studied in packet switching networks, where each traffic flow is allocated a reserved rate of server capacity [17], [13]. The guarantee provided by the virtual clock server [17] is conditional, it works only for on-time packets arrivals. In [10], the computation of the worst case response time of a message is based on fixed priority scheduling. Our worst case response time analysis is innovative. The analysis consists of three parts: 1) the computation of the worst case response time of a task set with a jitter for a uniprocessor non-preemptive EDF scheduling, 2) the extension of those results to the distributed case, where clocks are ε-synchronized, 3) the holistic approach [16] for the computation of the end-to-end response time. To our knowledge, the holistic approach has always been applied to a sequential processing of message [16], [15], [7]. It has never been applied to parallel processing: here the parallel processing by the relays. In [16], the scheduling is based on fixed priorities. In [15] the scheduling is preemptive EDF with a blocking factor. Here we use non-preemptive EDF.

4 The reliable multicast algorithm

In this section we design a Uniform Reliable Multicast protocol. In subsection 4.1 we first give the assumption made and an intuitive idea of the algorithm. The algorithm is given in subsection 4.2.

4.1 Assumption and principles

Informally a message m_i whose reliable multicast is requested is timestamped and put in the R_Multicast queue. The processing of that message by the Uniform Reliable Multicast module generates send and receive operations over the network, and finally the message is R_Delivered by all non-crashed controllers in $dest(m_i)$: the message is put in the R_Deliver queue of each non-crashed controller in $dest(m_i)$. We recall that the reliable multicast must tolerate up to f_c controller crashes and f_o network omissions. More precisely, we assume:

Assumption 1: any message m_i sent by any controller NC_j to $dest(m_i)$ is received by at least $card[dest(m_i)\text{-}\{NC_j\}]\text{-}f_o\text{-}f_c$ correct controllers in $dest(m_i)$ distinct from NC_j.

The reliable multicast algorithm relies on the concept of relays. They are introduced to mask the source crash and the network omissions: the relays of message m_i are in charge of repeating the message m_i initially sent by $src(m_i)$. In section 4.2 the reliable multicast algorithm is given with the number of relays per message. In the next subsection, properties *P1*, *P2* and *P3* are proved. We first give an idea of the algorithm. Informally the reliable multicast of message m_i is performed as follows:

- the source sends m_i to all controllers in $dest(m_i)$ except itself;
- if the source belongs to $dest(m_i)$, it delivers m_i.
- upon first receipt of m_i from $src(m_i)$, a relay sends the received message to all the controllers in $dest(m_i)$ except itself.
- upon first receipt of m_i, any controller in $dest(m_i)$ delivers m_i.

4.2 The reliable multicast algorithm

We recall that NC_j receives only messages m_i such that NC_j is in $dest(m_i)$, and when NC_j sends a message it does not send it to itself. NC_j runs the following algorithm:

upon R_Multicast queue not empty/* at step 0 */
{

    extract the msg. m_i with the earliest deadline $d(m_i)$ in R_Multicast queue
    $send(m_i, dest(m_i), src(m_i), ts(m_i), d(m_i))$
    if NC_j is in $dest(m_i)$ then $R\_Deliver(m_i, dest(m_i), src(m_i), ts(m_i), d(m_i))$
}
upon "receive queue not empty"
{

    extract the message m_i with the earliest deadline $d(m_i)$ in the receive queue
    if NC_j is $relay(m_i)$ and first receipt of m_i from $src(m_i)$ then
        $send(m_i, dest(m_i), src(m_i), ts(m_i), d(m_i))$
    if first receipt of the message m_i and $NC_j \neq src(m_i)$ then
        $R\_Deliver(m_i, dest(m_i), src(m_i), ts(m_i), d(m_i))$
    else discard (m_i)
}
to execute $R\_Deliver(m_i, dest(m_i), src(m_i), ts(m_i), d(m_i))$
{

    insert m_i in the R_Deliver queue
}

We now establish the minimum number of relays per source.

Lemma 1. *Each message m_i has, in $dest(m_i)$, f_c+f_o+1 relays distinct from $src(m_i)$. A feasibility condition is $card(dest(m_i) - \{src(m_i)\}) \geq f_c+f_o+1$.*

Proof. Any message m_i sent by its source ($src(m_i)$) is received, according to assumption 1, by at least $card[dest(m_i)-\{src(m_i)\}]-f_o-f_c$ correct controllers distinct from the source. To ensure that there is at least one correct controller, we must have $card[dest(m_i)-\{src(m_i)\}]-f_o-f_c \geq 1$. Hence the feasibility condition is $card[dest(m_i)-\{src(m_i)\}] \geq f_o-f_c+1$. That is why we associate with each message f_c+f_o+1 relays in $dest(m_i)$ (distinct from the source). Indeed at most f_c+f_o relays can have not received the message. Relays are chosen to share the workload in the destination group $dest(m_i)$.

The maximum number of messages sent over the network, is:

- in case of a multicast network, a total of f_c+f_o+2 messages per reliable multicast sent over a multicast network.

- in case of a point-to-point network, $(f_c+f_o+2)[card(dest(m_i))-1]$ messages per reliable multicast of message m_i sent over a point-to-point network, when $src(m_i)$ belongs to $dest(m_i)$.

4.3 Proofs of properties

We now prove that properties (P1), (P2) and (P3) are met with regard to primitives R_Multicast and R_Deliver: in other words, the algorithm achieves a Uniform Reliable Multicast.

Lemma 2. *The Validity property (P1) is met.*

Proof. If a correct source R_Multicasts a message m_i, it completes the execution of the R_Multicast algorithm because by definition of correct, that source does not fail. If it belongs to $dest(m_i)$, it eventually R_Delivers m_i. If it does not belong to $dest(m_i)$, at least one correct relay in $dest(m_i)$ eventually receives m_i by assumption 1 and Lemma 1 and hence R_Delivers m_i.

Lemma 3. *The Uniform Agreement property (P2) is met.*

Proof. Let us assume that there exists a message m_i such that a controller NC_j in $dest(m_i)$, whether correct or faulty, R_Delivers m_i. According to the algorithm run by any controller, a message cannot be R_Delivered before having been sent by its source. According to assumption 1, if p omissions have occurred, $0 \geq p \geq f_0$, message m_i has been received by at least $card(dest(m_i)-\{src(m_i)\})-f_c-p$ correct controllers distinct from $src(m_i)$. Among them there are at least f_o-p+1 correct relays. According to the algorithm, each of them sends m_i to all controllers in $dest(m_i)$ except itself. As the total number of omissions cannot exceed f_o during the execution of a reliable multicast, at most f_o-p omissions can occur during these f_o-p+1 sendings, any correct controller receives m_i, and R_Delivers it.

Lemma 4. *The Uniform Integrity property (P3) is met.*

Proof. According to the network failure model (omission) and the controller failure model (crash), a controller cannot forge a message. A source, whether correct or faulty, delivers its message m_i at most once at the end of the execution of the R_Multicast and only if it belongs to $dest(m_i)$. A controller in $dest(m_i)$, whether correct or faulty, which is not the source of the message delivers that message at most once: after the first receipt.

5 The real-time dimension

In this section we are concerned with the worst case response time of the reliable multicast of a message m_i. We present in section 5.2 the holistic approach adopted to perform the computation of that end-to-end response time. Hence as depicted on figure 2, the computation of the worst case response time, on controller NC_j in $dest(m_i)$, for the reliable multicast of a message m_i originated from $src(m_i)$ depends on the computation of the worst case response time on:

- $src(m_i)$,
- the relays of m_i,
- NC_j in $dest(m_i)$,
- the communication network.

We call direct receipt, a receipt where the message is directly received from the source. An indirect receipt corresponds to a receipt from a relay.

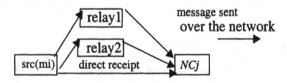

Fig. 2. Three possibilities for NC_j to receive m_i

On figure 2, there are three possibilities for message m_i to be received by NC_j in $dest(m_i)$: from $src(m_i)$, from $relay1$ or from $relay2$. In the following, all copies of m_i are considered as distinct messages, unless specified. By our assumption, the maximum transmission delay of the communication network is known and equal to Max and the minimum transmission delay is equal to Min. We could have considered a value depending on the message to transmit, but to keep the analysis simple we take the same time for all messages. We then focus on the assumptions taken for the network controllers (see section 5.1). Section 5.2 shows how the end-to-end response time between the R_Multicast request and the R_Deliver of a message m_i by a non-crashed controller NC_j can be computed using the holistic scheduling approach. Section 5.3 shows how to compute the worst case response time of a set of tasks scheduled EDF on a uniprocessor. Section 5.4 shows how the previous established results can be used to compute the end-to-end response times.

5.1 Assumptions related to network controllers

We assume that each network controller is controlled by an Application Specific Integrated Circuit (ASIC) that enables to send and receive messages in parallel (i.e receiving a message has no impact on the sending). This can be virtually seen as two processors working in parallel: one in charge of receiving messages from the network and another one in charge of sending messages in the network. The processing of a message by one of these processors is assumed to be non-preemptive. The scheduling policy of each processor of a network controller consists in serving the message with the earliest deadline in one of the two waiting queues, depicted in gray on figure 1: the R_Multicast queue and the receive queue. The processing of a message consists of basic actions. The times associated with these actions are given hereafter, the network controllers being assumed homogeneous for a sake of simplicity:

- P_i: time needed to put message m_i in the R_Deliver queue and to notify the host.

- R_i: time needed to receive message m_i from the receive queue.

- S_i: time needed to send message m_i.

5.2 The holistic approach

Tindell and Clark [16] have developed an interesting approach to establish feasibility conditions in a distributed system based on the computation of worst case end-to-end response times with fixed priority assignment. With the holistic approach, the analysis of end-to-end response times in real-time distributed systems is made easier by the concept of attribute inheritance.

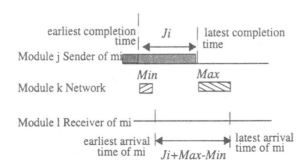

Fig. 3. Release jitter inheritance

In the following, a module is either a network controller or the communication network. Assume that a module j sends a message m_i with a period T_i to a module k. The release jitter J_i resulting from module j is equal to the maximum response time on module j minus the minimum response time. From module k point of view, the scheduling problem is to determine the worst case response time of m_i where m_i is a message with a period T_i and a release jitter J_i. That is the principle of attribute inheritance. Figure 3 shows how a receiver, *module l*, inherits for message m_i sent by module j, a release jitter of $J_i + Max-Min$.

With attribute inheritance, it is possible to reason on any module independently. The main problem is to be able to determine the worst case response time of a message subject to a release jitter on a module, where messages are scheduled EDF. Section 5.3 addresses that problem. The holistic approach is then iterative: the response time of all messages sent or received is computed on every network controller as a function of the current release jitter of the messages; a resulting release jitter is determined which in turn leads to new worst case response times. Those steps are iterated until the release jitters of messages in every queue of the network controllers stabilize. Notice that the response time of a message is an increasing function of the jitter (see section 5.3). This guarantees that either the system converges or a deadline on the receipt of a message is missed. We now apply this result to the computation of the response time of a message m_i sent by $src(m_i)$ through a reliable multicast service. Let us focus on the messages processed by any network controller NC_j. We identify two types of messages: the sent messages and the received messages. For the sent messages, we have:

- let τ_s^j be the set of messages whose source is NC_j. We have $\forall m_i \in \tau_s^j$, the duration on NC_j of the associated sending is $C_i = S_i + P_i$ if $NC_j \in dest(m_i)$, and $C_i = S_i$ otherwise.

- let τ_{sr}^j be the set of messages relayed by NC_j. We have $\forall m_i \in \tau_{sr}^j$, the duration on NC_j of the associated sending is $C_i = S_i$.

A network controller NC_j has to send messages belonging to $\tau_s^j \cup \tau_{sr}^j$. For the received messages, we have:

- let τ_r^j be the set of messages received by NC_j. Notice that a message m_i can be received either directly from $src(m_i)$ or indirectly from $relay(m_i)$. We have $\forall m_i \in \tau_r^j$, the duration on NC_j of the associated receipt is $C_i = R_i + P_i$ if $NC_j \neq src(m_i)$, and $C_i = R_i$ otherwise. Indeed we do not distinguish in the analysis the first receipt of m_i.

Section 5.3 describes how to compute the worst case response time of a set of tasks, subject to a release jitter and scheduled on a uniprocessor using EDF. This analysis will be used locally on any network controller to determine the worst case response time on the sending and on the receiving of a message and consequently the new release jitter of a message. Informally to compute the release jitter of m_i on every involved network controller NC_j, the holistic scheduling analysis proceeds by iterative steps:

- Step 0: on every network controller NC_j compute the initial jitter $J_i^{\tau_s^j \cup \tau_{sr}^j}(0)$ for every message m_i to be sent. For a message m_i whose source is NC_j, the release jitter is equal to 0. For a message m_i such that NC_j is a relay of m_i, the release jitter is at least equal to *Max-Min*.

- Step p: compute on every network controller NC_j the jitter for every received message m_i. If NC_j is a relay of m_i then the copy of m_i which is sent by NC_j is the one received from $src(m_i)$. We can now compute on every network controller the jitter $J_i^{\tau_s^j \cup \tau_{sr}^j}(p+1)$ for every message m_i to be sent. If for any network controller NC_j and for any message m_i in $\tau_s^j \cup \tau_{sr}^j$, the jitter stabilize (i.e $J_i^{\tau_s^j \cup \tau_{sr}^j}(p+1) = J_i^{\tau_s^j \cup \tau_{sr}^j}(p)$), we have found the release jitter for any message. If there exists a network controller such that the maximum end to end response time of a received message m_i is higher than D_i, the algorithm halts: the message set is not feasible. Otherwise step $p+1$ is run, and so on...

Before computing the worst case end-to-end response times (see section 5.4), we give hereafter an implementation of the holistic scheduling analysis; the function that returns the maximum response time on NC_j of a message m_i scheduled among other messages in τ^j is called $max\_rt(\tau^j, m_i)$ where τ^j is either $\tau_s^j \cup \tau_{sr}^j$ or τ_r^j. The function $max\_rt(\tau^j, m_i)$ is described in section 5.3.b. The release jitter is then equal to the maximum response time minus the minimum response time. The minimum response time for a message m_i in τ_{sr}^j is S_i and for a message m_i in τ_r^j is $R_i + P_i$ if $src(m_i)$ is not NC_j and R_i otherwise. The following procedures are a direct application of Step 0 and Step p.

- $init()$ determines the initial release jitter of any message to be sent.

- $compute\_sending()$ determines the worst case response time of any message to be sent on every network controller. The worst case response time computation is based on the analysis proposed in section 5.3.b.

- $compute\_receiving()$ determines on any network controller the new maximum release jitter of any received message.

```
init() /* at step 0 */
{
      let τⱼₛ = {mᵢ such that NCⱼ = src(mᵢ)}
      let τⱼₛᵣ = {mᵢ such that NCⱼ = relay(mᵢ)}
      let τⱼᵣ = {mᵢ such that NCⱼ ∈ dest(mᵢ)}
      for any NCⱼ
      /* messages R_multicast by NCⱼ */
            ∀mᵢ ∈ τⱼₛ, Jᵢ^(τⱼₛ∪τⱼₛᵣ)(0) := 0
      /* relayed messages inherit an initial release jitter from the network */
            ∀mᵢ ∈ τⱼₛᵣ, Jᵢ^(τⱼₛ∪τⱼₛᵣ)(0) := Max − Min
      endfor
}
compute_sending(p) /* at step p > 0 */
{
      for any NCⱼ
/* compute the resp. time of msg. sent by NCⱼ with jitter Jᵢ^(τⱼₛ∪τⱼₛᵣ)(p) */
```

$$\forall m_i \in \tau_s^j \cup \tau_{sr}^j, \; r_i^{\tau_s^j \cup \tau_{sr}^j}(p) := max\_rt(\tau_s^j \cup \tau_{sr}^j, m_i)$$

endfor

}

compute_receiving(p) /* at step $p > 0$ */

{

    for any NC_j

        for any $m_i \in \tau_r^j$ received from NC_k, $k \neq j$

          if $NC_k \in dest(m_i)$ then

$$J_i^{\tau_r^j} := r_i^{\tau_s^k \cup \tau_{sr}^k}(p) - S_i - P_i + Max - Min$$

          else $J_i^{\tau_r^j} := r_i^{\tau_s^k \cup \tau_{sr}^k}(p) - S_i + Max - Min$

          /* response time computed with the jitter $J_i^{\tau_r^j}(p)$ */

$$r_i^{\tau_r^j}(p) := max\_rt(\tau_r^j, m_i)$$

          if $NC_j \in relay(m_i)$ and $NC_k = src(m_i)$ then

$$J_i^{\tau_s^j \cup \tau_{sr}^j}(p+1) := r_i^{\tau_r^j}(p) - R_i - P_i$$

        endfor

    endfor

}

The following function main() is a direct application of the holistic scheduling approach.

main()

{

    p:=0 /* step number */, end:=0

    init()

    repeat

        compute_sending(p)

        compute_receiving(p)

        if for any NC_j and $\forall m_i \in \tau_s^j \cup \tau_{sr}^j$, $J_i^{\tau_s^j \cup \tau_{sr}^j}(p+1) := J_i^{\tau_s^j \cup \tau_{sr}^j}(p)$ then

          end:=1

        else if there is a message m_i and a controller $NC_j \in dest(m_i)$ such that

$$max\_rt(\tau_s^{src(m_i)} \cup \tau_{sr}^{src(m_i)}, m_i) + Max +$$

$$max_{NC_k \in relay(m_i) \; and \; k \neq j}(max\_rt(\tau_r^k, m_i) - J_i^{\tau_r^k} + max\_rt(\tau_s^k \cup \tau_{sr}^k, m_i) - J_i^{\tau_s^k \cup \tau_{sr}^k}) +$$

$$Max + max\_rt(\tau_r^j), m_i) - J_i^{\tau_r^j} > D_i$$

        then end:=1 else p:=p+1

    until end=1

}

At the end of the procedure, the value of the maximum release jitter of any message m_i in any queue of any network controller is known, or the system has diverged. Section 5.4 shows how to compute $r_i^{j,rel}$, the maximum time for any message m_i between the R_Multicast request and the time where the non-crashed controller NC_j in $dest(m_i)$ has R_Delivered the message m_i. Finally F_i, the maximum time between the R_Multicast request and the R_Deliver in the group $dest(m_i)$ is computed. We now focus on Non-Preemptive EDF (NP-EDF) scheduling on a uniprocessor.

5.3 Uniprocessor NP-EDF scheduling

a) Notations
We first define the notations used for the NP-EDF scheduling analysis.

- **NP-EDF** is the non-preemptive version of Earliest Deadline First non idling scheduling. We recall that EDF schedules the tasks according to their absolute deadlines: the task with the shortest absolute deadline has the highest priority.

- Time is assumed to be **discrete** (task arrivals occur and tasks executions begin and terminate at clock ticks; the parameters used are expressed as multiples of the clock tick); in [2], it is shown that there is no loss of generality with respect to feasibility results by restricting the schedules to be discrete, once the task parameters are assumed to be integers (multiple of the clock tick) i.e. a discrete schedule exists if and only if a continuous schedule exists.

We now introduce the busy period notion that identifies periods of activity of the processor. The aim of the analysis given in 5.3.b is to identify the worst case busy periods (where the maximum response time of any task can be obtained).

- An **idle time** t is defined on a processor as a time such that there are no tasks requested before time t pending at time t. An interval of successive idle times is called an **idle period**. Notice that a task subject to a release jitter is not supposed to be pending until the release jitter ends.

- A **busy period** is defined as a time interval $[a,b)$ such that there is no idle time in the interval (a,b) (the processor is fully busy) and such that both a and b are idle times.

- $U = \sum_{i=1}^{n} C_i/T_i$ is the **processor utilization factor**, i.e., the fraction of processor time spent in the execution of the task set [11]. In the following, we assume $U < 1$.

- Let time 0 be the beginning of a busy period bp. $\forall \tau_i$ and $\forall a \geq -J_i$, we define the sets: $hp_i(a) = \{\tau_k, k \neq i, D_k - J_k \leq a + D_i\}$ and $\overline{hp}_i(a) = \{\tau_k, D_k - J_k > a + D_i\}$. By construction, if $\tau_k \in hp_i(a)$, at least the occurrence of task τ_k whose activation is requested at time $-J_k$ and subject to a release jitter J_k has a higher priority than task τ_i whose activation is requested at time a. All occurrences of tasks in $\overline{hp}_i(a)$ (if any) have a priority lower than task τ_i whose activation is requested at time a whatever their release time in bp.

b) Worst case response time

We now consider the problem of scheduling by NP-EDF n sporadic tasks on a uniprocessor. This analysis is based on [5]. The worst case response time is reached for any task τ_i subject to a release jitter J_i in a scenario described in lemma 5.

Lemma 5. *Let $\tau_i, i \in [1, n]$ be a task requested at time a, subject to a release jitter J_i and executed according to NP-EDF in a busy period bp. The worst case response time of τ_i requested at time a, $a \geq -J_i$, is obtained in the first busy period of a scenario where:*

- *any task $\tau_k \in hp_i(a)$ executed in bp is requested for the first time at time $t_k^0 = -J_k$, with an initial release jitter J_k, and is then periodic.*

- *all the previous occurrences of τ_i executed in bp are periodic from t_i^0 to a, where $t_i^0 \in [-J_i, -J_i + T_i - 1]$.*

- *a task in $\overline{hp}_i(a)$ whose duration is maximum over $\overline{hp}_i(a)$ (if any) is released at time -1.*

Proof. see [5] for a detailed proof.

The following schema illustrates the worst case scenario of lemma 5 for a task requested at time a in a busy period bp.

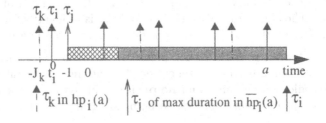

Fig. 4. Worst case scenario for task τ_i

Lemma 6. *If $U < 1$ then the longest busy period L is obtained in the first busy period of the scenario where all tasks $\tau_k, k \in [1, n]$ are subject to a release jitter J_k and are requested for the first time at time $-J_k$ and then at their maximum rate.*

Proof. Suppose there exists a busy period BP longer than L the first busy period of the scenario where all tasks $\tau_k, k \in [1, n]$ are requested at time $-J_k$. Let time 0 be the beginning of that busy period. Let t_k^0 be the first time task τ_k, is requested in the busy period. If $\forall k \in [1, n]$, t_k^0 is changed to $-J_k$ and task τ_k is subject to a release jitter J_k then the resulting busy period can only see more or the same number of tasks and thus its size cannot decrease invalidating the former hypothesis.

L is the first solution of the equation: $L = \sum_{i=1}^{n}\lceil\frac{L+J_i}{T_i}\rceil$. It is shown in [4] that L always exists when $U < 1$.

- Let $L_i(a)$ denotes the time when τ_i's instance requested at time $a \geq -J_i$ can start its execution in a scenario of lemma 5.

- The response time of the instance of τ_i requested at time a is: $r_i(a) = max\{C_i, L_i(a) + C_i - a\}$

The value of $L_i(a)$ can be determined by finding the smallest solution of the equation (1)

$$t = max_{\tau_k \in \overline{hp_i}(a)}\{C_k - 1\} + \overline{W}_i(a, t) + \lfloor\frac{a + J_i}{T_i}\rfloor C_i \qquad (1)$$

The first term on the right side accounts for the worst-case priority inversion w.r.t. the absolute deadline $a + D_i$. The second term is the time needed to execute the instances of tasks other than τ_i with absolute deadlines smaller than or equal to $a + D_i$ and request times before the execution start time of τ_i's instance. Finally, the third term is the time needed to execute the τ_i's instances requested before a. The rationale of the equation is to compute the time needed by the τ_i's instance released at time a to get the processor: every other higher priority instance released before this event will be executed earlier, thus its execution time must be accounted for. For the same reason, the function $\overline{W}_i(a, t)$ must account for all higher priority instances of task $\tau_j \in hp_i(a)$ requested in the interval $[-J_j, t]$ (according to scenario of lemma 5), thus also including those possibly requested at time t. For any task τ_j, the maximum number of instances requested in $[-J_j, t]$ is $1 + \lfloor\frac{t+J_j}{T_j}\rfloor$. However, among them at most $1 + \lfloor\frac{a+D_i-D_j+J_j}{T_j}\rfloor$ can have an absolute deadline less than or equal to $a+Di$. It follows that :

$$\overline{W}(a, t) = \sum_{\tau_j \in hp_i(a)} (1 + \lfloor\frac{min(t, a + D_i - D_j) + J_j}{T_j}\rfloor)C_j \qquad (2)$$

$\overline{W}_i(a, t)$ being a monotonic non-decreasing step function in t, the smallest solution of Equation (1) can be found using the usual fixed point computation:

$$L_i^{(0)} = 0 \qquad (3)$$

$$L_i^{(p+1)}(a) = max_{\tau_j \in \overline{hp_i}(a)}\{C_j - 1\} + \overline{W}_i(a, L_i^p(a)) + \lfloor\frac{a + J_i}{T_i}\rfloor C_i \qquad (4)$$

Having computed $L_i(a)$, we obtain $r_i(a)$. Notice that according to the lemma 6, $L_i(a)$ is upper bounded by L. Hence we conclude that the computation of $r_i(a)$ can be coherently limited to values of a smaller than L. That is, the worst-case response time of τ_i is finally

$$r_i = max\{r_i(a) : -J_i \leq a \leq L\}. \qquad (5)$$

5.4   End-to-end response times

We show how the notations used in the uniprocessor case are extended to the distributed case. We can then compute $r_i^{j,rel}$, the maximum time between the R_Multicast request and the R_Deliver of a message m_i by the non-crashed network controller NC_j in $dest(m_i)$.

We first study the effect of the clock precision ε:
Two messages timestamped by the same source are not affected by the clock precision. If two messages are timestamped by two different network controllers then the precision of the clock synchronization has an effect equivalent to an extra release jitter ε to add in the worst case analysis of section 5.3. In the following, we denote $\varepsilon_{i,k}$ the function that returns for any message m_i and m_k in the same waiting queue, ε if $src(m_k) \neq src(m_i)$ and 0 otherwise.
In the uniprocessor case, a task τ_i is defined by the parameters (C_i, T_i, D_i, J_i). In the distributed case, task τ_i is associated to a message m_i. The values of the former parameters must be adapted on any network controller NC_j as follows:

The execution time C_i: already given in section 5.2.

The release jitter J_i: if $J_i^{\tau^j}(p-1)$ is the release jitter obtained for message m_i in the waiting queue τ^j at step p-1 in the holistic scheduling approach (see section 5.2) then for any message m_k in τ^j, $J_i^{\tau^j} = J_i^{\tau^j}(p-1)+\varepsilon_{i,k}$. Indeed, the worst case behavior of sources different from $src(m_i)$ is to have timestamped their messages with a clock ε late compared to the local clock of $src(m_i)$.

The parameters Ti and Di are left unchanged.
With those adaptations, we can determine the worst case response time of any task τ_i in either the send queue or the receive queue. When the holistic scheduling iteration ends, the system has either converged or diverged. If the system has converged then the worst case release jitter of any message m_i in τ^j, with $\tau^j = \tau_s^j \cup \tau_r^j$ or $\tau^j = \tau_r^j$, is determined on any network controller NC_j.
We now show how to compute $r_i^{j,rel}$ defined in section 5.2 as the maximum time between the R_Multicast request of message m_i and the R_Deliver by the non-crashed network controller NC_j in $dest(m_i)$. According to figure 2, a message m_i can be received from different network controllers, either directly or through a relay. Then $r_i^{j,rel}$ is the maximum between:

- the maximum time between the R_Multicast request and the R_Deliver of message m_i by controller NC_j in $dest(m_i)$, after a direct receipt of message m_i;

- the maximum time between the R_Multicast request and the R_Deliver of message m_i by controller NC_j in $dest(m_i)$, after an indirect receipt of message m_i.

If m_i is received directly by NC_j, then the worst duration between the R_Multicast request of m_i and the R_Deliver of m_i on NC_j is equal to:

$$max\_rt(\tau_s^{src(m_i)} \cup \tau_{sr}^{src(m_i)}, m_i) + Max + max\_rt(\tau_r^j, m_i) - J_i^{\tau_r^j} \qquad (6)$$

If m_i is received indirectly by NC_j, then the worst duration between the R_Multicast request of m_i and the R_Deliver of m_i on NC_j is equal to:

$$max\_rt(\tau_s^{src(m_i)} \cup \tau_{sr}^{src(m_i)}, m_i) + Max +$$
$$max_{NC_k \in relay(m_i)}(max\_rt(\tau_r^k, m_i) - J_i^{\tau_r^k} +$$
$$max\_rt(\tau_s^k \cup \tau_{sr}^k, m_i) - J_i^{\tau_s^k \cup \tau_{sr}^k}) + Max +$$
$$max\_rt(\tau_r^j, m_i) - J_i^{\tau_r^j} \qquad (7)$$

$r_i^{j,rel}$ being computed for any message m_i. Finally the worst case end to end response time for the reliable multicast of message m_i is $F_i + \varepsilon$, where $F_i = max_{j \in dest(m_i)} r_i^{j,rel}$.

Hence the system is feasible if the worst case end to end response time of every message is less than its relative deadline, i.e.:

$$F_i + \varepsilon \le D_i \qquad (8)$$

where D_i is the end-to-end deadline required for the reliable multicast of message m_i in the group $dest(m_i)$.

6 Conclusion

In this paper, we have designed and proved a uniform reliable multicast protocol tolerating up to f_c processor crashes and up to f_o network omissions during the execution of a reliable multicast. The total number of messages generated per reliable multicast of message m_i is $f_c + f_o + 2$ in a broadcast network and $(f_c + f_o + 2)[card(dest(m_i)) - 1]$ in a point-to-point network, when the source of the multicast belongs to the destination group $dest(m_i)$. The fault-tolerance feasibility condition is $card[dest(m_i) - \{src(m_i)\}] \ge f_c + f_0 + 1$. The network transmission delay is assumed to be bounded. The end-to-end worst case response time is analysed using the holistic approach. We have established a necessary and sufficient condition for the feasibility on a uniprocessor, of a set of tasks subject to a release jitter and scheduled EDF. These results are then applied to the computation of the end-to-end response time. In [4] the complexity is shown to be pseudo-polynomial when $U < 1$, U being the processor utilization factor. This uniform reliable multicast service ensures that for any message m_i whose reliable multicast is requested at time t, no controller delivers m_i after time $t + F_i + \varepsilon$, where F_i is a constant depending on m_i and on the workload of processors involved by the multicast. The real-time feasibility condition is then $F_i + \varepsilon \le D_i$, where D_i is the deadline of message m_i.

References

[1] B. Charron-Bost, C. Delporte, H. Fauconnier, E. Ledinot, G. Le Lann, A. Marcuzzi, P. Minet, J.M. Vincent, "Spécification du problème ATR (Accord Temps Réel)", rapport du contrat DGA- DSP/MENSR/CNRS, Juin 1997.

[2] S. K. Baruah, R. R. Howell, L. E. Rosier, "Algorithms and Complexity Concerning the Preemptive Scheduling of Periodic Real-Time tasks on one processor", Real- Time Systems, 2, p 301-324, 1990.

[3] F. Cristian, "Synchronous atomic broadcast for redundant channels", IBM Research Report RJ 7203, Dec. 1989.

[4] L. George, "Ordonnancement en ligne temps réel critique dans les systèmes distribués", PhD Thesis, Université de Versailles Saint-Quentin, Janvier 1998.

[5] L. George, N. Rivierre, M. Spuri, "Preemptive and Non-Preemptive Real- Time Uniprocessor Scheduling" INRIA Rocquencourt, France, Research Report 2966, Sept. 1996.

[6] R. Guerraoui, A. Schiper, "Total Order Multicast to Multiple Groups", ICDCS'97, Baltimore, Maryland, pp 578- 585, May 1997.

[7] J. F. Hermant, M. Spuri, "End-to-end response times in real-time distributed systems", 9th int. conf. on Parallel and Distributed Computing Systems, Dijon, France, pp 413-417, Sept. 1996.

[8] V. Hadzilacos, S. Toueg, "A modular approach to fault-tolerant broadcasts and related problems", Technical Report TR 94-1425, Dept. of Computer Science, Cornell University, Ithaca, NY14853, May 1994.

[9] K. Jeffay, D. F. Stanat, C. U. Martel, "On Non-Preemptive Scheduling of Periodic and Sporadic Tasks", IEEE Real-Time Systems Symposium, San-Antonio, December 4-6, 1991, pp 129-139.

[10] D. D. Kandlur, K. G. Shin, D. Ferrari, "Real-time communication in multihop networks", IEEE Trans. on Parallel and Distributed Systems, 5(10), October 1994.

[11] C.L Liu, J. W. Layland, "Scheduling Algorithms for multiprogramming in a Hard Real Time Environment", Journal of the Association for Computing Machinery, 20(1), Jan. 1973.

[12] G. Le Lann, "A methodology for designing and dimensioning critical complex computing systems", IEEE Engineering of Computer Based Systems, Friedrichshafen, Germany, March 1996, pp 332-339.

[13] A. Parekh, R. Gallager, " A generalized processor sharing approach to flow control in integrated services networks- the single node case", INFOCOM92, Florence, Italy, 1992, pp915-924.

[14] F. Schmuck, F. Cristian, "Continuous clock amortization need not affect the precision of a clock synchronization algorithm", Research Report RJ7290, IBM Almaden, Jan. 1990.

[15] M. Spuri, "Holisitic analysis for deadline scheduled real-time distributed systems" Research Report 2873, INRIA, France, April 1996.

[16] K. Tindell, J. Clark "Holistic Schedulability Analysis for Distributed Hard Real-Time Systems", Microprocessors and Microprogramming 40, 1994.

[17] G Xie, S. Lam, "Delay Guarantee of virtual clock server", IEEE/ACM Trans. on Networking, 3(6), pp 683-689, Dec. 1995.

A Tool to Assist in Fine-Tuning and Debugging Embedded Real-Time Systems

Gaurav Arora[1] and David B. Stewart[2]

[1]Broadcast Products Division, Hughes Network Systems
11717 Exploration Lane, Germantown, MD 20876, U.S.A.
garora@hns.com

[2]Dept. of Electrical Engineering and Institute for Advanced Computer Studies
University of Maryland, College Park, MD 20742
dstewart@eng.umd.edu

Abstract: During the latter stages of a software product cycle, developers may be faced with the task of fine-tuning an embedded system that is not meeting all of its timing requirements. To aid in this process, we have created a tool called AFTER (Assist in Fine-Tuning Embedded Real-time systems) to help software designers fine-tune and debug their target real-time implementations. AFTER uses raw timing data collected from an embedded system, analyzes it by correlating the measured data with the system specifications, then provides a temporal image of the current implementation, highlighting actual and potential problems. AFTER is then used in an interactive predictor mode to help the developer fine-tune the application systematically.

1 Introduction

An extremely difficult task faced by system software developers is the fine-tuning and debugging of timing errors in an embedded system. We have developed a tool that merges the capabilities from software design CASE tools and runtime performance monitors, to assist engineers to systematically debug and fine-tune their embedded applications.

Most commercial CASE tools focus on the software specifications and design of an embedded system, but do not provide much support after the software has been implemented. The software design and real-time analysis is based only on hypothetical data, and does not take into account such practical concerns as operating system overhead, interrupt handling, and inaccuracies in estimating worst-case execution time of each process.

On the other hand, performance monitoring tools allow developers to obtain raw data from the underlying embedded system. Although these tools provide most, if not all, of the data needed to pinpoint the problem, such data is not provided in a very useful manner. It only shows exactly what happened during runtime, without correlating those results to the original specifications. As a result, there is no means to differentiate between parts of the execution that are "normal" versus those parts that have the timing errors. Only an expert can look at this raw data and make those differentiations.

The key contributions of our tool, called AFTER (*Assist in Fine-Tuning Embedded Real-time systems*), are the following:

- Correlates measured data with the original specifications, to analyze the real-time performance and highlight deviations of the execution from the original specifications.

- Predicts the effect of small fine-tuning adjustments to the code, to help a designer quickly zero-in on the best techniques for fixing the timing problems.

The remainder of this section presents related work in software tools for analyzing and monitoring embedded real-time systems. The design of AFTER is described in Section 2. The theoretical foundations of AFTER are detailed in Section 3. The predictor capabilities are presented in Section 4. Finally, future directions for this project are discussed in Section 5.

1.1 Related Work

AFTER is a CASE tool that provides real-time scheduling analysis *after* implementation. In contrast, other CASE tools provide real-time scheduling advice *before* implementation, and performance monitors only provide raw timing data – not analysis – after implementation.

Many commercial and non-commercial CASE tools aid real-time system developers in detecting and removing potential "timing bugs" from the system. Examples of tools that perform schedulability analysis on real-time systems are: PERTS, CAISARTS and, Scheduler 1-2-3.

PERTS [8] is a prototyping environment for real-time systems. It is a collection of tools and simulation environment for the analysis, validation, and evaluation of real-time systems. It focuses on the specification and design phase of the system lifecycle. It uses traditional real-time scheduling models for the analysis and ignores the effect of operating system overheads and overhead interrupt handling on the system performance. This tool has to rely on estimated timing parameters for the system evaluation which are not usually reflective of the actual system parameters.

CAISARTS [2] on the other hand is a rule-based tool used by real-time engineers to obtain expert advice for all aspects of system design related to scheduling. This advice is extracted from a knowledge-base of real-time system facts, theories and algorithms and is beneficial for the design and early implementation stage of a real-time system. This advice is *general* and not specific to any actual implementation. CAISARTS is a useful tool to obtain guidelines for designing a real-time system but it cannot assist an engineer in fine-tuning an already implemented system.

Scheduler 1-2-3 [12] uses hypothetical timing information, verifies the schedulability, and synthesizes a part of a test program, which is then downloaded onto the target system. In Scheduler 1-2-3, the schedulability analysis is done on a synthetic task set generated based on a workload table. Scheduler 1-2-3 has limited analysis capabilities. It can only analyze systems which use a fixed priority scheduling based on the Rate Monotonic algorithm. Also, it does not incorporate the operating system overheads in the analytical equations.

Another type of CASE tools are performance monitoring tools. They allow developers to obtain raw timing data from the underlying embedded system. Examples of such tools are: Stethoscope and ScopeProfile and, Chimera's Automatic Task Profiler (ATP).

StethoScope and ScopeProfile [13] are task profiling tools by WindRiver Systems. They do not perform any schedulability analysis on the gathered data. SthethoScope is a real-time graphical monitoring, performance analysis, and data collection tool. ScopeProfile is a dynamic execution profiler. It is used to calculate the CPU usage of a VxWorks program on a procedure-by-procedure basis. It can be used to extract timing information such as execution time of tasks and interrupts from an embedded system. Both these tools extract accurate timing information from the system but leave the more essential and time consuming job of analyzing this data and pin-pointing problems in the system to the engineer. The assumption is that embedded system engineers are experts in real-time systems analysis and will be able to use this extracted timing information to their benefit.

The automatic task profiling (ATP) mechanism in Chimera [11] minimizes the need for a developer to use specialized hardware to debug the temporal aspects of embedded systems. The Chimera microkernel was modified to maintain statistics every time a context switch is performed. The statistics are available immediately via shared memory to tasks executing on the same or remote processors, or to a GUI with shared memory access to the system. The ATP mechanism enabled implementing a timing error detection and handling capability in the Chimera microkernel. As is the case with Stetho-Scope and ScopeProfile, it does not analyze the timing information that it extracts and leaves that part to the engineer.

Current performance monitoring tools show exactly what happened during runtime, but they do not correlate those results to the original specifications.

The unique features of AFTER that distinguishes it from other CASE tools are:

1. AFTER combines two types of real-time CASE tools (performance monitoring and system analysis) into one integrated tool.
2. It has a novel prediction feature. It predicts the effect of small fine-tuning adjustments to the code, to help a designer zero-in on the best techniques for fixing the timing problems.
3. The analytical models of AFTER incorporate the operating system overheads such as context switch and interrupt handling hence, provide more accurate results.
4. It has an easy to use graphical user interface and can be used by system developers with little or no real-time scheduling theory knowledge, which is the case for many embedded system developers in industry.

2 Implementation of AFTER

A diagrammatic view of AFTER is shown in Figure 1. AFTER includes a *filter unit*, an *analysis unit*, and a *graphical user interface (GUI)*. The diagram also shows the integration of AFTER with the system specifications, implementation environment, and data collection tools. Numbers in *{brackets}* in this text represent the circled numbers in the diagram, and are used below to help explain the process.

First *{1}* software is implemented using the developer's favorite environment. Next, *{2}* the code is executed, and timing data is collected using a performance monitoring tool such as Wind River System's Stethoprofile, Chimera's Automated Task Profiling, or by using hardware such as a logic analyzer or in-circuit emulator.

The filter unit *{3}* extracts and pre-processes only the raw data needed to represent the temporal state of the target system, based on the specifications of the system *{4}*. Examples of parameters typically extracted by the filter unit are execution time, period of tasks, and minimum interarrival time of interrupts.

The results of the filter step are displayed to the user, as shown in Figure 2. In the display, *Number* refers to the number of complete execution cycles for a thread in the input raw data file. C_{min}, C_{max} and C_{avg} are the minimum, maximum and average execution time for a thread, respectively. Similarly, T_{min}, T_{max} and T_{avg} are the minimum, maximum and average period for a thread, respectively. The threads are classified as periodic tasks (T) or interrupts (I).

The filter modules are specific to the profiling method used, such that using a different monitoring mechanism results in only needing to create an appropriate filter module.

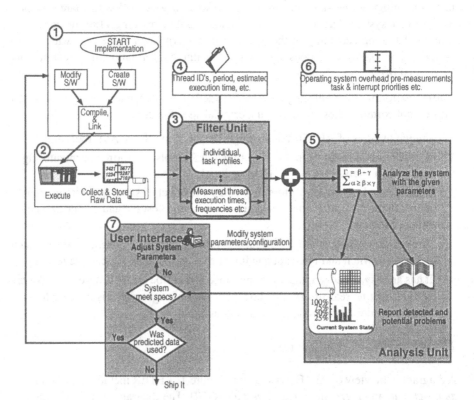

Fig. 1. Detailed view of AFTER

The filter unit can also be changed to provide different kinds of information to the analysis unit, depending on the type of analysis to be performed. For example, one filter unit may only extract worst-case execution times, while another may extract the entire timing history of a particular task.

2.1 Analysis Module

The analysis unit *{5}* is the core of AFTER, and operates in two modes: *analysis mode* and *predictor mode*. The inputs to the unit are the filtered data from the filter unit *{3}* and the pre-measured timing parameters of the target platform *{6}*.

In the analysis mode, the unit only uses real data collected from the embedded system, and performs a schedulability analysis using a mathematical model consistent with the scheduling algorithm and real-time operating system used in the underlying embedded system. The results of the analysis, as well as any actual problems such as tasks missing deadlines and processes using more CPU time than their allocated worst-case execution time, are displayed to the user.

In the predictor mode, the analysis unit uses a combination of real data and manually modified data to predict how a particular fine-tuning operation might change the timing

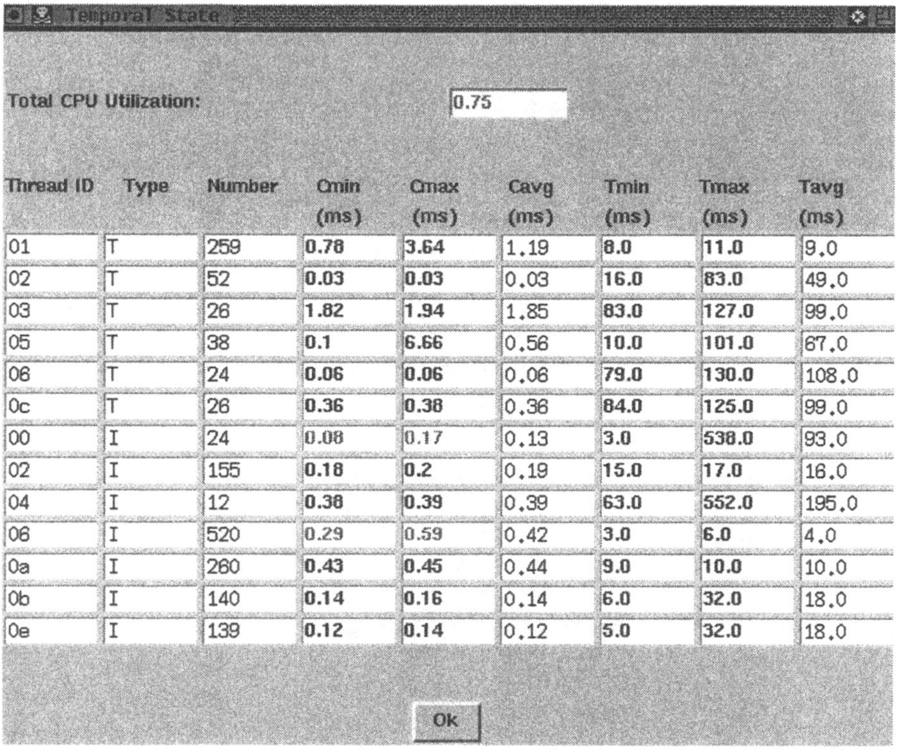

Total CPU Utilization: 0.75

Thread ID	Type	Number	Cmin (ms)	Cmax (ms)	Cavg (ms)	Tmin (ms)	Tmax (ms)	Tavg (ms)
01	T	259	0.78	3.64	1.19	8.0	11.0	9.0
02	T	52	0.03	0.03	0.03	16.0	83.0	49.0
03	T	26	1.82	1.94	1.85	83.0	127.0	99.0
05	T	38	0.1	6.66	0.56	10.0	101.0	67.0
06	T	24	0.06	0.06	0.06	79.0	130.0	108.0
0c	T	26	0.36	0.38	0.36	84.0	125.0	99.0
00	I	24	0.08	0.17	0.13	3.0	538.0	93.0
02	I	155	0.18	0.2	0.19	15.0	17.0	16.0
04	I	12	0.38	0.39	0.39	63.0	552.0	195.0
06	I	520	0.29	0.59	0.42	3.0	6.0	4.0
0a	I	260	0.43	0.45	0.44	9.0	10.0	10.0
0b	I	140	0.14	0.16	0.14	6.0	32.0	18.0
0e	I	139	0.12	0.14	0.12	5.0	32.0	18.0

Ok

Fig. 2. Temporal state of system, as extracted by filter unit

characteristics of the system. If the unit predicts that the change will likely result in an improvement in the system performance, the developer can implement those changes, then reanalyze the system using real data. The developer does not need to implement any changes that are not likely to improve the system.

The analysis unit is continually evolving as analysis based on a variety of computational models are being incorporated. The computational models and scheduling theory that has been included in the current prototype are discussed in more detail in Section 3.

2.2 Interactive Graphical Interface

The interactive graphical interface {7}, shown in Figure 3, allows the developer to inter-act with the analysis unit to request that it operates in the predictor mode.

The developer specifies one of a variety of fine-tuning optimizations that can possibly be made to fix the timing problems. The analysis unit then re-computes schedulability, but instead of using only measured data, it replaces the measured data directly pertain-ing to the user's request with manually modified data. It then predicts what kinds of tim-

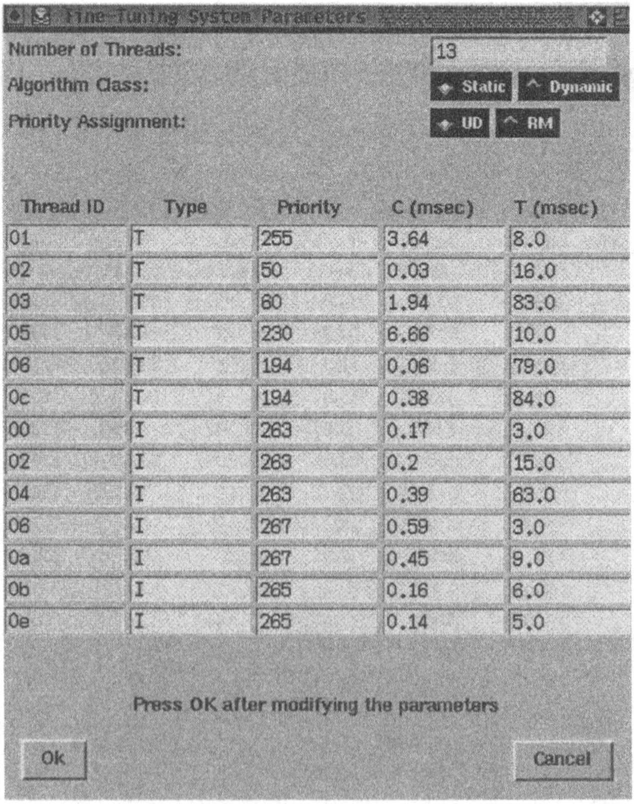

Thread ID	Type	Priority	C (msec)	T (msec)
01	T	255	3.64	8.0
02	T	50	0.03	16.0
03	T	60	1.94	83.0
05	T	230	6.66	10.0
06	T	194	0.06	79.0
0c	T	194	0.38	84.0
00	I	263	0.17	3.0
02	I	263	0.2	15.0
04	I	263	0.39	63.0
06	I	267	0.59	3.0
0a	I	267	0.45	9.0
0b	I	265	0.16	6.0
0e	I	265	0.14	5.0

Number of Threads: 13
Algorithm Class: Static / Dynamic
Priority Assignment: UD / RM

Press OK after modifying the parameters

Ok   Cancel

Fig. 3. Parameter modification window

ing errors, if any, may occur if the change was actually made. If the analysis unit indicates potential improvement, then the designer can modify the code, and repeat the steps {1} through {5}. If, however, the proposed change would have no effect on the final system, the designer does not need to spend any time implementing the change. The designer thus only performs a compile/link/download/execute iteration for fine-tuning changes that are likely to improve the system by reducing the number of timing problems in it.

The modifications that can currently be made through the interactive graphical interface are the following: changing the priority of a task; switching one or more interrupt handlers to aperiodic servers, or vice versa; changing the frequency of a task; lowering the execution time of a particular task to determine which modules most need to be optimized; and using dynamic instead of static scheduling. Many of the analytical models described in Section 3 pertain especially to supporting prediction. Additional prediction capabilities will be added later, as described in Section 5.

3 Theoretical Foundations of AFTER

The analysis unit is the core of AFTER. It performs schedulability analysis on the data provided by the filter unit based on a set of analytical equations. These equations are described in detail in this chapter. There are two operational modes for the AU, the *analysis mode* in which it uses only real data collected from the embedded application, and presents the current state of the system to the developer. The *predictor mode*, in which the unit uses a combination of real data and data modified by the developer, to predict how a particular fine-tuning operation might change the timing characteristics of the system. The main goal of AFTER is to assist in improving system performance in terms of predictability and efficiency. It does this by helping the engineer come up with the optimal set of timing parameters for the system so that even the low priority tasks such as the performance monitoring task, are able to execute in a predictable manner.

To test our first prototype, we focused on a commercial satellite modem embedded application. The modem receives encrypted bitstream from the satellite. This bitstream contains different types of packets such as video, audio and data. The modem de-multiplexes the bitstream after performing error correction and decryption. The different types of packets are then forwarded to their respective destinations which may be a television monitor for video and audio packets and a PC for the data packets. The modem software (runs on VRTX32 real-time operating system [9]) consists of fixed priority periodic tasks and interrupts. We used AFTER to determine whether dynamic priority scheduling or aperiodic servers would improve the application, and to identify which software modules need to be optimized the most.

The following notation is used throughout this section:

- A task set consists of n_{thr} periodic tasks, $\tau_1, \tau_2..., \tau_{nthr}$. We will use the term task and thread interchangeably throughout this discussion.
- An interrupt set consists of n_{intr} interrupts, $\iota_1, \iota_2..., \iota_{nintr}$.
- For periodic threads, C and T are execution time and period respectively.

- For aperiodic servers C is the server capacity and T is the minimum inter-arrival time.
- For interrupt handlers, C is the execution time and T is the minimum inter-arrival time.
- Each thread τ_i has a period T_i, a deadline D_i, where $D_i \leq T_i$.
- Each thread τ_i has a fixed priority P_i that is lower than the minimum priority of an interrupt. In dynamic scheduling models, P_i is ignored.
- The threads and interrupts are numbered in decreasing order of priority. For example, two threads τ_i, τ_j, with priorities P_i, P_j, if $P_i > P_j$, then $i < j$.
- Δ_{task} is the context switch overhead for a thread in VRTX32 and includes the time to execute the scheduler and to select the next thread.
- Δ_{intr} is the operating system overhead for servicing an interrupt.

Following are five models that have been implemented into the AFTER tool. They form a sufficient basis for the analysis and prediction capabilities described in this paper. Additional models can be added to AFTER, in order to support more analysis and prediction, as described in Section 5.

Model 1: VRTX32 Static Scheduling

This section presents the schedulability model for a task and interrupt set executing on the VRTX32 real-time kernel. It combines rate monotonic analysis [7] with operating system overheads, based on the method used by Katcher [4]. However, as compared to Katcher's work, the method in which operating system overheads are incorporated into the analysis needed to be modified, so that the overheads are measurable quantities given a commercial RTOS for which we do not have source code. To incorporate interrupts in this model, we model an interrupt service routine (ISR) as a sporadic server [10] with its capacity being the maximum execution time of the ISR and its period equal to the minimum inter-arrival time of the interrupt.

The VRTX32 scheduling model is described by the following equation. This model is capable of analyzing the target application which in this case happens to be the satellite modem.

A specific task and interrupt set under VRTX32 consisting of n_{thr} periodic tasks τ_1, τ_2..., τ_{nthr} and n_{intr} interrupts ι_1, ι_2..., ι_{nintr} is schedulable if and only if:

$$\forall i, 1 \leq i \leq n_{intr} + n_{thr},$$

$$S_i = \sum_{j=1}^{min(i, n_{intr})} \frac{C_j + \Delta_{intr}}{t} \left\lceil \frac{t}{T_j} \right\rceil ; S_t = \sum_{j = n_{intr} + 1}^{i} \frac{C_j + \Delta_{task}}{t} \left\lceil \frac{t}{T_j} \right\rceil \quad (1)$$

$$min_{(0 < t \leq D_i)}[S_i + S_t] \leq 1.$$

where Δ_{task} is the same as $C_{preempt}$ in Katcher's notation. The threads and interrupts in this equation are ordered in decreasing order of priority (with interrupt handler $j=1$ having highest priority in the system, and thread $j=n_{intr}+1$, having the highest priority among threads).

For detailed proofs of this and subsequent models, refer to [1].

Model 2: Dynamic Scheduling Model

The dynamic scheduling model can be used in analysis mode if the underlying system uses dynamic scheduling, or in predictor mode if the target system is using a static scheduling algorithm, to determine the likely effect if the scheduling algorithm is changed.

The primary advantage of a dynamic scheduling algorithm is an increase in schedulable bound to 100% for any task set. The dynamic scheduling model is described by the following equation:

Let τ be a task and interrupt set with n_{thr} dynamic priority periodic tasks and n_{intr} fixed priority interrupts with $U < 1$. τ will be feasible if and only if for all t, $t \in P$:

$$\left(\sum_{i=1}^{n_{thr}} \left\lfloor \frac{t}{T_i} \right\rfloor (C_i + \Delta'_{task}) + \sum_{j=1}^{n_{intr}} (C_j + \Delta'_{intr}) \left\lceil \frac{t}{T_j} \right\rceil \right) \leq t \qquad (2)$$

where, P is the set of non-negative multiples, less than B, of the periods of the periodic tasks.

$$B = \frac{\left(\sum_{j=1}^{n_{intr}} C_j \right)}{(1-U)} \qquad (3)$$

$$P = \langle kT_i | kT_i < B \wedge k \geq 0 \wedge 1 \leq i \leq n_{thr} \rangle$$

The above model was obtained by computing the availability function for a dynamic priority system with interrupts and combining it with Liu and Layland's mixed priority scheduling model [7]. To achieve a closed form equivalent of the model, we used the results provided by Jeffay and Stone [3].

Model 3: Static scheduling with aperiodic servers

This model represents the system which comprises of periodic tasks and aperiodic servers. Aperiodic servers are modelled as having a constant execution time for interrupt or signal handling (represented by S_{as}), in addition to the execution time of the server (S_t).

A system with n_{thr} periodic threads and n_{intr} aperiodic server threads executing under VRTX32 is feasible if and only if:

$$\forall i, 1 \leq i \leq n_{intr} + n_{thr},$$

$$S_{as} = \sum_{j=1}^{min(i, n_{intr})} \frac{K_{sig} + \Delta_{intr}}{t} \left\lceil \frac{t}{T_j} \right\rceil$$

$$S_t = \sum_{j=1}^{i} \frac{C_j + \Delta_{task}}{t} \left\lceil \frac{t}{T_j} \right\rceil \tag{4}$$

$$min_{(0 < t \leq D_i)} [S_{as} + S_t] \leq 1.$$

The overhead associated with an aperiodic server thread comprises of three components: overhead of signalling an aperiodic server from an interrupt handler, Δ_{task} and, Δ_{intr}. Adding these terms to the VRTX32 static scheduling model leads to this model.

Model 4: Frequency modification

The frequency modification module is used only in the predictor mode. It is used to analyze the target system if the frequency of one or more tasks is changed by the user through the graphical interface.

A specific task and interrupt set under VRTX32 consisting of n_{thr} periodic tasks τ_1, τ_2..., τ_{nthr} and n_{intr} interrupts ι_1, ι_2..., ι_{nintr} is schedulable if and only if:

$$\forall i, 1 \leq i \leq n_{intr} + n_{thr},$$

$$S_{t_k} = \frac{C_k + \Delta_{task}}{t} \left\lceil \frac{t}{T_k + \Delta T_k} \right\rceil$$

$$S_t = \sum_{j=n_{intr}+1}^{k-1} \frac{C_j + \Delta_{task}}{t} \left\lceil \frac{t}{T_j} \right\rceil + S_{t_k} + \sum_{j=k+1}^{i} \frac{C_j + \Delta_{task}}{t} \left\lceil \frac{t}{T_j} \right\rceil \tag{5}$$

$$S_i = \sum_{j=1}^{min(i, n_{intr})} \frac{C_j + \Delta_{intr}}{t} \left\lceil \frac{t}{T_j} \right\rceil$$

$$min_{(0 < t \leq D_i)} [S_i + S_t] \leq 1.$$

This model is obtained by replacing the time period of task τ_k in equation (1) such that $T_k = T_k + \Delta T_k$, where ΔT_k could be a positive or negative delta change in the time period. This leads to a modified value of S_t as given in equation (5). Similarly, modifying equations (2) and (4) allow us to make frequency modification predictions for other cases.

Model 5: Execution time modification

Execution time modification model is primarily used in the predictor mode in two ways: (1) If the execution time of a process is reduced (through either code optimization or removing some code), AFTER will predict the net effect on the overall timing of the system. (2) If more code needs to be added to a process, AFTER can aid in detecting whether or not the additional code will cause new timing problems.

A system with n_{thr} periodic threads and n_{intr} aperiodic server threads executing under VRTX32 is feasible if and only if:

$$\forall i, 1 \leq i \leq n_{intr} + n_{thr},$$

$$S_{t_k} = \frac{C_k + \Delta C_k + \Delta_{task}}{t} \left\lceil \frac{t}{T_k} \right\rceil$$

$$S_t = \sum_{j=1}^{k-1} \frac{C_j + \Delta_{task}}{t} \left\lceil \frac{t}{T_j} \right\rceil + S_{t_k} + \sum_{j=k+1}^{i} \frac{C_j + \Delta_{task}}{t} \left\lceil \frac{t}{T_j} \right\rceil \qquad (6)$$

$$S_{as} = \sum_{j=1}^{min(i, n_{intr})} \frac{K_{sig} + \Delta_{intr}}{t} \left\lceil \frac{t}{T_j} \right\rceil$$

$$min_{(0 < t \leq D_i)} [S_{as} + S_t] \leq 1.$$

This model is obtained by replacing the execution time of thread τ_k in equation (4) such that $C_k = C_k + \Delta C_k$, where ΔC_k could be a positive or negative delta change in the execution time. This leads to a modified value of S_t as given in equation (6).

4 Predictor Capabilities of AFTER

AFTER presents a temporal image of the system to the user, using an analysis that is based on a correlation of the system specifications with measured timing data. AFTER then fires up the interactive graphical interface and switches to its predictor mode.

AFTER provides two classes of prediction:

- Effect of changing the system configuration. For example, changing the scheduling algorithm from static to dynamic or vice versa. To make such a prediction, we use the same measured raw timing data, but use a different model to analyze the data.

- Effect of modifying the raw timing data. For example, modifying parameters such as execution time and period. For predicting the effect of such changes, we use the same model as in the analysis mode, but replace some of the measured data with the hypothetical data based on the user's request.

Given the five models and the numerous variables in each model, there are many types of predictions that can be performed. This section summarizes some of the fine-tuning decisions that AFTER can help a developer make.

Static vs. Dynamic Scheduling. AFTER provides the developer an option of evaluating the benefit of switching from a static to a dynamic scheduler, and vice-versa. The major advantage of switching to a dynamic scheduling algorithm is an increase in schedulable bound to 100% for any task set. If a system has interrupts or possible transient overloads, there is no guarantee that using a dynamic scheduler will improve the system. Before making such a change in the system, the developer can observe the likely benefits by using AFTER, and only implement the switch in scheduling strategies if there are worthwhile benefits. If AFTER suggests that such a change is not worthwhile, the developer can save a complete iteration of unnecessarily modifying the code, which could take considerable time to implement. To predict the effect of switching scheduling algorithms, we take the dynamic scheduling model (model 2) and use the real timing data gathered from the actual target system as input for this model. The result of this computation will tell us the outcome (positive or negative) of the switch from static to dynamic priority scheduling.

Interrupt vs. Aperiodic Server. There is a trade-off between interrupt handlers and aperiodic servers. Interrupt handlers are typically non-preemptive and execute with the highest priority, which decreases the predictability of the system. An aperiodic server, on the other hand, can be used to improve predictability, but at the cost of higher operating system overhead. Using the real data collected from the system, AFTER can predict the effect of converting one or more interrupt handlers to aperiodic servers. To perform such predictions, we can use model 3 on the real timing data. AFTER is also capable of the reverse prediction. That is, given data from a system already using aperiodic servers, it can determine the schedulability of the system if some of the servers are converted to high priority interrupt handlers.

Frequency and Period. AFTER allows a developer to request a prediction on whether or not a system will be schedulable if the period or frequency of one or more tasks is modified (model 4). In some cases, changing the frequency of tasks can improve the system performance, while in other cases (such as when using the rate monotonic algorithm), reducing the frequency of some tasks could in fact lower the schedulable bound [6].

Code Optimization. AFTER can be used by the software developer to estimate how much code optimization is needed (model 5). There are situations where after trying all possible modifications to the system parameters, the developer finds that the CPU is still overloaded. The only remaining option is to reduce the execution time of one or more tasks, either through optimization, by making some tasks soft real-time, or by removing some non-essential functionality. In either case, a major development effort is often required to perform these modifications. Unfortunately, even after this lengthy process, there is no guarantee that the system will meet the timing requirements. A major problem is that the designer does not have specific goals as to which modules need to be optimized – and more importantly by how much – in order to make a difference in the overall schedulability of the system. AFTER can be useful in such situations. For example, AFTER can help the developer determine that "if you reduce the execution of task A by 1 msec, and task B by 0.5 msec, then the system is likely to work; optimizing task C does not make any difference."

5 Summary and Future Work

During the latter stages of a software product cycle, developers may be faced with the task of fine-tuning a system which is not meeting all of its timing requirements. In some cases, the only thing needed would be a simple change of a task's period, but developers are reluctant to do that because it is quite difficult to gauge the effect of that change on other tasks in the system. In other cases, the modifications are more drastic and require significant effort in optimizing some code, but the designer does not know which code, nor by how much it must be optimized. This is where AFTER can have a major impact.

AFTER uses raw timing data collected from the embedded system, analyzes it, then provides a temporal image of the current implementation, highlighting actual and potential problems. AFTER is then used interactively through a graphical user interface to help the developer fine-tune the application effectively. If the predictor says that a particular fine-tuning optimization is going to improve the system performance, the developer still has to implement that change in the system and confirm that it makes a difference. At the very least, AFTER can be used to predict which changes are not going to have any positive impact, thus preventing the developer from unnecessarily wasting the time implementing and re-testing those changes.

Additional work to be performed includes the following:

- Validate the accuracy of all the models through substantial experimentation, by comparing predictions when a small change is proposed to actually implementing the change and performing a full analysis with the measured data.

- Create analytical models for other RTOS such as QNX, pSOS, VxWorks and for non-commercial RTOS that we are researching in our laboratories.

- Continually enhance the existing analytical models to better reflect the real characteristics of the target environment in order to improve the accuracy of analysis and prediction.

- Add the effect of synchronization overheads into the models. This will make the analytical models even more closely represent the implementation realities.

- Create a more comprehensive graphical user interface. The current prototype of AFTER is built using Tcl/Tk. A more portable user interface is now being developed using Java.

- Add more prediction features such as the effect of converting a polling based task to an interrupt-driven task or vice versa.

- Create models for non-preemptive scheduling policies. This is being done to support another project in our research group which uses a non-preemptive scheduling policy.

- Enhance AFTER to self-search through many possible fine-tuning operations, to suggest to the developer possible ways of solving the timing problems that it detects.

The current version of AFTER was developed for use with the VRTX32 real-time operating system, and used to analyze a satellite modem application.

References

1. G. Arora, "Automated analysis and prediction of timing parameters in embedded real-time systems using measured data," M.S. Thesis (Advisor: D. Stewart), Dept. of Electrical Engineering, University of Maryland, June 1997 (*www.ee.umd.edu/serts/bib/thesis/garora.html*).

2. M. Humphrey and J.A. Stankovic, "CAISARTS: A tool for Real-Time Scheduling Assistance," in *Proc. of IEEE Real-Time Technology and Applications Symposium*, June 1996.

3. K. Jeffay and D.L. Stone, "Accounting for Interrupt Handling Costs in Dynamic Priority Systems," in *Proc. of the 14th IEEE Real-Time Systems Symposium*, Raleigh-Durham, North Carolina, pp. 212-221, December 1993.

4. D.I. Katcher, "Engineering and Analysis of Real-Time Operating Systems," Ph.D. Dissertation, Dept. of Electrical and Computer Engineering, Carnegie Mellon University, Pittsburgh, PA, August 1994.

5. G. Krikor, T. Raza and D.B. Stewart, "Design of a Real-Time Co-Operation System for Multiprocessor Workstations," in *Proc. of Hawaii International Conference on System Sciences (Software Technology track)*, pp. 499-507, January 1996.

6. J. Lehoczky, L. Sha, and Y. Ding, "The rate monotonic scheduling algorithm: exact characterization and average case behavior," in *Proc. 10th IEEE Real-Time Systems Symposium*, Santa Monica, CA, pp. 166-171, December 1989.

7. C. L. Liu, and J. W. Layland, "Scheduling algorithms for multiprogramming in a hard real time environment," *Journal of the Association for Computing Machinery*, v.20, n.1, pp. 44-61, January 1973.

8. J.W.S. Liu, J.L. Redondo, Z. Deng, T.S. Tia, R. Bettati, A. Silberman, M. Storch, R. Ha, and W.K. Shih, "PERTS: A Prototyping Environment for Real- Time Systems," in *Proc. of 14th IEEE Real-Time Systems Symposium*, Raleigh-Durham, North Carolina, pp. 184-188, December 1993.

9. Microtec Research Inc., "VRTX32/86 User's Guide," San Jose, CA, May 1991. (*www.mri.com*)

10. B. Sprunt, L. Sha, and J. Lehoczky, "Aperiodic task scheduling for hard real-time systems," *Journal of Real-Time Systems*, v.1, n.1, pp. 27-60, November 1989.

11. D. B. Stewart and P. K. Khosla, "Policy-Independent RTOS mechanisms for timing error detection, handling, and monitoring," in Proc. of *IEEE High Assurance Systems Engineering Workshop*, Niagara, Ontario, Canada, Oct. 1996.

12. H. Tokuda and M. Kotera, "A Real-Time Tool Set for the ARTS Kernel," in *Proc. of the 9th IEEE Real-Time Systems Symposium*, Huntsville, Alabama, December 1988.

13. Wind River Systems, *www.wrs.com*.

Debugging Distributed Implementations of Modal Process Systems

Ken Hines and Gaetano Borriello

Department of Computer Science & Engineering, Box 352350
University of Washington, Seattle, WA 98195-2350
{hineskj,gaetano}@cs.washington.edu

Abstract. From the perspective of performance and parts cost, distributed architectures are often superior to single processor architectures for embedded systems designs. Despite this, embedded system designers still tend to use single processors whenever possible. One of the main reasons for this is that the additional costs in design and maintenance of distributed systems can far outweigh the lower parts cost and lower power consumption that might result from a distributed implementation. This is largely because most distributed models are limited in the system level abstraction that can be derived.

The modal process model [2] for embedded system design has been suggested as a way of addressing many of these issues. This model maps quite naturally to distributed implementations, while preserving unifying information from higher levels of abstraction. While this model provides numerous benefits as far as modularity and ease of composition, it also enhances the designers ability to debug such systems by enabling new debugging techniques. This paper discusses some debugging techniques enabled by the modal process model, and describes how these may be used.

1 Introduction

Distributed architectures are becoming increasingly important options for designers of embedded systems. In many cases, they provide better performance with respect to parts cost and power consumption than single processor architectures (several slower processors can cost less than single fast processors). Also, incorporating multiple processors into a design makes it possible to take advantage of the large number of special purpose embedded processors available. Some examples of these are Digital Signal Processors (DSPs), microcontrollers with built in interfaces such as IrDA, I^2C, Ethernet and so forth. These can be a major advantage to designers of embedded systems, but since it is often the case that none of them are exactly right by themselves, designers may need to include several in a single system. For example, cellular phones contain DSPs which support the data-flow aspect of cellular communication quite well. Unfortunately, much of the processing work in this application is control oriented, something that isn't well suited for DSPs. As a result, many modern cellular phones contain both a DSP and a general purpose processor. Even with single processor embedded system architectures, designers may still need to face to face distributed system issues. Individual embedded systems may be linked together to form networks which must function correctly as a unit. This is the case with personal appliances, automated homes, and again, cellular phones.

Although distributed embedded systems are becoming more common, they are still usually the exception rather than the rule. This is because with existing tools, the difficulty of a multi-processor design is much greater than that of a single-processor design. Some of the factors contributing to this are concurrent programming issues such as distributing control and synchronization, and implementation details such as interacting with operating systems, scheduling, interprocess communication and communication between software and hardware.

Modal processes [2] have shown promise as a new paradigm for the design of distributed embedded systems. An important aspect of this paradigm is that it allows designers to make many of their design decisions explicit, as opposed to conventional paradigms where many of these decisions are buried deeply in the code. Because of this, synthesis tools using modal processes designs as inputs, can automate many of the difficult tasks in implementing distributed designs. Furthermore, modal processes ease the difficulty of concurrent programming through *control composition*. In this paper, we investigate how these exposed design decisions aid in the task of debugging such systems.

We view debugging as an activity with three overlapping phases:

1. bug presence detection, which is usually performed through software testing. This phase is distinguished by the fact that the tester does not know for certain that there is a bug at the start of the phase.
2. bug pinpointing, which usually entails reverse engineering the system somewhat to arrive at the cause of the bug. A distinguishing factor of this phase is that when it begins, the designer knows that there is a bug and has some idea of how it affects an execution.
3. and finally, bug repair, and repeated testing in the vicinity of the bug (to ensure that this bug is really fixed). On completion of this phase, the process starts again.

The debugging techniques described in this paper are currently being incorporated into the Pia hardware/software co-simulator [4]. By using a co-simulation environment for debugging, we avoid introducing a significant probe effect. This means that the only difference between uninstrumented executions and those instrumented for debugging is in simulator performance. A remaining problem is that the accuracy of the simulation is limited by the accuracy of the estimates, but later in the paper we discuss obtaining traces from a physical implementation of the system, and using these to control the simulation for greater realism.

This paper is organized as follows: first, we provide a brief overview of the modal process model. Next, we discuss techniques for visualizing modal process executions. Finally we discuss practical aspects of using visualizations as an input to the simulator to force the system into buggy potentially states.

2 Modal Processes

In the modal process model for distributed embedded systems [2], systems are specified and implemented in several phases. First, reusable components (the modal processes) are either designed or are obtained from a library. Next, the modal processes are composed into a complete system. Finally, this composed system is mapped onto an architecture, and the communication and runtime system are synthesized[1].

2.1 Handlers and modes

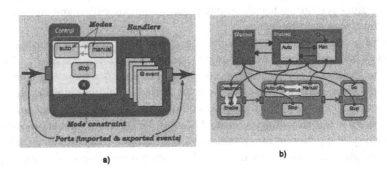

Fig. 1. A modal process for a mobile robot autopilot, and an example of control composition

Modal processes have several components such as code fragments called *handlers*, control abstractions called *modes*, local variables and constraints between modes. Handlers are triggered by events, which can be generated either locally or or on different processes. For modularity, all external events (events that are either generated externally, or internally generated events that are exported to the environment) are given local names which may be bound to other named events on other processes. An event name that refers to an imported or exported event is called a *port* and the bindings between event names on various processes are called *nets*. When a handler completes execution, it returns a request for activation and deactivation of modes. If the current mode configuration is not in line with this request, the system alters the configuration to make it so.

A mode contains the handlers that are enabled when the mode is active, and as such has some control over the execution of the system. Activating a new mode does not necessarily mean that any current modes must be exited. This depends on the mode constraints. For the example shown in Fig. 1a), there is a *mutual-exclusion* constraint wrapped around all modes in the process, signifying that only one mode may be active at a time. This means that activation of any of these modes forces deactivation of the rest.

2.2 System composition

The composition phase of modal process system design includes binding exported events on each process to imported events on other processes (*data composition*) and

---

[1] This paper discusses only the most fundamental aspects of modal processes. For more information, please see [1], [2], or [3].

binding and constraining exported modes on each process with modes on other processes (*control composition*). To aid in control composition, it may be useful for the designer to build a system level hierarchical mode diagram, and then bind the process level modes to those in the system level diagram, as shown in Fig. 1b). The hierarchy of the system level diagram implies type of constraint called *parent-child*. This works as follows: if a mode, for example *Auto* in Fig. 1b) has a *parent* mode (*Enabled* in this case) in the hierarchy, there is an implied parent-child constraint between *Enabled* and *Auto*, such that when *Auto* is activated, *Enabled* must also be activated. This constraint also implies that when *Enabled* is deactivated, *Auto* must be as well. A binding implies a *unification* constraint, such that the activation or deactivation of any mode in a binding activates or deactivates all the rest. In this example, there are also implied mutual-exclusion constraints between modes at the same level of hierarchy.

2.3 Mapping modal processes to distributed architectures

The final phase of designing an embedded system using this methodology involves mapping the system to an architecture. This involves binding processes to components such as processors, FPGAs, ASICs, or even off-the-shelf special purpose hardware like protocol chips, and so on. When this is completed, the designer must specify the paths to be used for events between different components and the timing constraints for these paths. Finally, the complete specification is used as input for communication and schedule synthesis tools.

3 Visualizing executions

The art of debugging systems usually requires designers to gain insight into certain obscure aspects of an execution. This is often aided by some instrumentation that selects certain aspects of an execution, and presents them to the designer in an intelligible format. In sequential systems, where the execution is entirely determined by a set of inputs and a single stream of code this can usually be done through examination of variables and following the program through its execution. In these sorts of systems, a textual interface (while not ideal) is still intelligible. The behavior of distributed systems, however, is determined by many streams of code executing on several processors simultaneously as well as the communication between these streams and inputs to the system's inputs. The additional complexity can make textual forms unintelligible for all but the most trivial sorts of details. In these systems, visualization tools can often be used to provide the required designer feedback.

Space/time diagrams are commonly used for visualizing executions in many distributed system debugging tools [7, 12, 9]. These diagrams include traces for each process, (although sometimes several processes may be clustered and represented by a single trace), events that occur locally on each process and messages that are passed between different processes. Fig. 2a) shows an example of a space time diagram. While these are good at displaying those aspects of an execution which pertain to interprocess communication and process activation and termination, they do not yield much information about other aspects. One of the main reasons for this is that the case is that communication behavior is often the only characteristic of arbitrary distributed processes that makes sense to observe from a global standpoint.

3.1 Several projections of an execution

One way to view space/time diagrams is as *projections* of a distributed execution, characterizing certain aspects of the execution without cluttering the visualization with needless details. In the general case, distributed systems don't allow for many meaningful projections. Modal processes, however, allow for a rich collection of these, several of which are depicted in Fig. 2.

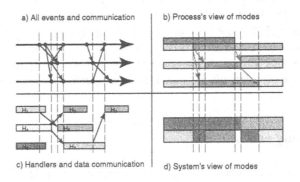

Fig.2. A number of projections from a single modal process system execution

The process level mode diagram in Fig. 2 *b*), shows the time evolution of mode on each process separately, as well as the control communication between processes to coordinate system wide mode consistency. Modes within a single process that are active at the same time are shown stacked on top of one another. This sort of projection could be used by the designer to monitor time evolution of mode, and as an aid in debugging control based problems.

Fig. 2 *d*) shows the time evolution of mode from the system's perspective. The lightly shaded regions represent periods when the system is in consistent modes and darkly shaded regions indicate that there is a system level modal inconsistency.

Finally Fig. 2 *c*) represents the data communication between processes in a system, as well as the code fragments, or handlers, that generate and act on these messages. In some cases, a designer may want to combine several projections in various ways. For example, one may want to look at the handler and mode views of the one process where a bug has been detected, but then observe only the modal projections of the rest of the processes in the system.

3.2 Causality vs. time

Modal process systems are not required to maintain a global clock and so simple event timestamping may not indicate the causal order of events. For example, it is entirely possible for an event e_1 to causally precede event e_2 on a different processor, but because of clock drift, e_2 may get an earlier timestamp than e_1. For most debugging activities, the *causal order* of events is more important than the approximate real-time order that would be obtained from local timestamps. We can characterize the causal order of an execution in terms of a space/time diagram by use of the *causal relation* [11] also called the *happened before* relation [8].

Definition 1 (Causal Relation) *For events a, b in the execution of a distributed system, the causal relation $a \rightarrow b$ is defined as the relation that holds if and only if b is reachable from a in the space/time diagram representing the execution in which they occur.*

Another important relation is the concurrence relation, which relates events whose real time ordering can be switched without changing the apparent behavior of an execution.

Definition 2 (Concurrence Relation) *For all events a, b, the concurrence relation $a \parallel b$ is defined as the relation that holds if and only if neither $a \rightarrow b$ nor $b \rightarrow a$ hold.*

It is important to note that these definitions apply only to single executions and the relationship between two events may not be the same in all executions. Since modal process systems are often real time systems, real time issues are still important factors to consider in executions. These issues, such as ensuring timing constraints are met, can usually be treated as orthogonal to the system functionality.

3.3 Consistent cuts in projections

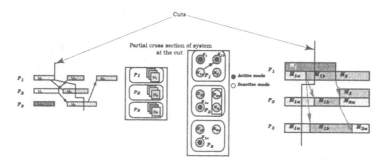

Fig.3. Cuts taken on two types of projections (handler-based and mode-based)

A *projection cut* is a collection of instantaneous single process states (one from each process) and can be represented as a jagged line across a projection that intersects each process exactly once. Cuts on handler and mode projections are shown in Fig. 3. In each of these events to the left of the cut are considered the *past*, and all events to the right are considered the *future*.

A *consistent cut* [10] is one that is consistent with causality. This means that there can be no messages (either data or control) that travel from the future to the past. Since many projections show only a subset of all messages, it may not be apparent on simple examination which cuts are inconsistent. It is not, however, difficult for a tool to determine this and alert the designer of inconsistencies. Consistent cuts indicate concurrent, and possibly simultaneous, local states which occur in the system. When the real time behavior of the system is considered, however, it may turn out that many consistent cuts represent concurrent states that can never be simultaneous.

Using a visualization tool, a designer can draw a cut on a projection, and observe the instantaneous state represented by this cut. Since there may be hidden information in particular projections that would cause a cut to be inconsistent, the tool displays any hidden communication that crosses from the future to the past, thus allowing the designer to choose consistent cuts. Fig. 3 shows the result of a pair of consistent cuts. On the left is shown a cut taken in a handler diagram, the right shows a cut in a mode diagram, and the center shows the instantaneous state at the moment of the cuts.

3.4 Different abstract views

In our discussion so far, we have considered only abstractions afforded by the modal process model. There are other ways in which systems may be abstracted, such as combining coherent processes into single traces, and grouping convex sets of events into single blocks processes as single units [6]. We allow designers to perform this sort of abstraction as well, but manually (the focus in [6] is on automating this process). This has made sense so far as the examples we have dealt with require relatively few processes.

3.5 Impact of architecture mapping

Upon mapping a system to an architecture, we complicate the issues of time, as the architecture can scramble many behavioral aspects of a system. These include changes in event ordering due to differing handler activation periods, mode durations, and message latency among other things. To some degree, Pia can provide realistic executions of such systems, but this realism is limited by the quality of timing estimates provided. It is possible that even with fairly accurate timing estimates, simulation can inadvertently avoid certain execution that may be possible on a real system.

4 Active debugging

So far only *passive* use of various projections has been discussed. Our discussion involved using projections to visualize executions in situations where our tool should have absolutely no impact on the execution, but it should simply tell us what is going on. This is because any interference introduced in viewing the execution can alter the ordering of events and hence the behavior of the system. For example, very intrusive instrumentation may synchronize certain pieces of a program, such that we are never able to repeat a synchronization bug in a debugging environment.

It can often make sense to use selected traces of a projection not only as a display of certain aspects of a particular execution, but also as an input to force the system to execute critical stages in order to evaluate it's behavior. For example, we can set up two traces in a mode-centric projection such that a suspected mode conflict occurs, and simulate from there to observe the results. In a sense, we generate a test bench for the system.

4.1 Setting up suspected conflicts

One case in which user-defined projections could be used to test for potential problems in a system is by setting up mode change conflicts. For example, the top part of Fig. 4a) shows two processes that asynchronously and concurrently activate conflicting modes. The outcome of such a conflict could result in transitions into several different modes before the system reaches a stable consistent state, as is shown in the bottom part. Some other possible outcomes could be endless transitions, never reaching a consistent state (livelock) or transitions into a stable inconsistent state (deadlock) [1].

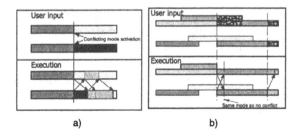

Fig.4. Two pairs of user-defined mode traces. a) shows a single activation conflict and b) shows several potential conflicts along a trace.

Using this partial projection as an input to the simulator, the designer can observe and evaluate the results of this conflict, and use this to guide changes in the specification.

4.2 Using projections to guide simulation

It is also possible for the programmer to enter longer traces consisting of several mode activations/deactivations, or handler invocations. When the designer enters such traces, it is possible to run an online mode consistency checker, and shade areas of the graph that are inconsistent with the constraints provided in the specification. These areas remain shaded until simulation, when the mode arbitration resolves these conflicts. It is possible that mode transitions with no apparent conflict may be changed during simulation depending on the interaction with the other, non-controlled processes.

5 Implementation issues

The current version of Pia is implemented as a Java application for many reasons including distributability and host independence (detailed in [5]). When executing unmapped specifications, Pia uses simple bi-level step-based execution semantics (*i.e. major-step, minor-step*). The execution of each handler occurs in the *major-step* in which the triggering event was received. Each event generated by a handler is separated by at least a *minor-step*, but these events cannot trigger handlers on other processes until the next major-step. In this way, the stepping is consistent with causality. Polling handlers are allowed to request a polling rate for each mode in terms of major-steps, and this rate persists while the relevant mode is active.

One issue mentioned in the introduction involves running executions based on traces obtained from actual hardware. Obtaining these traces requires some instrumentation, for example, the software could include code to stream out event representations. This instrumentation will introduce at least a small probe effect. There are ways to minimize this effect, such as using large queues and non-blocking communication for the event streamers. It is also possible to hide the probe effect altogether, by including the event streaming facility in the final implementation. This can be a reasonable choice if the additional overhead can be kept small, as may be the case when a large part of this facility is implemented in hardware.

The collected trace can then be used to ensure that every handler invocation, mode activation or deactivation in the simulation has the same history as in the corresponding real execution. This is done by stalling events until their entire history has been executed as shown in Fig. 5. Fig. 5a) shows both the mode and handler traces of the unaltered simulated execution of a three process system. As shown in Fig. 5b), we underestimated the speed of processes P_2 and P_3, and the real execution is significantly different. In fact, the locus of control for the real execution has shifted from P_1 to P_3. In this case, the mode change requested at the end of handler H_1 is denied locally because the competing mode change from handler H_8 is a higher priority. In simulation there was no contention for this mode change, since handler H_8 was never executed. Finally, Fig. 5c) shows what the simulator can do to compensate. It simply delays events until their causal history has been satisfied.

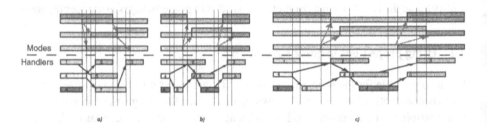

Fig.5. Combined handler and mode diagram from a) unhindered simulation, b) actual execution, and c) execution trace controlled simulation

We may also want to perform executions where the control stream contains an incomplete set of events. This would occur when, for example, a designer enters a mode control trace as described in Section 4. In this case, the simulator must either ignore data events generated as is the case with the mode conflict detection or it may need to deviate from the input mode change diagram as requests from handlers compete with the changes entered by the designer.

6 Conclusions

While modal processes were suggested as primarily a model for embedded system composition and synthesis, the abstractions provided by this model also enable many new debugging features which can aid the designer during several debugging phases. We have discussed these in terms of execution projections for visualization as well as control of distributed executions, and have discussed several issues pertaining to implementation.

References

1. CHOU, P., AND BORRIELLO, G. An analysis-based approach to composition of distributed embedded systems. In *Codes '98* (March 1998).
2. CHOU, P., AND BORRIELLO, G. Modal processes: Towards enhanced retargetability through control composition of distributed embedded systems. In *Proceedings of the 35th annual Design Automation Conference* (1998).
3. CHOU, P., HINES, K., PARTRIDGE, K., AND BORRIELLO, G. Control generation for embedded systems based on composition of modal processes. Submitted to ICCAD '98.
4. HINES, K., AND BORRIELLO, G. Dynamic communication models in embedded system co-simulation. In *Proceedings of the 34th annual Design Automation Conference* (June 1997).
5. HINES, K., AND BORRIELLO, G. Selective focus as a means of improving geographically distributed embedded system co-simulation. In *Rapid Systems Prototyping '97* (June 1997).
6. KUNZ, T. *Abstract Behaviour of Distributed Executions with Applications to Visualization.* PhD thesis, Technische Hochschule Darmstadt, Darmstadt, Germany, May 1994.
7. KUNZ, T. High-level views of distributed executions. In *Proceedings of the 2nd International Workshop on Automated and Algorithmic Debugging* (1995).
8. LAMPORT, L. Time, clocks and ordering of events in a distributed system. *Communications of the ACM 21*, 7 (July 1978), 558–563.
9. LEUNG, E. Event-based debugging for distributed internet applications. Master's thesis, University of Waterloo, Waterloo, Ontario, Canada, April 1997.
10. MATTERN, F. Efficient algorithms for distributed snapshots and global virtual time approximation. *Journal of Parallel and Distributed Computing*, 18 (1993), 423–434.
11. SCHWARZ, R., AND MATTERN, F. Detecting causal relationships in distributed computations: in search of the holy grail. *Distributed Computing*, 7 (1994), 149–174.
12. SIDE, R. S., AND SHOJA, G. C. A debugger for distributed programs. *Software - Practice and Experience 24*, 5 (1994), 507–525.

Using Inferno ™ to Execute
Java ™ on Small Devices

C. F. Yurkoski
L. R. Rau
B. K. Ellis
Bell Labs
600 Mountain Avenue
Murray Hill, NJ
{yurkoski, larryr, brucee}@bell-labs.com
http://www.chunder.com/

Abstract. This paper describes an implementation of Java [1] on the Inferno operating system.

There are applications for which object oriented designs are the appropriate solution. Java is an object oriented programming language in which these solutions can be written. But as always there are tradeoffs, and O-O designs in Java are not without theirs. Among the costs of using Java is that the memory and permanent storage required to run applications tends to be large, resulting in them not fitting on devices with limited capacity.

Inferno is a network operating system that was created to allow applications to be easily and dynamically distributed across networks. With Inferno, applications can easily take advantage of resources in the network such as persistent storage, memory, devices, cpu, server processes etc. as if they were local.

Here, we describe an implementation of Java on Inferno that minimizes the amount of local storage needed on a small device at the cost of a small increase in Inferno's text size. This work is explained and its performance characteristics are reported.

1. Introduction

First some background on Inferno. Inferno is an operating system designed for building distributed services. [2] It has three design principles. First, all resources are named and accessed like files in hierarchical file systems. Second, disjoint resource hierarchies can be joined together into a single, private hierarchical *namespace*. Third, a single communication protocol, *styx,* is used to access all resources, whether local or remote.

Inferno is small, less than 1 megabyte, including all of the kernel, graphics libraries, virtual machine and security code. Inferno is also highly portable running on many systems and processors (x86, sparc, mips, arm, powerpc and more).

Inferno applications have been written in a programming language called Limbo. [3] Limbo has a number of features that make it well suited for a heterogeneous network environment. It has a rich set of basic types, strong typing, garbage collection, concurrency, communications and runtime loadable modules. Limbo may be interpreted or compiled *just-in-time* for efficient and portable execution. Originally, Limbo was the only language available to application programmers under Inferno.

Object oriented designs can be the best way to solve some programming problems, but as with all engineering decisions there are trade-offs. O-O is no exception; the cost of the programming convenience of inheritance, polymorphism and information hiding can be increased program size. [4] On machines with ample memory and disk space, this trade-off may be worth it in terms of overall development costs. Even PCs these days often have over 100 megabytes of RAM and gigabytes of disk space; and workstations and servers have even more. However there are many devices on which you might like to run your applications that are equipped with significantly less. These devices include screen phones, nomadic and wireless computers and several flavours of "set top" boxes (web browsing set-top boxes, video on demand set-top boxes, next generation cable boxes, etc.). Typically these devices have four to eight megabytes of RAM and some flash storage. The effort described here addresses the problem of running on these small devices. To do so, two issues must be addressed: the device must have enough storage for the program text and enough memory in which to execute the application. Java is becoming the programming language of choice for object-oriented designs, but Java is not small. It is effected by both of these issues.

Start with storage. On a sparc, the total size of the 1.1.3 Java shared libraries from Javasoft needed to run the virtual machine is 1.6 megabytes. Under Windows 95, for the 1.1.4 version the size of the java.exe, DLLs and libs is 0.96 megabytes. Besides this, another 9.29 megabytes are needed to store the Java core classes in the *classes.zip* file. Then there is the operating system itself that is needed to execute this code. Together these numbers represent the static storage required by the Java run time environment.

A solution to the first issue, storage for the text for the Java runtime, could be to store it remotely and not on the device. The problem with this approach is that most of these small devices do not have high bandwidth network connections. Most will be equipped with at most a 56K modem. It takes too long to download the ten megabytes of code required to begin to run a Java application.

Second is the issue of the execution footprint needed to run a Java program, that is the memory needed to load the Java virtual machine, possibly just in time compile the classes, create the objects, etc. This, of course, will vary between programs. Even a minimal Java "hello world" on a sparc needs 4.3 megabytes in which to run (not counting any of the operating system). Any Java programs that use the graphical interface (AWT) are considerably larger. A trivial graphical clock program needs 1032 8K pages (8.24 megabytes) of user space memory in which to run. Devices that have only a total of 8 megabytes of memory cannot run such programs.

The small appliance world of screen phones, set top boxes and wireless computing is considerable different from the internet-centric desk top world in which Java grew up. What is good in one realm is not necessarily viable in the other. In an attempt to address this, Javasoft recently released its *Personal Java* [5] specification which is a slightly reduced subset of the original desk top Java. Implementations of Personal Java are scheduled to be available early in 1998. This slightly limited API reduces the size of the mandatory Java core classes somewhat. But it is still large and reducing the number or complexity of the required system classes has no effect on the size of the native shared object libraries needed to run the virtual machine. Nor does it have any effect on the run time footprint that is required.

The size of code needed for the Java run time makes it impossible to store it on these small devices and the network connections that they have make it impractical to download all the code to the devices on demand. A much smaller system is required, preferably a smaller system that can be easily segmented between the most important bits that could be stored locally on the device and the less important parts that have be to downloaded on demand. Ideally, it should be easy to distribute an application dynamically (what is where) to take advantage of different hardware configurations and network capacity. Inferno is designed to be a system that makes it easy to build such dynamically distributable services.

You might ask then why not just develop the application in a language that was designed for this environment - a language like Limbo. Given a clean sheet, that may often be the best solution. But there will be times when that is not practical. First, you might have already written the application in Java and if it is large enough, it may not be worth rewriting. Secondly, there may be externally produced programs that are written in Java and available to you on the web only as *.class* files that you would like to run on small devices. Third, there will be reasons, even on small devices, why writing a particular application in Java makes sense. Finally, programmers will program in whatever language they prefer. It is of no avail to tell them what you think is good for them.

2. Design Goals

Our goal was to allow Java to run on Inferno while requiring as little local persistent storage and memory as practical. We imposed the following design constraints:

- Adding Java support to Inferno should have no detrimental effect on Inferno. In particular, any increase in the operating system text size required to support Java system should be almost zero. Also any increase in OS data space when Java was not running had to be zero, and no changes required for Java in the operating system should make it run slower.

- The system should support Javasoft's *Personal Java* API.

- When running Java the system should use as little memory as possible and run as fast as practical.

- The resulting code must be completely portable, running everywhere Inferno runs. It could not be dependent on any platform specific features.

3. Implementation

The Inferno operating system has at its core a virtual machine (VM) called *Dis*. Dis is a memory-to-memory VM that allows small, simple just-in-time compilers to generate efficient code. The Limbo compiler produces virtual instructions for execution on the *Dis* VM.

Dis and the above considerations precipitated a design in which Limbo programs translate, resolve and provide the run time support needed for Java programs. Limbo modules provide the implementations of the native methods on which Java programs depend. Only some minor modifications were made to the Inferno kernel for Java.

The major components of this architecture are:

- A translator called *j2d*, written in limbo that converts the Java bytes codes in *.class* files into *Dis* instructions.

- A *loader*, also written in Limbo, which resolves the class hierarchy, provides a variety of run time support for the Java classes and uses *j2d* to translate the *.class* files as needed.

  To facilitate faster loading, system core classes can be pre-translated from Java byte codes into Dis instructions.

- Most Java implementations rely on a large body of native methods written in C/C++. In fact, the Personal Java proposal defines its JNI, which is in C/C++, as part of its standard. Although Inferno supports C code as drivers, in Inferno, user level code is written in Limbo. So we wrote our native methods in Limbo. This makes them smaller than if they were in C by a factor of 3 though it does make them slower.

  Also two particularly huge Java base classes were re-written in Limbo dramatically reducing their size. By rewriting it in Limbo, the memory needed for *Character.class* was shrunk from 139 K bytes to 48 Kbytes. The requirement for CharacterEncoding and character to byte conversion was reduce from 65K to 18K.

- Only nine simple instructions that required just 36 lines of C code to implement had to be added to the Dis virtual machine. Four of the new instructions support new type conversions and two provide previously unsupported shifts. The last three allocate new structures. These nine are:

```
cvtrf    convert real to float
cvtfr    convert float to real
cvtws    convert word to short
cvtsw    convert short to word
lsrw     logical shift right word
lsrl     logical shift right long
mnewz    allocate class
newaz    allocate (and zero) an array
newz     allocate object
```

It should be noted that none of these new instructions were required; the translation can be accomplished without them. However, they make the generated code more efficient. These new instructions are also not Java specific; the Limbo compiler can now generate them too.

- Finally, some minor modifications were required in the kernel. These exposed to user level code some interfaces that had previously only existed internal to the operating system. In general, these allow the loader to resolve modules and to create objects that the garbage collector can properly redeem. They were developed as a new *built-in* module that provides these interfaces:

```
ifetch    get a module's instructions
tdesc     get a module's type descriptors
newmod    create a new module
tnew      create a new type descriptor
link      create a new module link
ext       install links
dnew      create module data
compile   just in time compile a module
```

Several alternatives to this scheme were considered. The first was incorporating a Java virtual machine into Inferno. This was rejected not only because it would increase the size of the system by too much but because it would also result in too many duplicated sub-systems. There would be two virtual machines, two garbage collectors and two sets of just in time compilers. Getting them to all cooperate would be a challenge.

Another idea that was considered, was the creation of a hybrid virtual machine that could execute either Dis instructions or Java byte codes. Although this would not increase the size of the system by as much, it was would still make it much larger. Furthermore, since the two machines would now be integrated that cost would always have to be incurred, even when the Java functionality was not needed. The Java functionality could not be easily loaded only when it was needed.

Finally, we considered using Inferno's network capabilities and transparently use a "java server" in the network as if it is a local resource. This can be done, and in situations where there is sufficient bandwidth (for example, cable systems) can be the appropriate solution. But, as stated above, often there may only be a 56K connection into the device. If the application is graphics intensive this will not be enough. Also such a system does not scale well, so a solution that can also execute Java byte codes directly on the edge device needs to be also provided.

During this effort several problems encountered. The first was Java's "class spaghetti". We discovered that Java's system classes are not at all hierarchical. If you select any basic class and find all the classes it references, and find all those classes recursively, you will find yourself referencing every class in the system. This required us to abandon the idea of speeding execution by completely resolving the class when it is loaded. Instead the resolution is done during execution, resolving only what is needed.

A second problem is that translated text size of the *.dis* code that is the output of *j2d* process is larger than the *.class* code that was its input. This is because j2d does not have as much information available to it from the .class files as the Java compiler had at its disposal from the .java files. The best that j2d can do is one-to-one and the code can grow by as much as 100%. An alternative would be to provide a Java compiler that produced Dis instructions directly, instead of producing Java byte code, but that only helps if the Java source code is available, often only the class files will be. It turns out that for most Java programs running on Inferno this is not a problem because the total memory . footprint required to execute the Java program including not only the program text itself but all supporting operating system and virtual machine code is smaller using Inferno than it would be using another operating system and its virtual machine. For a sufficiently large Java program this would not be the case. How large the Java program has to be depends on how small the alternative system is, but it is on the order of several megabytes of class file text.

This system does not execute finalization routines. In general, this is not a problem because most of the functionality that the programmer might put in a finalization routine, such as closing open files is finessed by the garbage collector, the Inferno operating system takes care of them. Also the programmer cannot according to the Java language specification depend upon the finalization routine being executed at any specific point in time. The specification is nebulous enough in this respect that its letter if not its spirit can be met without ever executing these routines.

4. Results

The implementation that we selected resulted in a system that has the following characteristics:

- Kernel text size was increased by less than 11 Kbytes. This includes all the code for the new instructions and the new module built-in into the kernel. This adds less than 2% to the size of an Inferno kernel.

- Text space for the modules required to run Java on Inferno: j2d, the loader and assisting modules is just 176 Kbytes. This is distributed as follows:

105K bytes	for the Java to Dis translator
41K bytes	for the loader
3K bytes	dis assembly language utilities
27K bytes	miscellaneous

This 176K of code encompasses the functionality of about a megabyte of DLL or shared libraries. Several factors are responsible for this dramatic decrease in size. First, the Dis instructions are more concise than native machine code. In general Dis instructions sequences are a third the size of the corresponding native code. Second Limbo is an efficient language in which to develop an application like this. Third, doing this work on Inferno, allows the leveraging of much of the Inferno functionality. For example, the Inferno virtual machine and garbage collector can be used. A virtual machine or garbage collector need not be rewritten. This is significant savings.

If some local storage exists, using 176K of be practical in many situations where using several megabytes to store the shared libraries or DLLs would not be.

- Through the use of the Inferno namespace none of these modules need be resident on the small device. If hardware does not have this amount of local storage the modules can be remote but bound into the namespace of the application and be treated as if they are local. Of course, something analogous could be attempted through NFS, by mounting a remote file system that contains the Java virtual machine and its shared libraries and system classes. If your small device is also bandwidth poor using NFS would not be practical. Downloading the Java virtual machine, across a 33Kbit per second link, when you want to run a Java application would take too long. But downloading the entire 176K, even at that speed, is possible.

Of course it might not be possible to fit the code for NFS onto the device in the first place (whereas Inferno has its networking code built into it).

Furthermore, because Limbo modules are only loaded when the execution path of the program first requires them, often much of the 176K need not be loaded at all.

The same can be done for any pre-translated core system classes that are stored as .dis files. The entire contents of the *classes.zip* file need not traverse the link but only the classes that are used.

Also since the Inferno namespace allows disjoint hierarchies to be unioned into a single private hierarchy, some important classes can be local why others are in the network. Since the application, here the Java program, never sees the network, the distribution of what is where can vary between platforms, or even between executions on the same platform without requiring any change in the application.

- Both Limbo and Java allow modules to be "just in time" compiled on the target hardware. This *jitting* translates the machine independent codes into native machine instructions just before the code is executed. The goal of this late stage compiling is to maintain the portability of the code without incurring all the speed disadvantage of interpreted code. Jitting has two disadvantages: it increases the text size by a factor of about three and it incurs the execution time cost of the translation to native instructions. If the translated code is to be repeatedly executed this tradeoff may be worth it. Originally jitting Java code was an all or nothing decision, either the virtual machine compiled all the code it ran or none of it. More recently "hotspot" jitting has been proposed in which the virtual machine attempts to determine which pieces are most worthy of compiling. This scheme promises to address the all or nothing problem but further complicates and increases the size of the Java virtual machine. Inferno, in contrast, has always allowed the application module developer three choices on a per module basis:

  1. always compile the module,

  2. never compile the module, or

  3. let the virtual machine take its default. (The VM's default is an execution time option.)

These choices allow the developer to indicate to the system, considering speed and size constraints, exactly which modules should be compiled.

- Inferno has a hybrid garbage collecting algorithm that reference counts most data. [6] A background concurrent and incremental mark and sweep collector recovers any cyclic data that cannot be collected by reference counting. [7] This has several advantageous over stop the world memory recovery. Most important to us here is that on average less memory is needed since it is recovered as soon as it goes out of scope instead of having to wait for the next epoch.

Inferno is small even with the additional code for Java. Here is the size of Inferno operating system on several different platforms:

processor	text	data	bss	total (bytes)
386	466593	86944	62020	615557
arm	955168	99920	54200	1109288
sparc	911304	96496	45128	1052928

These numbers vary some with what device drivers are present, but these are typical values for actual systems.

The amount of memory, beyond that needed for the OS and virtual machine, required to run the application varies greatly with the application. But a growing number of small Inferno enabled devices have been built. From these we can see how much memory typical applications on Inferno require. These Inferno devices run as video-on-demand set top boxes, web browsing set top boxes, screen phones and network computers. They have between 2 and 8 meg of RAM. Running Java on them requires at least 8 megabytes, but for Java that is small. Tiny Java applications can use that much user space, without considering all the memory for the operating system support that they require. (For example, a minimally equipped Javastation, a sparc, comes with 32 Meg of memory.)

As stated at the beginning of this paper there are always tradeoffs. This design attempts to minimize memory usage and maximize portability. It runs on sparc, x86, arm and other processors. It runs on screen phones with as little as a total of 8 Megabytes of RAM. An implementation targeted for a specific processor and with no memory limit can always be made to out perform a system designed to run everywhere in limited memory. Here are some benchmarks for this system. As always mileage will vary, but to examine the performance of the system we used Pendragon's Embedded Caffeinemark ™ 3.0 [8] This benchmark is widely accepted as a measure of Java speed and is readily available on the web. It uses six sub-tests to quantify aspects of the Java virtual machine speed. The following is a brief description of each sub-test:

1. A sieve of Eratosthenes finds prime numbers.

2. The loop test measures compiler optimized loops.

3. The logic test tests the speed of decision making instructions.

4. The string test manipulates strings.

5. A float test simulates a 3D rotation around a point. And

6. The method tests recursive function call speed.

The following two tables show results for several specific platforms.

The first column of the first table is for a screen phone equipped with a 200 MHz strongARM processor, 8 megabytes of RAM and 2 megabytes of flash memory that appears as a disk. (In these tables larger values are better.)

Table 1 Inferno Caffeinemarks

	screen phone	set top box
Sieve score	83	22
Loop score	80	20
Logic score	80	58
String score	45	3
Float score	13	0
Method score	67	7
Overall score	329	0

The results for the screen phone running Inferno, are no where near the best Caffeinemarks in the world, but for a machine with just 8 megabytes of ram and 2 meg of flash they are impressive.

It would be interesting to compare these results with published reports of other Java virtual machines running on similar platforms. But such data does not yet exist.

For comparison, the first column second table column shows the results of the same test on a 200 megahertz Pentium running Javasoft's version 1.1.4 and the second column shows the results on the same machine running Inferno with the jit enabled.

Table 2 Pentium Caffeinemarks

	Javasoft jvm	Inferno
Sieve score	364	679
Loop score	278	992
Logic score	343	2676
String score	533	48
Float score	298	222
Method score	315	266
Overall score	346	415

As you can see Inferno's speed here is slightly better than Javasoft's JVM.

As a more extremely limited example, the second column of the first table contains the results on a set-top (web-browsing) box equiped with a 40 MHz 386 with 8 megabytes of memory, 8 megabyte of flash and a 28.8 hardware modem.

In this case the low score on the float test makes the overall score zero, but it is unlikely that another JVM would do better on this platform. The Pendragon web site that publishes the Caffeinemark results does not list any results for a 386 processor. This example shows that by using Inferno, Java can be executed even on extremely limited platforms.

5. Summary

The Inferno operating system is designed to allow distributed network applications to be easily developed and efficiently run on small devices. By taking advantage of Inferno's features we were able to develop a Java implementation that can run on small devices. This scheme is not the fastest Java engine but it is small both statically and dynamically. This allows Java to be used in places where it otherwise could not be.

References

1. Gosling: The Feel of Java. Computer IEEE V30, 6 (1997) 53-&

2. Dorward, Pike, Presotto et al.: Inferno. Proceedings IEEE COMPCOM (1997)

3. Dorward, Pike, Winterbottom: Programming in Limbo. Proceeding IEEE COMPCOM (1997)

4. Vazquez: Selecting A Software Development Process. Communications of the ACM (1994)

5. http://www.javasoft.com/products/personaljava/spec-1-0-0/personalJavaSpec.ht

6. Richard E. Jones and Rafel D. Lins: Garbage Collection: Algorithms for Automatic Dynamic Memory Management. Wiley (1996)

7. Kafura, Mukherji and Washabaugh: Concurrent and Distributed Garbage Collection of Active Objects. IEEE Transactions on Parallel and Distributed Systems Vol 6. No 4 (1995)

8. http://www.pendragon-software.com/pendragon/cm3/index.html

TurboJ, a Java Bytecode-to-Native Compiler

Michael Weiss, François de Ferrière, Bertrand Delsart, Christian Fabre,
Frederick Hirsch,
E. Andrew Johnson, Vania Joloboff, Fred Roy, Fridtjof Siebert, and Xavier
Spengler

Open Group Research Institute

Abstract. TurboJ is an off-line Java compiler, translating Java bytecodes to native code. TurboJ operates in conjunction with a Java Virtual
Machine (JVM); among the supported JVMs are those on HPUX, Linux,
and Wind River's Tornado for Java (running under VxWorks). Interfacing with a standard JVM entails benefits not enjoyed by the alternate
"standalone" approach; particularly important for embedded systems is
the opportunity to reduce the memory footprint via mixed-mode execution.

In this paper, we discuss the characteristics of TurboJ as currently implemented, focusing on two aspects of TurboJ: its interactions with the
JVM, and the optimizations it makes. We then briefly summarize TurboJ's current status, compare it with some other Java off-line compilers,
and outline future plans.

1   Introduction

TurboJ is an off-line Java-to-native compiler, translating Java bytecodes to native code. At run-time, the TurboJ-generated code interfaces with a standard
Java Virtual Machine (JVM), which provides memory and thread management,
and class and library loading services. This combination supports seamless mixed
mode execution, where some classes are compiled in advance, and others are interpreted or dynamically compiled by a Just-In-Time compiler (JIT). TurboJ
currently works with JVMs for HPUX, Linux, Solaris, ScoUNIX, and Wind
River's Tornado for Java under VxWorks.

We say a Java application is *closed* if all its class files are available at compile-
time, so it does not dynamically load classes over the net. This is an important
target area for TurboJ, and obviously for embedded systems. However, TurboJ
does support open applications as well.

In this paper, we focus on two aspects of TurboJ: its support for mixed-
mode execution of bytecode plus native binary, and the optimizations it makes.
We will see that mixed-mode execution helps deal with the space constraints of
embedded systems, and the optimizations of course help with the performance
needs. However, we will not address hard real-time requirements.

2 TurboJ and the JVM

A basic choice confronts the designer of an off-line Java-to-native compiler: either generate a standalone executable that "does it all", providing all its own run-time services, or else generate native code that will interface with a JVM for certain services. Toba[9] and IBM's HPC-Java[6] are examples of the former approach; TurboJ takes the latter approach.

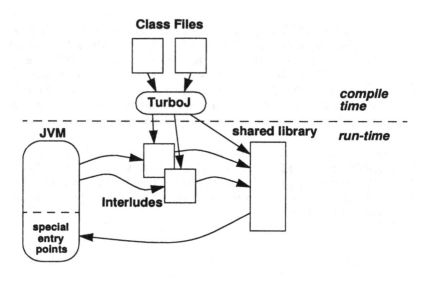

Figure 1: TurboJ inputs and outputs

In principle, the standalone approach offers the maximal opportunity for optimization: every aspect of execution is under the control of the generated native code. But the JVM-interface approach has compensating advantages. First, the entire Java application need not be available at compile-time: dynamic class-loading is permitted. Next, bytecode is a fairly compact format compared to native code. Most JVM instructions use only 1 or 2 bytes. Moreover, they are sophisticated instructions that cannot be translated into a single native processor instruction as a rule. For example, if every JVM instruction expands on average to two 32-bits instruction, the code will blow up by a factor of 4. In fact, most Java compilers that we know of expand code size by a factor of 5 to 10. For embedded systems where memory is scarce, space-time trade-offs are inevitable, and the ability to support mixed-mode execution (compiled with interpreted) is a definite plus. (TowerJ[12] supports dynamic loading by translating bytecodes into native code on-the-fly. Note that this does not reduce the run-time memory footprint.) Finally, this approach leads to increased robustness: the JVM furnishes a "fallback" mode of execution. (We discuss this further in Section 5. TurboJ enjoys these advantages while still achieving substantial speed-ups (typically 4 or more times JIT performance).

TurboJ relies on the JVM for object management, thread management, class and library loading, and the execution of any classes left in bytecode format. Everything else (including class initialization and exception handling) is handled by TurboJ.

The input to TurboJ consists of one or more class files; the output consists of new class files (called *interludes*), and C files. (See figure 1.) The C files are compiled with cc and linked into one or more shared libraries. Using C as an intermediate format eases the task of porting TurboJ to different platforms, and leverages the optimization technology of the native C compiler. We refer to the final result as "Turbo-ized code" here, since "compiled code" would be ambiguous. Bytecodes are, after all, the output of the javac compiler.

The interface between TurboJ and the JVM may be divided into two parts. First, the JVM invokes Turbo-ized methods via the interludes. Second, Turbo-ized code requests services from the JVM via special entry points in the JVM.

2.1 Interludes and Mixed Mode Execution

The interlude interface is relatively simple. If the original class file **Foo.class** declares a method **bar()**, then the corresponding interlude file is also named **Foo.class** and contains a method **bar()** with the **native** attribute. Although TurboJ compiled methods are declared native, the interface is not quite identical to that of user-written native methods. Fortunately, the JVM internal data structures include an *invoker attribute* for each method of a class. If the class is an interlude class, class initialization causes a TurboJ initialization routine to be called, and this routine sets the invoker attribute to point at a special TurboJ invoker. Figure 2 illustrates the generated files for a simple case.

There is significant overhead in going from Java code to native or compiled code and vice versa, especially when arguments have to be reformatted (or marshalled, in ORB parlance). For example, the JVM ABI requires that 64 bit quantities be passed in two 32 bit slots. TurboJ attempts to avoid this reformatting overhead via mechanisms discussed in the next paragraph. When it cannot be avoided entirely, it may be ameliorated by other optimizations. (See Section 3.3.)

Interludes allow interpreted code to call Turbo-ized code. Turbo-ized code can also call interpreted code; the JVM provides an entry point to support this. Of course, if a Turbo-ized caller needs to invoke a (known) Turbo-ized callee, it uses the standard C calling convention, i.e., it makes a direct call. A Turbo-ized caller may not know whether the callee has been Turbo-ized. In this case it calls

Java Source

```
public class foo {
  public void bar(double f, int i) {
    phoo(f + i);
  }
  .....
}
```

Generated Interlude

Note: the interlude is generated as classfile (i.e., bytecodes); this is the equivalent as Java source.

```
public class foo {
  public void bar(double f, int i) native;
}
.....
```

Generated C file (simplified outline)

```
// declarations of static constants, e.g., offsets

void TurboJ_foo_bar (
      JHandle* h_var_0, /* handle to "this" */
      double   d_var_1,
      int      var_2) {

  /* direct call */
  TurboJ_foo_phoo(h_var_0, d_var_1 + (double) var_2);

  /* but if a direct call was not possible, then something roughly
     like this: */
  double d_var_3 = d_var_1 + (double) var_2;
  /* reformat the argument */
  tmp.v = d_var_3;
  _args[1].i = tmp.a[0];
  _args[2].i = tmp.a[1];
  /* obtain info about method phoo from method table */
  method_info = method_table(...);
  callJavaMethod(_args[0].h, method_info, _args);
}
```

Figure 2: Example: Generated Interlude and C File

a special C routine we call a *trampoline*. The trampoline queries the JVM to find out the status of the callee; the JVM has this information by virtue of loading the interlude. The trampoline then dispatches the call appropriately, marshalling arguments as needed, and incidentally caching the result of the query for future use.

The Turbo-ized version of Sun's HotJava browser showcases the mixed-mode capabilities of TurboJ. The source for HotJava is a collection of 539 class files, and is one of the applications we use to test TurboJ. At run-time, dynamically loaded applets run in interpreted (or JIT) mode under the Turbo-ized HotJava, while the HotJava classes run as native code. The two sorts of classes communicate without difficulty.

Finally, we note that both the HPUX and Solaris JVMs contain JIT compilers. TurboJ works with both of these, dynamically loaded classes being compiled by the JIT.

2.2 Object Management

TurboJ currently relies on the JVM for all object allocation and garbage collection. The need to maintain consistency during garbage collection chiefly motivated this design choice. By entrusting the JVM with all aspects of heap management, we insure a robust implementation with minimal demands on the JVM. Indeed, one of TurboJ's primary design goals was that it work with off-the-shelf JVMs.

The attendant inefficiencies are alleviated in several ways, discussed in Sections 3.2 and 3.3.

3 TurboJ Optimizations

We divide these into three categories: whole-program optimizations, per-class optimizations, and per-method optimizations.

3.1 Whole-Program Optimizations

TurboJ attempts to compute the *closure* of the set of input class files: i.e., it follows references to external classes, recursively adding them to the input set. In the ideal scenario of a closed application, TurboJ will have available the bytecodes for all referenced classes when it generates the interludes and native code. TurboJ analyses the structure of the application as a whole, computing the class hierarchy tree and the class reference graph. However, TurboJ is not dependent on having total information: if only some classes are available, it will compute what it can and make conservative assumptions about the rest.

TurboJ uses this global information to make a number of optimizations:

Virtual-to-nonvirtual conversion: Virtual dispatches are converted to non-virtual dispatches if the apparent callee is "effectively final", i.e., not over-ridden. Since this optimization makes assumptions about what classes may appear at run-time, it is under the control of a switch, on a per-class basis.

Direct calls: Often TurboJ can determine the target of a call at compile-time. If the callee is slated for Turbo-ization, then the C calling convention is used, instead of going through the JVM.

Direct offsets: TurboJ can determine many field offsets at compile-time, and uses them in lieu of run-time resolution.

Inlining: TurboJ will inline calls when appropriate.

TurboJ also supports a distinction between "inside" and "outside" classes. An outside class is one whose class file is available for inspection, but which is not considered part of the application; i.e., TurboJ should not generate any code for it. System classes are typically treated as outside classes.

The "inside/outside" distinction can be employed to achieve separate compilation. The core system classes themselves have been Turbo-ized, resulting in a shared library and core interludes. If an application is Turbo-ized using these system interludes as outside classes (instead of the original system classes), then TurboJ will be able to make direct calls from the application into the system classes. This technique works in general for any pre-Turbo-ized collection of utility classes.

3.2   Per-Class Optimizations

In Java bytecodes, field references are kept in symbolic form; these are converted into offsets as part of *constant pool resolution*. For example, the JVM spec for the `getfield` instruction says that the operands of the instruction are used to construct an index into the constant pool of the class file; the indicated constant pool item is then "resolved, determining both the field width and the field offset" [7].

The JVM spec also describes the `getfield_quick` instruction, a optimized version of `getfield` which contains the field offset instead the index into the constant pool. The JVM can replace `getfields` with `getfield_quicks` when the class is loaded, insuring that field offsets are resolved only once. So the most obvious optimization is already performed by the interpreter.

TurboJ improves on this in two ways. The first was noted above: field offsets can often be computed when the code is Turbo-ized. For the rest, TurboJ generates initialization routines, both for the entire class and for each method in the class. (A method initialization routine are called the first time a method is invoked.) These routines do as much constant pool resolution as is possible "up-front"; although care must be taken to preserve the late-binding semantics of the JVM spec, in practice almost all resolution can be done when the class is initialized.

Performing up-front resolution reaps the same "resolve once" benefit as the `getfield_quick` optimization. But in addition, by collecting the initialization code in one spot, it becomes subject to common subexpression analysis by TurboJ, as well as the optimizations of the native C compiler.

Similar remarks apply to constant pool resolution for method names.

3.3   Per-Method Optimizations

To avoid the inefficient simulation of the Java-stack in the compiled C code, the bytecode instructions are first transformed into expression trees. The trees are then translated into nested C-expressions. TurboJ endeavors to create fewer larger trees instead of many small trees. A C compiler will generally do a good job of register allocation on code of this sort. Explicit assignments to local variables that simulate the Java-stack can be avoided in most cases.

The data and control flow optimizations should not simply be left to the C compiler. TurboJ possesses additional information which enables optimizations the C compiler cannot perform. In other words, we can take advantage of Java's tighter semantics vis-a-vis pointers. It is often possible to prove that an object's field has not changed between two accesses; the C compiler has to assume the worst. We give an example in the next section.

To exploit this additional potential, TurboJ runs an extra pass for common subexpression detection and removal. As usual in compilation, exposing more semantics enables better optimization. For example, a field access is split into three independent expressions: check for a null object pointer; dereference the pointer; access the field. In several consecutive accesses to different fields of the same object, the common null check and dereferencing need be done only once.

With surprisingly little effort, this scheme for common subexpression removal can be extended to hoist loop invariant expressions out of loops. Care has to be taken for exceptions, which still have to be checked during the execution of the loop. The generated code for the hoisted code is done conditionally only when no exception is thrown.

We discovered early on that Java bytecodes make heavy use of StringBuffer class methods, even when this system class is not explicitly mentioned in the Java source code. For example, a string concatentation expression such as **lastName** + **","** + **firstName** results in two StringBuffer appends. TurboJ recognizes such sequences and translates them into more efficient C code.

Finally, TurboJ performs certain optimizations with regard to exception handling, and miscellaneous peephole optimizations as it emits the actual code.

3.4   Example: Optimization of Field Accesses

We said above that TurboJ benefits from the fact that Java has tighter semantics than C, and as a consequence can often perform optimizations that the C compiler cannot. We give an example in this section.

Field accesses are implemented using pointers to arrays; these are indexed by a value that is usually constant. The C compiler cannot generally prove that these accesses are not aliased. Different fields in different objects cannot reference the same memory location, and this is obvious to TurboJ, but not to the C compiler in the generated code.

We illustrate this with the kernel of a bubblesort algorithm (taken from the CaffeineMark loop benchmark). Figure 3 gives the Java source for the main nested loops.

```
for(i=0; i<this.count; i++) {
  for(j=1; j<this.count; j++) {
    if (this.array[j-1] >= this.array[j]) {
      swap = this.array[j-1];
      this.array[j-1] = this.array[j];
      this.array[j] = swap;
    }
  }
}
```

Figure 3: Nested Loop Example, Java Source

We have loop-invariant reads to the fields this.count and this.array and read and write accesses to the elements of an array. Figure 4 gives a straightforward translation into C, ignoring runtime checks and other details.

```
for(i=0; i<this[count_offset]; i++) {
  for(j=1; i<this[count_offset]; j++) {
    if (this[array_offset][j-1] >= this[array_offset][j]) {
      swap = this[array_offset][j-1];
      this[array_offset][j-1] = this[array_offset][j];
      this[array_offset][j] = swap;
    }
  }
}
```

Figure 4: Naive translation into C

The C compiler would have severe difficulties in proving that the pointers this and this[array_offset] are not identical. Thus it would not be able to move the field accesses out of the loop body. But Java semantics states that an object and an array can never occupy the same memory location. TurboJ can thus safely perform two sorts of optimizations: the loop invariants this[count_offset] and this[array_offset] are hoisted out of the loop, and the common subexpressions this[array_offset][j-1] and this[array_offset][j] are each computed only once. The resulting code looks like figure 5, again ignoring runtime checks and other details.

The results on this benchmark are 50% better with these optimizations than without. Specifically, on an HP-UX 11 using HP's C compiler, the Caffeine loop score was 15122 with the optimizations and 10315 without.

```
loopinv_1 = this[count_offset];
loopinv_2 = this[array_offset];
for(i=0; i<loopinv_1; i++) {
  for(j=1; i<loopinv_1; j++) {
    cse_1 = loopinv_2[j-1];
    cse_2 = loopinv_2[j];
    if (cse_1 >= cse_2) {
      swap = cse_1;
      loopinv_2[j-1] = cse_2;
      loopinv_2[j] = swap;
    }
  }
}
```

Figure 5: Translation into C with Optimizations

4 Current Status

TurboJ supports the full JVM 1.1 instruction set. All required checks (null checks, bound checks, etc.) are enforced. It passes the JCK conformance suite, and has been used to process a number of substantial applications, e.g., HotJava, and the Java WorkShop.

The most up-to-date benchmark results may be found at our Website[13]. We mention here just a couple of results.

On an HP-UX B.10.10 A 9000/829, using the vendor's compiler with optimization level +O2 and the JVM HP-UX Java B.01.12.01, the overall embedded CaffeineMark 3.0 score is as follows (note that higher is better for CaffeineMark):

Caffeine	interpreted	JIT	TurboJ	TurboJ + JIT
	64	381	2084	2242

On an HP K6, 200 Mhz, 32 MB RAM, on VxWorks 5.3.1 with Tornado for Java 1.1 Beta, the results are:

Caffeine	interpreted	TurboJ
	149	3966

5 Related Work

We consider here the following off-line Java-to-native compilers: Harissa[8], jc1[1], Toba[9], JCC[10], jc1[1], TowerJ[12], and IBM's High Performance Compiler for Java[6]. Our information in all cases is taken from the cited references, the most recent we are aware of.

Harissa is a fairly mature research prototype from IRISA/INRIA. Like TurboJ, Harissa allows the mixing of compiled code and interpreted bytecode. Instead of interfacing to a JVM, however, Harissa achieves this by linking in its own version of the JVM. As a consequence, some functions of the Java virtual machine were missing as of December 1997.

Jc1 comes from Cygnus, and is intended for embedded applications. Like TurboJ, jc1 interfaces to a JVM, but unlike TurboJ, it requires a specific JVM, namely Kaffee[15]. As of July 1997, many bytecodes were not supported, nor was exception handling.

Harissa, jc1, and TurboJ are, to our knowledge, the only bytecode-to-native compilers that support mixed-mode execution. The remaining compilers all use some form of the standalone executable approach. Several of them (according to the cited references) do not support applets or graphics, or the JVM 1.1 spec, or differ from the standard in minor ways. While we expect that these defects will be remedied in time, they do illustrate a point made in the introduction: having a standard JVM around furnishes a graceful fallback mode of execution.

TowerJ is the only compiler (among the "standalone" group) that supports dynamic loading of bytecode; it does this by translating the bytecode into native code on-the-fly. We have noted the memory drawbacks of this approach in Section 2.

We are not sure to what extent these compilers can deal with incomplete information at compile-time. Harissa does support separate compilation.

6 Conclusions and Future Work

One of the pleasant surprises of our TurboJ work has been the degree to which good results can be obtained relatively cheaply. We believe this is largely due to the way the design of TurboJ piggybacks on pre-existing technologies. Our use of the JVM has been discussed sufficiently above. The other instance of this phenomenon is our use of the native C compiler, with its well-developed register allocation and code selection algorithms. This can be exploited however only if the generated code has a suitable shape. Hummel et al.[5] have noted that the single biggest penalty of a naive translation of bytecode to C comes from the inefficient use of registers. They remedy this by doing their own register allocation on the bytecodes; we solve it by converting the bytecodes into C expressions with significant nesting depth.

As another example, both our class hierarchy analysis and local optimization algorithms are not yet that sophisticated, but they harvest (we believe) a major portion of the benefit from more elaborate approaches.

Our future plans include several fairly standard optimizations. We will add local optimizations based on SSA-form[4, 11, 14]. We will also upgrade our class hierarchy analysis[3]. We believe there are synergistic possibilities in the combination of these technologies; for example, the inheritance tree can serve (with slight modification) as the lattice in the Wegman-Zadeck constant propagation algorithm[14]. We also intend to make further optimizations with regard to exception handling and synchronization.

As present, TurboJ makes use of no special features of the JVM. There are clear opportunities to be had in making this connection tighter: compiler-assisted garbage collection is an obvious example. However, there are also drawbacks. Adapting TurboJ to work with Tornado for Java (under VxWorks) involved relatively few changes, since the key issues of garbage collection and thread management are delegated to the JVM.

Object inlining[2] is one JVM-neutral optimization that can reduce the overhead of object management. Budimlic and Kennedy implemented this as a bytecode-to-bytecode optimization; this lead to certain protection difficulties that they had to work around. We note that these problems simply don't arise for a bytecode-to-native compiler.

References

1. BOTHNER, P. Compiling Java for embedded systems.
   http://www.cygnus.com/news/whitepapers/compiling.html.
2. BUDIMLIC, Z., AND KENNEDY, K. Optimizing Java: Theory and practice. *Concurrency: Practice and Experience* (June 1997).
   http://www.npac.syr.edu/projects/javaforcse/cpande/rice/JavaPaper.ps.
3. CHAMBERS, C., DEAN, J., AND GROVE, D. Whole-program optimization of object-oriented languages. Tech. Rep. 96-06-02, University of Washington, June 1996.
   http://www.cs.washington.edu/research/projects/cecil/cecil/www/Papers/whole-program.html.
4. CYTRON, R., FERRANTE, J., ROSEN, B. K., WEGMAN, M. N., AND ZADECK, F. K. Efficiently computing static single assignment form and the control dependence graph. *ACM Transactions on Programming Languages and Systems 13*, 4 (Oct. 1991), 451–490. http://www.acm.org/pubs/articles/journals/toplas/1991-13-4/p451-cytron/p451-cytron.pdf.
5. HUMMEL, J., AZEVEDO, A., KOLSON, D., AND NICOLAU, A. Annotating the Java bytecodes in support of optimization. In *Workshop on Java for Science and Engineering Computation, PPoPP97* (June 1997). http://www.npac.syr.edu/users/gcf/03/javaforcse/acmspecissue/finalps/1_hummel.ps.
6. IBM high performance compiler for Java: An optimizing native code compiler for Java applications.
   http://www.alphaworks.ibm.com/graphics.nsf/system/graphics/HPCJ/$file/highpcj.html.
7. LINDHOLM, T., AND YELLIN, F. *The Java Virtual Machine Specification.* Addison-Wesley, 1996.
8. MULLER, G., MOURA, B., BELLARD, F., AND CONSEL, C. Harissa: a flexible and efficient Java environment mixing bytecode and compiled code. In *COOTS97* (1997). available from http://www.irisa.fr/compose/ harissa/harissa.html.
9. PROEBSTING, T. A., TOWNSEND, G., BRIDGES, P., HARTMAN, J. H., NEWSHAM, T., AND WATTERSON, S. A. Toba: Java for applications. a *way ahead of time* (wat) compiler. available from http://www.cs.arizona.edu/sumatra/toba/.

10. SHAYLOR, N. JCC – a Java to C converter.
    http://www.geocities.com/CapeCanaveral/Hangar/4040/jcc.html.
11. SIMPSON, L. T. *Value-Driven Redundancy Elimination*. PhD thesis, Rice University, Apr. 1996. http://www.cs.rice.edu/ lts/thesis.ps.gz.
12. TowerJ release 2.0: A high performance compiler for server-side Java.
    http://www.twr.com/java/towerj2.html.
13. Turboj home page. http://www.opengroup.org/openitsol/turboj.
14. WEGMAN, M. N., AND ZADECK, F. K. Constant propagation with conditional branches. *ACM Transactions on Programming Languages and Systems 13*, 2 (Apr. 1991), 181–210.
15. WILKINSON, T. http://www.kaffe.org/.

Cache Sensitive Pre-runtime Scheduling

Daniel Kästner and Stephan Thesing *

Universität des Saarlandes, Fachbereich Informatik,
Postfach 15 11 50, D-66041 Saarbrücken, Germany
Phone: +49 681 302 5589   Fax: +49 681 302 3065
{kaestner,thesing}@cs.uni-sb.de
http://www.cs.uni-sb.de/~{kaestner,thesing}

Abstract. We present a novel pre-runtime scheduling method for uni-processors which precisely incorporates the effects of task switching on the processor cache into its decisions. Tasks are modelled as a sequence of non preemtable segments with precedence constraints. The cache behavior of each task segment is statically determined by abstract interpretation. For the sake of efficiency, the scheduling algorithm uses a heuristically guided search strategy. Each time a new task segment is added to a partial schedule, its worst case execution time is calculated based on the cache state at the end of the preceding partial schedule.

1   Introduction

Real-time systems consist of tasks which should be finished within given time bounds. In *hard* real-time systems it even has to be *guaranteed* that the time constraints are met. Otherwise, severe consequences may result in the physical environment, controlled by the system (nuclear power plants and flight control are examples of such environments).

Hard real-time systems are often constructed as a set of periodic tasks which have an *earliest release time*, a *period* and a *deadline* associated with them. Every task must not be started before its earliest release time and must be finished before its deadline. Execution repeats after the given period.

The problem is now to find a sequence for the task execution, i.e. to determine start times for all tasks, such that all deadlines are met and earliest release times are obeyed. The problem may further be complicated by the fact that some tasks must not be run before others due to, e.g., data dependencies.

Methods to find such a sequence, which we call a *schedule*, can be classified as *runtime* and *pre-runtime* approaches. Pre-runtime schedules are computed before the system is run and provide a fixed execution sequence. Scheduling methods may further be divided into methods that allow *preemption* and methods that do not. Preemption means that the execution of a task is interrupted and another task is run followed by the resumption of the original task. This

---

* This work was done while both authors were members of the Graduiertenkolleg "Effizienz und Komplexität von Algorithmen und Rechenanlagen" (supported by the DFG).

obviously extends the freedom of choosing task placements in a schedule. In the following, we focus on non preemptive pre-runtime scheduling for uniprocessors. However, we consider tasks as a sequence of *segments* and allow switching to a segment of a different task after a segment has finished its execution. A graphical example is given in Fig. 1.

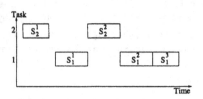

Fig. 1. A task schedule with segments S_j^i

Generating a schedule requires the *worst case execution time* (WCET) of each segment to be known. If the underlying programming language is restricted, the WCET can be calculated with different methods (see [15, 12]). However, cache memories and pipelines in modern microprocessors complicate the determination of the execution time of a single (machine) instruction, as this time depends on the execution path that leads to it (see [1, 6, 2, 11, 14, 13]). Although it is safe to count every memory access of an instruction as a cache miss, this strategy overestimates the execution time significantly[1].

In the following, we will present a pre-runtime, non preemptive scheduling method that takes the cache behavior into account. Its WCET predictions are much tighter than that of a native scheduling method. Our method is applicable to a wide range of cache architectures. Although this paper only considers instruction caches, the method can easily be extended to data or combined instruction/data caches.

1.1 Cache Architectures

In general, we are considering an *A-way set associative cache*, i.e. the cache is divided into n/A sets, and each set is fully associative. Here, n is the capacity of the cache, i.e. it describes how many different memory blocks can be stored in the cache, and A is the number of elements in one set. This includes as special cases direct mapped and fully associative caches. We are employing a *least recently used* (LRU) replacement strategy for each set (see Fig. 2).

1.2 Determining Cache Behavior

In [7] and [6] it was shown how *abstract interpretation* can be used to statically determine the cache behavior of a program. Abstract interpretation [5] is

---

[1] The access time for a cache hit is mostly 1 clock cycle and can be as high as 8-66 cycles for a miss [8].

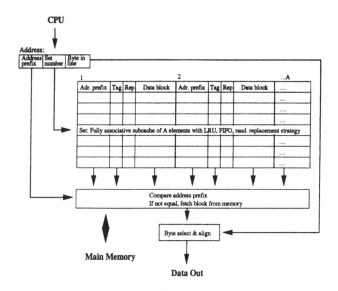

Fig. 2. *A*-way set associative cache architecture

a general framework for static program analyses. The main idea is to replace the concrete semantics operating on concrete values by an abstract semantics operating on abstract values. If the abstract versions of the concrete values and semantic functions satisfy certain conditions, a provably correct static analysis of a program can be constructed[2]. Based on this theory, a powerful tool, PAG (Program Analyzer Generator), has been constructed, which is used to generate the analyses described in this paper. PAG takes a concise specification of the analysis to be performed and generates an efficient program analyzer in the form of several **C** files that can be compiled and linked to the program in which the analysis is to be integrated. In order to perform the analysis, all that is needed is a call to the appropriate **C** function, which gets as an argument the control flow graph of the program to be considered. See [17] for details.

The analyses in [7] determine a classification of every memory access of a program as

- *always hit* (ah), if the access is guaranteed to be a cache hit,
- *always miss* (am), if the access is guaranteed to be a cache miss and
- *not classified* (nc), if the access cannot statically be determined to be a hit or a miss.

The analyses associate *abstract cache states* with every program point. The abstract cache state is the abstraction of concrete cache contents and describes a set of possible cache states that may occur at that point during the execution

---

[2] We are not dealing with the details of abstract interpretation here, see [5] or, with respect to cache memories, [7] for details.

of the program. For our needs, we will treat the above mentioned analysis as a function, taking an abstract start cache state and the control flow graph (CFG) of a segment and returning a function, which maps the nodes of the CFG to the set {ah, am, nc}, according to the previously mentioned classification. With this classification, we can compute the WCET of the segment, which is now dependent on the abstract start cache state, by using one of the methods from [15] or [12]. Since the analysis has to be conservative, each nc has to be accounted for as an am when calculating the WCET. Note that the nodes of a CFG may be annotated with additional information, e.g. the loop bounds from [15].

1.3 Related Work

In [2], it is pointed out that the interaction of different tasks on the cache, the so-called extrinsic cache behavior, can have considerable effects on the overall cache performance. An approach that tries to incorporate cache-related preemption delays into schedulability analysis in the context of preemtive scheduling was presented in [10]. There, Lee et al. extend the response time approach of [9, 18] by including an upper bound of the costs caused by cache reloading of preempted tasks into the recurrence equation for the response time R_i of task τ_i:

$$R_i = C_i + \sum_{\tau_j \in hp(i)} \left\lceil \frac{R_i}{T_j} \right\rceil C_j + PC_i(R_i) \qquad (1)$$

Here, C_i is the WCET of task τ_i, T_j the period of task τ_j and the set $hp(i)$ contains the tasks with higher priority than τ_i. $PC_i(R_i)$ denotes the preemption delay, which has to be considered when calculating the response time. This additional delay accounts for reloads of cache blocks during the execution of τ_i, that were caused by the preemption of τ_i by tasks from $hp(i)$.

To ensure the schedulability of a system, the response time of each task must be less than or equal to its deadline. The equations (1) are solved by iteration ([9]). The values for $PC_i(R_i)$ are determined by approximating the number of useful memory blocks, i.e. memory blocks that may be in the cache at the occurence of a task preemption and that may be referenced again after the resumption of the tasks execution.

The set of useful memory blocks can be determined by combining the results of two data flow analyses, *live memory blocks* and *reaching memory blocks*, see [10] for details. The preemption cost at a program point p may then be given by the number of useful memory blocks at p multiplied by the cache miss penalty time. This corresponds to the time required to reload the useful memory blocks into the cache, if the task is preempted at p. To incorporate the fact that a program point may be executed several times (e.g. the bodies of loops), they build a table of decreasing preemption costs for every task, where each program point p is considered e times, where e is the number of executions of p. In the second step, the equations (1) are solved, where the PC_i-values are determined by the cost table and the number of preemptions of the task by other tasks. For the computation of the number of preemptions, an integer linear program has to be formulated and solved in every iteration step.

In [10], only direct mapped caches are considered; moreover, their approach requires to solve an integer linear program at each iteration step. Since the computation of a single integer linear program is already $\mathcal{NP}$-hard in the worst case, this approach will be limited only to small task sets.

A similar approach for considering the extrinsic cache behavior in preemptive real-time systems is presented in [4]. Here, the preemption delays are modeled in a simpler way: either the time to refill the entire cache or the time to refill the lines misplaced by the preempting task is considered. The equation (1), however, is extended to incorporate the blocking time for a task, based on the Ceiling Semaphore Protocol [16].

An algorithm for the problem of pre-runtime scheduling for processes with precedence and exclusion relations was presented in [19]. The algorithm starts with a heuristically determined schedule that is obtained with the earliest-deadline-first strategy. This initial schedule is improved on until an optimal schedule is found. However, the cache behavior of the tasks is not taken into account.

2 Basic Definitions

2.1 Scheduling

We are considering a set $\mathcal{T}$ of N *tasks* $\mathcal{T} = \{\tau_i | 1 \le i \le N\}$. Every task consists of one or more *segments*, which are executed sequentially. The i-th segment of τ_j is annotated as $\mathcal{S}_j^i$, $1 \le i \le \eta_j$, where η_j is the number of segments of τ_j. The set of all segments is denoted by $\mathcal{S}$.

For every τ_j, D_j denotes the *deadline* and R_j the *earliest release time* of the task. In addition we assume that there is a precedence relation $<_p$ between segments: $\mathcal{S}_j^i <_p \mathcal{S}_{j'}^{i'}$, iff $\mathcal{S}_j^i$ must not be run after $\mathcal{S}_{j'}^{i'}$. $<_p$ has to be irreflexive, transitive and anti-symmetric. For the segments of a task τ_j, $<_p$ must satisfy $\mathcal{S}_j^i <_p \mathcal{S}_j^{i+1}$, $\forall 1 \le i \le \eta_j - 1$, i.e. the segments must execute sequentially.

It may be noted that a system of periodic tasks can always be transformed into the before mentioned form by considering an interval, which is the least common multiple (LCM) of the task periods, by creating LCM/p_j copies of each task with adjusted start times, where p_j denotes the period of the original task. By cfg_j^i, we denote the (annotated) *control flow graph* of $\mathcal{S}_j^i$. $start_j^i$ and end_j^i denote the (unique) start and end node of cfg_j^i. The *scheduling interval* $P = [0, t_{\max}] \subseteq \mathbb{Z}$ is the time interval that contains one complete execution of a schedule (we consider clock cycles as basic unit of the execution time). In most cases, $t_{\max}$ will be the least common multiple of all periods of the original problem. A *schedule* is a mapping T, which maps a segment in $\mathcal{S}$ to its starting time in the scheduling interval P. We represent T as a mapping $T : \mathcal{S} \to P$, where $T(\mathcal{S}_j^i) = t$ means that $\mathcal{S}_j^i$ starts execution at time t. The start time of τ_j is written r_j and given by $r_j = T(\mathcal{S}_j^1)$. By $C^T(\mathcal{S}_j^i)$ we denote the worst case execution time of S_j^i under the schedule T. A *valid* schedule is a schedule that obeys the following restrictions:

- $\forall S_j^i : T(S_j^i) + C^T(S_j^i) \leq t_{max} + 1$
- $\forall S_j^i : \nexists S_{j'}^{i'} : T(S_j^i) \leq T(S_{j'}^{i'}) < T(S_j^i) + C^T(S_j^i)$
- $\forall \tau_j : R_j \leq T(S_j^1)$
- $\forall S_j^i, S_{j'}^{i'} : S_j^i <_p S_{j'}^{i'} \Rightarrow T(S_j^i) < T(S_{j'}^{i'})$

The first condition forces the completion of all segments before the end of P. The next condition ensures that at most one segment is executed at any given time. The third condition states that tasks must not be started before their release times. The last condition demands that a valid schedule obeys the given precedence relation. A *feasible* schedule is a valid schedule under which all deadlines are met, i.e. $\forall \tau_j : T(S_j^{\eta_j}) + C^T(S_j^{\eta_j}) \leq D_j$. Finally, a *partial* schedule T^p is a valid schedule for a subset $S' \subseteq S$ (with $<_p$ restricted to S'). A segment S_j^i is called *scheduled* (in T^p), if $S_j^i \in S'$; otherwise, it is called *unscheduled*. A task τ_j is called *unscheduled*, iff S_j^1 is unscheduled. It is *(completely) scheduled*, iff $S_j^{\eta_j}$ is scheduled. If S_j^1 is scheduled but τ_j is not completely scheduled, it is called *partially scheduled*.

Note that for given T, a mapping $T' : P \to S \cup \{\text{Idle}\}$ can be constructed, mapping any time $t \in P$ to either a segment that is executed at t or Idle, meaning that the processor is idle:

$$T'(t) = \begin{cases} S_j^i \text{ , if } \exists S_j^i : T(S_j^i) \leq t < T(S_j^i) + C^T(S_j^i) \\ \text{Idle, otherwise} \end{cases}$$

2.2 Cache Memories

An A-way set associative cache with n lines consists of a sequence of (fully associative) sets. The store $M = \{m_1, \ldots, m_S\}$ consists of a set of memory blocks, whose addresses are determined by a function $adr : M \to \mathbb{N}$. The set $f_i \in F$, in which a memory block is cached, is determined by a function $set : M \to F$, where $set(m) = f_i$, iff $i = adr(m)\%(\frac{n}{A}) + 1$. Each set contains A *lines*; a line $l_i \in L$ is either empty (denoted by ϵ) or contains a memory block $m \in M$. We define $M' = M \cup \{\epsilon\}$. A function $\iota : L \to M'$, which maps each set line to its content, is called a concrete set state. Let I denote the set of all concrete set states. A concrete cache state $c : F \to I$ assigns a concrete set state to each set in the cache. Then, an abstract set state describes a set of concrete set states and can be represented as a function $\hat{\iota} : L \to \mathcal{P}(M')$. If we denote the set of all abstract set states by $\hat{I}$, we can represent an abstract cache state as a function $\hat{c} : F \to \hat{I}$ which assigns an abstract set state to each set in the cache. In the following we will use C to refer to the set of all cache states and $\hat{C}$ to refer to the set of all abstract cache states.

The MUST-Analysis, presented in [7], determines a set of memory blocks which are guaranteed to be in the cache, when the control flow reaches a given program point. In order to simulate the effect of a memory reference on the

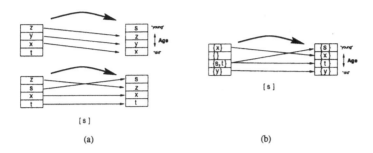

Fig. 3. a) Update of a concrete fully associative subcache, b) Update of an abstract fully associative subcache

abstract set and cache states, appropriate update functions have to be defined. Since set states as well as abstract set states depend on the associativity and the replacement strategy of the cache – assumed to be the LRU-strategy – we have to consider the relative age of each memory block in a set. The relative age of a memory block m in an abstract set state $\hat{\imath}$ must always be an upper bound on the relative ages of m in the concrete set states represented by $\hat{\imath}$. The relative age of a memory block m_a in the set can only be changed by references to memory blocks m_b, where $set(m_a) = set(m_b)$. Furthermore, memory block m_b must be as least as old as m_a for the relative age of m_a to be changed. These changes are modelled by an abstract set update function $\hat{U}_{\hat{I}} : \hat{I} \times M \rightarrow \hat{I}$, which describes the new abstract set state for a given abstract set state and a referenced memory block. The new abstract cache state is calculated by an abstract cache update function $\hat{U}_{\hat{C}} : \hat{C} \times M \rightarrow \hat{C}$ for a given abstract cache state and a referenced memory block. The update of a concrete fully associative cache for a referenced memory block s is shown in Fig. 3 (a). Two cases can be distinguished: in the first part of the figure, s enters the cache, in the second one, it is already contained in the cache and only its age has to be updated. The update of an abstract cache state for a referenced memory block s is shown in Fig. 3 (b).

When control flow joins exist in a program, abstract cache states have to be combined. A memory block only remains in an abstract set state, when it is contained in the abstract state of both operand set states. When these have different ages, the memory block is assigned the oldest one. This is modeled by a join function for abstract set states. A join function for abstract cache states applies the join function for abstract set states to all corresponding set states of its arguments. An example of an abstract join is given in Fig. 4.

In order to solve the MUST-Analysis for a given segment, a system of recursive equations is created from its control flow graph. The variables in the equation system represent abstract cache states for all program points. The least fixed point of this equation system is computed by fixed point iteration; it maps every node in the CFG to an abstract cache state. The fixed point $\mathcal{F}_{\hat{c}}(\mathcal{S}_j^i) : CFGNodes \rightarrow \hat{C}$ is computed relatively to the abstract cache state $\hat{c}$ at the start of the segment $\mathcal{S}_j^i$. This cache state $\hat{c}$ is given by $\mathcal{F}_{\hat{c}'}(\mathcal{S}_{j'}^{i'})(end_{j'}^{i'})$, if $\mathcal{S}_{j'}^{i'}$

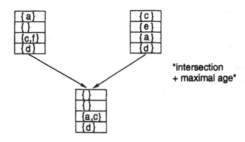

Fig. 4. Abstract join for the MUST analysis

is the segment executed before S_j^i, or by the empty abstract cache state for the first segment in the schedule.

3 Overview

We have integrated the static cache analysis into a pre-runtime scheduling algorithm, using a depth first search technique. The algorithm is based on a branch-and-bound algorithm which was presented in [3]. There the objective is to minimize the execution time of a set of tasks with given release times and deadlines. In our work, we extend this approach by considering precedence constraints and switching costs due to the inter-task cache interference. Since we have to deal with periodic tasks, we don't want to determine a feasible schedule with minimal execution time; instead we return the first feasible schedule found. Thus, the algorithm can be considered as a heuristically guided search where the search tree can be pruned under certain circumstances.

The schedule is computed incrementally. The root of the search tree corresponds to the empty schedule and the nodes of level k represent all valid schedules consisting of exactly k task segments. Clearly, the maximal depth of this tree corresponds to the number of task segments and without precedence constraints and without pruning, all $|S|!$ possible schedules are enumerated in the worst case. At each node n_μ, a *segment ready set* SRS_μ is computed which contains all yet unscheduled segments that can be appended to the schedule represented by n_μ. To be more precise, SRS_μ contains exactly those task segments, which are not contained in the partial schedule and whose predecessors with respect to the precedence relation have already been scheduled. A child of a node n_μ in the search tree is created for each task segment in SRS_μ which can be appended to the schedule corresponding to n_μ without exceeding its deadline. If the completion time of the newly added task segment S_i^j exceeds its deadline, then the tree can be pruned at node n_μ. The reason is the fact that, if S_i^j exceeds its deadline when appearing at the k-th position of the schedule, it will certainly miss its deadline when scheduled at an even later position. If at a node at level k in the search tree, the schedule length is less than or equal to the smallest release time among the unscheduled tasks, the problem decomposes at that node. The best schedule for the remaining $n - k$ task segments may not be started prior to the smallest release time among those tasks. Thus, there is no need to backtrack beyond level k. The order in which the children of a node in the search tree are visited can be determined by several heuristics. In our implementation, we have considered the earliest-deadline-first heuristic.

This approach allows us to consider cache effects in a straightforward way. At each node, the abstract cache state at the end of the partial schedule is calculated. Each instruction of a new segment is classified as either a cache miss or a cache hit. Thus, the worst case execution time of the task segments can be calculated taking their cache behavior into account. Since the abstract cache state at the end of the parent node in the search tree is used as initial cache state, the switching costs of different task sequences are considered.

4 Scheduling Algorithm

In this section, we present our scheduling algorithm in more detail. It can basically be described by two procedures: the procedure SCHEDULE and a recursive function RECSCHEDULE. These functions are given in a PASCAL-like pseudocode-notation as shown in Tables 1 and 2.

```
SCHEDULE(TASKSET p, SPEC spec)
begin
 Forall S ∈ p do
  cfg_S = CreateControlFlowGraph(S);
  InitDataFlow(cfg_S);
 od
 ReadTaskSetSpec(spec);
 l = CreateReadyList(p);
 schedule = ∅;
 Forall nodes n ∈ l do
 begin
  status = RecSchedule(n);
  if status == true then
   print schedule;
   return;
  fi
 end
 return("No feasible schedule found");
end
```

Table 1. The procedure SCHEDULE.

First, the control flow graphs of all task segments are created and the data flow values associated with each node are initialized. Then the specification of the actual task set is read in. This specification indicates for each task segment S_i^j its release time, deadline and the set of all task segments S_μ^ν which are directly dependent on S_i^j with respect to the precedence relation. Nodes are created for each task segment, the schedule can start with; these are inserted into a list l. Each node represents a partial schedule; it contains information about the last task segment in the corresponding schedule, the abstract cache state at the end of it and its end time. For all created nodes, the set $SRS(n)$ is calculated. This set contains all unscheduled segments that could be appended directly at the end of the schedule represented by n without violating any precedence constraints. For the nodes in l, the cache behavior prediction (see below) is performed starting from an empty cache state. The schedule is implemented as a list; it represents the path in the search tree from the root to the actual node. At the start of the algorithm, it is empty.

```
int RecSchedule(n)
begin
 Append n to schedule;
 if length(schedule) == N then
  return true;
 fi
 Forall S ∈ SRS(n) do
  if ReleaseTime(S)
       ≤ EndTime(n) then
   n' =CreateNode(S);
   n'→cache =
    CalcCacheBehavior(S, n→cache)
   n'→lastWcet = CalcWcet(S, cl);
   if (Endtime(n)+n'→lastWcet
       ≤Deadline(S) then
    append n' to Childlist(n);
   else
    remove n from schedule;
    return BACKTRACK;
   fi
  fi
 od
 if Childlist(n) == ∅ then
  Forall t ∈ SRS(n)
  with ReleaseTime(S)>Endtime(n)
  in incr. order of release time do
   n' = CreateNode(S);
   n'→root = true;
   n'→cache =
    CalcCacheBehavior(S, n→cache);
   n'→lastWcet = CalcWcet(S, cl);
   if (ReleaseTime(S)+n'→lastWcet
        ≤Deadline(S) then
    append n' to Childlist(n);
   else
    exit("No feasible Schedule can exist");
   fi
  od
 fi
 Sort Childlist(n) by heuristic h;
 Forall n' ∈ ChildList(n) do
  status = RecSchedule(n');
  if status == BACKTRACK then
   if n→root == true then
    exit("No feasible Schedule can exist");
   else
    remove n' from schedule;
    return false;
   fi
  fi
  if status == false then
   remove n' from ChildList(n);
  else
   return true;
  fi
 od
 if status == false
     and n→root == true then
  exit("No feasible Schedule can exist");
 else
  return false;
 fi
end
```

Table 2. The function RecSchedule.

The heart of the algorithm is the recursive function RecSchedule; it considers the nodes in the list l one after another as starting point until a feasible schedule is found. The node n passed as a parameter is appended to the actual schedule *schedule*. If all segments have been scheduled, the function returns *true*.

For each task segment S_i^j in the set SRS whose release time does not exceed the endtime of the actual schedule $schedule_n$, the following actions are performed: A new node n' is created which represents the schedule obtained by appending S_i^j to $schedule_n$. The cache behavior of that task segment is predicted starting with the cache state at the end of $schedule_n$ and the new abstract cache state at the end of S_i^j is saved. This is done by the function CalcCacheBehavior, which implements the static cache analysis as described in Section 2. Each instruction is either classified as a cache hit or a cache miss; the abstract cache state at the end of the actual task segment S_i^j is returned. Then the worst case execution time of S_i^j is calculated using the cache behavior prediction performed by CalcCacheBehavior. If S_i^j is guaranteed to complete before its deadline, the new information is registered in n' and n' is inserted into the childlist of n. Each node in $Childlist(n)$ represents a partial schedule where a task segment $S_\mu^\nu \in SRS(n)$ is executed after the segments in $schedule_n$ without exceeding its deadline. If any task segment exceeds its deadline, then no feasible schedule can be found starting from node n. Then RECSCHEDULE returns the value $BACKTRACK$. That means that we can stop considering node n and proceed with the next child in the childlist of the parent of n. If $Childlist(n)$ is empty, no task segment can be appended to $schedule_n$ without inserting idle time. Then the task segment with the earliest release time that is contained in SRS and does not exceed its deadline is appended to $schedule_n$. The flag $n' \rightarrow root$ is set to $true$ to indicate that no backtracking beyond that node need be performed. Subsequently, the childlist is sorted by increasing deadlines of the corresponding task segments. This way, the earliest deadline first strategy is incorporated into our algorithm, however other heuristics can be used, too. For the nodes in the childlist, the function RECSCHEDULE is called. No feasible solution is possible, when the return value of RECSCHEDULE for any of the children is $BACKTRACK$ and the root-flag is set to $true$. Otherwise, the actual incarnation of RECSCHEDULE returns $false$. Then the parent of n removes n from its childlist and proceeds with the next child. A feasible schedule has been found, when RECSCHEDULE(n') for a child n' of n returns $true$; then this return value is propagated and in the function SCHEDULE, the generated schedule is printed out. If the return value of all children was $false$ and the root-flag of n is $true$, again no feasible schedule can exist and the calculation stops; otherwise the function returns $false$ and the parent can proceed with its next child.

5   Experiments

For our experiments, we reused a C program collection, made available by the Real-Time research group of the Seoul National University, Korea[3]. The collection contains 17 programs consisting of 42 to 3224[4] SPARC instructions. From this collection, we extracted 18 test-functions, among these a cyclic redundancy

---

[3] See http://archi.snu.ac.kr/realtime/benchmark/index.html.
[4] compiled by gcc -O6

check function, fast fourier transformations, a finite impulse response filter, etc. We randomly selected calls to these test-functions to form the segments of a task set as follows: every segment is constructed as **C** code of the form

```
void Seg_i_j(void)    {
  glue code
  f(arguments)
  glue code
  }
```

The glue code contains declaration of variables, initializations, etc. f is one of the test-functions from the SNU collection, i is the task number and j is the segment number. The random selection was parameterized by the number of tasks to produce, the minimal and the maximal number of segments in a task. Another randomized parameter indicates the number of occurrences of a task within the scheduling interval to be considered; the deadlines and earliest release times have been chosen appropriately. The generated **C** code together with the code of the test-functions has been joined to form a single executable. This executable was given as input to our scheduler. The scheduler contains the cache analyzer, as generated by PAG (see 1.2). As described in Section 4, the analysis of a segment is simply performed by a call to the analysis function, with the actual task segment and the start cache state as arguments. The resulting cache state and the classification (ah,am,nc) for the code in the segment is returned by this function.

Since we did not dispose of an implementation of the WCET determination algorithms of [15, 12], we have used the qpt2 program tracer of the WARTS toolkit in order to determine the execution counts of each machine instruction in a segment. To obtain timing information, we used a simplified model. We assumed that every machine instruction that was classified as a cache hit takes one clock cycle to execute, whereas each miss or unclassified instruction takes 10 clock cycles. This is a realistic assumption for current RISC-architectures; in fact, for most architectures, the difference is even greater [8]. In order to obtain the WCET time of a segment, we combine the results of the classification of the cache analysis with the trace of that segment. The trace of each call to a test-function is static, as we have used static arguments. This way, an upper bound on the WCET is provided.

We have performed three scheduling runs on each task set:

1. The scheduling method proposed in this paper (C).
2. Scheduling is performed by the same method, but the empty cache is used as start cache for every cache analysis (I).
3. Finally, we completely ignored all cache effects during scheduling by considering every instruction fetch as a cache miss (N).

In our experimets, we have considered four randomly generated task sets for five distinct cache configurations where the number of recurrences of each segment lies between two and seven. The total number of task segments in our tasksets lies between 21 and 29. Each function may be called more than once during execution. Our results are summarized in Table 3. There, the column TS identifies the taskset, CS denotes the cache size (given in KB), A the associativity and LS the line size (given in bytes). The scheduling mode is specified in column MD and the length of the constructed schedule in machine cycles is given in column L. Finally, the last column labeled P indicates the performance loss in percent when substituting method C by method I.

TS	CS	A	LS	MD	L	P[%]	TS	CS	A	LS	MD	L	P[%]
1	0.5	1	16	C	47790	0.41	3	0.5	1	16	C	40126	0.54
				I	47988						I	40342	
	4	1	16	C	33687	10.1		4	1	16	C	24538	18.2
				I	37089						I	29002	
	4	4	16	C	33804	9.7		4	4	16	C	25537	28.2
				I	37089						I	28930	
	4	4	4	C	46899	19.9		4	4	4	C	44113	26.5
				I	58554						I	55822	
	20	5	16	C	33147	11.89		20	5	16	C	22558	28.2
				I	37089						I	28930	
	–	–	–	N	–			–	–	–	N	–	
2	0.5	1	16	C	12227	1.5	4	0.5	1	16	C	25204	0.29
				I	12416						I	25276	
	4	1	16	C	10715	9.6		4	1	16	C	22333	3.5
				I	11741						I	23125	
	4	4	16	C	10985	6.89		4	4	16	C	22225	3.8
				I	11741						I	23089	
	4	4	4	C	22964	5.56		4	4	4	C	37057	6.1
				I	24233						I	39352	
	20	5	16	C	9716	20.8		20	5	16	C	22027	4.8
				I	11741						I	23089	
	–	–	–	N	64310			–	–	–	N	164380	

Table 3. Experimental Results.

For the sake of simplicity, the deadlines and release times of the task segments have been chosen so, that no idle times need to be inserted. When the cache behavior is neglected, i.e. when all instructions are assumed to be cache misses, no feasible schedules could be found for the first and the third taskset. For taskset 2, a feasible scheduling taking 64310 clock cycles was found; the schedule calculated for taskset 4 ignoring all cache effects took 164380 clock cycles. These schedules are more than 5 times longer than the schedule length calculated by scheduling method C even for the smallest cache configuration considered (0.5 KB). Comparing the results of methods C and I, we can see that the difference increases with increasing cache size. This is a logical result since the benefits of extrinsic cache behavior will be the more important the larger the considered cache is. For the smallest cache size of 0.5 KB, the acceleration is on average 0.7%; considering a cache of 20 K size, we found an average acceleration of nearly

17%. Thus, we can conclude that considering the extrinsic cache behavior can have a significant impact on the length of the generated schedule and this way on the schedulability of a given task set.

6 Conclusion

In this paper, we have presented a pre-runtime scheduling algorithm which takes the extrinsic cache behavior of different tasks into account. Tasks are modeled as a sequence of segments in order to combine the flexibility of preemptive algorithms with the predictability of non-preemptive algorithms. The execution of segments of different tasks can be interleaved; the correctness of the resulting schedule is guaranteed by precedence constraints between the task segments. The intrinsic cache behavior is calculated by a static cache analyzer generated by the program analyzer generator PAG. The extrinsic cache effects are taken into account by analysing each task segment starting with the abstract cache state at the end of the preceding task segment in the schedule. This way, the switching costs can be incorporated into the scheduling process and the cache behavior of different task sequences can accurately be predicted.

7 Future Work

At the moment, the implementation of the timing scheme of [12] and its integration into our scheduler is under way. Also, we are considering the integration of data cache analysis into the scheduler, as well as a processor-pipeline analysis.

Further extensions concern the scheduling algorithm itself. Up to now, the extrinsic cache behavior is incorporated into the scheduling process, yet it cannot directly influence the scheduling decisions. The algorithm could benefit from a heuristic that takes the cache behavior of different task sequences into account, so that sequences with low switching costs would be preferred.

8 Acknowledgments

We would like to thank the Real-Time research group at SNU for making publically available their test programs. Special thanks go to Christian Ferdinand and Florian Martin for their help in the integration of the PAG analyzer into our scheduler.

References

[1] Martin Alt, Christian Ferdinand, Florian Martin, and Reinhard Wilhelm. Cache Behavior Prediction by Abstract Interpretation. *SAS'96 Static Analysis Symposium*, 1996.

[2] S. Basumallick and K. Nilsen. Cache Issues in Real-Time Systems. In *Proceedings of the ACM SIGPLAN Workshop on Language, Compiler and Tool Support for Real-Time Systems*, June 1994.

[3] P. Bratley, M. Florian, and P. Robillard. Scheduling with Earliest Start and Due Date Constraints. *Naval Res. Logist. Quart.*, 18:511–517, 1971.

[4] Jose Busquets-Mataix, Juan J. Serrano, Rafael Ors, Pedro Gil, and Andy Wellings. Adding Instruction Cache Effect to Schedulability Analysis of Preemptive Real-Time Systems. In *Proceedings of the 2nd Real-Time Technology and Applications Symposium*, pages 204–212. IEEE Computer Society Press, june 1996.

[5] Patrik Cousot and Radhia Cousot. A Unified Lattice Model for Static Analysis of Programs by Construction or Approximation of Fixpoints. In *Conference Record of the 4th ACM Symposium on Principles of Programming Languages*, pages 238–252, Los Angeles, CA, January 1977.

[6] Christian Ferdinand, Florian Martin, and Reinhard Wilhelm. Applying Compiler Techniques to Cache Behavior Prediction. In *Proceedings of the ACM SIGPLAN Workshop on Language, Compiler and Tool Support for Real-Time Systems*, pages 37–46, June 1997.

[7] Christian Ferdinand. *Cache Behavior Prediction for Real-Time Systems*. PhD thesis, Universität des Saarlandes, September 1997.

[8] J. Hennessy and D. Patterson. *Computer Architecture: A Quantitative Approach*. Morgan Kaufmann, second edition, 1996.

[9] M. Joseph and P. Pandya. Finding Response Times in a Real-Time System. *The BCS Computer Journal*, 29(5):390–395, January 1986.

[10] C.-G. Lee, J. Hahn, Seo Y.-M., S. L. Min, R. Ha, S. Hong, C. Y. Park, M. Lee, and C. S. Kim. Analysis of Cache-related Preemption Delay in Fixed-priority Preemptive Scheduling. In *Proceedings of the 16th Real-Time Systems Symposium*, 1996.

[11] S.-S. Lim, Y.H. Bae, G.T. Jang, B.-D. Rhee, S.L. Min, C.Y. Park, H. Shin, K. Park, S.-M. Moon, and C.S. Kim. An Accurate Worst Case Timing Analysis for RISC Processors. *IEEE Transactions on Software Engineering*, 21(7):593–604, July 1995.

[12] Y.-T. S. Li, S. Malik, and A. Wolfe. Efficient Microarchitecture Modeling and Path Analysis for Real-Time Software. In *Proceedings of the 16th IEEE Real-Time Systems Symposium*, pages 298–307, December 1995.

[13] F. Mueller, D.B. Whalley, and M. Harmon. Predicting Instruction Cache Behavior. In *Proceedings of the ACM SIGPLAN Workshop on Language, Compiler and Tool Support for Real-Time Systems*, 1994.

[14] F. Mueller. *Static Cache Simulation and its Applications*. PhD thesis, Florida State University, July 1994.

[15] P. Puschner and Ch. Koza. Calculating the Maximum Execution Time of Real-Time Programs. *Real-Time Systems*, 2(1):159–176, September 1989.

[16] L. Sha, R. Rajkumar, and J.P. Lehoczky. Priority Inheritance Protocols: An Approach to Real-Time-Synchronisation. *IEEE Transactions on Computers*, 39(9):1175–1185, September 1990.

[17] Stephan Thesing, Florian Martin, Oliver Lauer, and Martin Alt. *PAG: User's Manual*. Universität des Saarlandes, 1997.

[18] K. Tindell, A. Burns, and A. Wellings. An Extensible Approach for Analyzing Fixed Priority Hard Real-Time Tasks. *The Journal of Real-Time Systems*, 6(2):133–151, March 1994.

[19] Jia Xu and David Lorge Parnas. Scheduling Processes with Release Times, Deadlines, Precedence, and Exclusion Relations. *IEEE Transactions on Software Engineering*, 16(3):360–369, March 1990.

Priority Assignment for Embedded Reactive Real-Time Systems

Felice Balarin

Cadence Berkeley Labs

Abstract. We consider a model of reactive real-time systems in which tasks are enabled in reaction to external events or executions of other tasks, and enabled tasks are scheduled according to a fixed priority policy. For such a model, we propose a schedule validation method. The method is applicable to a class of priority assignments that require less total processor time than assignments that could be validated by previous methods. The method is safe in the sense that if it validates a system, then it is guaranteed that no timing violations occur. However, it is conservative, in the sense that it may not be able to validate some correct systems. Based on this method, we also propose a priority assignment algorithm. The algorithm is optimal in the sense that if an assignment that satisfies the proposed schedule validation method exists, the algorithm will find it.

1   Introduction

Embedded systems often consist of several tasks which need to share a common processor. Since more than one task may be ready to run at any given time, a *scheduling problem* arises: one has to decide which of the enabled tasks to execute. *Static priority scheduling* has long been a popular solution for embedded systems. In this approach, every task is assigned a fixed priority before the system is employed. These priorities are then used at run-time to decide which of the enabled tasks to execute.

There are two distinct classes of problems related to scheduling: *schedule validation*, and *schedule synthesis*. In case of static priority scheduling, the schedule validation problem is to check whether a set of tasks with assigned priorities satisfies all of its timing constraints. The schedule synthesis problem is to find a *priority assignment* which meets all the timing constraints.

Many embedded systems are *reactive*. In reactive systems, tasks are enabled in reaction to external events, or executions of other tasks, rather than in regular time intervals. Most of the previous formal approaches to schedule validation and synthesis are based on models of real-time systems which do not capture reactivity well. A notable exception is [6], where a schedule validation method is proposed for a model of embedded systems with explicit reactivity.

There are two main contributions of this paper. First, we propose an improved schedule validation method for the model of embedded systems introduced in [6].

The previously proposed method imposed some constraints on the priority assignments. We propose an alternative set of constraints, and show that newly proposed constraints can lead to a decrease in the required processor time.

Second, we propose a priority assignment algorithm based on the proposed schedule validation method. There is an obvious way to extend schedule validation to priority assignment: try all possible priority assignments and pick one that passes the test (if any). However, this naive approach requires an exponential number of tests. A dynamic programming approach that requires a polynomial number of tests was proposed by Audsley [1, 3]. We show that a similar approach can also be devised for the reactive model from [6].

The rest of this paper is organized as follows: We first survey the related work in section 2. Then, in section 3 we review the model of embedded systems and schedule validation tests proposed in [6]. We propose an improved schedule validation method in section 4, and then a priority assignment algorithm in section 5. Finally, some conclusions and ideas for future work are given in section 6.

2 Related Work

One of the earliest schedule validation and priority assignment assignment algorithms were proposed by Liu and Layland [7]. They have considered a model in which every task is enabled periodically, starting at time 0. They have proved that to validate the schedule, it suffice to simulate the system starting from time 0 until the processor becomes idle. They have also shown that the optimum priority assignment is *rate-monotonic*, i.e. tasks with shorter period get higher priority.

Many extensions of Liu and Layland model have been considered. Audsley et. al. [1, 2] have studied an extension where tasks are not necessarily enabled at time 0, but are allowed to have an arbitrary, known *offset*. In this case, rate-monotonic scheduling is not optimal. Audsley et. al. have proposed a schedule validation method for this model. Audsley [1] has also proposed a priority assignment algorithm for this model. Since the priority assignment algorithm proposed in this paper is an adaptation of Audsley's algorithm, we next describe this algorithm in details.

2.1 Audsley's algorithm

The algorithm is based on the assumption that a schedule validity test exists, and that it satisfies the following:

1. Given a priority assignment, it is possible to check whether some task t satisfies its timing constraints, and the result of the test for task t (pass or fail) does not change if two tasks which have a higher priority than t exchange their priorities. In other words the results of the test should only depend on which tasks have higher priority than t, and not on their exact priorities.

2. If some task t fails the test for some priority assignment in which task u has lower priority than t, then it also fails in the assignment where t and u switch their priorities. In other words, if t fails the test, we cannot make it pass by lowering its priority.

The algorithm divides a set of tasks into two groups: those that have already been assigned a priority, and those that have not. Similarly, priorities are divided into those that are already assigned and those that are still available. The algorithm always assigns the lowest available priority to any task which satisfies its timing constraint when assigned that priority. The algorithm may terminate in two ways. It either assigns priorities to all tasks, in which case a valid assignment has been found, or at some point, the lowest available priority (say p) cannot be assigned to any of the remaining tasks. In every priority assignment, at least one of these tasks must have priority p or lower, but:

- assigning priority p to any one of them results in a timing violation, as shown by the test results,
- assigning a priority less than p to any one of them also results in a timing violation, because (by assumption) test results cannot be improved by lowering the priority.

Therefore, we may conclude that there is no priority assignment satisfying the test. The algorithm is thus optimal, in the sense that it finds a valid priority assignment, if such an assignment exists. The number of required tests grows quadratically with the number of tasks, which is a vast improvement over the naive algorithm which checks all priority assignments and requires an exponential number of tests.

3 Schedule Validation for Reactive Systems

In this section we review the model of computation and the schedule validation method proposed in [6]. In this approach, a system is a collection of tasks with known priorities and execution times. Tasks are enabled either by external events or by executions of other tasks (internal events). Among the enabled tasks, the one with the highest priority is executed. We assume that there exists some known minimum time between two occurrences of external events. A system is correct if events are never "dropped", i.e. if tasks enabled by these events are executed before another event of the same kind occurs.[1]

Formally, a *system* is a 6-tuple (T, e, P, U, m, E) where

- T is the set of *internal tasks*,
- $e : T \mapsto \mathbb{R}$ assigns to every internal task its *execution time*,
- $P : T \mapsto \{1, \ldots, |T|\}$ assigns to every internal task its unique *priority*,

---

[1] This model is inspired by the model used in the hardware/software co-design system POLIS [4]. The correctness criterion emerged from a case-study in formal verification [5].

- U is the set of *external tasks*,
- $m : U \mapsto \mathbb{R}$ assigns to every external task *minimum time between two executions*.
- $E \subseteq (T \cup U) \times T$ is the set of *events*.

Intuitively, $(t, u) \in E$ indicates that an execution of task t enables task u. We say that the graph with nodes $T \cup U$ and edges E is the *system graph*. We consider only systems that have acyclic system graphs. If t is an external task, then we say that $(t, u) \in E$ is an external event. Otherwise, we say that (t, u) is an internal event.

A *run* of a system is any sequence of events that satisfies the following:

1. external tasks can execute at any time, as long as the time between two executions of any external task t is larger than or equal to $m(t)$,
2. immediately after the execution of task t, all the tasks u such that $(t, u) \in E$, are *enabled*, and task t is *disabled*,
3. at any time, the highest priority enabled task executes.

An event (t, u) is said to be *dropped* if after t is executed, task t is executed again before task u is executed. A run is *correct* if no events are dropped in it. A system is correct if all of its runs are.

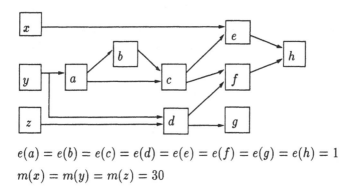

$$e(a) = e(b) = e(c) = e(d) = e(e) = e(f) = e(g) = e(h) = 1$$
$$m(x) = m(y) = m(z) = 30$$

Fig. 1. Example of a system.

An example of a system is shown in Figure 1. It has three external tasks (x, y, z) and eight internal tasks $(a-h)$. If the priority assignment is such that $P(c) > P(b) > P(a) > P(d) > P(e) > P(f)$, then a sequence of task executions $a, c, b, c, \ldots$ is a run triggered by task y. In that run events (c, e) and (c, f) are dropped.

3.1 Schedule validation

In [6], the schedule validation problem is divided into two sub-problems: checking that internal events are not dropped, and checking that external events are not dropped. To check internal events, [6] relies on static checks of priority assignments. In particular, it is observed there that (t, u) cannot be dropped if $P(t) < P(u)$. From this observation, it is quite easy to derive a priority assignment algorithm. However, this assignment may be sub-optimal in terms of the total processor work-load. To alleviate this problem, we propose an improved priority assignment check in the next section.

To check whether an external event (t, u) can be dropped, we seek a bound on the length of an interval (called $P(u)$-*busy interval*) in which neither the processor is idle, nor any tasks with priority lower than $P(u)$ execute. The first step in computing such a bound is to compute so-called *partial loads* [6]. Partial load $\delta(t, p)$ is the continuous work-load at priority p or higher caused by an execution of task t. To determine $\delta(t, p)$, one can simulate a run of the system that starts with an execution of t, and in which no external tasks execute and no other tasks are enabled prior to the execution of t. The simulation can be stopped at the first instance of time where either the processor is idle, or some task with priority less than p executes. However, computing partial loads is even simpler for the class of systems we consider in this paper, as shown in Section 4.1.

At the beginning of a p-busy interval some task of priority lower than p may be executing, and (in the worst case), it may be just finishing and enabling some tasks of priority p or higher. The total workload generated by such a task is bounded by $\max\{\delta(t, p) \mid P(t) < p\}$.

In a p-busy interval of length Δ, some external task u can be executed at most $\left\lceil \frac{\Delta}{m(u)} \right\rceil$ times,[2] and every execution generates a work-load (at priority p or higher) of $\delta(u, p)$. Combining these two arguments yields the following bound:

$$\Delta \leq \max\{\delta(t, p) \mid P(t) < p\} + \sum_{u \in U} \left\lceil \frac{\Delta}{m(u)} \right\rceil \delta(u, p) . \tag{1}$$

This implicit inequality can be solved by simple iteration to obtain an upper bound Δ on the length of a p-busy interval. If $p = P(u)$ and $\Delta < m(t)$, then (t, u) cannot be dropped.

4 Improved Schedule Validation

The requirement that $P(t) < P(u)$ holds for every internal event (t, u) may cause an increased total processor load. Consider, for example, the system in Figure 1. If $P(a) < P(b) < P(c)$ holds, then c will execute twice for every execution of a. However, if $P(c) < P(b) < P(a)$ holds, then c will execute only once. We will propose a priority assignment algorithm that generates such assignments, but first we need to introduce some definitions.

Given task t, its set of *immediate predecessors* $\mathrm{pre}(t)$ is the set $\{u \mid (u, t) \in E\}$. Similarly, its set of *predecessors* $\mathrm{pre}^*(t)$ is the set $\{u \mid (u, t) \in E^*\}$, where E^* is

---

[2] In this paper, we use $\lceil x \rceil$ to denote the smallest *positive* integer greater than or equal to x. Thus, according to this, slightly non-standard definition, $\lceil 0 \rceil = 1$.

the transitive and reflexive closure of E. Finally, its set of *external predecessors* $\text{pre}^U(t)$ is $\text{pre}^*(t) \cap U$. We say that task $t \in T$ is a *merge point* if it has more than one external predecessor, while some of its immediate predecessors has exactly one, i.e. $|\text{pre}^U(t)| > |\text{pre}^U(u)| = 1$ for some $u \in \text{pre}(t)$. We use $mp(t)$ to denote the predicate that is true if and only if t is a merge point. For example, in Figure 1 tasks c, d, and e are merge points.

We are now ready to propose a static priority check that induces lesser total processor load than previously proposed in [6].

Proposition 1. *If the priority assignment P is such that for every $(t, u) \in T \times T$:*

- $P(t) > P(u)$ *if* $(t, u) \in E$ *and t is not a merge point,*
- $P(t) < P(u)$ *if t is a merge point, $t \neq u$, and t is a predecessor of u,*

then no events in (t, u) such that $|\text{pre}^U(t)| > 1$ can be dropped.

Consider, for example, some event (t, u) such that t has more than one external predecessor. We argue that (provided P satisfies conditions in Proposition 1) when t is executed, none of its predecessors with priority higher than $P(u)$ can be enabled, unless a path from that predecessor to t goes through a merge point. Since the priority of that merge point must be lower than $P(u)$ (by the second condition in Proposition 1), we conclude that t cannot be enabled again before u is executed.

We may represent priority constraints in Proposition 1 with a graph in which nodes correspond to internal tasks, and in which there is an arc from task t to task u if t must have a lower priority than u. More precisely, such a *constraint graph* has nodes T and arcs:

$$\{(t, u) \mid u \neq t, t \in \text{pre}^*(u), mp(t)\} \cup \{(t, u) \mid u \in \text{pre}(t), \neg mp(u)\} . \quad (2)$$

It is not hard to check that the constraint graph is acyclic, if the system graph is.

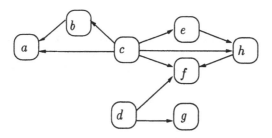

Fig. 2. Constraint graph.

For example, the constraint graph for the system in Figure 1 is shown in Figure 2. Notice that in this case $P(c) < P(b) < P(a)$ must hold. Thus, c will be executed only once for every execution of a.

However, even if the constraints in Proposition 1 are met, we still need to check not only external events, but also all internal events (t, u) such that t has a single external predecessor. For example, in Figure 1 we need to check whether external events and events (a, b), (a, c), and (b, c) can be dropped. To perform this check we use the busy-interval analysis from the previous section.

Proposition 2. *Let the priority assignment P of system (T, e, P, U, m, E) satisfy constraints in Proposition 1. If $t \in U$ and $(u, v) \in E$ are such that $\text{pre}^U(u) = \{t\}$, and the maximum length of a $P(v)$-busy interval is less than $m(t)$, then (u, v) cannot be dropped.*

Indeed, the first condition of Proposition 1 ensures that if the event (u, v) is such that $\text{pre}^U(u) = \{t\}$, then:

- both u and v will be executed in the same $P(v)$-busy interval in which t executes (since $\min(\text{pre}^*(u)) = P(u) > P(v)$),
- u will be executed exactly once for every execution of t (since $P(u) = \min(\text{pre}^*(u))$ implies that u is executed only after all of its predecessors are disabled).

Since the length of the $P(v)$-busy interval is assumed to be less then $m(t)$ it follows that t (and therefore also u) may execute in it at most once, and (u, v) cannot be dropped.

We can use Proposition 2 to check whether events not covered by Proposition 1 can be dropped. It may seem that to do that we need to compute the maximum length of $P(v)$-busy interval for every task v such that $|\text{pre}^U(u)| = 1$ for some event (u, v). In fact, we need to check only most critical such tasks. More precisely, we need to check the maximum length of $P(v)$-busy interval for every task v such that:

- either v is a merge point, or
- $|\text{pre}^U(v)| = 1$ and $v \notin \text{pre}(x)$ for any task x.

If a task does not satisfy either of these two conditions, we say that it is *safe*. If a task is safe, then it is either covered by Proposition 1 or it has a lower priority (thus more critical) successor that is not safe and will be checked. For example, in Figure 1 tasks a and b are safe, because they will be checked implicitly by computing the bound on a $P(c)$-busy interval. Tasks f, g and h are also safe because they are covered by Proposition 1.

4.1 Computing partial loads

In this section, we show that if the priority assignment satisfies conditions of Proposition 1, the partial loads are particularly easy to compute. Before that, we need to introduce some more terminology. We say that there is a *merge-free path* from t to u, and write $t \searrow u$ if there exists a sequence of tasks $t_0, \ldots, t_N$, such that $t_0 = t$, $t_N = u$, $(t_{i-1}, t_i) \in E$ for all $i = 1, \ldots, N$, and none of

$t_1, \ldots, t_{N-1}$ are merge points. Note that according to Proposition 1, $P(t_1) > P(t_2) > \ldots > P(t_N)$ must hold in this case (hence the notation $t \searrow u$).

We claim that if the priority assignment satisfies conditions of Proposition 1, then partial loads can be computed recursively as follows:

$$\delta(t, p) = \sum_{u \mid P(u) \geq p,\, t \searrow u} e(u) + \sum_{u \mid P(u) \geq p,\, t \searrow u,\, mp(u)} \delta(u, p) . \qquad (3)$$

To justify (3) it is key to observe that if a predecessor of a task is executed and there are merge-free paths between them, then the task will be executed once (and only once) before any merge points between them are executed. This is true even if there are multiple merge-free paths between the task and its predecessor. After that, some merge point between them will be executed, as captured by the recursive part of (3). Since we assume that the system graph is acyclic, (3) can be always evaluated by a single traversal of the system graph.

For example, in Figure 1 we have:

$$\delta(e, 1) = e(h) = 1 ,$$
$$\delta(c, 1) = e(e) + e(f) + e(h) + \delta(e, 1) = 4 ,$$
$$\delta(a, 1) = e(a) + e(b) + e(c) + \delta(c, 1) = 7 .$$

5   Priority Assignment Algorithm

We propose an adaptation of Audsley's priority assignment algorithm (shown in Figure 3) that searches for a valid priority assignment among all assignment satisfying constraints in Proposition 1.

Before we explain the algorithm, we need to introduce some graph operations. Given graph G with nodes N and arcs $A \subset N \times N$, we use $Src(G)$ to denote the set of *source* nodes in G, i.e. the set of nodes x such that $\forall y \in N : (y, x) \notin A$. Also, we use the phrase *"eliminate x from G"* to denote replacing G with the graph with nodes $N - \{x\}$ and arcs $\{(y, z) \in A \mid y \neq x, z \neq x\}$.

Arcs in graph G represent the constraints required by Proposition 1, so every task have to be assigned lower priority than any of its successors in G. As in Audsley's algorithm, we try to assign priorities sequentially, starting from the lowest (step 2 in Figure 3). At any point of the algorithm, graph G contains only tasks which have not been assigned a priority yet. We consider for assignment only source nodes in G (otherwise we would violate constraints in Proposition 1). We first try to find a safe source node in G (step 3), because assigning priority to such a task requires no checks. If such a task does not exist, then we try to assign priority p to a source node in G that is not safe (step 6). But, to perform required checks, we first need to compute a bound on the length of a p-busy interval (step 5).

It is not obvious that we can bound the length of a p-busy interval without a complete priority assignment. However, a closer examination of (1) and (3) reveals that we only need to know which tasks have priority lower than p, and

```
1    let G have nodes T and arcs determined by equation (2)
2    for each priority p = 1, . . . , |T|
3      if some task t ∈ Src(G) is safe then
4        assign priority p to such task t, and eliminate t from G
       else  /* no safe tasks in Src(G) */
5        let Δ be a bound on p-busy interval satisfying (1)
6        if ∃t ∈ Src(G) : ∀u ∈ preᵁ(t) : Δ < m(u) then
7          assign priority p to such task t, and eliminate t from G
         else
8          stop /* FAILURE */
         fi
       fi
     rof
```

Fig. 3. Priority assignment algorithm.

the relation between priorities of tasks t and u for each internal event (t, u). It is not hard to see that graph G contains this information. Furthermore, to compute (1) and (3), it does not matter which task has priority p, so we can compute Δ in step 5, even before we tentatively assign priority p to some task in step 6.

If we can find a task to assign priority p to (in steps 3 or 6), we do so, then we eliminate that task from graph G (steps 4 or 7), and continue the process with the next available priority. If such a task cannot be found, we terminate with failure (step 8).

For example, the graph in Figure 2 has two source nodes: c and d (both not safe). Assume that after bounding 1-busy interval, the algorithm assigns priority 1 to d. In the next iteration, priority 2 will be assigned to safe source node g. In the third iteration, the algorithm checks the bound on 3-busy interval to assure that c meets its timing constraints, and then it assigns priorities 4 and 5 to b and then a without any checks. The final bound computation is necessary before e is assigned priority 6. In the final two iterations h and f are assigned priorities 7 and 8 respectively, without any checks.

The algorithm in Figure 3 either finds a priority assignment that satisfies the schedule validity test from section 4, or such an assignment does not exist. Unfortunately, since the schedule validity test is conservative, it may be the case that a valid priority assignment exists, but our algorithm cannot find it. This may happen either because the valid assignment does not satisfy conditions of Proposition 1, or because (1) over-estimates the length of the p-busy interval for some priority p.

6   Conclusions

We have proposed a schedule validation method and a priority assignment algorithm for a model of reactive real-time systems. The algorithm is safe in the sense that whenever it finds a priority assignment, it is guaranteed that no timing violations occur in the system. However, it is conservative, in the sense that it may not be able to find a valid priority assignment, even if such an assignment exists.

Obviously, making the approach less conservative is an interesting future work. There are two areas where it is possible to improve the approach, and they both deal with the schedule validation (the priority assignment would not be conservative, if the schedule validation method was not). The proposed schedule validation method can be applied to a system only if the priority assignment satisfies some constraints. These constraints are not necessary, and it is not hard to construct an example in which every valid assignments violates these constraints. Therefore, finding weaker (and possibly even necessary) constraints is an open problem.

The second area in which the schedule validation method can be improved is better bounding of busy intervals. In our approach, partial loads are computed exactly, but combining partial loads from different tasks is done conservatively, ignoring the fact that some of their work-loads may overlap. A more precise combination could improve the validity test, and increase the utility of the overall approach.

References

1. N. C. Audsley. Optimal priority assignement and feasibility of static priority tasks with arbitrary start times. Technical report, University of York, England, 1991.
2. Neil C. Audsley, Alan Burns, M. Richardson, Ken W. Tindell, and Andy J. Wellings. Applying new scheduling theory to static priority pre-emptive scheduling. *Software Engineering Journal*, pages 284–292, September 1993.
3. Neil C. Audsley, Ken W. Tindell, and Alan Burns. The end of the line for static cyclic scheduling? In *Proceedings of the 5th Euromicro Workshop on Real-Time Systems*, pages 36–41, Oulu, Finland, 1993.
4. Felice Balarin et al. *Hardware-software co-design of embedded systems : the POLIS approach*. Kluwer Academic Publishers, 1997.
5. Felice Balarin, Harry Hsieh, Attila Jurecska, Luciano Lavagno, and Alberto Sangiovanni-Vincentelli. Formal verification of embedded systems based on CFSM networks. In *Proceedings of the 33th ACM/IEEE Design Automation Conference*, pages 568–571, June 1996.
6. Felice Balarin and Alberto Sangiovanni-Vincentelli. Schedule validation for embedded reactive real-time systems. In *Proceedings of the 34th ACM/IEEE Design Automation Conference*, June 1997.
7. C. L. Liu and James W. Layland. Scheduling algorithms for multiprogramming in a hard-realtime environment. *Journal of the Association for Computing Machinery*, 20(1):46–61, January 1973.

Mapping an Embedded Hard Real–Time Systems SDL Specification to an Analyzable Task Network — A Case Study*

Thomas Kolloch   Georg Färber

Laboratory for Process Control and Real–Time Systems, Prof. Dr.–Ing. G. Färber
Technische Universität München, Germany
{Thomas.Kolloch,Georg.Färber}@lpr.e-technik.tu-muenchen.de

Abstract. It is undoubtedly true, that the usage of a formal specification methodology in software design will reduce the development effort, particularly as embedded hard real–time systems show increasing functional complexity. We suggest the use of the language SDL even for the design of real–time systems with hard timing constraints. Emerging problems, caused by the non–deterministic semantics of SDL, can be solved by adding EDF process activation to the SDL system model. This paper describes the different steps necessary to map a SDL system specification to an analyzable task network. Considering a SDL process as a typical server process, the mapping rules are resolving the resulting interdependencies and delays, caused by possible priority inversion and blocking. Finally the study of an application example, the "Mine Control System" proofs the usabilty of the introduced methods.
Keywords: hard real–time, schedulability analysis, design methodology, Specification and Description Language SDL, EDF

1 Introduction

Rapid prototyping of embedded hard real–time systems requires a specification language as the basis for an automated design process. The "Specification and Description Language" (SDL), originally developed for the design of telecommunication systems, suits for this purpose. SDL [1] is very similar to ROOM [2], but is a standard of the ITU and has a larger user family. In contrast to the telecommunication domain, hard real–time systems require the proof that all timing constraints will be met even in a worst case scenario, because a deadline miss may result in loss of money or even in loss of lives. Unfortunately the semantics of SDL includes non–determinisms like unpredictable ordering of messages or unpredictable process activation. The addition of earliest deadline first scheduling (EDF) to the execution scheme of SDL can resolve this drawback. A survey of the rapid prototyping design methodology is given in

---

* The work presented in this paper is supported by the *Deutsche Forschungsgemeinschaft* as part of a research programme on "Rapid Prototyping for Embedded Hard Real–Time Systems" under Grant Fa 109/11-1.

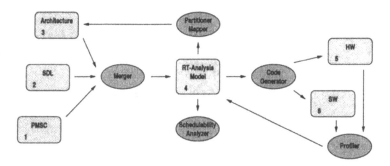

Fig. 1. Design Methodology

Fig. 1: An extended MSC [3] specification provides a description of the embedding process behaviour, i. e. describes the deadlines and the worst case scenario of the triggering external events. The architectural and detailed design is built with SDL blocks and processes. These two single models, complemented with information about the target architecture, specify all aspects of the complete system and have to be merged into the *"RT-Analysis Model"* (RTAM). In a partitioning and mapping step [4] the RTAM is linked to the target architecture [5]. Proceeding with HW/SW code generation [6], profiling should calculate the worst case execution times (WCET) of the single SDL state transitions. Now, all information, necessary for the schedulability analysis is available.

This paper is organized as follows: The next section surveys related work in the research area of timing analysis in combination with formal specification languages. Section 3 explains the schedulability proof based on EDF, followed by a description of the SDL to RTAM mapping rules. The "Mine Control System" case study (Sec. 5) evaluates the usability of the introduced methods. The last section gives a short conclusion and shows our future work.

2 Related Work

The design of embedded hard real–time systems requires a complete design methodology, which allows both the expression of functional and non–functional requirements and supports the verification of these system demands. HRT–HOOD [7] includes the explicit definition of application timing constraints and integrates appropriate scheduling paradigms with the design process, but lacks of the capability of specifying the behaviour of HOOD objects in an abstract and formal manner, e. g. with hierarchical statemachines.

Although ROOM [2] was developed for the design of real–time systems, the validation of timing properties is not included. [8] provide a heuristic, which leads to an analyzable implementation of ROOM models.

Supplementing SDL with a load and machine model, QSDL [9] uses queueing theory to calculate job and message queueing times and processor peak and average workloads.

Event Stream ES

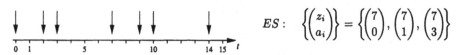

$$ES: \quad \left\{ \binom{z_i}{a_i} \right\} = \left\{ \binom{7}{0}, \binom{7}{1}, \binom{7}{3} \right\}$$

Fig. 2. Event Stream Example

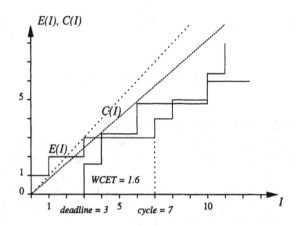

Fig. 3. Event Function $E(I)$ and Requested Computation Time $C(I)$

3 Schedulability Analysis

This section introduces the EDF based schedulability analysis for event driven hard real–time systems [10]. First, the characteristics of the embedding process have to be described, i. e. the timely behaviour of stimulating events using *Event Streams* (ES). ES describe the maximum possible number of events i of a certain type within an interval a_i [11]. Considering the occurrence of interrupts on the left side of Fig. 2, the resulting ES[1] is shown on the right. This leads to an *Event Function* $E(I)$, expressing the number of events per interval I (Fig. 3).

Single tasks are characterized by their WCET $c_{max,j}$ and a deadline d_j for the triggering event. The internal structure of an analysis task consists of atomic *receive* and *semaphore obtain* operations at the beginning of each task, a pre-emptive task body without calls to operating system services and finally atomic *send* (non–blocking), *semaphore release*, *timer* and *in*, *out* operations.

The $C(I)$ Function is defined as maximum computation time requested and due within interval I. For a single task $C_j(I)$ can be calculated easily from $E_j(I)$ by shifting by the deadline d_j and multiplication with the WCET $c_{max,j}$ (Fig. 3). While the resulting $C(I)$ for a number of *independent* tasks on a computing node is simply the sum of all $C_j(I)$ functions, Gresser developed an algorithm

---

[1] there are no 2 simultaneous events, i. e. only 1 event occurs in interval 0, a maximum of 2 events in interval 1 and a maximum of 3 events in interval 3, repetition with cycle 7

to determine $C(I)$ for a network of communicating tasks, taking into account dependencies[2] of the triggering events, precedence constraints, inter node communication and mutual exclusion. For EDF he proved, that all tasks on one node meet their deadlines, if the resulting $C(I)$ always runs under the bisector which specifies the available computing time in each interval.

$$C(I) \leq I \quad \forall \ I \geq 0 \qquad (1)$$

One crucial point in schedulabilty analysis is the avoidance of priority inversion in critical regions. For the analysis of complex structures of mutual exclusion, i.e. several tasks in different and overlapping critical regions, [10] explains two strategies to resolve the edges of a *"priority inversion graph"*: Either by shifting the deadline of the task to a new shorter, but during runtime fixed deadline or by taking into account a dynamic deadline inheritance protocol.

4 Mapping SDL to the RT–Analysis Model

There are prerequisites, which have to be satisfied for the translation of a SDL system to the RTAM: A static allocation of processes to processing units is mandatory and dynamic process instantiation can not be considered in the moment, i.e. most of the object oriented language extensions of SDL–92 are forbidden in a SDL model. Further language restrictions are: no usage of services and priority inputs, continuous signal trigger conditions and signal $SAVE$ statements. A general requirement — valid for all real–time systems — is saveness. Saveness means, that in spite of any possible stimulation the system will regain a save (rest) state, especially there are no receive/send – receive/send loops. For a save system the algorithm, described in Sec. 4.4 will terminate.

4.1 SDL Process — Server Behaviour

The similarity of the analysis model (Sec. 3) and the statemachine structure of the SDL process allows an automatical RTAM generation. For this purpose the hierarchical SDL block composition is transformed into a network of communicating (leaf) SDL processes. If there are no dependencies between these processes, the simple addition of the WCET $c_{max,j}$ will be allowed for the calculation of the overall $C(I)$. Therefore the interferences within this process structure have to be resolved.

Unfortunately, a SDL process (statemachine) has usually server process behaviour, with different sources of incoming messages and different destinations of outgoing messages. The RTAM, corresponding to a server process, has the process duplicated and protected in an area of mutual exclusion (Fig. 4(a)). Duplication takes into account a possible worst case delay, caused by an earlier message, mutual exclusion protects the ordering of execution. Preemption of

---

[2] *"event dependency matrix"* (EDM)

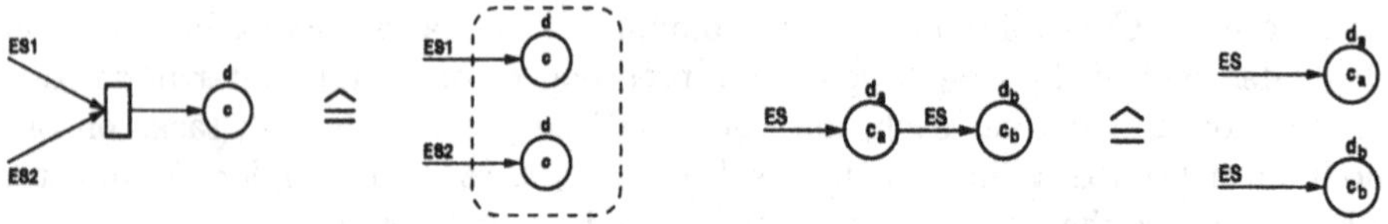

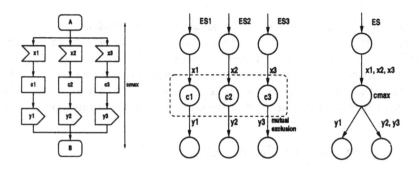

Fig. 4. (a) Server Process and (b) Process Precedences

Fig. 5. Analysis Model — (a) different and (b) same message source

a state transition is not allowed in SDL semantics, but can occur in the implementation. Depending on the type of implemented task system (Sec. 6), a transaction may be even preempted by a state transition of the same SDL process with shorter deadline, therefore the access to common SDL state information has to be synchronized by mutual exclusion. Using "tight integration" for code generation, which maps to one task per SDL process and one message queue per task, the order of computation is managed by the queue and therefore the mutual exclusion is not necessary in the implementation. But regarding the possible delay, caused by the computation of a reaction to an earlier received message, the analysis must take into account a mutual exclusion too.

4.2 Mapping SDL Statemachines

Depending on the source of the incoming messages (one single ES or serveral different ES), a statemachine has to be mapped to different RTAM trees, either with individual execution times c_i and mutual exclusion (Fig. 5 (a)) or to one single task (Fig. 5 (b)) with $c = c_{max} = Max(c_i)$.

If the same message triggers a transition in different states (Fig. 6, states A, B, C), the RTAM only takes into account the maximum computation time $c_{max} = Max(c_i)$. Depending on the destinations of the outgoing messages, the target analysis node can be derived. Assigning an asterix symbol to states and message receive statements, SDL syntax provides a kind of behavioural hierarchy like ROOMCharts [2]. This conforms to a state or a message enumeration and can be translated using the former explained mapping rules.

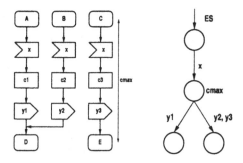

Fig. 6. Analysis Model — same message in different states

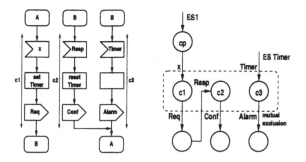

Fig. 7. Analysis Model — Dependent Timer

4.3 Mapping SDL Timers

SDL Timers are internal events, which can occur independently or dependently on external events. An example of a independent timer event is the cyclic activation of polling tasks in the case study (Sec. 5). A dependent timer event is e. g. the surveillance of a timely response to a server request. The first type has to be mapped to an analysis node with its own, the timer behaviour describing ES (2). The dependent timers mapping rule is identical to the former one, but supplemented with additional event dependency information ([10], Fig. 7). The minimum distance between the stimulating external event and the internal timer event results from the sum of minimum computation times of the tasks in the same precedence system plus the timer interval (3).

$$ES_{Timer} = ES_1 = \begin{pmatrix} z_1 \\ 0 \end{pmatrix} \quad (2) \qquad\qquad EDM = \begin{pmatrix} z_1 & c_p + T \\ 0 & z_1 \end{pmatrix} \quad (3)$$

4.4 Mapping Algorithm

The mapping algorithm starts the transformation at each triggering external event or each independent SDL Timer. Then, for each environment handling

Table 1. Mine Control System — Timing Constraints and Analysis Parameters

	P/S	Cycle z_i	Interv. a_i	Deadl. d_i	WCET c_i	Deadl. d_i	WCET c_i	Deadl. $d_{i,mutex}$	WCET $c_{i,mutex}$
CH_4 Sensor	P	$1\,s$	$0\,s$	$1\,s$	$0.350\,s$	$1\,s$	$0.350\,s$		
CO Sensor	P	$5\,s$	$0\,s$	$5\,s$	$0.125\,s$	$5\,s$	$0.075\,s$	$1\,s$	$0.050\,s$
Air Flow	P	$5\,s$	$0\,s$	$5\,s$	$0.125\,s$	$5\,s$	$0.075\,s$	$1\,s$	$0.050\,s$
H_2O Flow	P	$3\,s$	$0\,s$	$3\,s$	$0.075\,s$			$1\,s$	$0.075\,s$
H_2O Level	S	$100\,s$	$0\,s$	$20\,s$	$0.150\,s$	$20\,s$	$0.025\,s$	$1\,s$	$0.125\,s$
Operator	S	$10\,s$	$0\,s$	$1\,s$	$0.175\,s$	$1\,s$	$0.175\,s$		

SDL process, the consecutive SDL processes are identified by means of *SEND* statements. In a next step dependent SDL Timers have to be detected and the assignment of their own ES have to be prepared. Subsequently all state transitions, triggered by the same message, are eliminated, and a replacement with maximum computation time has to be defined. Finally, the analysis node, appropriate to the resulting dependent state transitions, has to be multiplied in an area of mutual exclusion. The algorithm continues with the next SDL process in the precedence system, until no more *SEND* statements can be found.

Applying this transformation to a SDL system, the resulting RTAM will consist of serveral independent analysis task precedence systems (Fig. 4 (b)), whereby each network is triggered by a different type of ES. The single branches of the RTAM tree are linked by regions with mutual exclusion. All analysis nodes in one precedence system have the same deadline, i. e. are fixed to the messages, sent through a precedence system. This leads to the fact, that different SDL state transitions in one SDL process may have different timing constraints.

5 The Mine Control System

The "Mine Control System" case study is originally described in [7, pp. 145–224] as an example of modelling a real–time system with HRT–HOOD. The purpose of the pump is to manage the water level in a mining environment.

5.1 Functional and Non–Functional Requirements

The pump monitors the water level in a sump. According to a high level detector or to operator interaction, the pump is turned on and the sump is drained, until a low level detector responses or the pump is turned off by the operator. The pump should only be allowed to operate, if the CH_4 concentration is below a critical level. The operator console and the level detectors communicate via interrupts with the pump control station. Additional sensors for monitoring the environment are polled in different cycles. Critical levels of CH_4, CO or an unsufficient air flow must be signalled to the operator as an alarm. In case of an operating pump, the water flow in the pump can be measured. A critical

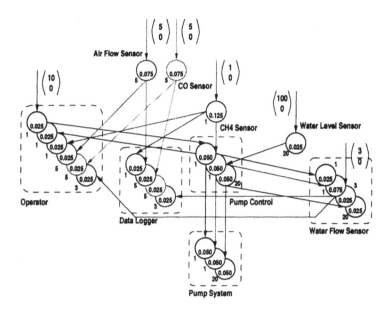

Fig. 8. Complete Analysis Model

CH_4 level must lead to an undelayed shut off of the pump. A summary of the tasks characteristics, their cycle times, respectively the minimum distance of the stimulating external events and the appropriate deadline is listed in Tab. 1.

5.2 Analysis Model and Analysis Results

As a representative, the analysis model of the pump control process (Fig. 9 (a)) will be explained. Although six different messages are consumed, the number of different message sources evaluates to three, therefore the analysis node must be tripled in an area of mutual exclusion. The upper left node in the pump control region of Fig. 8, triggered by an operators message, has three message outputs, whereby one is the response to the operators request. Since there are no further send statements in the consecutive processes, the forks of the analysis precedence tree (mapping algorithm) end in the next nodes.

The execution times are derived from the HRT–HOOD example [7, pp. 145–224]. To demonstrate the influence of priority inversion avoidance, the values of the WCETs are multiple oversized, compared to the complexity of the processes. The WCETs of the individual SDL state transitions can be seen in the appropriate analysis nodes in Fig. 8. Summing up the WCETs c_i of the nodes of one precedence system results in analysis parameters, summarized in Tab. 1.

In a next step a possible priority inversion in critical regions is considered by shifting the task deadlines to the shortest deadline in the region. The stimulating event stream remains untouched by this manipulation. The new deadlines calculate to $d_{i,mutex} = 1\,s$. The sums of the $c_{i,mutex}$ in the critical regions of one precedence system are shown in the last column of Tab. 1.

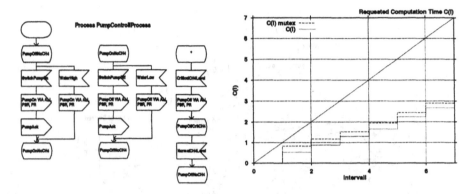

Fig. 9. (a) Pump Control SDL Statemachine and (b) Analysis Results

The result of the schedulability analysis can be seen in Fig. 9 (b). The distance between the $C(I)$ and the $C(I)_{mutex}$ functions shows the influence of the manipulated deadlines. By shortening the deadlines, the analysis has to schedule more computation time as possibly needed to meet all deadlines, i. e. the laxity, available for further tasks, may be lost. This leads to design rules to evade this effect: Keep computation times in critical region as small as possible; Minimize the number of nodes in critical region, i. e. avoid SDL process server behaviour, and minimize the number of critical regions by combining similar processes, e. g. combine the cyclic polling processes.

6 Conclusion

In this paper, we focused on the integration of a schedulabilty proof in the design flow for embedded hard real–time systems, based on the language SDL. This integration is done, by adding EDF semantics to SDL process activation to resolve non–predictable system behaviour and by mapping the SDL system to an analyzable task network.

The introduced SDL to RTAM mapping rules and algorithm allow the automation of this transformation and therefore the integration in a rapid prototyping design environment. To cover the complete syntax and semantic of SDL, further mapping rules are necessary. Forced by server behaviour of SDL processes, the mapping creates many areas of mutual exclusion. For this reason the system designer should get support by design rules, which help to develop an efficient and analyzable software architecture.

A trade–off appears, regarding the way of code generation,[3] done by the SDT CASE tool. Considering the fine granularity of a SDL process, — the transitions of a SDL statemachine are normally short — the generated task system is fine granular too. This leads to the phenomenon, that the resulting system will mainly do task switching, instead of processing real data. A solution for this

---

[3] tight integration to the "Real–Time Executive for Multiprocessor Systems RTEMS"

effect could be the implementation of a complete analysis precedence system in a single task (similar to [12]). The minimization of the number of context switches and the number of *receive* and *send* calls, should result in a more efficient implementation.

References

[1] ITU-T. *ITU-T Recommendation Z.100: CCITT Specification and Description Language (SDL)*, June 1994.

[2] Bran Selic, Garth Gullekson, and Paul T. Ward. *Real-Time Object-Oriented Modeling*. John Wiley & Sons, Inc., 605 Third Avenue, New York, 1994.

[3] ITU-T. *ITU-T Recommendation Z.120: Message Sequence Chart (MSC)*, September 1994.

[4] Georg Färber, Franz Fischer, Thomas Kolloch, and Annette Muth. Improving processor utilization with a task classification model based application specific hard real-time architecture. In *Proceedings of the 1997 International Workshop on Real-Time Computing Systems and Applications (RTCSA'97)*, Academia Sinica, Taipei, Taiwan, ROC, October 27–29 1997.

[5] Franz Fischer, Thomas Kolloch, Annette Muth, and Georg Färber. A configurable target architecture for rapid prototyping high performance control systems. In Hamid R. Arabnia et al., editors, *Proceedings of the International Conference on Parallel and Distributed Processing Techniques and Applications (PDPTA'97)*, volume 3, pages 1382–1390, Las Vegas, Nevada, USA, June 30 – July 3 1997.

[6] Franz Fischer, Annette Muth, and Georg Färber. Towards interprocess communication and interface synthesis for a heterogeneous real–time rapid prototyping environment. In *Proceedings of the 6th International Workshop on Hardware/Software Co-Design — Codes/CASHE '98*, pages 35–39, Seattle, Washington, USA, 15–18 March 1998. IEEE, IEEE Computer Society Press.

[7] Alan Burns and Andy Wellings. *HRT-HOOD: A Structured Design Method for Hard Real-Time Ada Systems*. Elsevier Science B. V., Amsterdam, The Netherlands, 1995.

[8] M. Saksena, P. Freedman, and P. Rodziewicz. Guidelines for automated implementation of executable object oriented models for real-time embedded control systems. In *Proceedings of the IEEE Real-Time Systems Symposium (RTSS'97)*, San Francisco, California, December 2–5 1997. IEEE Computer Society Press.

[9] Marc Diefenbruch, Elke Heck, Jörg Hintelmann, and Bruno Müller–Clostermann. Performance evaluation of sdl systems adjunct by queueing models. In *SDL'95 With MSC in CASE, Proceedings of the Seventh SDL Forum*, pages 231–242, Oslo, Norway, September 1995.

[10] Klaus Gresser. *Echtzeitnachweis ereignisgesteuerter Realzeitsysteme*. Number 268 in Fortschrittsberichte VDI, Reihe 10. VDI-Verlag, Düsseldorf, 1993. Dissertation am Lehrstuhl für Prozessrechner, Technische Universität München.

[11] Klaus Gresser. An event model for deadline verification of hard real–time systems. In *Proc. Fifth Euromicro Workshop on Real Time Systems*, pages 118–123, Oulu, Finland, June 1993. IEEE.

[12] Ralf Henke, Hartmut König, and Andreas Mitschele-Thiel. Derivation of efficient implementations from SDL specifications employing data referencing, integrated packet framing and activity threads. In *Proceeding of the Eighth SDL Forum, SDL'97 Time for Testing SDL, MSC and Trends*, pages 397–414, Evry, France, September 1997. Elsevier Science Publishers B.V.

Efficient User-Level I/O in the ARX Real-Time Operating System*

Yangmin Seo, Jungkeun Park, and Seongsoo Hong

School of Electrical Engineering,
Seoul National University, Seoul 151-742, Korea.
{seoym,jkpark,sshong}@redwood.snu.ac.kr
http://redwood.snu.ac.kr

Abstract. User-level I/O gets increasingly important for embedded real-time applications, since it can allow programmers to write flexible and efficient device drivers for proprietary devices. To support user-level I/O for embedded systems, an operating system must provide a mechanism to deliver an external interrupt from an I/O device to a process in a predictable and efficient manner. In this paper, we propose an efficient user-level I/O scheme which is based on a newly designed user-level signal mechanism. This scheme which exploits the multithreading architecture of the kernel such as dynamic stack binding and scheduling event upcalls can overcome the problems of traditional signal implementations.

We have fully implemented our scheme on the ARX real-time operating system that we already developed, and performed experiments to demonstrate its performance. The experiments clearly show that our user-level I/O scheme allows for a predictable delivery of external interrupts with a low overhead.

1   Introduction

User-level I/O becomes increasingly important for applications that require high performance. In a network of workstations environment, for example, data transfer between the system memory and a high speed network interface can be significantly sped up, if direct memory access (DMA) is supported at user-level, without involvement of the kernel. With user-level DMA, one can avoid costly context switches, protection mode crossings, and data copies between layers. In addition to this performance merit, user-level device handling allows for the following extra benefits.

- Flexibility: When new devices are added, programmers need not rebuild the kernel since device drivers are part of application code.

---

* The work reported in this paper was supported in part by Engineering Research Center for Advanced Control and Instrumentation (ERC-ACI) under Grant 96K3-0707-02-06-2, and KOSEF under Grants 981-0924-127-2 and 97-0102-05-01-3.

- Efficiency: Compact and efficient device drivers can be written, since they can be customized for an application at hand.
- Portability: User-level device drivers can be easily ported between vastly different operating systems such as MS-DOS and Unix.

These benefits render user-level device handling very attractive to device driver writers.

On the other hand, most of the conventional operating systems do not allow user-level I/O, since uncontrolled device accesses may jeopardize system security and consistency in the presence of malicious or negligent users. Such operating systems work as a device manager resolving conflicts among users that request the same device simultaneously.

However, even in general computer systems, one can find devices which are exclusively used by a dedicated process. For example, in a client/server window system like the X Window system, a graphics display device and a mouse input device are exclusively accessed by a server process. In embedded real-time systems where proprietary devices are commonly used, programmers can greatly benefit from user-level I/O, since most devices are exclusively accessed by dedicated processes.

For user-level I/O in embedded real-time systems, the operating system must be able to efficiently dispatch user interrupt handlers in a predictable manner in response to external interrupts. We could use Unix signal mechanisms for this purpose. Unfortunately, the traditional signal mechanism is not an excellent solution for embedded systems, since a signal delivery can be indefinitely delayed, if the receiving process is blocked in non-interruptible mode. In this paper, we propose a new signal mechanism that can eliminate this problem. It is designed to exploit the multithreading architecture of the ARX kernel, thus able to provide predictable signal delivery with a low latency. We have fully implemented the signal mechanism in the ARX kernel and report its performance.

2   Related Work

To allow user-level I/O, the kernel must provide a back door through which a user process can directly access I/O devices in user-mode. Moreover, the kernel must be able to dispatch user interrupt handlers in response to interrupts from I/O devices. Most of Unix variants including Linux do not support user-level interrupt dispatching. Thus, if programmers want user-level I/O in Linux, they need to use only polling-based I/O through the kernel-provided back door to device registers [3].

On the other hand, SGI's Irix with the REACT real-time capability allows kernel-dispatched user handlers [7]. A kernel interrupt handler of Irix performs a kernel/user mode change and then invokes a user interrupt handler. While this scheme allows a low interrupt latency due to its simplicity, it has a serious drawback: the execution of a user interrupt handler is severely restricted. Since

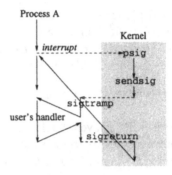

Fig. 1. Handling asynchronous signals in 4.3 BSD

a user interrupt handler is called and executed in a special context of the kernel interrupt handler, a user interrupt handler is prohibited from making system calls, performing floating-point calculations, or referring to memory locations that cause a page fault.

As an alternative to kernel dispatching, we could use any of event notification mechanisms such as Unix signal mechanisms. A signal is an operating system entity generated and delivered by the kernel on the occurrence of an event. A signal is received and handled by a user process via a user-defined signal handler. Figure 1 pictorially depicts signal handling in 4.3 BSD [4]. When an interrupt occurs, the kernel calls a user signal handler via a wrapper function called *signal-trampoline* code. As shown in the figure, a user signal handler is executed in the context of the receiving process. This causes serious problems that prevent us from using traditional signal mechanisms for embedded real-time systems. First, signal delivery can be indefinitely postponed, if the receiving process is blocked in non-interruptible mode. Second, signal delivery and handling incurs a large overhead, since it requires multiple protection mode crossings and context switches, as shown in Figure 1.

The ARX operating system solves these problems using its multithreading architecture. First, it allows a separate thread to handle asynchronous signals generated by external interrupts. Thus, asynchronous signals are immediately delivered and handled, even if a thread is blocked in kernel-mode. This is made possible, since the ARX kernel is designed to dynamically allocate kernel stacks to newly runnable threads. Second, the ARX kernel merely passes a signal to a user-level scheduler and gives it an absolute authority to dispatch a handler thread. Thus, the ARX signal handling mechanism can be implemented at user-level and be best optimized for user-level I/O. Our experimental results show the significant performance improvement of the scheme over conventional signal mechanisms.

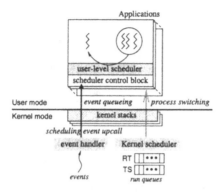

Fig. 2. Overall architecture of the ARX kernel

3 ARX Real-Time Operating System

ARX is a stand-alone operating system that we have developed for real-time and multimedia applications [2]. It was designed to support flexible two-level scheduling, versatile multithreading, and efficient user-level I/O. First, scheduling in ARX is done in a nested fashion such that the kernel schedules processes and a user-level scheduler schedules threads in a process, as shown in Figure 2. The kernel scheduler runs the weighted fair queuing algorithm in that processes are scheduled and run according to their shares of CPU bandwidth [6].

ARX supports pure user-level multithreading in that threads are hidden inside a process and are not visible to the kernel. A user-level scheduler that can directly manage threads can realize any of the well-known real-time scheduling algorithms such as rate-monotonic scheduling or earliest deadline first scheduling [5]. To support such preemptive scheduling polices at user-level, the ARX kernel relies on two mechanisms called *dynamic stack binding* and *scheduling event upcall*.

When a user-level thread blocks in kernel-mode, a kernel often gets confused and blocks an entire process possessing the thread, even if the process has other runnable threads. To avoid this problem, when a thread is blocked or preempted in kernel-mode, the ARX kernel creates a stack and binds it to the next runnable thread. We refers to this scheme as dynamic stack binding. When a blocked thread gets resumed, the kernel collects the used stack and recycles it.

To efficiently propagate kernel events to user-level schedulers, the ARX kernel provides the scheduling event upcall scheme. When an event occurs, the kernel enqueues it to the event queue and calls a user-level scheduler. Then it performs thread scheduling in response to that event. Currently, the ARX kernel supports following four types of events.

System time
Next TIMER upcall time
Head index of event queue
Tail index of event queue
Scheduler lock flag
Thread context
Event queue

Fig. 3. Scheduler control block

- BLOCK: When a thread is blocked in the kernel waiting for an event such as I/O events, the kernel sends a user-level scheduler a BLOCK event.
- WAKEUP: When a blocked thread wakes up in kernel-mode, the kernel sends a WAKEUP event.
- TIMER: When the timer expires at time preset by a user-level scheduler, the kernel sends a TIMER event to that particular scheduler. Upon receiving a TIMER upcall, a user-level scheduler reschedules threads or checks deadline misses of a thread according to the policy it implements.
- SIGNAL: When an event associated with a signal occurs, the kernel sends a SIGNAL event to a user-level scheduler. Upon receiving a SIGNAL upcall, a user-level scheduler dispatches a handler thread according to its priority.

To reduce the communication overhead incurred between a user-level scheduler and the kernel, the kernel communicates with the scheduler through shared memory mapped onto an application's address space. It is called a *scheduler control block*, and its contents are shown in Figure 3.

4 User-Level Signal Handling in ARX

4.1 Signal Classification

The ARX operating system supports signals conforming to POSIX 1003.1 [1] with real-time signal extensions including signal queuing and reliable and deterministic signal notification. These signals are numbered 1 through 31. Signals between 1 and 20 have predefined names, which include 13 signals required by POSIX, six job control signals, and one memory protection signal. The remaining signals numbered 21 (SIGRTMIN) through 31 (SIGRTMAX) are reserved for real-time applications.

For a single threaded process, the ARX kernel works in the same way as other Unix variants do – it dispatches signal handlers by itself. For a multithreaded process, on the other hand, the kernel simply passes signals to a user process, and its user-level scheduler dispatches signal handlers. For performance, the kernel intercepts and handles certain signals. They include job control signals and signals with default actions. A signal is subject to a default action such

```
void signal_thread(int signum)
{
    while (1) {
        q = find signal in the signal queue;
        if (q) {
            remove q from the signal queue;
            if (need siginfo)
                (sighandler[signum])(signum, q);
            else
                (sighandler[signum])(signum);
        } else
            thread_suspend(thread_self());
    }
}
```

Fig. 4. Structure of a signal handling thread

as *abort, exit,* and *ignore,* if no signal handler is registered for the signal. Such kernel filtering prevents from invoking a user-level scheduler to deal with signals to be ignored.

Signals are classified into synchronous and asynchronous. Synchronous ones are exceptions that happen in response to the execution of a process. They include SIGFPE, SIGILL, SIGSEGV, and SIGBUS. Asynchronous ones are external interrupts to a process's execution. All the signals except these four are asynchronous signals.

4.2 Handling Synchronous and Asynchronous Signals

The ARX kernel handles synchronous and asynchronous signals differently. For a synchronous signal, the kernel requires that the generating thread catch and handle it. Thus, each thread is allowed to have its own signal mask so that it can enable or disable a specific subset of synchronous signals.

An asynchronous signal is handled by a dedicated *handler thread* which is created when a user process calls `sigaction()` function to register a handler function. The structure of a handler thread is illustrated in Figure 4. Each asynchronous signal has its own delivery queue for an associated handler. Once invoked, a handler thread takes a signal from the signal queue and calls a real signal handler function. A signal thread is cancelled when the user process unregisters the signal handler through `sigaction()` function. Unlike synchronous signals, a process, instead of a thread, has a signal mask for asynchronous signals.

4.3 Delivering Signals and Dispatching Handlers

In Unix, a process becomes aware of the occurrence of a signal, (1) when the process is dispatched, (2) when it returns from an interrupt, or (3) when it returns

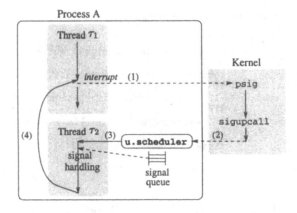

Fig. 5. Handling asynchronous signals in ARX

from a system call. In ARX, a process gets immediately notified regardless of the state of the current thread. To do so, the ARX kernel uses a SIGNAL upcall.

During a SIGNAL upcall, the kernel copies the signal-pending bitmask of the process into the event queue and clears the bitmask. It also moves signals queued at the process structure into the *signal queue* located in the scheduler control block. Each entry in the queue carries information such as a signal number, a signal code, and a signal value, as defined in the siginfo structure of POSIX 1003.1.

At the end of a SIGNAL upcall, the kernel invokes a user-level scheduler which, in turn, takes an entry out of the *signal queue*. It first looks at the signal code to determine if the signal is generated synchronously or asynchronously. If it is asynchronous, the user-level scheduler resumes a handler thread. Otherwise, it arranges the generating thread to handle the exception.

5   User-level I/O Interfaces and Implementation

The ARX kernel supports both kernel-dispatched user interrupt handlers and signal-based user interrupt handlers so as to allow programmers to choose the best I/O handling scheme for each device in the system. We recommend that programmers sparingly use kernel-dispatched user interrupt handlers only for the cases where a certain device cannot tolerate a large interrupt latency, or a handler is very short and takes little time to execute. In either case, programmers are required to write an interrupt handler with extreme care, since it runs on a special context of the kernel. On the other hand, if programmers want a safe and flexible interrupt handler or if a handler involves complex operations such as floating point calculations, kernel-dispatched user interrupt handlers cannot be used. We describe application programming interfaces (API) that support both types of user-level I/O. These APIs were implemented in the ARX operating system.

The first step to activate user-level I/O is to request a right to access the I/O device. The following functions are used to request and release the access right.

- uio_request(ioa_start, ioa_end, [type]): This function grants a user process a right to access I/O addresses from ioa_start to ioa_end. If these addresses correspond to memory-mapped devices, they must be page-aligned. If the microprocessor supports both I/O mapped and memory-mapped addresses for I/O devices, an addressing type (type parameter) must be specified as either IOMAP or MEMORYMAP. The kernel manages a list of address pairs granted to user processes. When invoked, this function checks user-level I/O collision using the list. If no collision is detected, it returns an integer handle to denote granted addresses. Otherwise, it returns zero. The ARX kernel realizes I/O address protection with the memory protection mechanism of the underlying microprocessor. If a page possesses memory addresses of several different devices, it is possible for a process to access devices owned by other processes. Thus, uio_request requires that memory-mapped devices be page-aligned.
- uio_release(handle): This function releases an access right for device addresses denoted by handle.

The second step is to install a user interrupt handler for the I/O device. The following functions are used to control interrupts at user-level.

- uio_int_request(irq, handler, type, flag): This function registers a user interrupt handler. The type can be either KERNEL_DISPATCH or USER_DISPATCH. If USER_DISPATCH is selected, this function assigns the interrupt a free signal number chosen between SIGRTMIN and SIGRTMAX. If the calling process is a multithreaded application, this function also creates a handler thread. If the flag is zero, it returns after disabling the interrupt. If the function is successful, it returns a pointer to an irq_info structure containing the irq number, a signal number, and a thread identifier. Otherwise, it returns zero indicating an error. The thread identifier is needed to allow the process to control the attributes of a handler thread such as a priority.
- uio_int_release(irq, flag): This function unregisters a user interrupt handler. If flag is one, it also cancels the associated handler thread.
- uio_int_enable(irq), uio_int_disable(irq): This function enables or disables an interrupt. If the registered handler is a signal-based handler, it simply masks or unmasks the associated signal without actually disabling a real interrupt.

6 Performance

The performance of the ARX user-level I/O scheme is critically dependent on the efficiency of the ARX signal handling mechanism. To demonstrate the per-

Table 1. Measured signal handling latencies in Linux and ARX

	Linux signal	ARX signal	Performance increase
In user-mode	19.15	17.07	11 %
In kernel-mode	30.80	17.07	45 %
Return from handler	11.97	1.85	85 %

(unit: μs)

formance improvement of the ARX signals over the Unix signals, we measured signal handling latencies in ARX and Unix. The signal handling latency is defined as a time duration between when the first instruction of a kernel interrupt handler starts to execute and when the first instruction of a signal handler starts to execute.

As a Unix system, we selected Linux version 2.0.31. Since user-level interrupt handling was not supported in Linux, we could not associate an arbitrary interrupt with a signal. Thus, we used an alarm signal in our experiment, since it was generated in response to a clock interrupt. To measure true signal handling latencies, we deducted the execution time of the clock interrupt handler from the measured latency.

For the experiment, we wrote a simple audio playback program that ran on a PC equipped with an Intel 100 MHz Pentium processor, 256K bytes of secondary cache, 32M bytes of EDO DRAMs, and a Sound Blaster card. The audio player program periodically transfered a block of 4K-byte audio data to the audio device using user-level DMA. The device issued an end-of-DMA interrupt at the end of each DMA transfer, and the player, in turn, started the next transfer.

Table 1 shows signal handling latencies measured in ARX and Linux. We listed latencies for two cases where the receiving process runs in user-mode and in kernel-mode. Table 1 clearly shows that the ARX signals experience much lower latencies than the Linux signals. More importantly, the signal handling latencies in ARX are constant regardless of the state of the receiving process, whereas those in Linux greatly vary up to 61%. This is because an interrupt is serviced by a dedicated handler thread in ARX. This allows predictable and deterministic signal handling which renders the ARX user-level I/O scheme ideal for embedded real-time systems. The last row of Table 1 shows times to take for control to return from a signal handler. Linux incurs much larger overhead than ARX, since a Linux signal handler needs to make a system call to restore the signal mask managed inside the kernel.

7 Conclusions

We have presented an efficient user-level I/O scheme that is based on a user-level signal mechanism designed for the ARX real-time operating system. This scheme which exploits the multithreading architecture of the kernel allows for predictable and deterministic signal delivery with a low latency. It overcomes the problems of traditional signal implementations by making the kernel simply pass a signal to a process via an upcall and letting a user-level scheduler dispatch a signal hander, and by dedicating a handler thread to an asynchronous signal.

This scheme allows for the following benefits. First, it offers fully configurable signals for a variety of applications. Since most signals are managed at user-level, we can implement distinct signal specifications such as 4.3 BSD, System V, and POSIX signals on a single operating system. As a result, programmers can use different sets of signals by changing the libraries. Second, this scheme significantly lowers the signal handling overhead, since it can reduce kernel intervention during signal handling. Third, this scheme is very suitable for I/O-driven real-time embedded systems where tasks are often triggered by interrupts from external devices such as sensors and actuators. Programmers can easily configure such systems by assigning a signal number to each external device interrupt and installing a handler function. Moreover, this scheme allows threads and interrupt handlers to run under a single scheduling policy such as fixed priority scheduling. This will greatly aid programmers in scheduling real-time tasks. Finally, this scheme enables threads and interrupt handlers to get easily synchronized via various synchronization primitives provided by a user library. The cost of such synchronization primitives will be very cheap, since such primitives do not require costly kernel supports.

We have fully implemented our scheme on the ARX real-time operating system, and performed experiments to demonstrate its performance. The experimental results clearly show that our user-level signal mechanism outperforms traditional signal implementations.

References

1. Institute for Electrical and Electronic Engineers. POSIX Part 1: System application program interface, 1996.
2. S. Hong, Y. Seo, and J. Park. ARX/ULTRA: A new real-time kernel architecture for supporting user-level threads. Technical Report SNU-EE-TR-1997-3, School of Electrical Engineering, Seoul National University, August 1997.
3. M.K. Johnson. The Linux kernel hackers' guide, 1997.
4. S. Leffler, M. McKusick, M. J. Karels, and J. Quarterman. *The Design and Implementation of the 4.3BSD UNIX Operating System*. Addison Wesley, 1990.
5. C. Liu and J. Layland. Scheduling algorithms for multiprogramming in a hard real-time environment. *Journal of the ACM*, 20(1):46–61, Jan 1973.
6. A. K. Parekh and R. G. Gallager. A generalized processor sharing approach to flow control in integrated services networks: The single-node case. *IEEE/ACM Transactions on Networking*, 1(3):344–357, December 1993.
7. Silicon Graphics, Inc. $REACT^{TM}$ in $IRIX^{TM}$ 6.4. Technical report, Jan 1997.

Machine Descriptions to Build Tools for Embedded Systems

Norman Ramsey and Jack W. Davidson

Department of Computer Science
University of Virginia
Charlottesville, VA 22903
nr@cs.virginia.edu   jwd@cs.virginia.edu

Abstract. Because of poor tools, developing embedded systems can be unnecessarily hard. Machine descriptions based on register-transfer lists (RTLs) have proven useful in building retargetable compilers, but not in building other retargetable tools. Simulators, assemblers, linkers, debuggers, and profilers are built by hand if at all—previous machine descriptions have lacked the detail and precision needed to generate them. This paper presents detailed and precise machine-description techniques that are based on a new formalization of RTLs. Unlike previous notations, these RTLs have a detailed, unambiguous, and machine-independent semantics, which makes them ideal for supporting automatic generation of retargetable tools. The paper also gives examples of λ-RTL, a notation that makes it possible for human beings to read and write RTLs without becoming overwhelmed by machine-dependent detail.

Machine Descriptions for Machine-Level Tools

Developers for embedded systems often work without the benefit of the best software tools. Embedded systems can have unusual architectural features, and new processors can be introduced rapidly. Development is typically done on stock processors, and cross-development can make it hard to get basic compilers, assemblers, linkers, and debuggers, let alone profilers, tracers, test-coverage analyzers, or general code-modification tools. One reason such tools are seldom available is that machine-dependent detail makes it hard to build them.

This paper describes work in progress on Computer Systems Description Languages (CSDL). CSDL descriptions are intended not only to provide precise, formal notations for describing machine-dependent detail, but also to support automatic generation of useful tools. Moreover, CSDL descriptions are intended to be *reusable*, so we can build up a body of descriptions, e.g., of popular embedded processors, that will be useful for building future as well as current tools.

The design goals for CSDL are

- CSDL should support a variety of machine-level tools while remaining independent of any one in particular.

- Descriptions should be composed from simple components. Each component should describe, as much as possible, a single property of the target machine. Such properties might include calling conventions, representations of instructions, semantics of instructions, power consumption, code size, pipeline implementations, memory hierarchy, or other properties.
- An application writer should be able to derive useful tools from partial descriptions. For example, an application writer working entirely at the assembly-language level or above should not have to describe binary representations of instructions.
- Components of descriptions should be reusable. For example, many different tools targeted to the ARM might benefit by reusing a standard formalization of the "ARM Thumb instruction set."

The contributions of this paper are semantic and notational. CSDL uses *register transfers* to specify the semantics of machine instructions. In previous work, the exact meaning of register transfers is known only in the context of a particular machine. By contrast, CSDL gives register transfers a detailed, unambiguous, and machine-independent semantics. The detail will make CSDL useful for building a variety of machine-level tools, because information (e.g., byte order) that is left implicit in other formalisms is made explicit in CSDL. The notational contribution is a metalanguage, called λ-RTL, which makes it possible to write register-transfer semantics without having to write all of the detail explicitly. The *λ-RTL translator* bridges the gap between the concise metalanguage and the fully explicit register transfers. λ-RTL also has a semantic abstraction mechanism that gives the author of a specification some freedom to choose the level of detail at which to specify the effects of particular instructions. This paper describes our detailed form of register transfers, then shows how λ-RTL makes it possible to omit much of the detail from the form of specification that is read and written by people. The paper is illustrated with excerpts from our semantic descriptions of popular microprocessors.

Related Work

Machine descriptions have been successful in building retargetable compilers, but the descriptions used in compilers are hard to reuse, because they typically combine information about the target machine with information about the compiler. For example, "machine descriptions" written using tools like BEG (Emmelmann, Schröer, and Landwehr 1989) and BURG (Fraser, Henry, and Proebsting 1992) are actually descriptions of code generators, and they depend not only on the target machine but also on a particular intermediate language. In extreme cases (e.g., gcc's md files), the description formalism itself depends on the compiler. CSDL separates machine properties from compiler concerns.

Some existing languages for machine description, like VHDL (Lipsett, Schaefer, and Ussery 1993) and Verilog (Thomas and Moorby 1995) do describe only properties of machines, but they are at too low a level, describing implementations as much as architectures. These description languages require too much detail that is not needed to build systems software.

CSDL and the nML description language (Fauth, Praet, and Freericks 1995) address similar goals and use similar techniques, but they differ significantly. nML requires explicit attribute equations to write assembly-language syntax and binary representations; the CSDL language SLED uses an implicit syntax for assembly language and a more sophisticated, less error-prone sublanguage for describing binary representations (Ramsey and Fernández 1997). nML has no mechanism for abbreviating common idioms, making it harder to specify semantics in detail. The published papers suggest that the register transfers used in nML do not carry as much information as the register transfers described in this paper.

LISAS (Cook and Harcourt 1994) is another specification language that includes distinct semantic and syntactic descriptions. It specifies binary representations by mapping sequences of named fields onto sequence of bits, a technique that works well for RISC machines, but is awkward for CISC. The underlying model of instructions used in LISAS is less general and flexible than the model used in CSDL and nML. LISAS supports only "instructions" and "addressing modes," and LISAS addressing modes lump together values and side effects. CSDL copes with side effects more cleanly by enabling specification writers to use different attributes for describing values and side effects. LISAS also permits "overlapping register sets," which imply that two apparently different registers can be aliased to the same location. In CSDL, any aliasing is purely notational; the λ-RTL translator eliminates apparent aliasing, making the resulting register transfers easier to analyze.

The Core of CSDL

All languages in the CSDL family have the same view of two core aspects of machines: instructions and state. We chose these aspects based on our study of descriptions used to help retarget a variety of systems-level tools. These tools included an optimizer (Benitez and Davidson 1988), a debugger (Ramsey and Hanson 1992), an instruction scheduler (Proebsting and Fraser 1994), a call-sequence generator (Bailey and Davidson 1995), a linker (Fernández 1995), and an executable editor (Larus and Schnarr 1995). We saw no single aspect used in descriptions for all of these tools, but we did see that all the descriptions refer either to a machine's instruction set or to its storage locations. For example, the descriptions used by the scheduler and linker refer only to the machine's instructions and the properties thereof. The descriptions used in the call-sequence generator and in the debugger's stack walker refer only to storage, explaining in detail how values move between registers and memory. Some descriptions, like those used in the optimizer and the executable editor, refer both to instructions and to storage, and in particular, they show how the execution of instructions changes the contents of storage.

Given these observations, we require that languages in the CSDL family refer to instructions, storage, or both, and that they use the models of instructions and storage presented below.

Instructions

In CSDL, an *instruction set* is a list of instructions together with information about their operands. The model is based on experience with the New Jersey Machine-Code Toolkit (Ramsey and Fernández 1997), which has been used to build several machine-level tools. Although instruction names in assembly languages are typically overloaded, CSDL requires instructions to have unique names, because tools often need uniquely named code for each instruction in an instruction set. For example, an assembler might use a unique C procedure to encode each instruction, or an executable editor might use a unique element of a C union to represent an instance of each instruction.

An individual instruction is viewed as a function or constructor that is applied to operands. Instruction descriptions include the names and types of the operands of each instruction. Operand types include integers of various sizes; it is also possible to introduce new types to define such machine-dependent concepts as effective addresses. Values of these new types are created by applying suitable constructors, as defined in a CSDL description. For example, the SPARC supports two addressing modes,[1] the semantics of which can be specified as follows:

```
default attribute of
  indexA(rs1, rs2)    : Address  is  $r[rs1] + $r[rs2]
  dispA (rs1, simm13) : Address  is  $r[rs1] + sx simm13
```

indexA and dispA are the names of the constructors, and they create values of type Address. Such values denote 32-bit addresses. Values of type Address can be used as operands to instructions like store:

```
default attribute of  st (rd, Address)  is  $m[Address] := $r[rd]
```

The semantics shows that the store moves data from register rd into memory.

We also use CSDL constructors to describe 9 of the addressing modes used on the Pentium,[2] but because the meanings of the Pentium effective addresses depend on context, the description is more complicated, requiring 35 lines of λ-RTL.

As shown above, we specify attributes of instructions in a compositional style; instructions' attributes are functions of the attributes of their operands. In addition to the unnamed default attribute, there may be arbitrarily many named attributes. Attributes might describe not only semantics but also binary representations, assembly-language representations, power consumption, code size, cycle counts, or other costs.

---

[1] The SPARC assembly language appears to support four addressing modes, but the other two are variations of the ones shown, obtained in the special case when rs1 is 0. We have chosen not to define constructors for these modes, since the semantics specifies elsewhere that register 0 is always zero.

[2] These are the effective addresses available in 32-bit mode without using the address-prefix byte.

Storage

In CSDL, a *storage space* is a sequence of mutable cells. A storage space is like an array; cells are all the same size, and they are indexed by integers. Each cell contains either a bit vector or the distinguished value ⊥, which is used to model the results of instructions whose effects are undefined. The number of cells in a storage space may be left unspecified. For example, we specify the general-purpose registers and memory of the Intel Pentium as follows:

```
storage
  'r' is 8 cells of 32 bits called "registers"
  'm' is   cells of  8 bits called "memory"
                 aggregate using littleEndian
```

The Pentium has a register file made up of 32-bit cells and a memory made up of 8-bit cells (bytes). The **aggregate** directive tells the λ-RTL translator the default byte order to use with references to memory.

The state of a machine can be described as the contents of its storage spaces. We use storage spaces to model not only main memory and general-purpose registers, but also special-purpose registers, condition codes, and so on.

Languages in the CSDL family may refer to individual *locations*. Ways of writing locations may vary, but each one must resolve to a name of a storage space and an integer offset identifying a cell within that storage space. For example, on the Pentium, $r[0] stands for general-purpose register 0, i.e., register EAX.

Combining instructions and storage

Specifications of instructions and storage come straight out of architecture manuals. Manuals list instructions, their operands, and the storage locations that constitute the state of a processor. Most importantly, manuals say what instructions do; i.e., they explain how each instruction affects the state of the processor. We believe that a formal description of this information will enable us to build many different kinds of tools, including control-flow analyzers, code-editing tools like EEL (Larus and Schnarr 1995) and ATOM (Srivastava and Eustace 1994), code improvers in the style of PO (Davidson and Fraser 1980), vpo (Benitez and Davidson 1988), and gcc (Stallman 1992), and even emulators like SPIM (Larus 1990) and EASE (Davidson and Whalley 1990).

In λ-RTL, we specify the effect of each instruction as a *register-transfer list* (RTL), which describes a way of modifying storage cells. Like other properties of instructions, the RTL is a synthesized attribute.

Register Transfer Lists

CSDL's register transfer lists designed to be used by tools, not by people. To simplify analysis, we make their form simple, detailed, and unambiguous. We insist that as much information as possible be explicit in the RTL itself. It doesn't matter if individual RTLs grow large, as long as they are composed from simple

```
ty = (int) -- size of a value, in bits
exp      = CONST (const)
         | FETCH (location, ty)
         | APP   (operator, exp*)
location = AGG   (aggregation, cell)
cell     = CELL  (space, exp)
effect   = STORE (location dst, exp src, ty)
         | KILL  (location)
guarded  = GUARD (exp, effect)
rtl      = RTL   (guarded*)
```

const	bit vector
operator	function
aggregation	bijection
space	mutable store

Meanings of unspecified
terminal symbols

Fig. 1. ASDL specification of the form of RTLs

parts using only a few rules. This design choice distinguishes CSDL's RTLs from earlier work, which has used smaller RTLs that make implicit assumptions about details like operand sizes and byte order. In CSDL,

- RTLs are represented as trees.
- All operators are fully disambiguated, e.g., as to type and size.
- There is no covert aliasing of locations—locations with different spaces or offsets are always distinct.
- Fetches are explicit, as are changes in the size or type of data.
- Stores are annotated with the size of the data stored.
- Explicit tree nodes specify byte order. More generally, they specify how to transfer data between storage spaces with different cell sizes.

Figure 1 uses the Zephyr Abstract Syntax Description Language (Wang *et al.* 1997) to show the form of RTLs. Working from the bottom, a register transfer list is a list of guarded effects. Each effect represents the transfer of a value into a storage location, i.e., a store operation. The transfer takes place only if the guard (an expression) evaluates to **true**. Effects in a list take place simultaneously, as in Dijkstra's multiple-assignment statement; an RTL represents a single change of state. For example, we can specify swap instructions without introducing bogus temporaries. Locations may be single cells or aggregates of consecutive cells within a storage space. Values are computed by expressions without side effects. Eliminating side effects simplifies analysis and transformation. Expressions may be integer constants, fetches from locations, or applications of *RTL operators* to lists of expressions.

Not every effect assigns a value; a *kill* effect stores ⊥ in a location. Kill effects are needed to specify instructions that change values in an undefined way; for example, Intel (1993) states that "the effect of a logical instruction on the AF flag is undefined."

As an example of a typical RTL, consider a SPARC load instruction using the displacement addressing mode, written in the SPARC assembly language as

```
ld [%sp-12], %i0
```

Although we would not want to specify just a single instance of a single instruction, the effect of this load instruction might be written in λ-RTL as follows:[3]

```
$r[24] := $m[$r[14]+sx(~12)]
```

because the stack pointer is register 14 and register i0 is register 24. (Throughout the paper we use the Pascal assignment operator := to write the built-in store operation.) The corresponding RTL is much more verbose, with the sizes of all quantities identified explicitly, as a fully disambiguated tree:

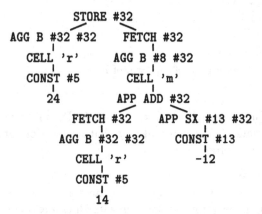

The constants labeled with hash marks, like #32, indicate the number of bits in arguments, results, or data being transferred. Such constants fit into a generalization of the Hindley-Milner type system (Milner 1978).

Figure 2 shows the meanings and types of the operators used in this tree. The left child of the STORE is a subtree representing the location consisting of the single register i0, which is register 24. The right-hand child represents a 32-bit word (a big-endian aggregation of four bytes) fetched from memory at the address given by the subtree rooted at APP ADD. This node adds the contents of the stack pointer (register 14) to the constant −12. The constant is a 13-bit constant, and applying the SX operator sign-extends it to 32 bits, so it can be added to the stack pointer.

In a real machine description, we wouldn't specify just one instance of a load instruction; we would give the semantics of all possible instances:

```
default attribute of ld (Address, rd) is $r[rd] := $m[Address]
```

This specification relies on the semantics of Address, which denotes a 32-bit address, as shown above.

We can also use λ-RTL to specify exceptional behaviors of instructions. The following lines specify that load instructions cause traps unless they load from addresses that are aligned on 4-byte boundaries.

```
fun alignTrap (address, k) is address modu k <> 0 --> trap(not_aligned)
attribute trap of ld (address, rd) is alignTrap(address, 4)
```

---

[3] The ~ in ~12 is a unary minus.

STORE : ∀#n.#n loc × #n bits → effect

> Store an n-bit value in a given location. The type indicates that for any n, STORE #n takes an n-bit location and an n-bit value and produces an effect.

FETCH : ∀#n.#n loc → #n bits

> For any n, FETCH #n takes an n-bit location and returns the n-bit value stored in that location.

AGG B : ∀#n.∀#w.#n cells → #w loc

> For any n and w, AGG B #n #w aggregates an integral number of n-bit cells into a w-bit location, making the first cell the most significant part of the new location, i.e., using big-endian byte order. w must be a multiple of n. (w and n are mnemonic for wide and narrow.)

CELL 'm' : #32 bits → #8 cells

> Given a 32-bit address, CELL 'm' returns the 8-bit cell in memory referred to by that address.

CELL 'r' : #5 bits → #32 cells

> Given a 5-bit register number, CELL 'r' returns the corresponding 32-bit register (a mutable cell).

ADD : ∀#n.#n bits × #n bits → #n bits

> For any n, ADD #n takes two n-bit values and returns their n-bit sum. ADD ignores carry and overflow, which can be computed using other RTL operators.

SX : ∀#n.∀#w.#n bits → #w bits

> For any n and w, SX #n #w takes an n-bit value, interprets it as a two's-complement signed integer, and sign-extends it to produce a w-bit representation of the same value. w must be greater than n.

CONST : ∀#n.⟨constant⟩ → #n bits

> For any n, CONST #n k represents the n-bit constant k. k must be representable in n bits. The same k could be used with different ns.

Fig. 2. Some RTL operators and their types

Throughout the paper we use the right arrow --> to write the built-in GUARD operator, which connects a guard to an effect. If the address is properly aligned, the guard on the effect returned by the alignTrap function ensures that nothing happens. The alignTrap function can be used with other values of k to specify the trapping semantics of load-halfword and load-double instructions.

CSDL RTLs are typed. Tools like compilers and analyzers may work directly with RTLs, and because optimizations and other semantics-preserving transformations should also preserve well-typedness, type-checking RTLs can help find bugs (Morrisett 1995). Figure 3 shows the types used in the λ-RTL type system. We have extended Milner's type inference to this system; λ-RTL specifications omit types and widths. Unlike in ML, type inference alone does not always guarantee that terms make sense; in general, there are additional constraints. For example, in the sample tree, the signed integer −12 must be representable using 13 bits, and 32 must be a multiple of both 8 and 32.

#*n* bits   A value that is *n* bits wide.

#*n* loc   A location containing an *n*-bit value.

#*n* cells One of a sequence of *n*-bit storage cells, which can be aggregated together
to make a larger location, as by the AGG B nodes in the example tree.

bool   A Boolean condition.

effect A state transformer (side effect on storage).

Fig. 3. Types in λ-RTL's type system

In contrast to RTLs used in earlier work, CSDL's RTLs have detailed and precise semantics independent of any particular machine. Space limitations prevent us from giving a formal semantics here, but the basic idea should be clear: CSDL **storage** declarations specify the state of a machine as a collection of mutable cells, and each RTL denotes a function from states to states. Figure 1 leaves four elements of RTLs unspecified. **space** is an identifier denoting one of the storage spaces declared with **storage**. **const** must denote a bit vector. The denotations of **operator** and **aggregation** warrant more discussion.

RTL operators, written in Fig. 1 as **operator**, must be interpreted as pure, strict functions on values. In particular, the result of applying an RTL operator cannot depend on processor state, and if an RTL operator is applied to ⊥, it must produce ⊥. Within these restrictions, users may introduce any RTL operators that seem useful—this abstraction mechanism gives users the ability to say that *something* specific happens, without saying exactly *what*. For example, the rules for determining when a SPARC signed divide instruction overflows are both complicated and implementation-dependent. Rather than attempt to write them using primitives like remainder, absolute value, etc., we might simply introduce a new RTL operator:

```
rtlop sparc_sdiv_overflow : #64 bits * #32 bits -> #1 bits
```

This operator accepts a 64-bit dividend and a 32-bit divisor, and it produces a 1-bit value, which is stored in the V bit by the SPARC SDIVcc instruction.

Most users won't define new RTL operators; they will use the 57 operators defined in our basic RTL library (Ramsey and Davidson 1997). This library includes integer arithmetic and comparison, bitwise operations, and IEEE floating-point operations and rounding modes.

RTL aggregations, written in Fig. 1 as **aggregation**, specify byte order. For example, in the sample tree, the AGG B #8 #32 between FETCH and CELL 'm' specifies that the machine builds a 32-bit word by aggregating four 8-bit bytes in big-endian order. In general, aggregations make it possible to write an RTL that stores a w-bit value in (or fetches a w-bit value from) k consecutive n-bit locations, provided that $w = kn$. Such an aggregation has type #*n* cells → #*w* loc, and its interpretation must be a bijection between a single w-bit value and k n-bit values. Moreover, when $w = n$, the bijection must be the identity function. Storing uses the bijection, and fetching uses its inverse, making it possible to combine RTLs using forward substitution. Little-endian and big-endian aggregations are built into λ-RTL, as is an "identity aggregation" that is defined only when $w = n$. We imagine that users could define other aggregations by giving systems of equations, e.g., using the bit-slicing operators of Ramsey (1996).

The precise, machine-independent semantics of RTLs will simplify construction of many useful software tools. A processor simulator is one such tool that is useful for embedded-system development and for architectural research. For development, a simulator allows software to be written, tested, and debugged in a mature programming environment. For research, a simulator gathers detailed measurements of the performance and behavior of the processor. Because CSDL's RTLs are meaningful independent of any machine, they will support the creation of a single interpreter capable of simulating any program expressed in RTL form. Previous versions of register-transfer lists required some machine-dependent code for each target machine of interest.

Precise, simple RTLs also make it easier to build tools that analyze RTL programs. For example, access to the mutable state of a machine is available only through the built-in fetch and store operations, so we can easily tell what state is changed by an RTL and how that change depends on the previous state. For embedded and real-time systems, we are interested in developing retargetable tools that analyze RTL programs to determine upper bounds on execution speed, power consumption, and space requirements. Such tools need detail about memory accesses and about the sizes of constants. For mobile code applications, we are interested in performing on-the-fly analysis to detect possible security violations. Of critical importance are the RTLs' lack of aliasing, explicit trap semantics, exposure of fetches, and explicit changes in size or type of data.

Using λ-RTL to Specify Register Transfer Lists

Bare RTLs are both spartan and verbose. Expressions do not include if-then-else, so conditionals must be represented by using guards on effects. There is no expression meaning "undefined;" assignments of undefined values must be specified using a kill effect. These restrictions, and the requirement that operations be fully disambiguated, make RTLs good for manipulation by tools but not so good for writing specifications.

The λ-RTL metalanguage enables specification writers to attach RTL trees to the CSDL constructors that describe instructions and addressing modes. Tools and tool generators have access to all the details of the full RTLs, but people can write λ-RTL specifications *without* having to write everything explicitly, because λ-RTL operates at a slightly higher level of abstraction. The *λ-RTL translator* bridges the gap.

λ-RTL is a higher-order, strongly typed, polymorphic, pure functional language based on Standard ML (Milner, Tofte, and Harper 1990). λ-RTL descriptions are easier to write than bare RTLs; higher-order functions help eliminate repetition, and the type system infers sizes of operands. Also, λ-RTL relaxes several of the restrictions on the form of RTLs:

- In λ-RTL, one need not write fetches explicitly.
- λ-RTL gives the illusion that bit slices (subfields) are locations that can be assigned to.
- λ-RTL gives the illusion that aggregates of cells are locations that can be assigned to. It is seldom necessary to write aggregations explicitly.
- One can define RTLs by sequential composition. The λ-RTL translator uses forward substitution to rewrite a sequence of RTLs into a single RTL.

Implicit Fetches. Most programmers are used to writing $x := x + 1$ and having the x on the left denote a location while the x on the right denotes the value stored in that location. Typical programming languages define "lvalue contexts" and "rvalue contexts," and compilers automatically insert fetches in rvalue contexts. λ-RTL works similarly, but instead of using syntax to identify the contexts, it uses types. This technique enables the specification writer to define arbitrary functions that change the state of the machine (e.g., to set condition codes), instead of restricting state change to a few built-in assignment constructs. For example, in our Pentium specification, we have written a function that implements the common pattern

$$l \leftarrow l \oplus r$$

where $\oplus$ is a generic binary operator:

```
fun llr (left, op, right) is left := op(left, right)
```

The λ-RTL translator infers that left must refer to a location, and it inserts a fetch above the instance that is passed to op.

To define the precise meaning of fetches and stores, including implicit fetches, users can attach fetch and store methods to each storage space. This technique makes it possible to model resources that are almost, but not quite, sequences of mutable cells. For example, SPARC registers can be viewed as a collection of 32 mutable cells, except that register 0 is not mutable because it is always 0. The fetch and store methods needed to implement this behavior are simple:

```
storage
  'r' is 32 cells of 32 bits called "registers"
    fetch using \n. if n = 0 then 0 else RTL.TRUE_FETCH $r[n] fi
    store using \(n, v). n <> 0 --> RTL.TRUE_STORE($r[n], v)
```

The \ represents λ-abstraction, which is a way of defining functions without requiring that they be named. The fetch method accepts a value n, representing the offset within storage space r, i.e., the register number. If n is zero, the result of the fetch is zero, otherwise it is the result of the true fetch (RTL.TRUE_FETCH) from that location. (The if-then-else-fi construct is present in λ-RTL, but the λ-RTL translator converts it into guarded effects, so tools that analyze RTLs need not deal with conditionals, only guards. Guards are easier to analyze because they appear only at the top level.) The store method accepts a register number n and a value v, and it returns an effect that stores v into register n, except when n is zero, in which case it does nothing.

Fetch and store methods offer substantial power and flexibility. For example, we could use fetch and store methods to describe the true implementation of

SPARC registers, in which "registers" 8 through 31 denote locations accessed indirectly through the register-window pointer (CWP). For our current specification, however, we have chosen a more abstract view of register windows (Ramsey and Davidson 1997, Chap. 5).

Slices. Many machine instructions manipulate fragments of words stored in mutable cells. For example, some machines represent condition codes as individual bits within a program status word, and user instructions may change only those bits. Some machines have instructions that, for example, assign to the least-significant 8 bits of a 32-bit register. To make it easy to specify such instructions, λ-RTL creates the illusion that a sub-range or "slice" of a cell is a location that is can be used in a fetch or store operation. This illusion helps keep machine descriptions readable; for example, an effect that sets the SPARC overflow bit simply assigns to it, hiding the fact that it is buried in a program status word that has to be fetched, modified, and stored.

λ-RTL uses a special syntax for slices, which can be applied to locations or to values. Examples include

x@loc[k]   Bit k of x. (Bit 0 is the least significant bit. In a future version of λ-RTL, it may be possible to change the numbering.)

x@loc[k_1..k_2]   Bits k_1 to k_2 of x, inclusive.

x@loc[k bits at e] A k-bit slice of x, with the least significant bit at e. k's denote integer constants, e's denote expressions, and x's denote locations. (If @bits is used instead of @loc, x's denote values.) In all cases, the size of the slice is known statically, so its type can be computed automatically. For example, Pentium programmers are accustomed to thinking of AX as a register in its own right, but it is in fact the least significant 16-bit word of register EAX:

    locations AX is EAX@loc[16 bits at 0]

Henceforth AX has type #16 loc, and it can be used anywhere any other 16-bit location can be used. The illusion that slices are locations is implemented by rewriting fetches and stores so that all slices operate on values and all fetches and stores operate on true locations. Invocation of user-defined fetch and store methods takes place *after* the rewriting of slices. This ordering makes it possible to use fetch and store methods to define cell-like abstractions, while ensuring that the meaning of slicing is always consistent with respect to such abstractions.

Implicit Aggregation. λ-RTL provides the special syntax $space[offset] for references to mutable cells. The *offset* can be an arbitrary expression, but the *space* must be a literal name, which λ-RTL can use to identify the storage space and the appropriate fetch and store methods. To make this cell a location, λ-RTL applies an aggregation, which is also associated with the storage space as a method. The default method is the identity aggregation, which permits only one-cell "aggregates."

Boolean constants:

true	Truth
false	Falsehood

Functions used to create RTLs:

RTL.TRUE_STORE	Takes location and value, produces effect.
RTL.STORE	Invokes a space's store method.
RTL.TRUE_FETCH	Fetches value from location.
RTL.FETCH	Invokes a space's fetch method.
RTL.SKIP	The empty RTL; an effect that does nothing.
RTL.GUARD	Takes a Boolean expression and an effect and produces an effect.
RTL.NOT	Boolean negation.
RTL.PAR	Takes two effects (RTLs) and composes them so they take place simultaneously (list append on list of effects).
RTL.SEQ	Takes two effects (RTLs) and composes them so they take place sequentially (forward substitution).
RTL.AGGB	Big-endian aggregation.
RTL.AGGL	Little-endian aggregation.

Functions on vectors:

sub	Vector subscript.
Vector.spanning	Vector.spanning x y produces the vector $[.x, x+1, \ldots, y.]$.
Vector.foldr	A higher-order function used to visit every element of a vector.

Fig. 4. λ-RTL's initial basis

When little-endian, big-endian, or other aggregations are used, the λ-RTL translator will infer the size of the aggregate. We have tentatively decided to infer aggregates of a size up to the largest cell size in an RTL, so, for example, the translator will infer a 32-bit aggregation in $r[rd] := $m[Address]$, but a 64-bit aggregation (for a doubleword load) would have to be given explicitly. In the translator's output, all aggregations are explicit. Explicit aggregations are especially useful for building tools like binary translators, which must transform non-native aggregations into byte-swapping.

Writing λ-RTL

λ-RTL provides expressive power with few restrictions. Most of the RTL-specific content of λ-RTL is in the initial basis, i.e., the collection of predefined functions and values. Most of the basis, shown in Fig. 4, is used to create RTLs in the form we have prescribed. The rest contains vector functions that substitute for looping and recursion constructs. (As a way of making sure specifications are well defined, λ-RTL omits looping and recursion.) Loops whose sizes are known in advance can be simulated by using Vector.foldr and Vector.spanning. Because this style is familiar only to those well versed in functional programming, we expect eventually to provide syntactic sugar for it. We hope that a similar strategy will help specify instructions that are normally considered to have internal control flow, e.g., string-copy instructions.

In addition to using the initial basis, specification writers can introduce new RTL operators. They can also define functions, but the functions are interpreted by the λ-RTL translator and do not appear in the resulting RTLs. Functions are useful only for making specifications more concise and readable. The freedom to define functions and to introduce abstract RTL operators gives us ample scope for experimenting with different styles of description.

Status

Our prototype translator implements λ-RTL as described in this paper, except it omits some size checks, and it does not implement forward substitution. We have used about 300 lines of λ-RTL to describe 160 SPARC instructions, including register windows, control flow, load and store, and all integer and floating-point ALU instructions, including effects on condition codes. The only instructions omitted are some coprocessor instructions, a few privileged load and store instructions, and cache flush. In this description, we used 37 of the 57 RTL operators defined in our machine-dependent library. We also introduced two new, SPARC-specific operators to avoid having to specify exactly how the machine decides when signed and unsigned integer division have overflowed. The Appendix gives some excerpts from this description.

On the Pentium, we have described the registers and their aliases, effective addresses (which may have three different meanings depending on the contexts in which they are used), and the logical instructions. We have also explored ways of using λ-RTL to make descriptions concise; given suitable auxiliary functions, we can specify the semantics of 42 logical instructions, including effects on condition codes, in 7 lines of λ-RTL. The descriptions, as well as more lengthy expositions of RTLs and λ-RTL, are available in a technical report (Ramsey and Davidson 1997).

Acknowledgements

This work has been supported by NSF Grant ASC-9612756 and by DARPA Contract MDA904-97-C-0247. Members of the program committee provided useful suggestions about presentation.

Appendix: Excerpts from the SPARC description

This appendix presents a few more excerpts from our SPARC description. The basic RTL library has been omitted, as have the declarations of the 'r' and 'm' spaces, which appear in the text. With these omissions restored, the excerpts (as extracted from the source of this paper) compile with our prototype translator. The complete description, with commentary, is available as part of a technical report (Ramsey and Davidson 1997).

The excerpts begin with more storage spaces and locations.

```
storage 'i' is 6 cells of 32 bits called "control/status registers"
locations [PSR WIM TBR Y PC nPC] is $i[[0..5]]
structure icc is struct
  locations [N Z V C] is PSR@loc[1 bit at [23 22 21 20]]
end
storage 'f' is 32 cells of 32 bits called "floating-point registers"
```

Here are some simple instructions. Control transfer is by assignment to nPC.

```
default attribute of
  ldstub(address, rd) is $r[rd] := zx $m[address] | $m[address] := 0xff
  call (target)       is nPC := target | $r[15] := PC
  jmpl (address, rd)  is nPC := address | $r[rd] := PC
  [sll srl sra] (rs1, reg_or_imm, rd) is
    $r[rd] := [shl shrl shra](32, $r[rs1], reg_or_imm@bits[5 bits at 0])
```

Here is machinery for setting condition codes and for specifying binary operators that may set condition codes.

```
fun set_cc(result, overflow, carry) is
  icc.N := bit (result < 0) | icc.Z := bit (result = 0) |
  icc.V := overflow         | icc.C := carry
fun dont_set_cc _ is RTL.SKIP
fun binary_with_cc (operator, rs1, r_o_i, rd, special_cc) is
  let val result is operator(RTL.FETCH $r[rs1], r_o_i)
  in  $r[rd] := result | special_cc result
  end
```

Here are the logical instructions, which set condition codes. Operators and, or, and xor must be parenthesized because the basic library declares them to be infix. The square brackets are an iterative grouping construct that enables repeated specification in a single expression; this code specifies 4 functions and 12 constructors.

```
fun logical_cc (result) is set_cc(result, 0, 0)
fun [andn orn xnor] (a, b)  is  [(and) (or) (xor)](a, com b)
default attribute of
  [and or xor andn orn xnor]^[cc ""] (rs1, reg_or_imm, rd) is
    binary_with_cc([(and) (or) (xor) andn orn xnor], rs1,
                    reg_or_imm, rd, [logical_cc dont_set_cc])
```

These functions pair an ordinary register with the Y register, to hold a 64-bit value.

```
structure Reg64 is struct
  fun set (reg, n) is
    Y := n@bits[32 bits at 32] | $r[reg] := n@bits[32 bits at 0]
  fun get reg is bitInsert {wide is zx #32 #64 $r[reg], lsb is 32} Y
end
```

Here are signed and unsigned division, which operate on 64-bit values.

```
fun div_like((operator, overflow), rs1, r_o_i, rd, ccguard) is
  let val result is operator(Reg64.get rs1, r_o_i)
      val V      is overflow(Reg64.get rs1, r_o_i)
  in $r[rd] := result | ccguard --> set_cc (result, V, 0)
  end
rtlop sparc_sdiv_overflow : #64 bits * #32 bits -> #1 bits
rtlop sparc_udiv_overflow : #64 bits * #32 bits -> #1 bits
default attribute of
  [u s]^div^["" cc] (rs1, reg_or_imm, rd) is
    div_like([((divu), sparc_udiv_overflow)
              ((quots), sparc_sdiv_overflow)],
                rs1, reg_or_imm, rd, [false true])
```

References

Bailey, Mark W. and Jack W. Davidson. 1995 (January). A formal model and specification language for procedure calling conventions. In *Conference Record of the 22nd Annual ACM Symposium on Principles of Programming Languages*, pages 298–310, San Francisco, CA.

Benitez, Manuel E. and Jack W. Davidson. 1988 (July). A portable global optimizer and linker. *Proceedings of the ACM SIGPLAN '88 Conference on Programming Language Design and Implementation,* in *SIGPLAN Notices*, 23(7):329–338.

Cook, Todd and Ed Harcourt. 1994 (May). A functional specification language for instruction set architectures. In *Proceedings of the 1994 International Conference on Computer Languages*, pages 11–19.

Davidson, Jack W. and Christopher W. Fraser. 1980 (April). The design and application of a retargetable peephole optimizer. *ACM Transactions on Programming Languages and Systems*, 2(2):191–202.

Davidson, Jack W. and David B. Whalley. 1990 (May). Ease: An environment for architecture study and experimentation. In *Proceedings of the 1990 ACM Sigmetrics Conference on Measurement and Modeling of Computer Systems*, pages 259–260, Boulder, CO.

Emmelmann, Helmut, Friedrich-Wilhelm Schröer, and Rudolf Landwehr. 1989 (July). BEG — a generator for efficient back ends. *Proceedings of the ACM SIGPLAN '89 Conference on Programming Language Design and Implementation,* in *SIGPLAN Notices*, 24(7):227–237.

Fauth, Andreas, Johan Van Praet, and Markus Freericks. 1995 (March). Describing instruction set processors using nML. In *The European Design and Test Conference*, pages 503–507.

Fernández, Mary F. 1995 (November). *A Retargetable Optimizing Linker.* PhD thesis, Dept of Computer Science, Princeton University.

Fraser, Christopher W., Robert R. Henry, and Todd A. Proebsting. 1992 (April). BURG—fast optimal instruction selection and tree parsing. *SIGPLAN Notices*, 27(4):68–76.

Intel Corporation. 1993. *Architecture and Programming Manual.* Vol. 3 of *Pentium Processor User's Manual.* Mount Prospect, IL.

Larus, James R. and Eric Schnarr. 1995 (June). EEL: machine-independent executable editing. *Proceedings of the ACM SIGPLAN '95 Conference on Programming Language Design and Implementation,* in *SIGPLAN Notices,* 30(6):291–300.

Larus, James R. 1990 (September). SPIM S20: A MIPS R2000 simulator. Technical Report 966, Computer Sciences Department, University of Wisconsin, Madison, WI.

Lipsett, R., C. Schaefer, and C. Ussery. 1993. *VHDL: Hardware Description and Design.* 12 edition. Kluwer Academic Publishers.

Milner, Robin, Mads Tofte, and Robert W. Harper. 1990. *The Definition of Standard ML.* Cambridge, Massachusetts: MIT Press.

Milner, Robin. 1978 (December). A theory of type polymorphism in programming. *Journal of Computer and System Sciences,* 17:348–375.

Morrisett, Greg. 1995 (December). *Compiling with Types.* PhD thesis, Carnegie Mellon. Published as technical report CMU–CS–95–226.

Proebsting, Todd A. and Christopher W. Fraser. 1994 (January). Detecting pipeline structural hazards quickly. In *Conference Record of the 21st Annual ACM Symposium on Principles of Programming Languages,* pages 280–286, Portland, OR.

Ramsey, Norman and Jack W. Davidson. 1997 (November). Specifying instructions' semantics using CSDL (preliminary report). Technical Report CS-97-31, Department of Computer Science, University of Virginia. Revised, May 1998.

Ramsey, Norman and Mary F. Fernández. 1997 (May). Specifying representations of machine instructions. *ACM Transactions on Programming Languages and Systems,* 19(3):492–524.

Ramsey, Norman and David R. Hanson. 1992 (July). A retargetable debugger. *ACM SIGPLAN '92 Conference on Programming Language Design and Implementation,* in *SIGPLAN Notices,* 27(7):22–31.

Ramsey, Norman. 1996 (April). A simple solver for linear equations containing nonlinear operators. *Software—Practice & Experience,* 26(4):467–487.

Srivastava, Amitabh and Alan Eustace. 1994 (June). ATOM: A system for building customized program analysis tools. *Proceedings of the ACM SIGPLAN '94 Conference on Programming Language Design and Implementation,* in *SIGPLAN Notices,* 29(6):196–205.

Stallman, Richard M. 1992 (February). *Using and Porting GNU CC (Version 2.0).* Free Software Foundation.

Thomas, Donald and Philip Moorby. 1995. *The Verilog Hardware Description Language.* 2nd edition. Norwell, USA: Kluwer Academic Publishers.

Wang, Daniel C., Andrew W. Appel, Jeff L. Korn, and Christopher S. Serra. 1997 (October). The Zephyr abstract syntax description language. In *Proceedings of the 2nd USENIX Conference on Domain-Specific Languages,* pages 213–227, Santa Barbara, CA.

Non-local Instruction Scheduling
with Limited Code Growth*

Keith D. Cooper and Philip J. Schielke

Department of Computer Science, Rice University, Houston Texas
keith@cs.rice.edu, phisch@cs.rice.edu

Abstract. Instruction scheduling is a necessary step in compiling for many modern microprocessors. Traditionally, global instruction scheduling techniques have outperformed local techniques. However many of the global scheduling techniques described in the literature have a side effect of increasing the size of compiled code. In an embedded system, the size of compiled code is often a critical issue. In such circumstances, the scheduler should use techniques that avoid increasing the size of the generated code. This paper explores two global scheduling techniques, extended basic block scheduling and dominator path scheduling, that do not increase the size of the object code, and, in some cases, decrease it.

1 Introduction

The embedded systems environment presents unusual design challenges. These systems are constrained by size, power, and economics; these constraints introduce compilation issues not often considered for commodity microprocessors. One such problem is the size of compiled code. Many embedded systems have tight limits on the size of both RAM and ROM. To be successful, a compiler must generate code that runs well while operating within those limits.

The problem of code space reduction was studied in the 1970's and the early 1980's. In the last ten years, the issue has largely been ignored. During those ten years, the state of both processor architecture and compiler-based analysis and optimization have changed. To attack the size of compiled code for embedded systems, we must go back and re-examine current compiler-based techniques in light of their impact on code growth.

This paper examines the problem of scheduling instructions in a limited-memory environment. Instruction scheduling is one of the last phases performed by modern compilers. It is a code reordering transformation that attempts to hide the latencies inherent in modern day microprocessors. On processors that support instruction level parallelism, it may be possible to hide the latency of some high-latency operations by moving other operations into the "gaps" in the schedule.

* This work has been supported by DARPA and the USAF Research Laboratory through Award F30602-97-2-298.

Scheduling is an important problem for embedded systems, particularly those built around DSP-style processors. These microprocessors rely on compiler-based instruction scheduling to hide operation latencies and achieve reasonable performance. Unfortunately, many scheduling algorithms deliberately trade increased code size for improvements in running time. This paper looks at two techniques that avoid increasing code size and presents experimental data about their effectiveness relative to the classic technique—local list scheduling.

For some architectures, instruction scheduling is a necessary part of the process of ensuring correct execution. These machines rely on the compiler to insert NOPs to ensure that individual operations do not execute before their operands are ready. Most VLIW architectures have this property. On these machines, an improved schedule requires fewer NOPs; this can lead to a direct reduction in code space. If, on the other hand, the processor uses hardware interlocks to ensure that operands are available before their use, instruction scheduling becomes an optimization rather than a necessity. On these machines, NOP insertion is not an issue, so the scheduler is unlikely to make a significant reduction in code size.

In this paper, we focus on the VLIW-like machines without hardware interlocks. (Of course, good scheduling without code growth may be of interest on any machine.) For our discussion, we need to differentiate between *operations* and *instructions*. An operation is a single, indivisible command given to the hardware (*e.g.* an add or load operation). An instruction is a set of operations that begin execution at the same time on different functional units.

Traditionally, compilers have scheduled each basic block in the program independently. The first step is to create a data precedence graph, or DPG, for the block. Nodes in this graph are operations in the block. An edge from node a to node b means that that operation b must complete its execution before operation a can begin. That is, operation a is data dependent on operation b. Once this graph is created it is scheduled using a list scheduler [17, 11].

Since basic blocks are usually rather short, the typical block contains a limited amount of instruction-level parallelism. To improve this situation, regional and global instruction scheduling methods have been developed. By looking at larger scopes, these methods often find more instruction-level parallelism to exploit. This paper examines two such techniques, *extended basic block scheduling* (EBBS) and *dominator path scheduling* (DPS). Both methods produce better results than scheduling a single basic block; this results in fewer wasted cycles and fewer inserted NOPs.

We selected these two techniques because neither increases code size. In the embedded systems environment, the compiler does not have the luxury of replicating code to improve running time. Instead, the compiler writer should pay close attention to the impact of each technique on code size. These scheduling techniques attempt to improve over local list scheduling by examining larger regions in the program; at the same time, they constrain the movement of instructions in a way that avoids replication. Thus, they represent a compromise between the desire for runtime speed and the real constraints of limited memory machines.

Section 2 provides a brief overview of prior work on global scheduling. In section 3 we explain in detail the two techniques used in our experiments: namely *extended basic block scheduling* (EBBS) and *dominator-path scheduling* (DPS). Section 4 describes our experiments and presents our experimental results.

2   Global Scheduling Techniques

Because basic blocks typically have a limited amount of parallelism [20], global scheduling methods have been developed in the hopes of improving program performance. All the global techniques we will be describing increase the *scope* of scheduling, but do not change the underlying scheduling algorithm. Each technique constructs some sequence of basic blocks and schedules the sequence as if it were a single basic block. Restrictions on moving operations between basic blocks are typically encoded in the DPG for the sequence.

The first automated global scheduling technique was trace scheduling, originally described by Fisher [8]. It has been used successfully in several research and industrial compilers [7,18]. In trace scheduling, the most frequently executed acyclic path through the function is determined using profile information. This "trace" is treated like a large basic block. A DPG is created for the trace, and the trace is scheduled using a list scheduler. Restrictions on inter-block code motion are encoded in the DPG. After the first trace is scheduled, the next most frequently executed trace is scheduled, and so on. A certain amount of "bookkeeping" must be done when scheduling a trace. Any operation that moves above a join point in the trace must be copied into all other traces that enter the current trace at that point. Likewise, any operation that moves below a branch point must be copied into the other traces that exit the branch point, if the operation computes any values that are live in that trace.

One criticism of trace scheduling is its potential for code explosion due to the introduction of bookkeeping code. Fruedenberger, *et al.*, argue that this does not arise in practice [10]. They show an average code growth of six percent for the SPEC89 benchmark suite and detail ways to avoid bookkeeping (or compensation) code altogether. Restricting the trace scheduler to produce no compensation code only marginally degrades the performance of the scheduled code.

Hwu, *et. al.*, present another global scheduling technique called *superblock scheduling* [14]. It begins by constructing traces. All side entrances into the traces are removed by replicating blocks between the first side entrance and the end of the trace. This *tail duplication* process is repeated until all traces have a unique entry point. This method can lead to better runtime performance than trace scheduling, but the block duplication can increase code size. Several other techniques that benefit from code replication or growth have been used. These include Bernstein and Rodeh's "Global Instruction Scheduling" [4,2], Ebcioglu and Nakatani's "Enhanced Percolation Scheduling" [6], and Gupta and Soffa's "Region Scheduling" [12].

3 The Two Techniques

In this section we examine two non-local scheduling techniques specifically designed to avoid increasing code size, namely dominator-path scheduling (DPS), and extended basic block scheduling (EBBS). We assume that, prior to scheduling, the program has been translated into an intermediate form consisting of basic blocks of operations. Control flow is indicated by edges between the basic blocks. We assume this control-flow graph (CFG) has a unique entry block and a unique exit block.

3.1 Extended basic block scheduling

Little work has been published on extended basic block scheduling. Freudenberger, *et. al.* show some results of scheduling over extended basic blocks, but only after doing some amount of loop unrolling [10]. Since we are striving for zero code growth, such loop unrolling is out of the question.

An extended basic block (or EBB) is a sequence of basic blocks, $B_1, \ldots, B_k$, such that, for $1 \leq i < k$, B_i is the only predecessor of B_{i+1} in the CFG, and B_1 may or may not have a unique predecessor [1]. For scheduling purposes, we view extended basic blocks as a partitioning of the CFG; a basic block is a member of only one EBB. (This differs from the view in much of the literature.)

The first step in EBBS is to partition the CFG into extended basic blocks. We define the set of *header* blocks to be all those blocks that are the first block in some EBB. Initially, our set of headers consists of the start block and all blocks with more than one predecessor in the CFG. Once this initial set of headers has been found, we compute a weighted *size* for each basic block. The size for a header is set to zero. The size for all other blocks equals the total number of operations in the block weighted by their latencies plus the maximum size of all the block's successors in the CFG. To construct the EBB's, we maintain a worklist of header blocks. When a block B is pulled off the worklist, other blocks are added to its EBB based on sizes computed earlier. The successor of B in the CFG with the largest size is added to B's EBB. The other successors of B are added to to the worklist to become headers for some other EBB. This process continues for the new block, until no more eligible blocks are found for the current EBB. For each EBB, a DPG is constructed, and the EBB is scheduled with a list scheduler.

To avoid code growth, we prohibit some operations from moving between the blocks of an EBB. Assume a block B_1 has successors $B_2, B_3, \ldots, B_n$ in the CFG. Further assume that B_2 is placed in the same EBB as B_1. We prohibit moving an operation from B_2 to B_1, and vice versa, if that operation defines a value that is live along some path from B_1 to B_i where $i \neq 2$. We call this set of values *path-live* with respect to B_2, or PL_{B_2}. The set is a portion of the set $liveout(B_1)$ as computed by the following equation:

$$PL_{B_2} = \bigcup_{B_i = B_3}^{B_n} livein(B_i)$$

Intuitively, we can't move the operation if any value it defines is used in some block other than B_1 or B_2 and that block is reachable from B_1 via some path not containing B_2. The operations that can be moved are called *partially dead* if they are in B_1 [16].

3.2 Dominator-path scheduling

DPS was originally described in Sweany's thesis [21]. Other work was done by Sweany and Beaty [22], and Huber [13].

We say a basic block B_1 *dominates* block B_2 if all paths from the start block of the CFG to B_2 must pass through B_1 [19]. If B_1 dominates B_2, and block B_2 executes on a given program run, then B_1 must also execute. We define the *immediate dominator* of a block B (or $idom(B)$) to be the dominator closest to B in the CFG. Each block must have a unique immediate dominator, except the start block which has no dominator. Let $G = (N, E)$ be a directed graph, where the set N is the set of basic blocks in the program, and define $E = \{(u, v) \mid u = idom(v)\}$. Since each block has a unique immediate dominator, this graph is a tree, called the *dominator-tree*. A dominator-path is any path in the dominator-tree.

We now define two sets, $idef(B)$ and $iuse(B)$. For a basic block B, $idef(B)$ is the set of all values that may be defined on some path from $idom(B)$ to B (not including B or $idom(B)$.) Likewise $iuse(B)$, is the set of all values that may be used on some path from $idom(B)$ to B. The algorithm for efficiently computing these sets is given by Reif and Tarjan [23].

DPS schedules a dominator-path as if it were a single basic block. First, the blocks in the CFG must be partitioned into different dominator-paths. Huber describes several heuristics for doing path selection and reports on their relative success. We use a size heuristic similar to the one described above for EBBS. This is done via a bottom-up walk over the dominator-tree. The size of a leaf equals the latency-weighted number of operations in the block. For all other blocks, size equals the latency-weighted number of operations in the block plus the maximum size of all the block's children in the dominator-tree. When building the dominator-paths, we select the next block in the path by choosing the child in the dominator-tree with the largest size. All other children become the first block in some other dominator-path. Once the dominator-paths are selected, a DPG is created for each path, and the path is scheduled using a list scheduler. After each path is scheduled, liveness analysis and the $idef$ and $iuse$ sets must be recomputed to insure correctness.

When the compiler builds the DPG for the dominator-path, it adds edges to prevent motion of certain operations between basic blocks. Assume B_1 is the immediate dominator of B_2. Sweany's original formulation prohibits moving an operation from B_2 up into B_1 if the operation references a value in $idef(B_2)$ or defines a value in $idef(B_2) \cup iuse(B_2)$. That is, we don't want to move an operation that defines a value V above a use or definition of V in the CFG. Likewise, an operation that references V is not allowed to move above a definition of V. This strategy is safe when B_1 dominates B_2 *and* B_2 postdominates B_1.

Huber showed that, in the general case, this strategy is unsafe. Figure 1(a) illustrates the problem. In this simple CFG we show only the operations that use or define r1. Assume blocks B_1 and B_2 will be scheduled together. Clearly r1 is not a member of $iuse(B_2)$ or $idef(B_2)$ since there are no blocks between B_1 and B_2. Thus, the definition of r1 in B_2 could be unsafely hoisted into block B_1 causing the use of r1 in B_4 to use the wrong value. Thus, Huber adds the restriction that any operation that defines a value in

$$idef(B_2) \cup iuse(B_2) \cup (liveout(B_1) - livein(B_2))$$

cannot be moved up from B_2 into B_1.

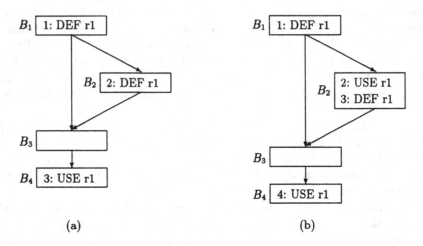

(a)   (b)

Fig. 1. DPS example

However, we have found that this formulation too is unsafe. Figure 1(b) demonstrates the problem. Again, assume that blocks B_1 and B_2 will be scheduled together. Note that $r1 \in liveout(B_1)$ and $r1 \in livein(B_2)$ since it is referenced before it is defined in B_2. Therefore, r1 is not in the set $liveout(B_1) - livein(B_2)$. Assuming operation 2 does not define anything that causes movement to be unsafe, we can move it up into block B_1. It would then be legal to move the operation 3 into B_1. Thus both operations in B_2 could be moved into block B_1, which would cause operation 4 in block B_4 to potentially get the wrong value. Once a dominator-path is selected for scheduling, no updating of the liveness information is done during the scheduling of that dominator-path. Some sort of incremental update would be one way to solve this problem, since moving operation 2 into B_1 would cause r1's removal from the set $livein(B_2)$.

We use an approach that doesn't require incremental updates. What we really want to capture are those values that are live along paths other than those from B_1 to B_2. This is fairly straightforward if B_1 is the only parent of B_2 in the CFG; we simply use the path-live notion discussed in the previous section. In

$dontdef = idef(B_2) \cup iuse(B_2)$
if B_2 does not post-dominate B_1
    then if B_1 is the predecessor of B_2 in CFG
        $dontdef = dontdef \cup PL_{B_2}$
    else
        $dontdef = dontdef \cup liveout(B_1)$
if B_2 and B_1 are in different loops
    then $dontdef = dontdef \cup liveout(B_1)$
        $dontdef = dontdef \cup memory\_values$

Fig. 2. Summary of prohibited moves between B_1 and B_2

other cases, we take the conservative approach and don't allow any operation that defines a value in $liveout(B_1)$ to move up.

Now we consider motion of an operation in the downward direction. Sweany does not allow an operation to move down the CFG, that is into block B_2 from its dominator B_1, but he does mention that this could be done if B_2 *post-dominates* B_1. A block B_2 post-dominates B_1 if every path from B_1 to the end of the CFG must pass through B_2 (simply the dominance relation in reverse). Huber allows operations to move down into the post-dominator if they don't define anything in $idef(B_2) \cup iuse(B_2)$ or use anything in $idef(B_2)$. No downward motion is allowed if B_2 does not post-dominate B_1. We take this one step further by allowing motion of an operation from B_1 into B_2 if B_1 is the predecessor of B_2 in the CFG, and the operation computes values that are only live along the edge (B_1, B_2). (This is the path-live notion from section 3.1.) In any other case where B_2 does not post-dominate B_1, we take the conservative approach and disallow any motion of operations that compute a value in $liveout(B_1)$.

Loops pose additional concerns. We must be careful not to allow any code that defines memory to move outside of its current loop or to a different loop nesting depth.[1] In addition to the restrictions described above, we disallow any operation that defines memory from moving between two blocks if they are in different loops or at different loop nesting levels. Finally, we don't allow an operation that defines registers in $liveout(B_1)$ to move between the two blocks.

To summarize, we disallow motion of an operation between block B_2 and its immediate dominator B_1 (forward or backward) if that operation defines a value in the set $dontdef$. This set is defined in figure 2. Additionally any operations that use a value in $idef(B_2)$ are not allowed to move.

4 Experimental Results

Our research compiler takes C or Fortran code as input and translates it into our assembly-like intermediate form, ILOC [5]. ILOC code can then be passed to various optimization passes. All the code for these experiments has been heavily

---

[1] Recall that scheduling follows optimization. We feel strongly that code motion should be done in the optimizer with appropriately strong tools like lazy code motion [15].

optimized prior to scheduling. These optimizations include pointer analysis to disambiguate memory references in the C codes, constant propagation, global value numbering, dead code elimination, operator strength reduction, lazy code motion, and register coalescing. No register allocation was performed before *or* after scheduling, as we wanted to completely isolate the effects of the scheduler. After optimization, the ILOC is translated into C, instrumented to report operation and instruction counts, and compiled. This code is then run. Our results are reported as instruction counts.

A variety of C and Fortran benchmark codes were studied, including several from various versions of the SPEC benchmarks and the FMM test suite [9]. The C codes used are, clean, compress, dfa, dhrystone, fft, go, jpeg, nsieve, and water. All other benchmarks are Fortran codes. clean is an optimization pass from our compiler. dfa is a small program that implements the Knuth-Morris-Pratt string matching algorithm. nsieve computes prime numbers using the Sieve of Eratosthenes. water is from the SPLASH benchmark suite, and fft is a program that performs fast-fourier transforms.

4.1 A Generic VLIW Architecture

In the first set of experiments, we assume a VLIW-like architecture. This hypothetical architecture has two integer units, a floating point unit, a memory unit, and a branch unit. Up to four operations can be started in parallel. Each ILOC operation has a latency assigned to it. We assume that the latency of every operation is known at compile time. The architecture is completely pipelined, and NOPs must be inserted to ensure correct execution. We compare DPS and EBBS to scheduling over basic blocks. In each case the underlying scheduler is a list scheduler that assigns priorities to each operation based on the latency-weighted depth of the operation in the DPG. For both DPS and EBBS we select which blocks to schedule based on the size heuristic described above. We add one final restriction on code movement; we do not allow any operations that could cause an exception to be moved "up" in the CFG. In practice this means that divide operations, and loads from pointer memory (ILOC's PLDor operations), do not move upwards.

Table 1 shows the dynamic instruction counts for our benchmark codes. This value can be thought of as the number of cycles required to execute the code. Both EBBS and DPS produced consistently better code than basic block scheduling, though neither technique dominated. Slightly better than fifty per cent of the time DPS outperformed EBBS, and a few of these wins were substantial. On average EBBS produced a 6.5 per cent reduction in the number of dynamic instructions executed, and DPS produced a 7.5 per cent reduction.

Table 2 shows the static instruction counts for the same experiments. This corresponds to the "size" (number of instructions) of the object code. Note that all the object codes have the same number of operations; only the number of instructions changes. DPS did better by this metric in roughly the same number of experiments. However, the static and dynamic improvements did not necessarily occur on the same codes. This demonstrates that smaller more compact code

Table 1. Dynamic Instruction Counts for VLIW

Benchmark	Basic Block Dynamic Insts	EBBS Dynamic Insts	EBBS % decrease	DPS Dynamic Insts	DPS % decrease
clean	4515619	4113837	8.9	3969926	12.1
compress	10641037	9511683	10.6	9489915	10.8
dfa	696450	592836	14.9	625166	10.2
dhrystone	3660102	3340092	8.7	3220092	12.0
fft	22469970	22138422	1.5	22193147	1.2
go	589209782	527762311	10.4	521628685	11.5
jpeg	45900780	44107954	3.9	44040659	4.1
nsieve	2288889385	2254236158	1.5	2254236164	1.5
water	36111497	33544010	7.1	33253230	7.9
fmin	5370	4495	16.3	4100	23.6
rkf45	818884	731155	10.7	749565	8.5
seval	3340	3264	2.2	3261	2.4
solve	2813	2652	5.7	2627	6.6
svd	14649	13805	5.8	13921	5.0
urand	1117	1081	3.2	1093	2.1
zeroin	4603	4088	11.2	4035	12.3
applu	884028559	865609968	2.1	866257750	2.0
doduc	16953587	16122745	4.9	15248824	10.1
fpppp	95701038	90578189	5.4	89483748	6.5
matrix300	43073238	42802715	0.6	42803515	0.6
tomcatv	436717483	436706995	0.0	408090942	6.6

does not always results in enhanced runtime performance. On average EBBS reduced static code size by 12.2 per cent and DPS by 12.8 per cent.

When performing basic block scheduling, we found each block had an average of 6.8 operations (over all benchmarks). On average, an EBB consisted of 1.8 basic blocks and 12.4 operations. Dominator paths averaged 2.2 basic blocks and 15.1 operations each.

We also measured the amount of time required to schedule. The scheduling times for each benchmark are shown in table 3. In two runs, the average scheduling time for all benchmarks was 88 seconds for basic block scheduling, 92 seconds for EBBS, and 2297 seconds for DPS. This comparison is a bit unfair. Several of our C codes have many functions in each ILOC module. Thus DPS is performing the dominator analysis for the whole file every time a dominator-path is scheduled. The **go** benchmark contributed 2109 seconds alone. This effect can certainly be engineered out of the implementation. We totaled times for the Fortran benchmarks (all ILOC files contain a single function), and a random sampling of the single function C codes (about 24 functions). The scheduling times were 56 seconds for basic block scheduling, 50 seconds for EBBS, and 105 seconds for DPS. If we eliminate **fpppp**, which actually scheduled faster with EBBS than basic block scheduling, we get times of 8 seconds, 10 seconds, and 49 seconds, respectively.

Table 2. Static Instruction Counts for VLIW

	Basic Block	EBBS		DPS	
Benchmark	Static Insts	Static Insts	% decrease	Static Insts	% decrease
clean	11429	10283	10.0	10322	9.7
compress	1597	1378	13.7	1386	13.2
dfa	1356	973	28.2	1007	25.7
dhrystone	525	470	10.5	458	12.8
fft	2708	2469	8.8	2449	9.6
go	73456	62102	15.5	61497	16.3
jpeg	19785	18220	7.9	18316	7.4
nsieve	271	254	6.3	252	7.0
water	6469	6032	6.8	5927	8.4
fmin	712	502	29.5	446	37.4
rkf45	2387	1934	19.0	2023	15.2
seval	1055	988	6.4	1008	4.5
solve	1007	927	7.9	922	8.4
svd	2481	2176	12.3	2220	10.5
urand	192	172	10.4	168	12.5
zeroin	545	444	18.5	441	19.1
applu	13334	12898	3.3	12816	3.9
doduc	42127	38275	9.1	37187	11.7
fpppp	10521	9765	7.2	9608	8.7
matrix300	429	346	19.3	348	18.9
tomcatv	953	904	5.1	881	7.6

Table 3. Scheduling times in seconds

Benchmark	BB	EBBS	DPS
clean	5.10	6.49	44.54
compress	1.31	1.37	3.26
dfa	0.19	0.24	3.75
dhrystone	0.20	0.24	0.31
fft	0.37	0.47	5.15
go	12.07	20.86	2108.22
jpeg	12.83	14.85	41.29
nsieve	0.08	0.08	0.13
water	0.89	1.00	1.75
fmin	0.06	0.06	0.11
rkf45	0.18	0.22	0.57
seval	0.09	0.10	0.15
solve	0.12	0.12	0.31
svd	0.19	0.25	1.54
urand	0.03	0.03	0.04
zeroin	0.04	0.05	0.07
applu	1.84	2.34	7.03
doduc	4.01	5.20	22.24
fpppp	47.93	39.48	55.91
matrix300	0.08	0.08	0.14
tomcatv	0.13	0.15	0.26

4.2 The TI TMS320C62xx Architecture

The Texas Instruments TMS320C62xx chip (which we will refer to as TMS320) is one of the newest fixed point DSP processors [24]. From a scheduling perspective it has several interesting properties. The TMS320 is a VLIW that allows up to eight operations to be initiated in parallel. All eight functional units are pipelined, and most operations have no delay slots. The exceptions are multiplies (two cycles), branches (six cycles), and loads from memory (five cycles). NOPs are inserted into the schedule for cycles where no operations are scheduled to begin. The NOP operation takes one argument specifying the number of idle cycles.

This architecture has a clever way of "packing" operations into an instruction. Operations are always fetched eight at a time. This is called a *fetch packet*. Bit zero of each operation, called the p-bit, specifies the execution grouping of each operation. If the p-bit of an operation o is 1, then operation $o + 1$ is executed in parallel with operation o (*i.e.*, they are started in the same cycle.) If the p-bit is 0, then operation $o + 1$ begins the cycle after operation o. The set of operations that execute in parallel are called an *execute packet*. All operations in an execute packet must run on different functional units, and up to eight operations are allowed in a single execute packet. Each fetch packet starts a new execute packet, and execute packets cannot cross fetch packet boundaries. This scheme and the multiple-cycle NOP operation described above, allow the code to be quite compact.

We have modified our scheduler to target an architecture that has the salient features of the TMS320. Of course, there is not a one-to-one mapping of ILOC operations to TMS320 operations, but we feel our model highlights most of the interesting features of this architecture from a scheduling perspective. Our model has eight fully pipelined functional units. The integer operations have latencies corresponding to the latencies of the TMS320. Since ILOC has floating point operations and the TMS320 does not, these operations are added to our model. Each floating point operation is executed on a functional unit that executes the corresponding integer operation. Latencies for floating point operations are double those for integer operations. All ILOC intrinsics (cosine, power, square root, *etc.*) have a latency of 20 cycles. The experiments in the last section assumed perfect branch prediction. However, the TMS320 has no mechanism for predicting branches. Thus, every control-flow operation (including an unconditional jump) incurs a five cycle delay to refill the pipeline. We simulate this by adding five cycles to the dynamic instruction count each time a branch, jump, subroutine call, or subroutine return is executed.

Our static instructions counts reflect the TMS320 fetch packet/execute packet scheme. We place as many execute packets as possible in each fetch packet. NOPs in consecutive cycles are treated as one operation to be consistent with the multiple-cycle NOP on the TMS320. Each basic block begins a new fetch packet.

Table 4 shows the dynamic instruction counts for our TMS320-like architecture. Static instruction counts (*i.e.*, fetch packet counts) are reported in table 5. In dynamic instruction counts, we see improvements over basic block scheduling similar to those seen for the previous architectural model. On average, EBBS

Table 4. Dynamic Instruction Counts for TMS320

Benchmark	Basic Block Dynamic Insts	EBBS Dynamic Insts	% decrease	DPS Dynamic Insts	% decrease
clean	7120834	6809472	4.4	6759302	5.1
compress	6451078	5865494	9.1	5860732	9.2
dfa	1234284	1163901	5.7	1187176	3.8
dhrystone	6310416	6040418	4.3	5940418	5.9
fft	19134370	18881224	1.3	18896041	1.2
go	873164337	826369843	5.4	824064415	5.6
jpeg	59600121	58496774	1.9	58629470	1.6
nsieve	3810982127	3793649623	0.5	3793649623	0.5
water	37216606	34821429	6.4	34575067	7.1
fmin	4363	3852	11.7	3590	17.7
rkf45	621932	561135	9.8	564360	9.3
seval	2515	2443	2.9	2441	2.9
solve	2819	2692	4.5	2674	5.1
svd	12716	12023	5.4	12160	4.4
urand	1504	1487	1.1	1494	0.7
zeroin	3710	3391	8.6	3292	11.3
applu	676079366	658466445	2.6	658542326	2.6
doduc	13510434	12693031	6.1	12111705	10.4
fpppp	57174493	49772531	12.9	49523545	13.4
matrix300	33652694	33362954	0.9	33363754	0.9
tomcatv	291504852	291494375	0.0	265479402	8.9

showed a 5.0 per cent improvement over basic block scheduling, and DPS a 6.1 per cent improvement. Since the same number of control-flow operations are executed regardless of the scheduling method used, these percentages would improve if the architecture could take advantage of branch prediction information.

The reductions in static code size were not as dramatic as before and the size of the code actually increased in several cases. The average code size reduction due to EBBS was 2.2 per cent and 1.8 per cent from DPS. These results are due, at least in part, to the hardware code compaction scheme described above. Consider a basic block that has eight operations all packed into one instruction. If six of these operations are moved into another block, and the number of instructions in that block is increased by one, the overall length of the code will increase by one instruction. While we have not added any operations to the compiled code, the number of instructions can increase due to the code motion. This shows how effective the TMS320 design is at keeping object code compact. It also highlights the need for improved scheduling techniques to keep the static code size small for these architectures, while still improving runtime performance.

5   Conclusions and Observations

This paper has examined the problem of scheduling instructions without increasing code size. We looked at two techniques that consider regions larger than a

Table 5. Static Instruction Counts for TMS320

Benchmark	Basic Block	EBBS		DPS	
Benchmark	Static Insts	Static Insts	% decrease	Static Insts	% decrease
clean	1910	1886	1.3	1888	1.2
compress	302	293	3.0	292	3.3
dfa	344	289	16.0	302	12.2
dhrystone	109	106	2.8	111	-1.8
fft	358	352	1.7	350	2.2
go	12708	12619	0.7	12768	-0.5
jpeg	3011	2905	3.5	2932	2.6
nsieve	49	50	-2.0	50	-2.0
water	733	713	2.7	721	1.6
fmin	61	64	-4.9	63	-3.3
rkf45	185	175	5.4	179	3.2
seval	80	79	1.3	79	1.3
solve	117	110	6.0	113	3.4
svd	243	229	5.8	232	4.5
urand	23	25	-8.7	23	0.0
zeroin	40	40	0.0	41	-2.5
applu	1874	1847	1.4	1857	0.9
doduc	3760	3786	-0.7	3723	1.0
fpppp	1556	1543	0.8	1547	0.6
matrix300	77	69	10.4	69	10.4
tomcatv	127	127	0.0	128	-0.8

single basic block, but do not replicate code. We compared the performance of these two methods against that of list scheduling over single basic blocks. We reformulated the safety conditions for DPS to avoid problems that arose in our implementation of the algorithm.

1. Both techniques improved on the single block list scheduling by about seven percent. DPS produced better results, on whole, than EBBS. This may be due to the fact that DPS generated larger regions for scheduling.
2. Both EBBS and DPS required more compile time than list scheduling. EBBS was reasonably competitive with list scheduling, taking up to thirty percent longer. DPS required much more time–the worst case slowdown was two orders of magnitude. This suggests that better implementation techniques are needed for DPS.
3. On machines that require the compiler to insert NOPs for correctness, the improvement in running time may shrink the code. Our measurements showed that this averaged roughly eleven percent for the codes used in our study. The experiments with the TMS320 showed some negative results for code size; that machine's hardware strategy for achieving compact instructions makes the arithmetic of compiler-based code compaction very complex.

Taken together, these findings suggest that, even in a memory constrained environment, non-local scheduling methods can achieve significant speedups compared to a purely local approach. For machines that require NOPs, the accompanying reduction in code size may be important.

This study suggests two directions for future work.

- Techniques that quickly generate larger acyclic regions may lead to further reductions in running time (and code space), even when code growth is prohibited. These warrant investigation.
- A more efficient implementation of DPS is needed. This may be a matter of engineering; on the other hand, it may require some significant re-thinking of the underlying algorithms.

If code size is an issue, these techniques deserve consideration. In fact, the compiler writer should consider using EBB as the baseline scheduling technique, and using a best-of-several approach for final, production compiles. This approach has proved profitable on other problems [3]; Huber has recommended it for finding the best dominator-paths.

6 Acknowledgements

The scheduler was implemented inside the experimental compiler built by the Massively Scalar Compiler Group at Rice; the many people who have contributed to that effort deserve our heartfelt thanks. Also, thanks to Phil Sweany for his pointer to Brett Huber's work, to the referees for their helpful comments, and to DARPA and the USAF Research Laboratory for their support of this work.

References

1. Alfred V. Aho, Ravi Sethi, and Jeffrey D. Ullman. *Compiler: Principles, Techniques, and Tools.* Addison Wesley, 1986.
2. David Bernstein, Doron Cohen, and Hugo Krawczyk. Code duplication: An assist for global instruction scheduling. *SIGMICRO Newsletter*, 22(12):103–113, December 1991. *Proceedings of the 24th Annual International Symposium on Microarchitecture.*
3. David Bernstein, Dina Q. Goldin, Martin C. Golumbic, Hugo Krawczyk, Yishay Mansour, Itai Nahshon, and Ron Y. Pinter. Spill code minimization techniques for optimizing compilers. *SIGPLAN Notices*, 24(7):258–263, July 1989. *Proceedings of the ACM SIGPLAN '89 Conference on Programming Language Design and Implementation.*
4. David Bernstein and Michael Rodeh. Global instruction scheduling for superscalar machines. *SIGPLAN Notices*, 26(6):241–255, June 1991. *Proceedings of the ACM SIGPLAN '91 Conference on Programming Language Design and Implementation.*
5. Preston Briggs. The massively scalar compiler project. Technical report, Rice University, July 1994.
6. Kemal Ebcioglu and Toshio Nakatani. A new compilation technique for parallelizing regions with unpredictable branches on a VLIW architecture. In *Proceedings of the Workshop on Languages and Compilers for Parallel Computing*, August 1989.
7. John R. Ellis. *Bulldog: A Compiler for VLIW Architectures.* The MIT Press, 1986.

8. Joseph A. Fisher. Trace scheduling: A technique for global microcode compaction. *IEEE Transactions on Computers*, C-30(7):478–490, July 1981.

9. G. E. Forsythe, M. A. Malcolm, and C. B. Moler. *Computer Methods for Mathematical Computations*. Prentice-Hall, Inc., Englewood Cliffs, NJ, 1977.

10. Stefan Freudenberger, Thomas R. Gross, and P. Geoffrey Lowney. Avoidance and supression of compensation code in a trace scheduling compiler. *ACM Transactions on Programming Languages and Systems*, 16(4):1156–1214, July 1994.

11. Phillip B. Gibbons and Steven S. Muchnick. Efficient instruction scheduling for a pipelined architecture. *SIGPLAN Notices*, 21(7):11–16, July 1986. *Proceedings of the ACM SIGPLAN '86 Symposium on Compiler Construction*.

12. Rajiv Gupta and Mary Lou Soffa. Region scheduling: An approach for detecting and redistributing parallelism. *IEEE Transactions on Software Engineering*, 16(4):421–431, April 1990.

13. Brett L. Huber. Path-selection heuristics for dominator-path scheduling. Master's thesis, Computer Science Department, Michigan Technological University, Houghton, Michigan, 1995.

14. Wen-Mei W. Hwu, Scott A. Mahlke, William Y. Chen, Pohua P. Chang, Nancy J. Warter, Roger A. Bringmann, Roland G. Ouellette, Richard E. Hank, Tokuzo Kiyohara, Grant E. Haab, John G. Holm, and Daniel M. Lavery. The superblock: An effective technique for VLIW and superscaler compilation. *Journal of Supercomputing – Special Issue*, 7:229–248, July 1993.

15. Jens Knoop, Oliver Rüthing, and Bernhard Steffen. Lazy code motion. *SIGPLAN Notices*, 27(7):224–234, July 1992. *Proceedings of the ACM SIGPLAN '92 Conference on Programming Language Design and Implementation*.

16. Jens Knoop, Oliver Rüthing, and Bernhard Steffen. Partial dead code elimination. *SIGPLAN Notices*, 29(6):147–158, June 1994. *Proceedings of the ACM SIGPLAN '94 Conference on Programming Language Design and Implementation*.

17. David Landskov, Scott Davidson, Bruce Shriver, and Patrick W. Mallett. Local microcode compaction techniques. *ACM Computing Surveys*, pages 261–294, September 1980.

18. P. Geoffrey Lowney, Stephen M. Freudenberger, T. J. Karzes, W. D. Lichtenstein, Robert P. Nix, J. S. O'Donnell, and J. C. Ruttenburg. The Multiflow trace scheduling compiler. *Journal of Supercomputing – Special Issue*, 7:51–142, July 1993.

19. R.T. Prosser. Applications of boolean matrices to the analysis of flow diagrams. In *Proceedings of the Eastern Joint Computer Conference*, pages 133–138. Spartan Books, NY, USA, December 1959.

20. B. Ramakrishna Rau and Joseph A. Fisher. Instruction-level parallel processing: History, overview, and perspective. *Journal of Supercomputing – Special Issue*, 7:9–50, July 1993.

21. Philip H. Sweany. *Inter-Block Code Motion without Copies*. PhD thesis, Computer Science Department, Colorado State University, Fort Collins, Colorado, 1992.

22. Philip H. Sweany and Steven J. Beaty. Dominator-path scheduling – A global scheduling method. *SIGMICRO Newsletter*, 23(12):260–263, December 1992. *Proceedings of the 25th Annual International Symposium on Microarchitecture*.

23. Robert E. Tarjan and John H. Reif. Symbolic program analysis in almost-linear time. *SIAM Journal on Computing*, 11(1):81–93, February 1982.

24. Texas Instruments. *TMS320C62xx CPU and Instruction Set Reference Guide*, January 1997. Literature Number: SPRU189A.

An Efficient Data Partitioning Method for Limited Memory Embedded Systems *

Sundaram Anantharaman and Santosh Pande

Department of ECECS, University of Cincinnati, Cincinnati, OH 45221–0030
E-mail: {asundara,santosh}@ececs.uc.edu

Abstract. In this work we propose a framework to carry out an efficient data partitioning for arrays on limited memory embedded systems. We introduce a concept of footprint to precisely calculate the memory demands of references and compute a profit value of a reference using its access frequency and reuse factor. We then develop a methodology based on 0/1 knapsack algorithm to partition the references in local/remote memory. We show the performance improvements due to our approach and compare the results.

1 Introduction

Embedded systems are often characterized by limited resources. The architectures developed around embedded devices attempt to augment the limited on-chip resources with the additional ones. Memory on embedded systems (such as TMS320C2x series) is especially limited due to its high power consumption [12] . On the other hand, most of the applications (such as image processing codes, data compression/uncompression codes etc.) that execute on these systems are memory–intensive. In such cases, the data segment of such applications is split across the on-chip and off chip memory. This results in remote memory references which are expensive and can lead to significant degradation in real time response for these devices.

In this work, we propose a compiler optimization methodology that analyzes the memory demands and the frequency of references generated within the loops and performs efficient partitioning of data segments of codes. The issue of data segment partitioning must be addressed in conjunction with the need for low run time overheads for fast real time response and also the code size. One of the key issues is that part of the local memory of the embedded device is used up by the code generated for an application and this makes lesser memory available to the data segment. The issue of compact code generation has been addressed by other researchers [8] and is not focus of this work. However, one of the important implications of compact code generation and real time response stipulation is that addressing mechanisms for arrays must be simple. In particular, no run time address resolution should be carried out since that would result in extra code which can consume memory and can also slow down execution dramatically. Due to this reason, we undertake compile time partitioning of data segments and through an efficient algorithm based on 0/1 knapsack problem,

---
* This work was partially supported by NSF grant # CCR 9696129 and DARPA contract # ARMY DABT63-97-C-0029

we map these partitions on local/remote memory. The partitions are chosen to reflect the underlying *data footprints* of the references within a loop nest. We introduce a concept of data footprint of a reference which defines a smallest lattice polytope whose boundaries are compile time defined for address calculation purposes. In other words, for all the references that fall within this polytope, we are guaranteed that no *run time address resolution* will be needed and thus, we can carry out local/remote mapping of these footprints using 0/1 knapsack algorithm. References in remotely mapped footprints can then be suitably prefetched by hoisting code at the top of loop nest for which no run time resolution is needed.

The next section discusses the related work in the area of data partitioning and locality, while the section 3 discusses the outline of our approach. Section 4 defines terms and definitions. In section 5 we discuss our methodology and algorithms to solve the problem. Finally section 6 discusses results and conclusions.

2 Related work

Most compiler optimizations have focussed on decreasing the code size or have focussed on techniques to fit the code in the available memory on an embedded device through different techniques. Bowman et al [3] have attempted code mapping problem by overlapping program portions. Devadas et al [8] have attempted code size optimization by addressing the problem of instruction selection in code generation. They achieve this by formulating instruction selection as a binate covering problem for Directed Acyclic Graphs(DAGs). Recently, Kolson, Nicolau, Dutt and Kennedy have developed an optimal register allocation algorithm through loop unrolling [7]. However, these approaches focus on code size or register allocation and not on data segment partitioning.

Data partitioning has been extensively examined in parallel computing focusing on the issues of data alignment and interprocessor communication [14]. Some of the other typical uses of data partitioning are to enhance cache performance [9] and data locality [6]. Wolf and Lam [13] have achieved data locality of a loop nest in parallel programs, by transforming the code via interchange, reversal, skewing and tiling to minimize memory latency.

Data partitioning on memory scarce embedded devices is a challenging problem mainly due to a very limited amount of available memory and also due to tight requirements on real time response and code size. Thus, a new approach needs to be designed so that an efficient code could be generated obeying all these constraints. In this paper, we develop an approach based on a concept of compile time definable data partitions (called footprints) to carry out an effective data partitioning.

3 An Outline of Approach

Following is the outline of our approach:
• We first identify the footprint to be associated with each array reference within loop nest. In order to do this, we first classify the references for a given array within the loop nest and determine their overlaps and then compute the footprint

associated with them. A footprint associated with a group of references represents the tightest polytope that surrounds lattice elements accessed by those references. We then precisely compute the size of footprint in terms of the number of lattice points enclosed.

• After identifying the footprints, we associate a profit value that reflects the access frequency of lattice points enclosed in them corresponding to the underlying references.

• Using the size of footprint, profit-value and memory available on the embedded device as input parameters to a variation of 0/1 Knapsack algorithm we determine the set of footprints that can be fitted locally.

• We then relax the problem for simpler address calculation. We calculate a simple bounding box enclosing each footprint. The following is the motivation behind the relaxation. All data accesses of a array reference can be served by the footprint of the reference. Consequently fitting just the footprint on the local machine can suffice the needs of a array reference. However the address calculation within the footprint will be very complex due to the the shape of the footprint. We overcome this by using a bounding box which is rectangular in shape aligned parallel to each axis of the index variable.

• Using the above set of footprints, we enumerate the set of corresponding bounding boxes that can be fitted on the local machine. An exhaustive version of 0/1 knapsack is used in this case to find the optimal solution viz. the set of bounding boxes that could be locally fitted. An exhaustive solution is justified since the size of input that we are dealing with is small in this case due to elimination done using footprints in the previous step.

We thus first compute precise footprint values and use them to compute a 0/1 solution and then relax the solution to corresponding bounding boxes. An alternative approach could be used to identify the bounding boxes associated with each reference and use them directly to compute 0/1 solution. We claim that our approach of identifying the set of bounding boxes from a the set of footprints is more beneficial than using just the bounding boxes in the 0/1 knapsack algorithm. This is due to the fact that the knapsack is more closely packed by using object with small granularity in a 0.5-bounded solution (one may note that 0/1 knapsack problem is NP-hard and we have to resort to such a bounded solution to make this analysis tractable). This was concluded by a study by Sarkar et al [11]. Please refer to section 5.7 for an example which demonstrates the superiority of our approach based on precise footprints as against using the bounding boxes. The major contribution of our work is thus, the identification of the footprint of each reference, and devising a framework for its 0/1 solution and then relaxing it to enclosing bounded boxes for simplifying address calculation.

4 Terms and Definitions

Definition of G matrix: The statement in the loop body can have array references of the form A[g(i_1, i_2, i_3)] where the index function is g $:Z^l \longrightarrow Z^d$, l is the loop nesting with indices i_1, i_2 and i_3 and d is the dimension of the array A. We also assume that the array index expressions are affine function of loop indices. In other words, the index function can be expressed as g(i) = iG + a

where **G** is a l x d matrix with integer entries and a is an integer constant vector of length d, termed offset vector.

Definition of L matrix: An l dimensional square integer matrix **L** defines the l dimensional iteration space.

Null space of a matrix: Null space of a matrix $\mathbf{A}^{n \times m}$ is the set $\{\boldsymbol{x} | \boldsymbol{Ax} = 0\}$.

Data footprint of a reference: Data footprint of a reference g(i) is the polytope P in real space obtained by substituting the bounds of the loop index vector $\boldsymbol{i}$. Thus polytope P can be defined by a set of hyper-planes $\{A\boldsymbol{x} \geq \boldsymbol{k} | \boldsymbol{x}, \boldsymbol{k} \in I\!R^d\}$, where, $\boldsymbol{k} = g(\boldsymbol{I})$ where $\boldsymbol{I}$ is the extreme value of $\boldsymbol{i}$.

Intersecting references: Two references A[$g_1(\boldsymbol{i})$] and A[$g_2(\boldsymbol{i})$] are said to be intersecting if there are two integer vectors $(\boldsymbol{i_1})$, $(\boldsymbol{i_2})$ such that $g_1(\boldsymbol{i_1}) = g_2(\boldsymbol{i_2})$.

Uniformly generated references: Two references A[$g_1(\boldsymbol{i})$] and A[$g_2(\boldsymbol{i})$] are said to be uniformly generated if $g_1(\boldsymbol{i}) = (\boldsymbol{i})\mathbf{G} + \boldsymbol{a_1}$ and $g_2(\boldsymbol{i}) = (\boldsymbol{i})\mathbf{G} + \boldsymbol{a_2}$ where **G** is a linear transformation and $\boldsymbol{a_1}$ and $\boldsymbol{a_2}$ are integer constants.

Uniformly intersecting references: Two array references are uniformly intersecting if they are both intersecting and uniformly generated.

Spread of a set of vectors: Given a set of d-dimensional offset vectors $a_r 1 \leq r \leq R$, $spread(a_1, \dots \dots a_R)$ is a vector of the same dimension as the offset vectors, whose k-th component is given by $max_r(a_{r,k}) - min_r(a_{r,k}), \forall k \in 1, \dots \dots d$.

5 Theoretical framework of our approach

We first develop the criteria for classification of references. After classification we develop a methodology to calculate the footprint of each reference. We then discuss how to compute profit-values that can be associated with a footprint and methods to calculate them. Finally we present a partitioning algorithm based on 0/1 knapsack problem.

5.1 Classification of references

We classify references according to Fig. 1. This classification of references is done so as to identify references that can be combined depending upon the category they fall. After representing each reference in matrix format resulting in the **G** and offset matrices, we classify each reference as either Uniformly generated or Non-uniformly generated. This can be established after examining the **G** matrix of each reference. Uniformly generated references can be further classified as intersecting or non-intersecting by examining the **G** matrix. We use Omega Test [10] based on Fourier-Motzkin projections to determine whether there exists a non-empty integer solution. If a non empty integer solution exists the references are intersecting.

Uniformly generated intersecting references with offset differences: References which are uniformly generated and are intersecting have offset differences and are combined together and the cumulative footprint is determined. These references are treated together and the size of the cumulative footprint is determined to be used by the knapsack algorithm.

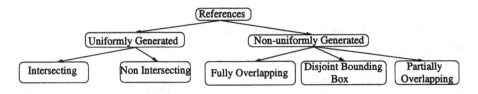

Fig. 1. Classification of references

Uniformly generated but non-intersecting references: References uniformly generated but which are non-intersecting are considered as separate references. This leads to evaluating the size of footprint, profit-value for each reference separately. The enclosing bounding box and their size is determined for each reference.

Non-uniformly generated but fully overlapping references: Two references are fully overlapping references, if the footprint of one of the references completely encloses the footprint of the other reference. This can be easily determined by checking the corresponding polytopes first in real spaces and then (if needed) in integer spaces. We use Fourier-Motzkin projections to determine whether references are overlapping. References that overlap are combined.

5.2 Bounding Box

Every footprint associated with a reference is a polytope, whose sides/edges need not be parallel to the coordinate axes. Fitting such an footprint on the embedded device, will demand a complex address translation mechanism. This is due to the fact that array elements are accessed linearly from the base of the array. We overcome this issue by considering a bounding box that will enclose the footprint. This bounding box has all its sides/edges parallel to the coordinate axes. Data elements within this bounding box can be accessed linearly from the base of this bounding box. Array references that were combined after classification are treated together, thus a combined bounding box is calculated for these set of references.

Building bounding box: Array-slice of each reference is found by calculating the vertices of the polytope. These vertices can be determined by substituting the lower and upper bounds of the loop on to the index expression. Bounding box that encloses this polytope is established by considering the extreme vertices on each coordinate axes.

Size of Bounding box: Once the extreme vertices of the bounding box is obtained the number of lattice points in the bounding box can be determined by primitive techniques. This will be used by the data partitioning algorithm to determine the actual amount of memory needed to fit the array locally on the embedded device. After determining the bounding boxes of each reference or each set of reference the Non-uniformly generated references can be further classified depending upon their bounding boxes.

Non-uniformly generated references with disjoint bounding box: References that are non-uniformly generated and with disjoint bounding box are considered separately for evaluating the size of the footprint profit-value, and

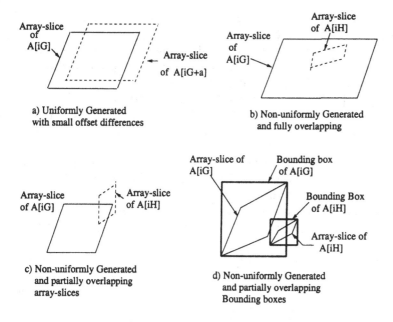

Fig. 2. Overlapping and intersecting footprints

size of bounding box.

Non-uniformly generated references with partial overlapping: References which are non-uniformly generated, but have their footprints overlapping partially fall in this category. Partial overlapping can also happen due to the overlapping of the bounding boxes, but not the footprints. We will consider each reference in this category as a separate reference thus calculating the size of footprint, profit-value and the bounding box for each reference. Figure 2 illustrates the different overlapping cases discussed above.

5.3 Calculating the size of an footprint of a reference

After the above classification, each reference or the set of references that are combined is associated with a footprint. The next step is to calculate the size of the footprint. To calculate the size of the footprint we need to determine the number of lattice points in the corresponding polytope. In order to determining the number of lattice points, we classify references according to their **G** matrices.

- **G** matrix that is Unimodular and Invertible.
- **G** matrix that is Non-unimodular and Invertible.
- **G** matrix that is Non-unimodular and Non-invertible.

G matrix that is Unimodular and Invertible: We will consider two cases :

1. **Single reference**

   The number of lattice points in the footprint of this reference is given by $|\det(\mathbf{D})|$, where $\mathbf{D} = \mathbf{LG}$.

2. **Cumulative number of lattice points in the footprint of a set of uniformly intersecting references**

Consider the case of two references, in which one of the offset vectors is (0,0). The cumulative number of lattice points in the footprint of these two uniformly intersecting references can be found by

$| det\mathbf{D} | + \sum_{k=1}^{d} | det\mathbf{D_{k\longrightarrow a}} |$ where $\mathbf{D}$ is the matrix obtained by the product of $\mathbf{L}$ and $\mathbf{G}$ and $D_{k\longrightarrow a}$ is the matrix obtained by replacing the k th row of $\mathbf{D}$ by 'a'.

Consider the case of multiple references. The basic approach for estimating the cumulative footprint size involves deriving an effective offset vector 'a' that captures the combined effects of multiple offset vectors when there are several overlapping footprints resulting from a set of uniformly intersecting references. According to a theorem stated by Agarwal et. al. [1,2] we have the following:

Given a matrix $\mathbf{L}$ representing the loop bounds and a unimodular reference matrix $\mathbf{G}$, the size of the cumulative footprint with respect to a set of uniformly intersecting references specified by the reference matrix $\mathbf{G}$ and a set of offset vectors $a_1, ...a_r$ is approximately

$| detD | + \sum_{k=1}^{d} | det\mathbf{D_{k\longrightarrow \hat{a}}} |$ where $\hat{a} = spread_D(a_1, a_2..., a_r)$ and $\mathbf{D_{k\longrightarrow \hat{a}}}$ is the matrix obtained by replacing the k th row of $\mathbf{D}$ by $\hat{a}$.

G matrix that is Non-unimodular and Invertible: A $\mathbf{G}$ matrix that is non-unimodular and invertible implies that not every integer point in the hyper-parallelepiped $\mathbf{D}$ is an image of an iteration point in $\mathbf{L}$. We are however interested in the total number of points enclosed by polytope, which also includes the points that are not referenced, but are within the polytope. The number of lattice points can be calculated by the same methodology used to calculate the number of lattice points when the $\mathbf{G}$ matrix is unimodular and invertible.

G matrix that is Non-unimodular and Non-invertible: In this subsection we calculate the number of lattice points when $\mathbf{G}$ matrix is non-unimodular and non-invertible. We restrict this case only to two dimensional references since the calculation in higher dimensions is highly combinatorial. In order to determine the number of lattice points enclosed by the corresponding polygon, we use Pick's theorem [4].

Pick's Theorem: The area of any simple polygon $\mathbf{P}$ in $I\!\!R^2$ (not necessarily convex) whose vertices are lattice points is

$Area = l_1 + \frac{l_0}{2} - 1$ where l_1 : Number of lattice points in the interior of the polygon and l_0 : Number of lattice points on the boundary of the polygon

Given the vertices of a line, n_0-number of points on this line can be calculated by using the formula

$n_0 = 1 + gcd((x_2 - x_1)(y_2 - y_1))$ where (x_1, y_1) and (x_2, y_2) are the end points of a line.

The number of lattice points on the boundary of the polygon can be determined using the above formula and the vertices of the polygon. The area of any polygon can be determined using primitive techniques of geometry. Once the number of lattice points on the boundary and the area of the polygon is found, Pick's theorem can be used to calculate the total number of lattice points.

This theorem is general for n-dimension space. However in dimensions greater than two, Pick's theorem uses the number of lattice points on the surface, edges of the polytope to calculate the volume. Calculating the number of lattice points for the surface and edge of a polytope is very complex. Therefore this method for calculating the number of lattice points using Pick's theorem is intractable except in 2 dimensional cases.

5.4 Profit-value of a reference

Each array reference is associated with a profit-value to reflect the benefit of fitting the footprint associated with this reference on the embedded device. In other words the profit-value of a reference will exhibit the reuse of an footprint. To calculate the profit-value we use the following two approaches.

Profit-value using the loop size: Every reference within a loop has a footprint associated with it. Therefore during each iteration of the loop, a reference will access one data element from the footprint. Thus the trip-count of the enclosing loop is the count of the number of times the footprint is referenced. This gives a measure of the profit-value. However, the profit value computed in this manner is not a precise measure of the remote references saved. A more precise measure is obtained by estimating the exact number of distinct references within the footprint of an array reference [1].

Profit-value using the number of distinct references: In this approach to calculate the profit-value, we find the number of distinct references within an footprint. Not every data element in an footprint is accessed during the execution of the loop. We determine the profit-value of a reference by computing the number of distinct accesses made by the reference. Consider the following example.

```
for i = 1 to 10
    for j = 1 to 10
        A[2i, 2i] = .... ;
    end for
end for
```

Trip-count of the loop = $10 * 10 = 100$.
Size of the footprint = $20 * 20 = 400$.
Number of distinct references = 10 (
Only alternative diagonal elements of
the footprint are accessed).
Profit-value = Number of distinct
references = 10.

We have devised an empirical algorithm to compute the number of distinct data elements accessed in an footprint. This empirical algorithm finds the number of distinct elements accessed by array references that are 2-dimensional. The motivation behind the following algorithm is that the distinct references are a reflection of temporal reuse which depends upon the null vector of the reference matrix **G**.

---

[1] The justification of using the distinct references is that remote references could always be cached on the local memory the first time they are used; thus, *actual* number of remote accesses is given by the number of distinct references

Algorithm for computing the number of distinct references

1. Compute the determinant of the reference matrix-**G**.
2. If determinant is not 0, then there does not exists a Null vector for this reference. This means there is no temporal reuse and the number of data elements accessed is equal to the total trip count of the enclosing loops.
3. Determine the reference matrix-**G** matrix, Null Vector for this reference-**N** matrix, and the loop size matrix-**B** matrix.
4. Initialize the DistRef (DistRef is a counter for distinct references) to 0.
5. Initialize rn to 1, where rn is the row number.
6. Multiply the rn^{th} row of the **N** matrix with all rows of **B** matrix excepting the rn^{th} row.
7. Add the value obtained from step 4 to DistRef.
8. Subtract the rn^{th} row of the **B** matrix by the rn^{th} row of the **N** matrix
9. Increment rn and repeat steps 4,5,6 as long as rn is lesser or equal to the number of rows in **N** matrix.

This algorithm can be illustrated by an example.

```
for i= 1 to k1
    for j = 1 to k2
        arr[a*i+b*j, d*i+e*j];
    }
}
```

For this code fragment :
$$G = \begin{pmatrix} a & b \\ d & e \end{pmatrix} \quad N = \begin{pmatrix} n_1 \\ n_2 \end{pmatrix} \quad B = \begin{pmatrix} k1 \\ k2 \end{pmatrix}$$
DistRef = 0 and rn = 1

Stepping through the algorithm :
First iteration through step 4
$n1 \times k2$
First iteration through step 5
DistRef = DistRef + $n1 \times k2$
First iteration through step 6
$$B = \begin{pmatrix} k1 - n1 \\ k2 \end{pmatrix}$$

Second iteration will result in
DistRef = DistRef + $n2 \times (k1 - n1)$
$$B = \begin{pmatrix} k1 - n1 \\ k2 - n2 \end{pmatrix}$$

5.5 0/1 Knapsack Algorithm

Finally we should use the above information about footprint sizes and profit values to decide 0/1 partitioning which is a 0/1 knapsack problem. In the 0/1 knapsack problem we are given n objects and a knapsack of finite capacity **M**. Object i, $(1 \le i \le n)$, has a weight **W**[i] and a profit **P**[i]. The problem is to maximize the total profit of the subset of the objects which can be packed into the knapsack without exceeding its capacity **M**. Stated more formally, the problem is to maximize $\sum_{i=1}^{n}$ **P**[i]**X**[i] subject to $\sum_{i=1}^{n}$ **W**[i]**X**[i] $\le$ **M**, and **X**[i] ϵ {0, 1}, $1 \le i \le$ n. The knapsack problem is similar to our problem of selecting the footprints that can be fitted in the local embedded device. The objects in the knapsack problem can be mapped to footprints in ours, the weight to the size of array slices, the profit to profit-value of a reference, and the capacity to the memory available on the embedded device.

The 0/1 knapsack problem is known to be NP-hard [5] and hence any algorithm which guarantees to provide optimal solution is believed to be computationally no less than semi-exhaustive in nature. We use the algorithm proposed by U.K. Sarkar et al [11](please refer to this paper for a detailed discussion about the algorithm), which is a greedy procedure whose solution is guaranteed to be 0.5-bounded.

5.6 Data partitioning

We now describe the data partitioning algorithm:

1. For each footprint evaluate the ratio $\frac{Profit-value}{Footprintsize}$
2. The sorted ratios above and the size of the memory are given as input to the 0/1 knapsack algorithm proposed by Sarkar et al [11]. This knapsack algorithm should output the set of footprints that can be accommodated on the local machine.
3. For the set of footprints selected we then relax the condition by computing their bounding boxes to simplify address calculation. If the all corresponding bounding boxes can be fitted in the memory, then the solution is found; else, we select the optimal subset of bounding boxes by exhaustively enumerating solutions.
4. Compute the resulting profit by adding up the corresponding profit of each bounding box chosen by the algorithm.

Extended case for Non-uniformly generated references with partial overlapping: After the data partitioning algorithm has computed the solution, it is possible that there is some memory not occupied in the embedded device. This may happen because the amount of memory remaining is not sufficient to accommodate any remaining footprint (bounding box). Under this scenario, we determine any of the remaining references (not accommodated) which have a partial overlap with any reference that has been accommodated. When a non-accommodated reference has a partial overlap with an accommodated reference, we determine a bounding box that can accommodate both of these references and attempt to fit the resulting bounding box on the embedded device. However if the resulting bounding box cannot be fitted on the embedded device, then we proceed with the original data partitioning.

5.7 Illustration of the algorithm

We now illustrate the data partitioning algorithm for the code fragment below. Table 1 lists the profits, footprint sizes and the bounding box sizes associated with the references in the code fragment. Let us assume this code is to be executed in an device with a memory capacity of 30. If we decide to perform the selection by using just the bounding boxes, the 0.5-bounded knapsack algorithm will select references B and C. Thus the profit achieved is 230. Using footprint sizes as a criteria results in the selection of references A, B, and C. Relaxing this to fit the corresponding bounding boxes will let us fit the bounding boxes of reference A and B on the device. The profit achieved by this method is 240 as against 230 obtained by using bounding boxes showing that our method based on precise footprints is superior.

```
1 for j = 1 to 10            8    for i = 1 to 4
2   for i = 1 to 6           9        C[1,i] = C[2, i+1]
3     A[ i/3, i] = i ;                    + A[i/2, i]
4   endfor                               + B[1, i]
5   for i = 1 to 8                        + B[2, i+1];
6       B[1,j] = B[2, i+1]   10 endfor
                 + 2*i;      11 C[1,j/4] = j;
7   endfor                   12 endfor
```

	Ref A	Ref B	Ref C
Profit	100	240	90
Footprint size	6	16	8
Bounding Box size	12	18	10

Table 1. table of references

Reference in Line	Lattice Pts	Bndg. Box pts	Cumm. pts
c's in 27	2400	2952	2572
d in 32	1680	2232	NA
a in 12	19	361	NA
b in 17	870	1682	NA
b in 22	3334	5074	NA
a in 7	5986	5986	NA

Table 2. table of references

6 Performance Evaluation

We evaluated our methodology by simulating an embedded system framework
discussed above using the Tiny Loop Restructuring Research Tool. We also assumed the memory latency to be 150 nanosecs for local access and 150 millisecs
for remote access. We tested our implementation using the sample test routine
below.

```
1    real a(1:300, 1:300)          18       endfor
2    real b(1:300, 1:300)          19     endfor
3    real c(1:300, 1:300)          20   for i = 1,15 do
4    real d(1:300, 1:300)          21     for j = 1,30 do
5    for i = 1,10 do               22       b(4*i+j, 2*j) =
6      for j = 2,20 do                        b(2*i + 2*i+j)
7        a(9*i-6, 4*j+3) =         23     endfor
                 i + j            24   endfor
8      endfor                      25   for i = 1,100 do
9    endfor                        26     for j = 2,25 do
10   for i = 1,10 do               27       c(i+j, j) =
11     for j = 1,10 do                         c(i+j+1,j+2)
12       a(i+j, i+j) =             28     endfor
                 a(i+5, j+11)      29   endfor
13     endfor                      30   for i = 1,70 do
14   endfor                        31     for j = 2,25 do
15   for i = 1,15 do               32       d(i+j, j)=a(j+5, j+10)
16     for j = 1,30 do                          + b((i mod 10)+2,
17       b(2*i,2*i+j) =                            (i mod 10)+3)
                 i * j                          + c(i+j,j)
                                   33     endfor
                                   34   endfor
```

In our sample code fragment there are 12 array references. Array references c(i+j, j) and c(i+j+1,j+2) are classified as uniformly intersecting , while other references are classified as non-uniformly generated. The uniformly intersecting references are combined and treated as a single reference. The cumulative footprint and the cumulative bounding box is determined for these references. Other references are treated separately. Array references 'a' in line 12 is Non-unimodular and non-invertible. The 'd' array reference is unimodular and invertible while array reference 'a' in line 7, array reference 'b' in line 17 and 22(b(4*i+j, 2*j)) are non-unimodular and invertible. References to array 'a', 'b' and 'c' in line 32 are totally overlapped by footprints of array references in lines 7, 17, and 27. Similarly array reference a(i+5, j+11) in line 12 is fully overlapped by reference in line 7 while array reference in line 22(b(2*i + 2*i+j)) is fully overlapped by the reference in line 17. After classifying the respective footprints and bounding boxes of references are determined. Table 2 gives the final list of references and the corresponding number of lattice points in the footprints(lattice pts), number of lattice points in the bounding box(Bndg. Box pts), and the cumulative number of points in cases where the footprints are combined(Cumm. pts). References to array 'c' being uniformly intersecting are combined which results in cumulative footprint. These precise footprints are input to the 0/1 knapsack algorithm to determine a subset that can be fitted locally. We further select references from this set whose bounding box can be accommodated in the local machine. We have examined the behavior of our methodology by varying the local memory available on the device. Following are the results obtained from using our methodology.

In graph (a), we observe that the loop completion time is lesser in cases when the distinct references are used instead of trip-count of the loop. This is due to the fact that distinct reference reflects reuse. Therefore the number of data elements is less than the trip-count. This allows us to pack more references locally. This results in better loop completion time as can be observed. However when the availability of memory increases, they converge. This implies that at low memory availability using distinct reference as the profit-value is better than using trip count as the profit-value.

In graph (b), we compare the percentage of memory utilized against the available memory. When the available memory is less, using either distinct references or trip-count for profit-value does not make a difference, but as memory increases the plots diverge. However the divergence is not in favor of any particular methodology of using distinct reference or trip-count for profit-value. The reason for this behavior is that the solutions found by our approach are non-optimal and the remnant capacity of the knapsack exhibits arbitrary behavior for non-optimal solutions (the remnant capacity can be shown to be bounded only in case of optimal solution [11].) In graph(c), at low memory availability considering distinct references for profit-value results in lesser number of remote accesses while at higher memory availability, they converge. This along with graph(a) suggests that distinct references for profit-value is effective in when available memory is low.

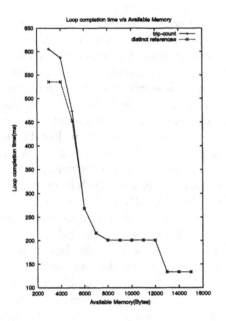

Fig. 3. graph (a)

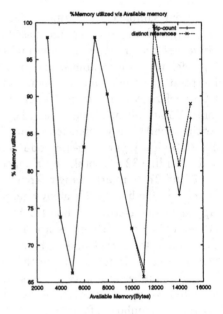

Fig. 4. graph (b)

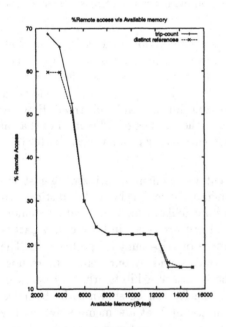

Fig. 5. graph (c)

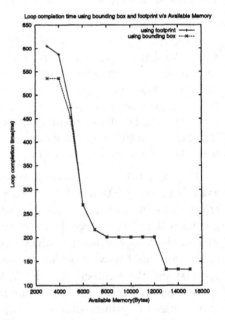

Fig. 6. graph (d)

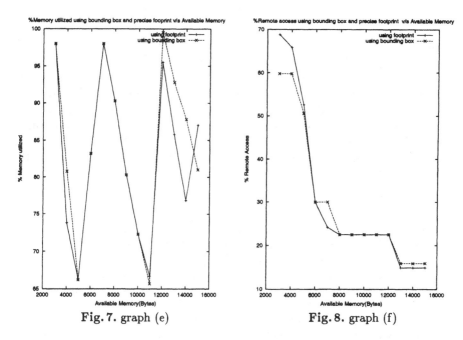

Fig. 7. graph (e) **Fig. 8.** graph (f)

In graphs (d) (e) and (f), we compare two approaches. The first approach is based on first computing the local/remote partition using precise footprint sizes and then relaxing the problem for choosing an appropriate subset of corresponding bounding boxes; whereas the second one is based on directly choosing a set of bounding boxes that could fit locally.

We observe that when the memory available is high, using the precise footprint and then the bounding box results in better performance. This is due to the fact that at high memory availability the footprints are more granular relative to the memory available. In Graph (e) our approach performs similar to the direct approach of using bounding boxes. However in all these graphs the second approach performs better than first approach at extreme low memory availability. This anomaly could be explained by the non-optimality of the solutions that are 0.5-bounded. An approach based on bounding boxes guarantees a solution that is 0.5–bounded from optimal; whereas an approach based on footprints would guarantee 0.5–bounded solution from the corresponding optima. However, when one relaxes the condition to corresponding bounding boxes, the second solution could degrade due to relatively higher granularity of selected bounding boxes that are in fact a sub–set of the complete set of bounding boxes. Thus, in some cases, it could be good to use precise footprints as starting inputs whereas in some others, bounding boxes could serve as better starting inputs. We are formalizing this problem to decide when in fact it is good to use footprint based approach and when is it better to use a bounding box based approach.

7 Conclusion

In this work, we have developed a framework for performing compile time analysis to determine efficient data partitioning of array references in loops on limited memory embedded systems. The tight demands on memory and real time response requirements make this problem especially challenging. Our methodology first attempts to determine precise values of footprints of references occuring within loop nests. We then use a variation of 0/1 knapsack problem to partition the reference into local/remote. Finally we relax the footprints to the corresponding bounding boxes and use exhaustive enumeration to determine the corresponding solution.

References

1. Anant Agarwal, David Kranz, and Venkat Natarajan. Automatic partitioning of parallel loops and data arrays for distributed shared memory multiprocessors. In *International Conferrence on Parallel Processing*, 1993.
2. Rajeev Barua, David Kranz, and Anant Agarwal. Communication-minimal partitioning of parallel loops and data arrays for cache-coherent distributed-memory multiprocessors. In *Languages and Compilers for Parallel Computing*, August 1996.
3. R. L. Bowman, E. J. Ratliff, and D. B. Whalley. Decreasing process memory requirements by overlapping program portions. In *Proceedings of the Hawaii International Conference on System Sciences*, pages 115–124, January 1998.
4. R.L. Graham, M. Grotschel, and L.Lovasz. Handbook of combinatorics-volume 1, The MIT Press. page 947.
5. E. Horowitz and S. Sahni. Fundamentals of computer algorimthms (Computer Science Press, Rockville, MD, 1984).
6. M. Kandemir, J. Ramanujam and A. Choudhary. A Compiler Algorithm for Optimizing Locality in Loop Nests. In *Proc. of 11th ACM International Conference on Supercomputing*, pages 269–278, Vienna, Austria, July 1997.
7. David J. Kolson, Alexandru Nicolau, Nikil Dutt, and Ken Kennedy. Optimal register assignment to loops for embedded code generation. In *ACM Transaction on Design Automation of Electronic Systems*, pages 251–279, April 1996.
8. Stan Liao, Srinivas Devadas, Kurt Keutzer, and Steve Tjiang. Instruction selection using binate covering for code size optim ization. In *International Conference on Computer-Aided Design*, 1995.
9. Frank Mueller. Compiler support for software-based cache partitioning. In *Workshop on Languages, Compilers and Tools for Real-time Systems*, June 1995.
10. W. Pugh. The Omega Test: A fast and practical integer programming algorithm for dependence analysis. In *Supercomputing '91*, 1991.
11. U. K. Sarkar, P. P. Chakrabarti, S. Ghose, and S. C. DeSarkar. A simple 0.5-bounded greedy algorithm for the 0/1 knapsack problem. In *Information Processing Letters*, pages 173–177, May 1992.
12. Texas Instruments. *TMS320C2x User's Guide*, 1993.
13. Michael E Wolf and Monica S Lam. A data locality optimizing algorithm. In *Programming Language Design and Implementation*, June 1991.
14. Hong Xu and Lionel M. Ni. Optimizing data decomposition for data parallel programs. In *International Conference on Parallel Processing*, 1994.

A Design Environment for Counterflow Pipeline Synthesis

Bruce R. Childers, Jack W. Davidson

Department of Computer Science, University of Virginia, Charlottesville, Virginia 22903
{brc2m, jwd}@cs.virginia.edu

Abstract. The Counterflow Pipeline (CFP) organization may be a good target for synthesis of application-specific microprocessors for embedded systems because it has a regular and simple structure. This paper describes a design environment for tailoring CFP's to an embedded application to improve performance. Our system allows exploring the design space of all possible CFP's for a given application to understand the impact of different design decisions on performance. We have used the environment to derive heuristics that help to find the best CFP for an application. Preliminary results using our heuristics indicate that speedup for several small graphs range from 1.3 to 2.0 over a general-purpose CFP and that the heuristics find designs that are within 10% of optimal.

1 Introduction

Application-specific microprocessor design is a good way to improve the cost-performance ratio of an application. This is especially useful for embedded systems (e.g., automobile control systems, avionics, cellular phones, etc.) where a small increase in performance and decrease in cost can have a large impact on a product's viability. A new computer organization called the *Counterflow Pipeline* (CFP), proposed by Sproull, Sutherland, and Molnar [8], has several characteristics that make it a possible target organization for the synthesis of application-specific microprocessors. The CFP has a simple and regular structure, local control, high degree of modularity, asynchronous implementations, and inherent handling of complex structures such as result forwarding and speculative execution.

Our research uses an application expressed algorithmically in a high-level language as a specification for an embedded microprocessor. The counterflow pipeline is a good candidate for this type of fast, aggressive synthesis because of its extreme composability and simplicity. This substantially reduces the complexity of synthesis because a CFP synthesis system does not have to design control paths, determine complex bus and bypass networks, etc.

We have built a framework for exploring the design space of application-specific counterflow pipelines. The environment includes tools for program optimization, synthesis experimentation, performance analysis, and design simulation. This paper describes how we used our environment to develop heuristics to narrow a CFP design space to pipeline configurations with good performance.

1.1 Synthesis Strategy

Most high-performance embedded applications have two parts: a control and a computation-intensive part. The computation part is typically a kernel loop that accounts for the majority of execution time, and increasing the performance of the computation part increases overall performance. Thus, synthesizing custom hardware for the computation-intensive portion may be an effective technique to increase performance.

The type of applications we are considering need only a modest kernel speedup to effectively improve overall performance. For example, the function j_rev_dct() accounts for 60% of total execution time in JPEG. This function consists of applying a single loop twice (the inverse discrete cosine transformation), so it is a good candidate for CFP synthesis. Figure 1 shows a plot of Amdahl's Law for various speedup values of j_rev_dct(). The figure shows that a small speedup of the kernel loop of 6 or 7 achieves most of the overall speedup.

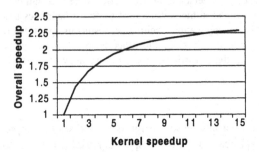

Figure 1. Overall speedup plotted using Amdahl's law for kernel loop speedups of 1 to 15.

Our synthesis system uses the data dependency graph (DDG) of an application's kernel to determine processor functionality and interconnection. Processor functionality is determined from the type of operations in the graph and processor topology is determined by exploring the design space of all possible interconnection network.

1.2 Related Work

Recently there has been much interest in automated design of application-specific integrated processors (ASIPs) because of the increasing importance of high-performance and quick turn-around in the embedded systems market. ASIP techniques address two problems: instruction set and microarchitecture synthesis. Instruction set synthesis tries to discover microoperations in a program that can be combined to create instructions [6]. The synthesized instruction set is optimized to meet design goals such as minimum code size and execution latency. Microarchitecture synthesis derives a microprocessor implementation from an application. Some microarchitecture synthesis methodologies generate a custom coprocessor for a portion of an application and integrate the coprocessor with an embedded core [5,7]. Another approach tailors a single processor to the resource requirements of the target application [3]. Although instruction set and microarchitecture synthesis can be treated independently, many codesign systems attempt to unify them into a single framework [2,4].

Our research focus is microarchitecture synthesis. We customize a CFP microarchitecture to an application using the SPARC instruction set and information about the data flow of the target application. Our microarchitecture synthesis technique has the advantage that the design space is well defined, making it easier to search for pipeline configurations that meet design goals.

1.3 Counterflow Pipeline

The counterflow pipeline has two pipelines flowing in opposite directions. One is the instruction pipeline. It carries instructions from an instruction fetch stage to a register file stage. When an instruction issues, an *instruction bundle* is formed that flows through the pipeline. The instruction bundle has space for the instruction opcode, operand names, and operand values. The other is the results pipeline that conveys results from the register file to the instruction fetch stage. The instruction and results pipelines interact: instructions copy values to and from the result pipe.

Functional units (or *sidings*) are connected to the pipeline through *launch* and *return* stages. Launch stages issue instructions into functional units and return stages extract results from functional units. Instructions may execute in either pipeline stages or functional units.

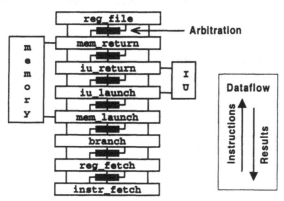

Figure 2. An example counterflow pipeline with memory and integer functional sidings.

A memory unit connected to a CFP pipeline is shown in Figure 2. Load instructions are fetched and issued into the pipeline at the instr_fetch stage. A bundle is created that holds the load's memory address and destination register operands. The bundle flows towards the mem_launch stage where it is issued into the memory subsystem.

When the memory unit reads a value, it inserts the value into the result pipeline at the mem_return stage. In the load example, when the load reaches the mem_return stage, it extracts its destination operand value from the memory unit. This value is copied to the destination register value in the load's instruction bundle and inserted into the result pipe. A *result bundle* is created whenever a value is inserted into the result pipeline. A result bundle has space for the result's register name and value. Results from sidings or other pipeline devices flow down the result pipe to the instr_fetch stage. Whenever an instruction and a result bundle meet in the pipeline, a comparison is done between the instruction operand names and the result name. If a result name matches an operand name, its value is copied to the corresponding operand value in the instruction bundle. When instructions reach the `reg_file` stage, their destination values are written back to the register file and when results reach the `instr_fetch` stage, they are discarded. In effect, the register file stores register values that have exited the pipe.

The interaction between instruction and result bundles are governed by special *pipeline* and *matching rules* that ensure sequential execution semantics. These rules govern the execution and movement of instructions and results and how they interact.

Arbitration is required between stages so that instruction and result bundles do not pass each other without a comparison of their operand names. In Figure 2, the blocks between stages depict arbitration logic. A final mechanism controls purging the pipeline on a branch misprediction or exception. A *poison pill* is inserted in the result pipeline whenever a fault or misprediction is detected. The poison pill purges both pipelines of instruction and result bundles.

As Figure 2 shows, stages and functional units are connected in a very simple and regular way. The behavior of a stage is dependent only on the adjacent stage in the pipeline, which permits local control of stages and avoids the complexity of conventional pipeline synchronization.

1.4 Execution Model

Our synthesis system models asynchronous counterflow pipelines by varying computational latencies. Table 1 shows the latencies we use for simulation.

Table 1. Computational latencies

Operation	Latency
Stage copy	1
Garner, kill, update	3
Return, launch	3
Instruction operation	5

The table's values are relative to the latency of moving an instruction or result between pipeline stages. From Table 1, we derive other pipeline latencies. such as an addition operation which takes 5 time units. High latency operations are scaled relative to low latency ones, so multiplication—assuming it is four times slower than addition—takes 20 time units.

2 Experimental Framework

Figure 3 depicts the synthesis framework. The system accepts a C source file containing a loop that drives customizing a CFP processor. The loop is compiled by the optimizer *vpo* [1] into instructions for the SPARC instruction set. During optimization, *vpo* builds the dependency graph for the kernel loop. The graph serves as an input to the rest of the synthesis system, which consists of phases for hardware allocation, processor topology determination, instruction scheduling, simulation, and performance analysis.

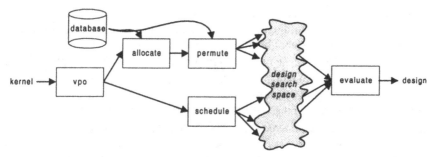

Figure 3. The synthesis system accepts a kernel loop and searches for a design that matches the loop's data flow and resource requirements.

2.1 Hardware Allocation

The first step of CFP synthesis is hardware allocation, which is done by the *allocate* phase. Hardware allocation determines processor functionality by assigning computational elements to data dependency graph (DDG) nodes.

allocate uses a design database of pipeline stages and functional sidings to determine what hardware devices to assign graph nodes. A database entry has fields for a name, a list of instruction opcodes, operation latency, siding depth, and device type. The name uniquely identifies devices in the database and the opcode gives the semantics of a device. *allocate* uses the opcode list to select the kind of device to assign a graph node. The latency field is device execution latency and the depth field is the pipeline length of a siding. The type field gives a device's kind and is one of: STAGE, LU, and RLU. STAGE identifies a device as a pipeline stage, LU as a siding that does not return a result (e.g., a unit for stores) and RLU as a siding that does return a result.

```
database "example" {
    entry "add" { type=STAGE; latency=5;
        opcodes={add, addcc}; };
    entry "branch" { type=STAGE; latency=5;
        opcodes={bne, be, bg, ble, bge, bl, bgu, bleu}; };
    entry "multiply" { type=RLU; latency=20; depth=4;
        opcodes={umul, smul}; };
    entry "memory" { type=RLU; latency=15; depth=3;
        opcodes={ldsb, ldsh, ldsw, stb, sth, stw}; }; }
```

Figure 4. An example design database with add, branch, multiply and memory devices.

An example database is shown in Figure 4. The first two entries are pipeline stages for addition and branch resolution. The add stage handles two addition opcodes, one that generates a condition code and one that does not. The branch stage resolves branch predictions for eight different branch opcodes. The database also has entries for two functional sidings. The multiply siding does either signed or unsigned multiplication in 20 cycles and has a siding depth of 4. The memory siding has a pipeline depth of 3 and executes load and store instructions in 15 cycles. This siding handles load and store instructions, including variants for word, halfword, and byte data types.

The design database makes it easy to partition processor functionality among pipeline stages and functional sidings. We use a database that consists of unique devices for every opcode group in the SPARC instruction set. For example, there is a single device in the database for unsigned and signed multiplication. We also partition functionality according to operation latency: pipeline stages execute low latency operations and sidings execute high latency operations.

Pipeline stages in the synthesized processor are determined from the type of device a graph node is assigned. *allocate* generates an unique pipeline stage of an appropriate type for every graph node that is assigned a STAGE device. If a node is assigned a functional siding, then *allocate* generates two stages for RLU devices and one stage for LU devices. An RLU device has two stages since it launches an instruction and returns a result. An LU siding needs only a single stage to launch instructions since it does not return results to the main pipeline. Pipeline stages for instruction fetch, a register cache, and a register file are always included in a CFP.

allocate may constrain the position of pipeline stages in a given processor topology. For example, *allocate* ensures that a siding's return stage appears after the siding's launch stage. It further ensures that the return stage appears at least the siding's *depth* stages later than the launch stage. *allocate* also consults design heuristics to determine stage position constraints. These constraints limit the number of topologies considered by the synthesis system.

A hardware functionality description is emitted by *allocate* that lists the types of functional elements a synthesized processor should contain and their position constraints. The description is a list of instantiated computational elements from the device database and the mapping of graph nodes to pipeline stages and sidings.

2.2 Processor Topology

The *permute* phase uses the specification from *allocate* to derive CFP topologies that obey the position constraints imposed by *allocate*. The topologies are determined by permuting the order of pipeline stages.

permute emits a processor design specification for each topology it generates. The specification includes the order of pipeline stages and the functional characteristics of each device in the synthesized processor. The specification has attributes for pipeline stages and sidings that specify device latency, type, siding depth, and instruction opcodes. The attributes are used by the CFP simulator to model device behavior and pipeline resources.

Figure 5 shows a processor specification with stages for instruction fetch, multiply launch and return, addition, and register file write-back. It also has a siding for multiplication. The addition stage has a latency of 5 and executes add and addcc instructions. The multiply launch and return stages (mulL0 and mulR0) launch and return multiplication operations into and from the multiplier siding. The multiplier has a latency of 20 and a pipeline depth of 4.

```
pipeline "example" {
  stage "fetch" { type=instr_fetch; };
  stage "mulL0" { latency=3; type=launch;
    operations={smul, umul}; };
  stage "add0" { latency=5; operations={add, addcc}; };
  stage "mulR0" { latency=3; type=return;
    operations={smul, umul}; };
  stage "rf" { type=reg_file; };
  siding "mul" { latency=20; depth=4; type=RLU;
    launch="mulL0"; return="mulR0";
    operations={smul, umul}; }; }
```

Figure 5. An example CFP specification with five stages and one functional siding.

2.3 Instruction Scheduling

vpo emits optimized SPARC instructions that serve as input to *schedule*, which determines all legal instruction schedules. Branch and bound techniques can be used during design evaluation to reduce the number of schedules considered for each pipeline configuration.

2.4 Processor Simulation

cfpsim is a behavioral simulator for counterflow pipelines. A CFP simulation is specified by a pipeline configuration (from *permute*), an instruction schedule (from *schedule*), and a mapping of instructions to pipeline devices (from *allocate*). The simulator generates an execution trace used by performance analysis that indicates the state of pipeline resources on every clock cycle.

The simulator models resource usage and instruction and result flow; it does not model microarchitecture devices. This makes the simulator fast and easy to reconfigure. Reconfiguration is simple because *cfpsim* needs to know only what resources are present in a CFP organization and their interconnection to simulate a design.

cfpsim models a counterflow pipeline using a *tiling strategy*. For every instruction executed, a *resource tile* is placed in a time-resource diagram that gives the instruction's usage of functional sidings, instruction pipeline registers, and result pipeline registers. The tile is a reservation table that depicts the usage of devices by an instruction for an empty pipeline. Results generated by an instruction are modeled in the reservation table as the resource usage of result pipeline registers.

2.5 Performance Analysis

The cross-product of pipelines from *permute* and schedules from *schedule* define a CFP design space. This space is large. For example, the finite impulse response filter data dependency graph (12 nodes) produces 2,580,480 pipelines and 42,735 schedules.

Our analysis tool, *evaluate*, traverses the design space to collect performance statistics for every processor/schedule combination. *evaluate* post-processes the execution traces from *cfpsim* to gather statistics about instruction and result flow, pipeline utilization and throughput. These statistics are used to pick the best pipeline/schedule combination and to emit a visual representation of the design space. The visual representation shows the overall design space and simulation details for each design point.

3 Synthesis Methodology

Our synthesis technique generates all processor topologies for a given set of functional units and pipeline stages to pick the best one. Although it is not apparent how to build the full design space for a traditional microprocessor organization, it is straightforward for the CFP since pipeline stage order specifies processor topology.

It is not practical to exhaustively search the entire design space for most DDG's because the space is not likely to be small when aggressive instruction-level parallelism transformations such as speculative execution, software pipelining, if-conversion, etc. are used. We are evaluating heuristics that reduce the size of the space while finding pipeline/schedule combinations with good performance.

3.1 Performance Factors

From preliminary work, we have identified several factors that affect performance. The distance results flow between their production and consumption affects a CFP's performance because the latency of executing instructions includes the time it takes to acquire source operands. This is affected by the result flow distance; the further a result flows, the greater the latency of the instruction. For example, widely separated producer and consumer stages can cause the consumer instruction to stall waiting for its source operands, which may also delay subsequent instructions. Although careful instruction scheduling can mask a portion of result flow latency, it is not likely to hide the entire latency. Thus, it is important to find the pipeline structure *and* instruction schedule that best hides result flow latency.

The latency of conveying a result is also affected by the number of instructions a result encounters as it flows from its producer stage to its consumer stage. A result moves more slowly through a stage containing an instruction than it does through an empty stage because the result's register names must be compared with the instruction's source and destination names. This suggests producer and consumer instructions should be placed close together in the instruction schedule (the opposite of what traditional scheduling does) to minimize flow latency. However, our experiments indicate it is not always necessary for producer and consumer to be immediately adjacent. They can be separated by up to a few instructions because there is usually "enough time" to overlap the movement of the consumer instruction and its source operands, ensuring they meet before the consumer reaches its execution stage.

From our studies, it appears that overlapping the movement of results and instructions is very important for good performance. The effect of adjusting both the pipeline structure and instruction schedule is to balance the pipeline using the program's dynamic instruction and result flow. A traditional synchronous pipeline is balanced *a priori* by a designer; however, this is not possible with the CFP because it has dynamically varying latencies.

The importance of pipeline balancing is demonstrated by the effect of adding *blank stages* that do not perform any operation to a CFP. One way to balance the pipeline is to insert blank stages before pipeline regions that have high resource contention. Inserting blanks allows an instruction contending for a busy pipeline stage to move up one position, occupying a blank stage (or series of blanks). By ensuring that instructions always make progress, subsequent instructions are more likely to flow to stages where they can begin executing.

It may not be necessary to insert actual blank stages. Instead, stages that are unused during a period of execution can be arranged to serve as pipeline queues. Such stages have the dual purpose to execute instructions and to act as place-holders. Using our design environment we have found that stages executing off-critical path instructions can effectively serve as queues and execute instructions in the "delay" of the critical path. It is, however, difficult to statically predict where placing these stages is most effective.

Another important performance issue is overlapping the execution of adjacent loop iterations to expose instruction-level parallelism. A CFP microarchitecture can be arranged to achieve hardware loop unrolling by ensuring that hardware resources needed by the following loop iteration are available early in the pipeline. It is best to place resources for operations which do not have loop carried dependences near the beginning of the pipeline because they are the least likely to stall while waiting for source operands.

A question related to hardware loop unrolling is where to resolve branches in the pipeline. If branches are resolved near the instruction fetch stage, then very little speculative execution is possible and an opportunity to execute operations across loop iterations may be lost. However, if branch resolution is done late in the pipeline, then the misprediction penalty is high. The location of branch resolution is important because a good CFP design should not over or under speculatively execute instructions. The ideal location for branch resolution can be found by trying the branch in all possible places in the pipeline and picking the best one.

3.2 Design Heuristics

Heuristics that use the factors mentioned above to guide the exploration of a CFP design space may narrow the space sufficiently and accurately so a good stage order and schedule are found. We do not presently consider the instruction schedule because the data dependency graph constrains the number of schedules.

This paper discusses two pipeline layout heuristics. The first confines the search space to designs that have pipeline stages in order of the critical path :

Heuristic 1: For nodes $\{n_1, n_2, ..., n_k\}$ and edges $\{(n_1, n_2), (n_2, n_3), ..., (n_{k-1}, n_k)\}$ on the critical path, evaluate only designs that have the partial order $\{n_1 \ll n_2, n_2 \ll n_3, ..., n_{k-1} \ll n_k\}$ wrt. pipeline stages ($x \ll y$ is the relation that x comes before y).

The pipeline order is with respect to the instruction fetch stage, so the root of the critical path is the closest to instruction fetch. This order overlaps the execution of instructions from different loop iterations while minimizing the distance results flow along the critical path. If the pipeline is arranged in the reverse order so the root of the critical path is placed near the register file, then there is no overlap between loop iterations. In this case, an entire iteration flows into the pipeline with the last critical path instruction stalled at the bottom of the pipeline. This keeps the next iteration from entering the pipeline and beginning execution.

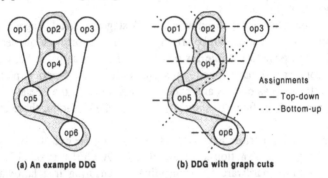

(a) An example DDG   **(b) DDG with graph cuts**

Figure 6. An example dependency graph is shown in (a) and the same graph is shown in (b) with greedy assignment of graph nodes from top-down and bottom-up.

This heuristic lets stages that execute non-critical path instructions occur any place in the pipeline. This ensures that the synthesis system finds the position for each stage that both executes instructions in the delay of the critical path and serves as a place-holder to let instructions move up the pipeline.

Figure 6 shows a DDG with the critical path highlighted. The partial order for this graph using heuristic 1 is: {$op2 \ll op4$, $op4 \ll op5$, $op5 \ll op6$}. For example, $op1$ can appear any place, while $op5$ must appear after $op4$ and before $op6$. Hardware allocation imposes this partial order on stage positions. Although this heuristic determines good pipeline layouts, in many cases is considers a large number of design points.

A second heuristic considers many fewer pipeline configurations by generating a more refined partial order. The heuristic preserves critical path order using the DDG to define operation partitions by drawing cuts across each level of the graph.

Heuristic 2: For the graph $G = (N, E)$, divide N into K partitions, where K is the maximum path length in E. Use the partitions to impose a partial order on pipeline stages such that $\forall n_i \in partition_k$ and $\forall n_j \in partition_{k+1}$ then $n_i \ll n_j$ is in the partial order. Assign nodes to a partition according to an assignment heuristic and the dependence edges E. Evaluate only designs that have the partial order wrt. pipeline stages.

The cuts determine a partial order that places operations from level n before operations from level $n+1$ (root is level 0) in a pipeline. Figure 6 shows the assignment of nodes to partitions in (b).

In the figure, the "top-down" assignment of operations gives the partial order: {$op1 \ll op4$, $op2 \ll op4$, $op3 \ll op4$, $op4 \ll op5$, $op5 \ll op6$}. In this example, $op1$, $op2$, and $op3$ all must occur within the first three pipeline stages (in any order), $op4$ occurs in the fourth position, $op5$ in the fifth, and $op6$ in the sixth position.

Assignment of nodes to instruction partitions can proceed top-down or bottom-up.

Top-down assigns nodes to early instruction cuts so operations begin executing as soon as possible, while bottom-up minimizes the distance results flow between their definition and use. In Figure 6, the bottom-up assignment works best since it minimizes the distance results move between their production and consumption. We have found that bottom-up assignment works well for most graphs.

Heuristic 2 forms instruction groups that execute in parallel in a way similar to very long instruction word (VLIW) formation. After forming instruction partitions, there is a single path through the DDG and the instruction groups are arranged in the order of this path. The order of operations is not constrained within a partition to let the synthesis system find the optimal local arrangement of pipeline stages in a partition while minimizing result flow distance between partitions.

4 Results

Preliminary results for several graphs are shown in Figure 7. The speedup in the figure is relative to a general-purpose pipeline that has separate sidings for memory, multiplication, and integer operations, and a pipeline stage for branch resolution. The figure shows speedup for three pipeline orders: *optimal*, *heuristic 1*, and *heuristic 2*. In all cases, the partitioning of functionality is the same: every graph node is assigned an unique pipeline stage or siding. The *optimal* pipeline had the best performance from all pipeline stage permutations. The *heuristic 2* pipelines use late assignment to allocate graph nodes to partitions.

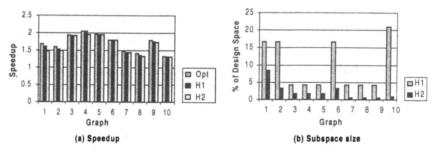

Figure 7. Speedup of custom pipelines over a general-purpose CFP is shown in (a) and the size of the design space searched by each heuristic is shown in (b).

The graphs in Figure 7 have less than 8 nodes. The nodes are mostly integer operations, except for graph 10 which has memory and multiplication operations. We selected these benchmarks because they were small enough to generate the full design space and demonstrate the effectiveness of the search heuristics. As we evaluate more realistic kernels with more instruction-level parallelism we expect that greater speedups will be achieved. Furthermore, a CFP may be faster than conventional processors due to the absence of global signals and better implementation technology.

The figure shows that the search heuristics find pipelines that are nearly as good as optimal. The performance difference between the heuristically determined pipelines and the optimal pipeline is less than 10%. This difference is influenced by start-up cost: The optimal stage orders have a lower start-up penalty because they order stages to favor requesting source operands from the register file.

Both search heuristics work well. *Heuristic 2* does nearly as well as *heuristic 1*, while evaluating fewer designs. Indeed, for graphs 3, 5, 7, and 10, *heuristic 2* finds the same pipelines as *heuristic 1*. Figure 7(b) shows a comparison of the number of designs evaluated by each heuristic as a percentage of the overall design space. Both heuristics reduce the size of the search space from up to several thousand design points to just a few hundred points that can be searched very quickly. Indeed, our current environment evaluates up to 1800 pipeline/schedule combinations per hour on a Sun 167 MHz UltraSPARC 1 workstation and we expect a production version of our synthesis technique could achieve even faster search speeds.

The graphs in Figure 7 show that the heuristics constrain the search space to a small number of pipelines and find designs that are nearly as good as optimal. Although these initial experiments are small, we expect the heuristics to also work for full applications. Future work however, must include heuristics for instruction scheduling as well as pipeline layout.

5 Conclusion

This paper describes a design environment for studying counterflow pipeline organizations. Our preliminary experiments demonstrate that the CFP is a flexible target for high-level synthesis of embedded microprocessors. The work also shows the importance of exploring a large design space to further understanding of a new computer organization.

References

1. Benitez M. E. and Davidson, J. W., "A portable global optimizer and linker", *1988 Symp. on Programming Lang. Design and Implementation*, pp. 329–338, Atlanta, Georgia, June 1988.

2. Binh N. N., Imai M, Shiomi A, et al., "A Hardware/software partitioning algorithm for designing pipelined ASIPs with least gate counts", *Proc. of 33rd Design Automation Conf.*, pp. 527–532, Las Vegas, Nevada, June 1996.

3. Corporaal H. and Hoogerbrugge J., "Cosynthesis with the MOVE framework", *Symp. on Modelling, Analysis, and Simulation*, pp. 184–189, Lille, France, July 1996.

4. Gupta R. K. and Micheli G., "Hardware-software cosynthesis for digital systems", *IEEE Design and Test of Computers*, Vol. 10, No. 3, pp. 29–41, Sept. 1993.

5. Hauser J. R. and Wawrzynek J., "Garp: A MIPS processor with a reconfigurable coprocessor", *IEEE 5th Annual Symp. on Field-Programmable Custom Computing Machines*, pp. 12–21, Napa Valley, California, April 1997.

6. Huang I-J and Despain A. M., "Synthesis of application specific instruction sets", *IEEE Trans. on Computer-Aided Design of Integrated Circuits and Systems*, Vol 14, No. 6, pp. 663–675, June 1995.

7. Razdan R. and Smith M. D., "A high-performance microarchitecture with hardware-programmable functional units", *Proc. of 27th Annual Int'l Symp. on Microarchitecture*, pp. 172–180, San Jose, California, Dec. 1994.

8. Sproull R. F., Sutherland I. E., and Molnar C. E., "The counterflow pipeline processor architecture", *IEEE Design and Test of Computers*, pp. 48–59, Vol. 11, No. 3, Fall 1994.

End-to-End Optimization in Heterogeneous Distributed Real-Time Systems

Seonho Choi

Department of Computer Science, Bowie State University, Bowie, MD 20715, U.S.A.

Abstract. In this paper we address an end-to-end optimization problem in a distributed real-time system when a set of pipelined task chains are given. End-to-end deadlines and end-to-end jitter constraints are assumed to be given for task chains, in addition to an objective function to be optimized throughout the optimization process. The objective of the optimization process is to obtain local deadlines and other system parameters that not only satisfy all the given end-to-end constraints but also minimize a given objective function.

A *separable programming* technique is used to solve the resulting nonlinear programming problems. If an objective function and constraints satisfy a certain condition, it is shown that those problems can be solved by using a linear programming technique which already has well-established theories and results. Also, it is shown that the condition is general enough that a wide class of optimization problems can be solved in designing distributed real-time systems by using this technique.

1 Introduction

Distributed real-time systems usually consist of heterogeneous resources like CPUs with different scheduling algorithms, local area networks (LAN) with various real-time multiple access control (MAC) protocols. End-to-end requirements may exist in such systems like end-to-end deadline and jitter constraints, dependability(reliability) constraints, etc. In designing such systems, decisions should be made on allocating resources to real-time streams and on selecting system parameters in each resource (e.g. local deadlines) such that the required end-to-end requirements are satisfied.

A considerable amount of study has been carried out on real-time scheduling and analysis techniques on single processor and on single communication network. For example, utilization based schedulability tests were obtained for various processor scheduling algorithms and real-time MAC protocols in LANs. Even though some of them provide only sufficient conditions, they provide unified mechanisms to test schedulabilities in heterogeneous resources.

In this paper we employ a system model similar to those given in [4, 9]. A set of pipelined task chains are assumed to be given with each task in the chain mapped to a designated CPU or network resource. In previous papers [8, 4, 9] it has been shown that this abstraction can be used in many real-time applications. End-to-end deadlines and end-to-end jitter constraints are assumed to be given for task chains, in addition to an objective function to be optimized throughout the optimization process. The objective of our optimization is to select parameters, including local deadlines and other system parameters like $TTRT$ [1] in a timed-token protocol for ring networks, that minimize a given objective function and satisfy all the end-to-end constraints.

An optimization technique, called *separable programming* [2], is employed in this paper to solve nonlinear problems resulting from the system model. Separable programming technique can be applied to any nonlinear programming problem as long as the objective function and constraint functions can be represented as sums of one-variable functions. As a special case, if those functions satisfy certain convexity[2] assumptions, it will be shown that the problems can be solved by using a linear programming technique like a *simplex algorithm*.

There have been a lot of recent activities in end-to-end design and analysis of real-time systems. The problem of scheduling with end-to-end deadlines was addressed in several papers[18, 3, 16]. Jeffay [8] introduced a real-time producer/consumer paradigm for expressing task precedence constraints and for reasoning about end-to-end timing behavior. Gerber et. al. [6] provided a comprehensive uni-processor design methodology for guaranteeing end-to-end timing requirements through calibrating parameters of periodic tasks.

Multi-resource end-to-end scheduling problem were addressed by several papers for different applications. Huang and Du [7] extended the uni-processor real-time producer/consumer paradigm and provided a multi dimensional bin-packing approach to resource allocation and task scheduling. Limitations of their approach is that only CPU and disk resources were considered, each executing rate-monotonic algorithm. Also, no end-to-end timing analysis were provided. Chatterjee et. al. [4] proposed a distributed pipeline scheduling paradigm for real-time and multimedia systems. They refined producer consumer paradigm and developed a mechanism to implement the paradigm in heterogeneous distributed systems. However, automated optimization issues were not addressed in their works. In [9], a design method was presented for distributed systems with statistical, end-to-end real-time constraints, and with statistical resource requirements.

The contribution made in this paper is that an efficient optimization technique is introduced that can be used to solve many nonlinear problems in end-to-end design of heterogeneous distributed real-time systems. This technique is general enough to be applied to a wide class of optimization problems even though we applied the technique to a simple example problem in this paper.

In Section 2 a system model is presented with a problem definition. In Section 3 and 4 results (schedulability conditions) on real-time processor and communication scheduling are summarized. Using these results, a simple example problem is formulated in Section 5. In Section 6 a separable programming technique is explained in detail with some useful theorems. A solution to the example problem is shown at the end of this section. Finally, a conclusion follows.

---

[1] Target Token Rotation Time

[2] A function f is convex if $f(\lambda x_1 + (1-\lambda)x_2) \leq \lambda f(x_1) + (1-\lambda)f(x_2)$ for all $\lambda \in [0,1]$ and all $x_1 < x_2$. f is *strictly convex* if $f(\lambda x_1 + (1-\lambda)x_2) < \lambda f(x_1) + (1-\lambda)f(x_2)$ for all $\lambda \in [0,1]$ and all $x_1 < x_2$.

2 System Model and Problem Definition

The following is a formal description of our system model:

Resources: A set of resources, $\{R_1, R_2, \ldots, R_\alpha\}$, where a given resource R_i corresponds to a CPU or a network resource in the system. Associated with R_i are scheduling algorithm(arbitration protocol) and its schedulability condition that can be expressed as a conjunction of inequalities whose properties will be given later. The schedulability condition for a resource is a function of its associated scheduling algorithm, or arbitration protocol (in the case of a network resource).

Task Chains: A set of N task chains, denoted as $\Gamma_1, \ldots, \Gamma_N$, are given where the jth task in a chain Γ_i is denoted τ_{ij}. A task may be a computational task in a CPU or a message transmission task in a network resource like a local area network(LAN). Γ_i can be characterized as $(\mathcal{P}_i, \mathcal{D}_i, \mathcal{J}_i)$, where

- $\mathcal{P}_i$ is a minimum inter-arrival time between two consecutive invocations of Γ_i.
- $\mathcal{D}_i$ is a *relative end-to-end deadline* of Γ_i, i.e., the maximum amount of time that can elapse between an invocation of one instance of Γ_i and completion of its tasks.
- $\mathcal{J}_i$ is a *jitter constraint* on consecutive output times of Γ_i relative to their invocation times. That is, suppose that two consecutive instances of τ_{i1} have been invoked at t_1 and t_2, respectively, at a source resource. Then, the difference between their completion times should lie in the interval $[t_2 - t_1 - \mathcal{J}_i, t_2 - t_1 + \mathcal{J}_i]$.

And τ_{ij} is characterized as $(C_{ij}, P_{ij}, D_{ij}, \rho_{ij})$, where

- C_{ij} is a maximum execution(transmission[3]) time that may be spent for τ_{ij}.
- P_{ij} is a minimum inter-invocation time of τ_{ij}. P_{ij} is set to be equal to P_i.
- D_{ij} is a relative deadline for τ_{ij}. That is, if one instance of τ_{ij} is invoked at time t_1, then it should be completed within $t_1 + D_{ij}$. It is assumed that $D_{ij} \leq P_{ij}$, and D_{ij}'s are decided by our optimization process, i.e., D_{ij}'s are the input variables to our optimization algorithm.
- ρ_{ij} denotes a resource to which τ_{ij} is mapped.

A producer/consumer relationship exists between each connected pair of tasks $\tau_{i(j-1)}$ and τ_{ij}, and we assume there exists an one-slot buffer between each such pair. The flow control algorithm presented next guarantees that no data in the buffer is lost during the system operation.

Flow Control: If the data traffic in a chain is not regulated at each intermediate resource, then jitters between consecutive chain output times will be very

---

[3] This includes the time to transmit both the data and message headers. It is assumed that a propagation delay is not included.

large if the number of resources in the chain increases. This paper assumes that every pair of adjacent resources in a chain uses a flow control mechanism similar to the Jitter Earliest Due Date [19] to regulate the data arrival times from the previous resource. After a task $\tau_{i(j-1)}$ has completed its execution, its output data is stamped with difference between its deadline and actual finishing time. A regulation algorithm in the next adjacent resource will delay the invocation of τ_{ij} by that difference even though its input data has already arrived. By using this regulation algorithm, the jitter on consecutive output times of Γ_i may be restricted by an upper bound of D_{il} where τ_{il} is the last task in Γ_i.

An *effective utilization* of a resource R_k, $1 \leq k \leq \alpha$, is defined to be $U_k = \sum_{\tau_{ij} \text{ is mapped into } R_k} \frac{C_{ij}}{D_{ij}}$

Suppose that every parameter defined above is known except D_{ij}, then our objective in this paper is to obtain an optimal values of D_{ij} and other system parameters that satisfy all the timing constraints and minimize a given objective function.

Example

As an example optimization problem, we consider the problem of designing a distributed real-time system which consists of 3 stations(S_1, S_2, S_3) connected through an FDDI network as is shown in Figure 1.

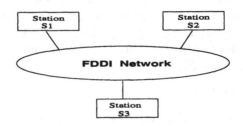

Fig. 1. Example Distributed Real-time System

We assume that stations 1 and 3 use a fixed priority (deadline monotonic) scheduling algorithm with an optimal priority inheritance protocol[15], and that station 2 uses an EDF scheduling algorithm with a stack based protocol[1]. Also, a timed-token protocol [11] is assumed to be used in an FDDI network with a token walk time $\tau = 1.0$. There exist 3 task chains as follows.

$$\Gamma_1: \ \tau_{11} \text{ at } S_1 \longrightarrow \tau_{12} \text{ at FDDI} \longrightarrow \tau_{13} \text{ at } S_3 \tag{1}$$
$$\Gamma_2: \ \tau_{21} \text{ at } S_2 \longrightarrow \tau_{22} \text{ at FDDI} \longrightarrow \tau_{23} \text{ at } S_3$$
$$\Gamma_3: \ \tau_{31} \text{ at } S_1 \longrightarrow \tau_{32} \text{ at FDDI} \longrightarrow \tau_{33} \text{ at } S_2$$

The parameters for the task chains and their constituent tasks are as follows.

$$\Gamma_1: \ \mathcal{P}_1 = 20 \ \mathcal{D}_1 = 48.3 \ \mathcal{J}_1 = 10 \tag{2}$$
$$C_{11} = 8 \ C_{12} = 2 \ C_{13} = 2 \ PD_{13} = 0.3$$

$$\Gamma_2: \quad \mathcal{P}_2 = 15 \quad \mathcal{D}_2 = 45.3$$
$$C_{21} = 8 \quad C_{22} = 2 \quad C_{23} = 7 \quad PD_{23} = 0.3$$
$$\Gamma_3: \quad \mathcal{P}_3 = 20 \quad \mathcal{D}_3 = 55.4$$
$$C_{31} = 6 \quad C_{32} = 3 \quad C_{33} = 6 \quad PD_{12} = 0.4$$

Note that PD_{ij} denotes a propagation delay from a station S_i to S_j.

3 Background — Processor Scheduling

In this section we present rate-based schedulability tests for various real-time processor scheduling algorithms. First, the schedulability conditions for fixed priority scheduling algorithms are presented, and then those for dynamic-priority scheduling algorithms are given.

3.1 Fixed Priority Scheduling Algorithm

Suppose that a set of tasks are given whose relative deadlines are less than or equal to their minimum inter-arrival times. In this case, a deadline monotonic scheduling algorithm is known to be optimal, where a task with a shorter deadline is assigned a higher priority than the task with a longer deadline. But, because the deadlines are variables in our optimization process, we can't assign the optimal priorities until the optimization process is completed and the deadlines are decided. However, the following theorem [15] allows us to represent the schedulability constraint in terms of the deadline variables.

Suppose that a set of n sporadic tasks $\{\tau_1, \tau_2, \ldots, \tau_n\}$ are given.

Theorem 1 *A set of n sporadic tasks with deadlines less than or equal to their periods can be scheduled by the deadline monotonic algorithm with a priority ceiling protocol, for all task phasings, if the following conditions are satisfied:*

$$\forall i, \ 1 \le i \le n, \ \frac{C_1}{D_1} + \ldots + \frac{C_n}{D_n} + \frac{B_i}{D_i} \le n(2^{1/n} - 1) \tag{3}$$

where B_i is the maximum time τ_i can be blocked by another task when τ_i is assigned a highest priority.

In the original formula given in [15], B_i is defined as the maximum time τ_i can be blocked waiting for a lower-priority task to complete its use of protected data. However, in this theorem, B_i is defined in a more pessimistic manner, i.e., the maximum time τ_i can be blocked by another task in any priority assignment scenario. This is because D_i's are to be decided by our optimization algorithm and the priorities cannot be assigned before the optimization process completes.

3.2 Dynamic Priority Scheduling Algorithm

In this section schedulability conditions for an Earliest Deadline First(EDF) scheduling algorithm are given. Other dynamic priority scheduling algorithms exists, but EDF is a most well-known algorithm, and many results are already obtained about this algorithm in real-time systems.

Several concurrency control protocols have been developed for EDF, including Dynamic Priority Ceiling Protocol [5] and Stack based Resource Allocation Protocol [1]. The schedulability conditions with these protocols are summarized in the following two theorems.

Theorem 2 *A set of n sporadic tasks are schedulable by an EDF algorithm with a dynamic priority ceiling protocol if*

$$\sum_{i=1}^{n} \frac{C_i + B_i}{D_i} \le 1 \qquad (4)$$

Theorem 3 *A set of n sporadic tasks are schedulable by an EDF algorithm with a stack-based protocol if*

$$\forall i,\ 1 \le i \le n,\ \sum_{j=1}^{i} \frac{C_j}{D_j} + \frac{B_i}{D_i} \le 1 \qquad (5)$$

4 Background – Communication Scheduling

In this section, several Multiple Access Control(MAC) protocols and their utilization based schedulability tests are briefly presented. Note that we present only some of the results, and others may also be used in our optimization process as long as the separable programming technique can be applied. For example, utilization based schedulability condition is found for slotted ring network in [12] which can also be used in our optimization procedure.

4.1 Priority Driven Protocol

Fixed-priority scheduling algorithm may be extended to schedule arriving real-time sporadic messages in distributed systems connected through a common bus or a ring network. The following theorem [14] presents a rate-based schedulability testing mechanism. In this theorem the definition of *transmission schedulability* is used [17].

Theorem 4 *For the priority-driven protocol using the IEEE 802.5 standard, a set of n sporadic messages is t-schedulable ,for all message arrival phasings, if the following conditions are satisfied [14]:*

$$\forall i,\ 1 \le i \le n, \qquad (6)$$

$$\sum_{j=1}^{n} \frac{C_j + Overhead_j}{D_j} + \frac{B_i}{D_i} \le n(2^{1/n} - 1)$$

where C_i, $Overhead_i$, D_i, and B_i are the worst-case message transmission time of τ_i, the overheads in terms of transmission time[4], t-Deadline of τ_i, and the worst-case blocking time during which τ_i may be delayed by lower priority tasks when τ_i is assigned a highest priority, respectively.

In [14] the schedulability conditions are given for Conventional Token Release(CTR) and Early Token Release(ETR) scheduling models for the IEEE 802.5 token ring network. Details on how $Overhead_i$ and B_i can be obtained from system parameters are given in the paper.

4.2 Transmission Control Based Approach – The Timed-token Protocol

In this paper, the result developed by Malcolm and Zhao is presented and extended [11]. They proposed a simple local bandwidth allocation scheme:

$$H_i = \frac{C_i}{\lfloor \frac{D_i}{TTRT} - 1 \rfloor} \tag{7}$$

The *worst case achievable utilization*[5] is found to be [11]:

$$U^* = (1 - \frac{2}{\lfloor \frac{D_{min}}{TTRT} \rfloor + 1})(1 - \frac{\tau}{TTRT}) \tag{8}$$

Note that the following holds:

$$U^* \geq (1 - \frac{2}{\frac{D_{min}}{TTRT}})(1 - \frac{\tau}{TTRT}) = (1 - \frac{2TTRT}{D_{min}})(1 - \frac{\tau}{TTRT}) \tag{9}$$

Hence, if the total effective utilization $U = \sum_{i=1}^{n} C_i/D_i$ is less than or equal to $(1 - \frac{2TTRT}{D_{min}})(1 - \frac{\tau}{TTRT})$, then the task set is schedulable according to the above result. This is true under the assumption that TTRT value is given prior to optimization. However, as is seen in (9), the lower bound on U^* depends not only of D_{min} but also of TTRT. In designing real-time systems the parameters like TTRT and H_is should also be chosen such that the resource usage is optimized. For this purpose, the value of TTRT will be obtained in terms of D_{min} that maximizes the right-hand side function of (9):

$$(1 - \frac{2TTRT}{D_{min}})(1 - \frac{\tau}{TTRT}) \tag{10}$$

If we differentiate this function with respect to TTRT, we obtain a derivative $\frac{-2}{D_{min}} + \frac{\tau}{TTRT^2}$. If we set this derivative equal to 0, we obtain $TTRT^2 = \frac{\tau D_{min}}{2}$. Then, the value of TTRT that maximizes the function in (10) is $TTRT =$

---

[4] The overhead is from transmission of header and trailer fields of packets and from transmission of control token around the ring.

[5] If a total effective utilization is less than or equal to the worst case achievable utilization, then the task set is schedulable for any task phasing.

$\sqrt{\frac{\tau D_{min}}{2}}$. If we substitute this expression for $TTRT$ in (10), we obtain the following maximized approximate lower bound function of U^* in terms of D_{min}:

$$U^* \geq (1 - \sqrt{\frac{2\tau}{D_{min}}})^2 \qquad (11)$$

It can be easily proved that the function $(1 - \sqrt{\frac{2\tau}{D_{min}}})^2$ is *concave*[6] for $3.556\tau \leq D_{min}$ by examining the second derivative. The second derivative of this function is less than 0 for $3.556\tau \leq D_{min}$.

The optimal value of $TTRT$ that maximizes the original U^* function in (8) is as follows [11]:

$$TTRT = \frac{D_{min}}{\lceil \frac{-3 + \sqrt{9 + \frac{8D_{min}}{\tau}}}{2} \rceil} \qquad (12)$$

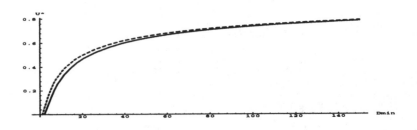

Fig. 2. Worst case achievable utilization(U^*) versus minimum deadline(D_{min}) when $\tau = 1$. Dashed curve shows a function in (8) with optimal $TTRT$. Solid curve shows an approximate lower bound function given in (11).

From Figure 2 we figure out that there exist some differences between two curves even though they are small. Hence, a curve fitting algorithm is employed to find out a better lower bound function that more closely approximates the original function. Note that the approximating function given in (11) can be expressed as $1 - 2\frac{\sqrt{2\tau}}{\sqrt{D_{min}}} + \frac{2\tau}{D_{min}}$. Functions in $\{1, 1/\sqrt{D_{min}}, 1/D_{min}\}$ are used as basis functions to obtain the following approximating function, which is a linear combination of those basis functions. Here, it is assumed that $\tau = 1$.

$$U^* \geq 0.9535 - \frac{2.367}{\sqrt{D_{min}}} + \frac{1.418}{D_{min}} \qquad (13)$$

---

[6] A function f is concave if and only if $-f$ is convex.

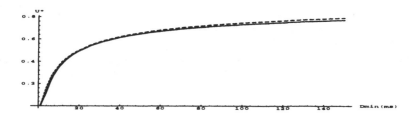

Fig. 3. Worst case achievable utilization(U^*) versus minimum deadline(D_{min}) when $\tau = 1$. Dashed curve shows a function in (8) with optimal $TTRT$. Solid curve shows a new approximating function given in (13).

Figure 3 shows the newly obtained curve from (8).

From the above results, the following theorem follows(Again, $D_j \leq P_j$ is assumed.). Also, $\tau = 1$ is assumed in this theorem. For other values of τ similar results may be derived.

Theorem 5 *A set of n sporadic messages can be successfully transmitted with timed-token protocol if the following condition is satisfied:*

$$\forall i, \ 1 \leq i \leq n \ :: \tag{14}$$

$$\sum_{j=1}^{n} \frac{C_j}{D_j} - 0.9535 + \frac{2.367}{\sqrt{D_i}} - \frac{1.418}{D_i} \leq 0$$

Note that the function $-0.9535 + \frac{2.367}{\sqrt{D_{min}}} - \frac{1.418}{D_{min}}$ is a convex function with one variable D_i for $2 \leq D_i$.

5 Example

A nonlinear programming problem is derived for the example problem given in Section 2. In this formulation, it is assumed that no objective function is given and the problem is formulated as a feasibility problem for the purpose of simplicity.

Various objective functions may be defined and used such as a sum of weighted effective utilizations, or a sum of weighted remaining capacities(in terms of utilization) of all resources for load balancing purpose. In this example, it is assumed that the blocking times B_{ij} are assumed to be equal to 0.3 for tasks.

The variables, k_1, k_2, k_3, k_4, are redundant slack variables (≥ 0) that may be useful in some cases. For example, if the objective is to maximize the weighted sum of remaining capacities(utilizations) of all resources, the objective of the optimization would be to minimize $\sum_{j=1}^{5} -w_j k_j$. where w_j is a weight assigned for resource R_j.

Example P: (15)

Find a feasible solution satisfying:

$$\frac{8.3}{D_{11}} + \frac{6}{D_{31}} + k_1 \leq 0.8284 \qquad \frac{8}{D_{11}} + \frac{6.3}{D_{31}} + k_1 \leq 0.8284$$

$$\frac{8.3}{D_{21}} + \frac{6}{D_{33}} + k_2 \leq 1 \qquad \frac{8}{D_{21}} + \frac{6.3}{D_{33}} + k_2 \leq 1$$

$$\frac{2.3}{D_{13}} + \frac{7}{D_{23}} + k_3 \leq 0.8284 \qquad \frac{2}{D_{13}} + \frac{7.3}{D_{23}} + k_3 \leq 0.8284$$

$$\frac{0.582}{D_{12}} + \frac{2}{D_{22}} + \frac{3}{D_{32}} - 0.9535 + \frac{2.367}{\sqrt{D_{12}}} + k_4 \leq 0$$

$$\frac{2}{D_{12}} + \frac{0.582}{D_{22}} + \frac{3}{D_{32}} - 0.9535 + \frac{2.367}{\sqrt{D_{22}}} + k_4 \leq 0$$

$$\frac{2}{D_{12}} + \frac{2}{D_{22}} + \frac{1.582}{D_{32}} - 0.9535 + \frac{2.367}{\sqrt{D_{32}}} + k_4 \leq 0$$

$$8 \leq D_{11} \leq 20 \quad 2 \leq D_{12} \leq 20 \quad 4 \leq D_{13} \leq 10$$

$$8 \leq D_{21} \leq 15 \quad 2 \leq D_{22} \leq 15 \quad 7 \leq D_{23} \leq 15$$

$$6 \leq D_{31} \leq 20 \quad 3 \leq D_{32} \leq 20 \quad 6 \leq D_{33} \leq 20$$

$$D_{11} + D_{12} + D_{13} + 0.3 \leq 48.3$$

$$D_{21} + D_{22} + D_{23} + 0.3 \leq 45.3$$

$$D_{31} + D_{32} + D_{33} + 0.4 \leq 55.4$$

6 Separable Programming

We can use a separable programming technique [2] to obtain solutions to non-linear programs where the objective function and the constraint functions can be expressed as the sum of functions, each involving only one variable. Such a separable nonlinear program *Problem P* can be expressed as follows:

Problem P: (16)

$$\text{Minimize} \quad \sum_{j=1}^{m} f_j(x_j)$$

$$\text{subject to} \quad \sum_{j=1}^{m} g_{ij}(x_j) \leq q_i \quad \text{for } i = 1, \ldots, l$$

$$x_j \geq 0 \qquad \qquad \text{for } j = 1, \ldots, m$$

The set of constraints derived from our system model fits into this model since the linear and nonlinear functions in the constraints involve only one variable.

We now discuss how one can define a new problem that approximates the original problem P. The new problem is obtained by replacing each nonlinear function by an approximating piecewise linear functions. We wish to define a piecewise linear function $\hat{f}(\mu)$ that approximates $f(\mu)$ over the interval $[a, b]$. The interval $[a, b]$ is first partitioned into smaller intervals, via the grid points $a = \mu_1, \mu_2, \ldots, \mu_k = b$. The function f is approximated in the interval $[\mu_\nu, \mu_{\nu+1}]$ as follows. Let $\mu = \lambda\mu_\nu + (1 - \lambda)\mu_{\nu+1}$ for some $\lambda \in [0, 1]$. Then

$$\hat{f}(\mu) = \lambda f(\mu_\nu) + (1 - \lambda)f(\mu_{\nu+1})$$

Note that the grid points may or may not be equidistant, and also that the accuracy of the approximation improves as the number of grid points increase. However, a major difficulty may arise in using the above linear approximation to a function. This is because a given point μ in the interval $[\mu_\nu, \mu_{\nu+1}]$ can be alternatively represented as a convex combination of two or more nonadjacent grid points. To illustrate, consider the function f defined by $f(\mu) = \mu^2$. The graph of the function on the interval $[-2, 2]$ is shown in Figure 4.

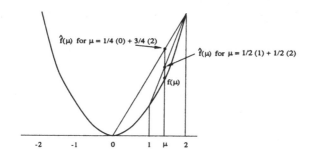

Fig. 4. Importance of adjacency in approximation

Suppose that we use the grid points -2, -1, 0, 1, and 2. The point $\mu = 1.5$ can be written as $(1/2) \cdot (1) + (1/2) \cdot (2)$ and also as $(1/4) \cdot (0) + (3/4) \cdot (2)$. The value of the function f at $\mu = 1.5$ is 2.25. The first approximation gives $\hat{f}(\mu) = 2.5$, whereas the second approximation gives $\hat{f}(\mu) = 3$. Clearly, the first approximation using adjacent grid points yields better approximation. In general, therefore, the function f can be approximated over the interval $[a, b]$ via the grid points $\mu_1, \ldots, \mu_k$ by the piecewise linear function $\hat{f}$ defined by

$$\hat{f}(\mu) = \sum_{\nu=1}^{k} \lambda_\nu f(\mu_\nu), \qquad \sum_{\nu=1}^{k} \lambda_\nu = 1, \tag{17}$$
$$\lambda_\nu \geq 0 \quad \text{for } \nu = 1, 2, \ldots, k$$

where at most two adjacent λ_ν's are positive.

We now present a problem that approximates the separable *Problem P* defined in (16). This is done by considering each variable x_j for which either f_j or g_{ij} is nonlinear for some $i = 1, 2, \ldots, m$ and replacing it with the piecewise linear approximation defined by (16). We first define a set L as

$$L = \{j : f_j \text{ and } g_{ij} \text{ for } i = 1, \ldots, l \text{ are linear}\}$$

Then, for each $j \notin L$, we consider the interval of interest $[a_j, b_j]$, where $a_j, b_j \geq 0$. We can now define the grid points $x_{j\nu}$ for $\nu = 1, 2, \ldots, k_j$, where $x_{1j} = a_j$ and $x_{k,j} = b_j$. Note that the grid points need not be spaced equally and that different grid lengths could be used for different variables. Using the grid points for each $j \notin L$, from (17) the functions f_j and g_{ij} for $i = 1, \ldots, l$ could be replaced by their linear approximations given below. Note again $j \notin L$ below.

$$\hat{f}_j(x_j) = \sum_{\nu=1}^{k_j} \lambda_{j\nu} f_j(x_{j\nu}) \tag{18}$$
$$\hat{g}_{ij}(x_j) = \sum_{\nu=1}^{k_j} \lambda_{j\nu} g_{ij}(x_{j\nu}) \text{ for } i = 1, \ldots, l$$
$$\sum_{\nu=1}^{k_j} \lambda_{j\nu} = 1$$
$$\lambda_{j\nu} \geq 0 \qquad \text{for } \nu = 1, \ldots, k_j$$

By definition, both f_j and g_{ij} for $i = 1, \ldots, l$ are linear for $j \in L$. Hence no grid points need to be defined, and in this case the linear approximations are given by

$$\hat{f}_j(x_j) = f_j(x_j), \quad \hat{g}_{ij}(x_j) = g_{ij}(x_j)$$
$$\text{for } i = 1, \ldots, l \text{ and } j \in L$$

By using the definition of $\hat{f}_j$ and $\hat{g}_{ij}$ for $j \notin L$, the problem can be restated in an equivalent more manageable form as *Problem LAP* defined as follows.

Problem LAP: (19)

$$\text{Minimize } \sum_{j \in L} f_j(x_j) + \sum_{j \notin L} \sum_{\nu=1}^{k_j} \lambda_{j\nu} f_j(x_{j\nu})$$

$$\text{subject to } \sum_{j \in L} g_{ij}(x_j) + \sum_{j \notin L} \sum_{\nu=1}^{k_j} \lambda_{j\nu} g_{ij}(x_{j\nu}) \leq q_i$$
$$\text{for } i = 1, 2, \ldots, l$$

$$\sum_{\nu=1}^{k_j} \lambda_{j\nu} = 1 \qquad \text{for } j \notin L$$

$$\lambda_{j\nu} \geq 0 \qquad \text{for } \nu = 1, \ldots, k_j, \ j \notin L$$

$$x_j \geq 0 \qquad \text{for } j = 1, 2, \ldots, m$$

At most two adjacent $\lambda_{j\nu}$'s are positive for $j \notin L$.

Solving the Approximating Problem

With the exception of the constraint that, at most two adjacent $\lambda_{j\nu}$'s are positive for $j \notin L$, Problem *LAP* is a linear program. For solving Problem *LAP*, one can use the simplex method with the following *restricted basis entry rule*. A non-basic variable $\lambda_{j\nu}$ is introduced into the basis only if it improves the objective function and if the new basis has no more than two adjacent $\lambda_{j\nu}$'s that are positive for each $j \notin L$ [2]. The following theorem shows that for $j \notin L$, if g_{ij} is convex for $i = 1, \ldots, l$ and if f_j is strictly convex, we can discard the restricted basis entry rule and adopt the simplex method for linear programming [10].

Theorem 6 *Suppose that for $j \notin L$, f_j is strictly convex and that g_{ij} is convex for $i = 1, \ldots, l$. Let $\hat{x}_j$ $(j \in L)$ and $\hat{\lambda}_{j\nu}$ $(\nu = 1, \ldots, k_j$ and $j \notin L)$ be the solutions found from Problem LAP defined in (19). Then, the following is true:*

1. *For each $j \notin L$, at most two $\hat{\lambda}_{j\nu}$'s are positive, and they must be adjacent.*
2. *Let $\hat{x}_j = \sum_{\nu=1}^{k_j} \hat{\lambda}_{j\nu} x_{j\nu}$ for $j \notin L$. Then the vector $\hat{x}$ whose jth component is $\hat{x}_j$ for $j = 1, \ldots, m$, is feasible to the original Problem P.*

Since the problems derived from our system model satisfy the convexity conditions of this theorem, we can apply any linear programming technique to obtain a feasible solution to *Problem LAP* without using the restricted basis entry rule.

However, note that the above theorem only provides a sufficient condition for finding out the solution for the original *Problem P*. That is, the above theorem is useful only if we can find a feasible solution for *Problem LAP*, and if we can't find a feasible solution then we have to increase the number of grid points and re-apply the simplex algorithm to find a feasible solution for the extended *problem LAP*. By increasing the number of grid points, better solution can be found that more closely approximates the optimal solution. For example, in solving the problem (15), it is possible that the solution obtained with given grid points may have negative values for some slack variables, which is not a feasible solution. In that case, new grid points have to be added until a feasible solution is found, or until it turns out that no feasible solution exists.

The problem of how additional grid points have to be chosen is explained in more detail at the end of this section, and at this point, we just assume that after each iteration 1 additional grid point is added to the system in an optimal manner. Our algorithm used in our paper is stated next.

1. Set the number of grid point, k_j, for each x_j to 2. (start and end points of the interval)
2. Transform the problem into *Problem LAP* using the grid points.
3. Apply a simplex algorithm.
   (a) If a feasible solution is found, then exit.
4. Add 1 more grid point to some variable x_j where $j \notin L$.
5. Go to Step 2.

Example

A feasible solution to the example problem given in (15) can be found by using a separable programming technique. Problem (15) is approximated by the following problem where only two grid points (end points) are used for each D_{ij} variable.

The problem defined in (15) is transformed into a linear programming problem defined in (19) with 22 variables (including slack variables) and 21 constraints (including 9 additional constraints, $\sum_{\nu=1}^{2} \lambda_{ij\nu} = 1$). The actual set of constraints is not given here because of space limitations. The feasible solution obtained by applying a linear programming technique is as follows:

$D_{11} = 18.82$ $D_{12} = 20$ $D_{13} = 9.18$
$D_{21} = 15$ $D_{22} = 15$ $D_{23} = 15$
$D_{31} = 18.96$ $D_{32} = 18.92$ $D_{33} = 17.11$

Also, an optimal $TTRT$ value for FDDI network is obtained from (12):

$$TTRT = 3$$

It can be shown, at each iteration of our algorithm, that the number of variables in the transformed linear programming problem (LAP) is $O(GM)$, and the number of constraints is $O(M)$, w here G is a total number of grid points used for all variables and M is the total number of tasks in the system. The number of constraints doesn't vary even if the number of grid points is incremented at each iteration. This is a good property since the number of constraints affects the computation times of simplex algorithm more than the number of variables[13].

Generation of the Grid Points

It should be noted that the accuracy of the procedure discussed above largely depends upon the number of grid points for each variable. However, as the number of grid points is increased, the number of variables in the approximating linear program also increases. One approach is to use a coarse grid initially and then to use a finer grid around the optimal solution obtained with the coarse grid. An attractive alternative is to generate grid points when necessary. The detailed procedure can be found in page 463-467 in [2], and is not given due to the space limitation. Performance of such algorithms should be experimentally evaluated for our system model, and it is left as one of our future works.

7 Conclusion

An efficient end-to-end optimization algorithm is developed in this paper for designing heterogeneous distributed real-time systems. A separable programming technique is utilized as a basic solution approach in this paper, and it is shown that, under certain convexity conditions, the derived nonlinear programming problems can be solved by using a linear programming algorithm. We used a simple example to show its applicability. System parameter values like $TTRT$ for FDDI network were obtained as well as local deadlines satisfying all the end-to-end constraints.

References

1. T. P. Baker. A Stack-Based Resource Allocation Policy for RealTime Processes. In *Proceedings, IEEE Real-Time Systems Symposium*, 1990.
2. M. Bazaraa. *Nonlinear Programming: Theory and Algorithms*, chapter 11. Separable Programming, pages 453–471. John Wiley & Sons, 1979.
3. R. Bettati and J. Liu. End-to-end scheduling to meet deadlines in distributed systems. In *Proceedings, IEEE International Conference on Distributed Computing Systems*, 1992.
4. S. Chatterjee and J. Strosnider. Distributed Pipeline Scheduling. *The Computer Journal*, 38.
5. M. Chen and K. Lin. Dynamic Priority Ceilings: A Concurrency Control Protocol for Real-Time Systems. *Real-Time Systems*, 2(4):325–346, 1990.
6. R. Gerber, S. Hong, and M. Saksena. Guaranteeing End-to-End Timing Constraints by Calibrating Intermediate Processes. In *Proceedings IEEE Real-Time Systems Symposium*, 1994. Also available as University of Maryland CS-TR-3274, UMIACS-TR-94-58.
7. J. Huang and D. Du. Resource management for continuous mutimedia database applications. In *Proceedings, IEEE Real-Time Systems Symposium*, Dec. 1994.
8. K. Jeffay. The real-time producer/consumer paradigm. In *ACM/SIGAPP Symposium on Applied Computing*, Feb. 1993.
9. D. Kang, R. Gerber, and M. Saksena. Performance-based design of distributed real-time systems. In *Proceedings, IEEE Real-Time Technology and Applications Symposium*, June 1997.
10. D. Luenberger. *Linear and Nonlinear Programming*, chapter The Simplex Method, pages 30–84. Addison-Wesley, 1984.
11. N. Malcolm and W. Zhao. The timed-token protocol for real-time communication. In *IEEE Computer*, Jan. 1994.
12. S. Mukherjee, D. Saha, M. Saksena, and S. Tripathi. A bandwidth allocation scheme for time constrained message transmission on a slotted ring lan. In *Proceedings, IEEE Real-Time Systems Symposium*, pages 44–53, Dec. 1993.
13. K. Murty. *Linear and Combinatorial Programming*, chapter Appendix 1, pages 541–552. John Wiley & Sons, 1976.
14. S. S. Sathaye and J. K. Strosnider. Conventional and Early Token Release Scheduling Models for the IEEE 802.5 Token Ring. *Real-Time Systems*, 7:5–32, 1994.
15. L. Sha, R. Rajkumar, and J. P. Lehoczky. Priority Inheritance Protocols: An Approach to Real-Time Synchronization. *IEEE Transactions on Computers*, 39(9):1175–1185, September 1990.
16. L. Sha and S. Sathaye. A systematic approach to designing distributed real-time systems. In *IEEE Computer*, Sep. 1993.
17. L. Sha, S. Sathaye, and J. Strosnider. Scheduling real-time communication on dual link networks. In *Proceedings, IEEE Real-Time Systems Symposium*, pages 188–197, Dec. 1992.
18. J. Sun, J. Liu, and R. Bettati. And End-to-End Approach to Scheduling Periodic Tasks with Shared Resources in Multiprocessor Systems. Technical report, University of Illinois at Urbana-Champaign, Department of Computer Science, 1994.
19. D. Verma, Hui Zhang, and D. Ferrari. Guaranteeing delay jitter bounds in packet switching networks. In *Proceedings of Tricomm'91*, April 1991.

Using UML for Modeling Complex Real-Time Systems

Bran Selic

ObjecTime Limited, 340 March Rd.
Kanata, Ontario, Canada K2K 2E4
bran@objectime.com

Abstract. Real-time software systems encountered in telecommunications, aerospace, and defense often tend to be very large and extremely complex. It is crucial in such systems that the software has a well-defined architecture. This not only facilitates construction of the initial system, it also simplifies system evolution. We describe a set of modeling constructs that facilitate the specification of complex software architectures for real-time systems. These constructs are derived from field-proven concepts originally defined in the ROOM modeling language. Furthermore, we show how they can be represented using the industry-standard Unified Modeling Language (UML) by using the powerful extensibility mechanisms of UML.

1 Introduction

Perhaps the only characteristic common to all real-time software systems is *timeliness*; that is, the requirement to respond correctly to inputs within acceptable time intervals. Beyond that, the term "real-time" covers a surprisingly diverse spectrum of systems, ranging from purely time-driven to purely event-driven systems, and from soft real-time systems to hard real-time systems. Each of these different categories of systems has highly specialized idioms, proven design patterns, and modeling styles.

We focus on a major subset of real-time systems that are characterized as complex, event-driven, and, possibly distributed. Complexity implies not only magnitude but also significant diversity. Such systems are most frequently encountered in telecommunications, aerospace, defense, and automatic control applications. The effort required to design and realize these systems typically involves large development teams. Because of the high initial development cost, when major new requirements are identified for these systems, their software tends to be modified rather than rewritten.

Under such circumstances an overriding concern is the *architecture* of the software. This refers to the essential structural and behavioral framework on which all other aspects of the system depend. This is the software equivalent of the load-bearing frames in buildings – any changes to this foundation necessitates complex and costly changes to substantial parts of the system. A well-designed architecture not only simplifies construction of the initial system, but more importantly, it promotes evolution.

To facilitate the design of good architectures, it is extremely useful to capture the proven architectural design patterns of the domain as first-class modeling constructs. As our primary source for this we have selected the Real-time Object-Oriented Modeling Language (ROOM) [1]. ROOM is an architectural definition language developed specifically for complex real-time software systems. Its architectural modeling constructs have been in use for over a decade and have proven their effectiveness in hundreds of different large-scale industrial projects.

We have chosen to represent these constructs using the industry-standard Unified Modeling Language (UML) [2] [3] to obtain the benefits of a popular and widely-supported notation. UML has proven very well suited to this purpose since it has built-in extensibility mechanisms that allow domain-specific extensions [4]. With these mechanisms it was possible to represent the necessary constructs relying exclusively on standard UML semantics.

In effect, the modeling constructs described in this document represent a type of library of applied UML concepts intended primarily for use in modeling the architectures of complex real-time systems. They can be used in combination with the more basic UML modeling concepts and diagrams to provide a powerful and comprehensive modeling facility.

2 Modeling Structure

The *structure* of a system identifies the major components of that system and the relationships between them (communication relationships, containment relationships, etc.). For our purposes, we define three principal constructs for modeling structure:
- capsules
- ports
- connectors

Capsules correspond to the ROOM concept of *actors*. They are complex, physical, possibly distributed architectural objects that interact with their surroundings through one or more signal-based boundary objects called ports. A *port* is a physical part of the implementation of a capsule that mediates the interaction of the capsule with the outside world—it is an object that implements a specific interface. Each port of a capsule plays a particular role in a collaboration that the capsule has with other objects. To capture the complex semantics of these interactions, each port has an associated *protocol* that defines the valid flow of information (signals) through that port. In a sense, a protocol captures the contractual obligations that exist between capsules. Protocols are discussed in more detail later in the document. By forcing capsules to communicate solely through ports, it is possible to fully de-couple their internal implementations from any direct knowledge about the environment. This makes them highly reusable.

Connectors, which correspond to ROOM *bindings*, are abstract views of signal-based communication channels that interconnect two or more ports. The ports bound by a connection must play mutually complementary but compatible roles in a protocol. If we abstract away the ports from this picture, connectors really capture the key communication relationships between capsules. These relationships have architectural significance since they identify which capsules can affect each other through direct communication.

The functionality of simple capsules is realized directly by the state machine associated with the capsule. More complex capsules combine the state machine with an *internal* network of collaborating *sub-capsules* joined by connectors. These sub-capsules are capsules in their own right, and can themselves be decomposed into sub-capsules. This type of decomposition can be carried to whatever depth is necessary, allowing modeling of arbitrarily complex structure. The state machine (which is optional for composite capsules), the sub-capsules, and their connections network represent parts of the *implementation* of the capsule and are hidden from external observers.

2.1 Ports

Ports are objects whose purpose is to act as boundary objects for a capsule instance. They are "owned" by the capsule instance in the sense that they are created along with their capsule and destroyed when the capsule is destroyed. Each port has its identity and state that are distinct from the identity and state of their owning capsule instance (to the same extent that any part is distinct from its container).

Each port plays a specific role in some protocol. This *protocol role* defines the *type* of the port, which simp'y means that the port implements the behavior specified by that protocol role.

Because ports are on the boundary of a capsule, they may be visible both from outside the capsule and inside. When viewed from the outside, all ports present the same impenetrable object interface and cannot be differentiated except by their identity and the role that they play in their protocol. However, viewed from within the capsule, we find that ports can be either *relay ports* or *end ports*. These two differ in their internal connections—relay ports are connected to sub-capsules while end ports are connected directly to the capsule's state machine. Generally speaking, relay ports serve to selectively export the "interfaces" of internal sub-capsules while end ports are boundary objects for the state machine of a capsule. Both relay and end ports may appear on the boundary of the capsule and, as noted, are indistinguishable from the outside.

Relay ports. *Relay ports* are ports that simply pass all signals through. They provide an "opening" in the encapsulation shell of a capsule that can be used by its sub-capsules to communicate with the outside world without actually being exposed to the outside world (and vice versa). A relay port is connected, through a connector, to a sub-capsule and is normally also connected from outside to some other "peer" capsule. They receive signals coming from either side and simply relay it to the other side keeping the direction of signal flow.

Relay ports allow the direct (zero overhead) delegation of signals destined for a capsule to a sub-capsule without requiring intervention by the state machine of the capsule. Relay ports can only appear on the boundary of a capsule and, consequently, always have *public* visibility.

End Ports. To be useful, a chain of connectors attached via relay ports must ultimately terminate in an end port that is attached to a state machine. End ports are boundary objects for the state machines of capsules. They are the ultimate sources and sinks of all signals sent between capsules. To send a signal, a state machine invokes a send or call operation on one of its end ports. The signal is then relayed through the attached connector, possibly passing through one or more relay ports and connectors, until it finally strikes another end port in a different capsule. The end port has a queue to hold asynchronous messages that have been received but not yet processed by the state.

Like relay ports, end ports may appear on the boundary of a capsule with public visibility. These ports are called *public end ports*. Such ports are boundary objects of both the state machine and the containing capsule. However, end ports may also appear completely inside the capsule as part of its internal implementation structure. The state machine uses these ports to communicate with its sub-capsules or with external implementation-support layers. Internal end ports are called *protected end ports* since they have protected visibility.

End ports that are connected to supporting layers are called *service access points*. Implementation support *layers* represent run-time services, such as operating system services, that may be shared by multiple capsules and, hence, cannot be incorporated directly into any particular one of the capsules. This is used to model *run-time layering* relationships.

UML Modeling. In UML terms, a port object is modeled by the «*port*» stereotype, which is a stereotype of the UML Class concept. As noted earlier, the type of a port is defined by the protocol role played by that port. Since protocol roles are abstract classes, the actual class corresponding to this instance is one that *implements* the protocol role associated with the port. In UML the relationship between the port and the protocol role is referred to as a "realizes" *relationship*. The notation for this is a dashed line with a solid triangular arrowhead on the specification end (Figure 1). It is a form of generalization whereby the source element—the port—inherits only the behavior specification of the target—the protocol role—but not its structure.

A capsule is in a composition relationship with its ports. (This means that ports cannot exist independently of their capsule.) If the multiplicity of the target end of this relationship is greater than one, it means that multiple instances of the port exist at run time, each participating in a separate instance of the protocol. If the multiplicity is a range of values, it means that the number of ports can vary at run time and that ports can be dynamically created and destroyed (possibly subject to constraints).

Notation. In UML class diagrams, the ports of a capsule are listed in a special labeled list compartment as illustrated in Figure 2. The *ports* list compartment normally appears after the attribute and operator list compartments. This notation takes advantage of the UML feature that allows the addition of specific named compartments.

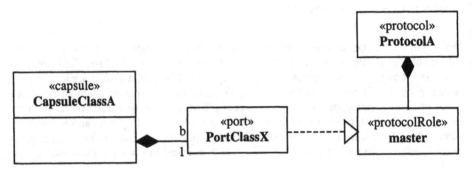

Fig. 1. The relationship between capsules, ports, protocols, and protocol roles in UML notation

All external ports (relay ports and public end ports) have public visibility while internal ports have protected visibility (e.g., port b2 in Figure 2). The protocol role (type) of a port is normally identified by a pathname since protocol role names are unique only within the scope of a given protocol. For the most frequent case of protocols involving just two parties (binary protocols), a simpler notational convention is used: a suffix tilde symbol ("~") is used to identify the conjugated protocol role (e.g., port b2) while the base role name is implicit with no special annotation (e.g., port b1). Ports with a multiplicity other than 1 have the multiplicity factor included between square brackets. For example, port b1[3] has a multiplicity factor of exactly 3 whereas a port designated by b5[0..2] has a variable number of instances not exceeding 2.

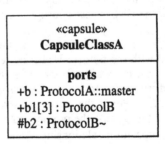

Fig. 2. Special list compartment listing all the ports attached to a capsule class in a UML class diagram

Figure 2 shows how ports are indicated in class diagrams. However, they also appear in collaboration diagrams. In these diagrams, objects are represented by the appropriate classifier roles—sub-capsules by *capsule roles* and ports by *port roles*. To reduce visual clutter, port roles are generally shown in iconified form, represented by small black or white squares (Figure 3). Public ports are represented by port role icons that straddle the boundary of the corresponding capsule. This shorthand notation allows them to be connected both from inside and outside the capsule without unnecessary crossing of lines and also identifies them clearly as boundary objects.

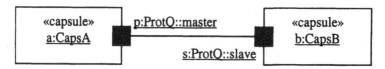

Fig. 3. Iconified notation for ports in collaboration diagrams

For the case of binary protocols, the port playing the conjugate role is indicated by a white-filled (versus black-filled) square. In that case, the protocol name and the tilde suffix are sufficient to identify the protocol role as the conjugate role; the protocol role name is redundant and can be omitted. Similarly, the use of the protocol name alone on a black square indicates the base role of the protocol. This convention makes it easy to spot when complementary protocol roles are connected.

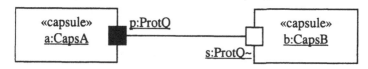

Fig. 4. Notation for the port roles of binary protocols

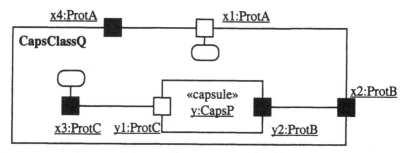

Fig. 5. Port notation in a collaboration diagram (internal capsule view)

When the decomposition of a capsule is shown, we can see the implementation inside the capsule using a UML collaboration diagram (Figure 5). In this case, an end port is distinguished by a small rectangle with rounded corners ("roundtangle") that symbolizes the state machine behind the end port. For example, port x1 is a public (conjugated) end port and port x3 is a protected end port. Ports without a roundtangle that are bound to a sub-capsule's port (e.g., port x2) or another end port are relay ports. Ports that are not connected to either a state machine roundtangle or to a sub-capsule port, such as port x4 above, are *indeterminate*.

2.2 Connectors

A connector represents a communication channel that provides the transmission facilities for supporting a particular signal-based protocol. A key feature of connectors is that they can only interconnect ports that play complementary roles in the protocol associated with the connector.

The similarity between connectors and protocols might suggest that the two concepts are equivalent. However, this is not the case, since protocols are abstract specifications of desired behavior while connectors are physical objects whose function is merely to convey signals from one port to the other. Typically, the connectors themselves are passive conduits.

UML Modeling. In UML, a connector is modeled directly by a standard UML association. This association is defined between two or more ports of the corresponding capsule classes. In a collaboration diagram, it is represented as an association role. No UML extensions are required for representing connectors.

2.3 Capsules

Capsules are the central architectural modeling construct. They represent the major architectural elements of complex real-time systems. Typically, a capsule has one or more ports through which it communicates with other capsules. It cannot have operations or public parts other than ports, which are its exclusive means of interaction with the external world. As noted, a capsule may contain one or more sub-capsules joined together by connectors. This internal structure is specified as a collaboration.

A capsule may have a state machine that can send and receive signals via the end ports of the capsule and that has control over certain elements of the internal structure such as the optional dynamic creation and destruction of sub-capsules.

The Internal Structure. A capsule's *complete* internal decomposition, that is, its implementation, is represented by a collaboration. This collaboration includes a specification of all of its ports, sub-capsules, and connectors. Like ports, the sub-capsules and connectors are strongly owned by the capsule and *cannot* exist independently of the capsule. They are automatically created when the capsule is created and automatically destroyed when their capsule is destroyed.

Some sub-capsules in the structure may not created at the same time as their containing capsule. These may be created subsequently, when and if necessary, by the state machine of the capsule.

An important feature for modeling complex dynamically created structures is the concept of so-called *plug-in* roles in a collaboration diagram. These are placeholders for sub-capsules that are filled in *dynamically* at run time. A collaboration diagram with plug-ins represents a dynamic architectural template or pattern. Plug-ins are necessary because it is not always known in advance which specific objects will play those roles. Once this information is available, the appropriate capsule instance (which is owned by some other composite capsule) can be "plugged" into such a slot and the connectors joining its ports to other sub-capsules in the collaboration automatically established. When the dynamic relationship is no longer required, the capsule is "removed" from the plug-in slot, and the connectors to it are taken down.

The Capsule State Machine. The optional state machine associated with a capsule is just another part of a capsule's implementation. However, it has certain special properties that distinguish it from the other constituents of a capsule:
- It cannot be decomposed further into sub-capsules.
- There can be at most one such state machine per capsule, although each sub-capsule can have its own state machine. Capsules that do not have state machines are simple containers for sub-capsules.
- It responds to signals arriving on an end port of a capsule and can send signals through those ports.
- It acts as a controller of all sub-capsules. It can create and destroy sub-capsules that are identified as dynamic, and it can plug in and remove external sub-capsules into the plug-in slots.

UML Modeling. In UML, a capsule is represented by the «*capsule*» stereotype of Class. The capsule is in a composition relationships with its ports, sub-capsules (except for plug-ins), and internal connectors. This means that they only exist while their capsule is instantiated. Except for public ports, all the various capsule parts, including sub-capsules and connectors, have protected visibility.

The internal structure of a capsule is modeled by a UML collaboration. Sub-capsules are indicated by appropriate sub-capsule (classifier) roles. Plug-in slots are also identified by sub-capsule roles. The type of the sub-capsule for a plug-in slot identifies the set of protocol roles (pure interface type) that must be satisfied by capsules that can be plugged into the slot.

Dynamically created sub-capsules are indicated simply by a variable multiplicity factor. Like plug-in slots, these may also be specified by a pure interface type. This means that, at instantiation time, any implementation class that supports that interface can be instantiated. This provides for genericity in structural specifications.

Notation. The class diagram notation for capsules uses standard UML notational conventions. Since it is a stereotype, the stereotype name may appear above the class name in the name compartment of the class rectangle. An optional special icon associated with the stereotype may appear in the upper right-hand corner of the name compartment (Figure 6). Sub-capsules are indicated by composition associations while plug-ins are rendered through aggregation relationships. Alternatively, the structure of a class can be shown as a collaboration as in Figure 7.

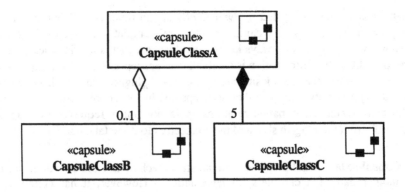

Fig. 6. Capsule notation - class diagram view

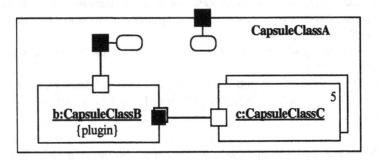

Fig. 7. Collaboration diagram view of the capsule class shown in Figure 6

3 Modeling Behavior

Behavior at the architectural level is captured using the concept of protocols.

3.1 Protocols

A protocol is a specification of desired behavior that can take place over a connector—an explicit specification of the contractual agreement between the participants in the protocol. It is pure behavior and does not specify any structural elements. A protocol consists of a set of participants, each of which plays a specific role in the protocol. Each protocol role is specified by a unique name and a set of signals that are received by that role as well as the set of signals that are sent by that role (either set could be empty). As an option, a protocol can also have a specification of the valid communication sequences; a state machine can be used to specify this. Finally, a protocol may also have a set of prototypical interaction sequences (these can be shown as sequence diagrams). These must conform to the protocol state machine, if one is defined.

Binary protocols, involving just two participants, are by far the most common and the simplest to specify. One advantage of these protocols is that only one role, called the *base role*, needs to be specified. The other, called the *conjugate*, can be derived from the base role simply by inverting the incoming and outgoing signal sets. This inversion operation is known as *conjugation*.

UML Modeling. A protocol role is modeled in UML by the *«protocolRole»* stereotype of ClassifierRole. A protocol is modeled by the *«protocol»* stereotype of Collaboration with a composition relationship to each of its protocol roles. This collaboration does not have any internal structural aspects (i.e., it has no association roles).

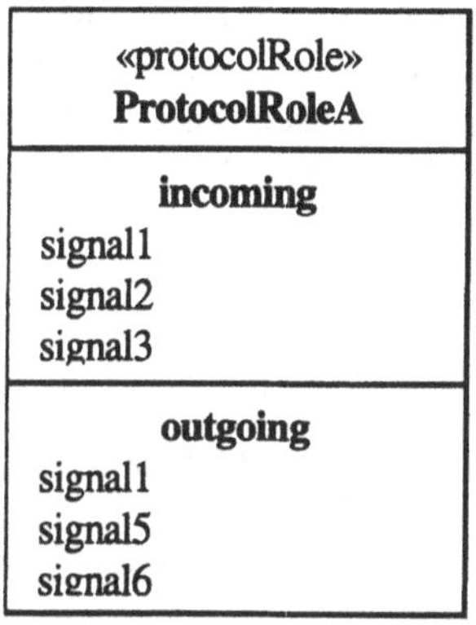

Fig. 8. Protocol role notation in class diagrams

Notation. Protocol roles can be shown using the standard notation for classifiers with an explicit stereotype label and two optional specialized list compartments for incoming and outgoing signal sets, as shown in Figure 8. The state machine and interaction diagrams of a protocol role are represented using the standard UML state machines.

4 Summary

We have defined a set of structural modeling concepts that are suitable for modeling the architectures of complex real-time systems. They were derived from similar constructs defined originally in the field-proven ROOM modeling language. The semantics and notation for representing these constructs are based on the industry-standard Unified Modeling Language. The result is a domain-specific "library" of predefined UML patterns that can be used directly as first-class modeling constructs.

An important aspect of these modeling constructs is that they have fully formal semantics. The definition of the static and dynamic semantics of the individual modeling constructs is outside the scope of this document but can be found in reference [1]. This means that models created using these constructs can be formally verified for correctness. Furthermore, they can be used to construct executable models to achieve early validation of high-level design and even analysis models. Finally, such models can be, *and have been*, used to automatically generate complete implementations. This bypasses the error-prone and lengthy step of manually converting a design model into a programming language realization.

Acknowledgements

The author would like to express his gratitude to James Rumbaugh of Rational Software whose contribution to the work described in this paper was instrumental. In addition, Grady Booch and Ivar Jacobson (also of Rational) provided invaluable and crucial feedback and suggestions on optimal ways to render these constructs in UML.

References

1. Selic, B., Gullekson, G., and Ward, P.: Real-Time Object-Oriented Modeling. John Wiley & Sons, New York, NY (1994)
2. OMG: UML Semantics. Version 1.1. The Object Management Group, Doc. no. ad/97-08-04. Framingham MA. (1997)
3. OMG: UML Notation Guide. Version 1.1. The Object Management Group, Doc. no. ad/97-08-05. Framingham MA. (1997)
4. OMG: UML Extension for Objectory Process for Software Engineering. Version 1.1. The Object Management Group, Doc. no. ad/97-08-06. Framingham MA. (1997)

Evaluating ASIC, DSP, and RISC Architectures for Embedded Applications

Marc Campbell

Northrop Grumman Corporation

Abstract. Mathematical analysis and empirical evaluation, based on solid state physical behavior, identifies a Architecture-Technology Metric for measuring the relative specialization of ASIC, DSP, and RISC architectures for embedded applications. Relationships are examined which can help predict relative future architecture performance as new generations of CMOS solid state technology become available. In particular, Performance/Watt is shown to be an Architecture-Technology Metric which can be used to calibrate ASIC, DSP, & RISC performance density potential relative to a solid state technology generations, measure & evaluate architectural changes, and project a architecture performance density roadmap.

The full paper is under IEEE copyright and can be found in the IPPS/SPDP'98 proceedings [1].

References

1. Campbell, M. E.: Evaluating ASIC, DSP, and RISC Architectures for Applications. In *Proceedings of the 12th Int. Parallel Processing Symposium and 9th Symposium on Parallel and Distributed Processing*, pages 600–603, IEEE, 1998.

Springer
and the
environment

At Springer we firmly believe that an international science publisher has a special obligation to the environment, and our corporate policies consistently reflect this conviction.

We also expect our business partners – paper mills, printers, packaging manufacturers, etc. – to commit themselves to using materials and production processes that do not harm the environment. The paper in this book is made from low- or no-chlorine pulp and is acid free, in conformance with international standards for paper permanency.

Lecture Notes in Computer Science

For information about Vols. 1–1415

please contact your bookseller or Springer-Verlag

Vol. 1416: A.P. del Pobil, J. Mira, M.Ali (Eds.), Tasks and Methods in Applied Artificial Intelligence. Vol.II. Proceedings, 1998. XXIII, 943 pages. 1998. (Subseries LNAI).

Vol. 1417: S. Yalamanchili, J. Duato (Eds.), Parallel Computer Routing and Communication. Proceedings, 1997. XII, 309 pages. 1998.

Vol. 1418: R. Mercer, E. Neufeld (Eds.), Advances in Artificial Intelligence. Proceedings, 1998. XII, 467 pages. 1998. (Subseries LNAI).

Vol. 1419: G. Vigna (Ed.), Mobile Agents and Security. XII, 257 pages. 1998.

Vol. 1420: J. Desel, M. Silva (Eds.), Application and Theory of Petri Nets 1998. Proceedings, 1998. VIII, 385 pages. 1998.

Vol. 1421: C. Kirchner, H. Kirchner (Eds.), Automated Deduction – CADE-15. Proceedings, 1998. XIV, 443 pages. 1998. (Subseries LNAI).

Vol. 1422: J. Jeuring (Ed.), Mathematics of Program Construction. Proceedings, 1998. X, 383 pages. 1998.

Vol. 1423: J.P. Buhler (Ed.), Algorithmic Number Theory. Proceedings, 1998. X, 640 pages. 1998.

Vol. 1424: L. Polkowski, A. Skowron (Eds.), Rough Sets and Current Trends in Computing. Proceedings, 1998. XIII, 626 pages. 1998. (Subseries LNAI).

Vol. 1425: D. Hutchison, R. Schäfer (Eds.), Multimedia Applications, Services and Techniques – ECMAST'98. Proceedings, 1998. XVI, 532 pages. 1998.

Vol. 1427: A.J. Hu, M.Y. Vardi (Eds.), Computer Aided Verification. Proceedings, 1998. IX, 552 pages. 1998.

Vol. 1429: F. van der Linden (Ed.), Development and Evolution of Software Architectures for Product Families. Proceedings, 1998. IX, 258 pages. 1998.

Vol. 1430: S. Trigila, A. Mullery, M. Campolargo, H. Vanderstraeten, M. Mampaey (Eds.), Intelligence in Services and Networks: Technology for Ubiquitous Telecom Services. Proceedings, 1998. XII, 550 pages. 1998.

Vol. 1431: H. Imai, Y. Zheng (Eds.), Public Key Cryptography. Proceedings, 1998. XI, 263 pages. 1998.

Vol. 1432: S. Arnborg, L. Ivansson (Eds.), Algorithm Theory – SWAT '98. Proceedings, 1998. IX, 347 pages. 1998.

Vol. 1433: V. Honavar, G. Slutzki (Eds.), Grammatical Inference. Proceedings, 1998. X, 271 pages. 1998. (Subseries LNAI).

Vol. 1434: J.-C. Heudin (Ed.), Virtual Worlds. Proceedings, 1998. XII, 412 pages. 1998. (Subseries LNAI).

Vol. 1435: M. Klusch, G. Weiß (Eds.), Cooperative Information Agents II. Proceedings, 1998. IX, 307 pages. 1998. (Subseries LNAI).

Vol. 1436: D. Wood, S. Yu (Eds.), Automata Implementation. Proceedings, 1997. VIII, 253 pages. 1998.

Vol. 1437: S. Albayrak, F.J. Garijo (Eds.), Intelligent Agents for Telecommunication Applications. Proceedings, 1998. XII, 251 pages. 1998. (Subseries LNAI).

Vol. 1438: C. Boyd, E. Dawson (Eds.), Information Security and Privacy. Proceedings, 1998. XI, 423 pages. 1998.

Vol. 1439: B. Magnusson (Ed.), System Configuration Management. Proceedings, 1998. X, 207 pages. 1998.

Vol. 1440: K.S. McCurley, C.D. Ziegler (Eds.), Advances in Cryptology 1981 – 1997. Proceedings. Approx. XII, 260 pages. 1998.

Vol. 1441: W. Wobcke, M. Pagnucco, C. Zhang (Eds.), Agents and Multi-Agent Systems. Proceedings, 1997. XII, 241 pages. 1998. (Subseries LNAI).

Vol. 1442: A. Fiat. G.J. Woeginger (Eds.), Online Algorithms. XVIII, 436 pages. 1998.

Vol. 1443: K.G. Larsen, S. Skyum, G. Winskel (Eds.), Automata, Languages and Programming. Proceedings, 1998. XVI, 932 pages. 1998.

Vol. 1444: K. Jansen, J. Rolim (Eds.), Approximation Algorithms for Combinatorial Optimization. Proceedings, 1998. VIII, 201 pages. 1998.

Vol. 1445: E. Jul (Ed.), ECOOP'98 – Object-Oriented Programming. Proceedings, 1998. XII, 635 pages. 1998.

Vol. 1446: D. Page (Ed.), Inductive Logic Programming. Proceedings, 1998. VIII, 301 pages. 1998. (Subseries LNAI).

Vol. 1447: V.W. Porto, N. Saravanan, D. Waagen, A.E. Eiben (Eds.), Evolutionary Programming VII. Proceedings, 1998. XVI, 840 pages. 1998.

Vol. 1448: M. Farach-Colton (Ed.), Combinatorial Pattern Matching. Proceedings, 1998. VIII, 251 pages. 1998.

Vol. 1449: W.-L. Hsu, M.-Y. Kao (Eds.), Computing and Combinatorics. Proceedings, 1998. XII, 372 pages. 1998.

Vol. 1450: L. Brim, F. Gruska, J. Zlatuška (Eds.), Mathematical Foundations of Computer Science 1998. Proceedings, 1998. XVII, 846 pages. 1998.

Vol. 1451: A. Amin, D. Dori, P. Pudil, H. Freeman (Eds.), Advances in Pattern Recognition. Proceedings, 1998. XXI, 1048 pages. 1998.

Vol. 1452: B.P. Goettl, H.M. Halff, C.L. Redfield, V.J. Shute (Eds.), Intelligent Tutoring Systems. Proceedings, 1998. XIX, 629 pages. 1998.

Vol. 1453: M.-L. Mugnier, M. Chein (Eds.), Conceptual Structures: Theory, Tools and Applications. Proceedings, 1998. XIII, 439 pages. (Subseries LNAI).

Vol. 1454: I. Smith (Ed.), Artificial Intelligence in Structural Engineering. XI, 497 pages. 1998. (Subseries LNAI).

Vol. 1456: A. Drogoul, M. Tambe, T. Fukuda (Eds.), Collective Robotics. Proceedings, 1998. VII, 161 pages. 1998. (Subseries LNAI).

Vol. 1457: A. Ferreira, J. Rolim, H. Simon, S.-H. Teng (Eds.), Solving Irregularly Structured Problems in Prallel. Proceedings, 1998. X, 408 pages. 1998.

Vol. 1458: V.O. Mittal, H.A. Yanco, J. Aronis, R-. Simpson (Eds.), Assistive Technology in Artificial Intelligence. X, 273 pages. 1998. (Subseries LNAI).

Vol. 1459: D.G. Feitelson, L. Rudolph (Eds.), Job Scheduling Strategies for Parallel Processing. Proceedings, 1998. VII, 257 pages. 1998.

Vol. 1460: G. Quirchmayr, E. Schweighofer, T.J.M. Bench-Capon (Eds.), Database and Expert Systems Applications. Proceedings, 1998. XVI, 905 pages. 1998.

Vol. 1461: G. Bilardi, G.F. Italiano, A. Pietracaprina, G. Pucci (Eds.), Algorithms – ESA'98. Proceedings, 1998. XII, 516 pages. 1998.

Vol. 1462: H. Krawczyk (Ed.), Advances in Cryptology - CRYPTO '98. Proceedings, 1998. XII, 519 pages. 1998.

Vol. 1463: N.E. Fuchs (Ed.), Logic Program Synthesis and Transformation. Proceedings, 1997. X, 343 pages. 1998.

Vol. 1464: H.H.S. Ip, A.W.M. Smeulders (Eds.), Multimedia Information Analysis and Retrieval. Proceedings, 1998. VIII, 264 pages. 1998.

Vol. 1465: R. Hirschfeld (Ed.), Financial Cryptography. Proceedings, 1998. VIII, 311 pages. 1998.

Vol. 1466: D. Sangiorgi, R. de Simone (Eds.), CONCUR'98: Concurrency Theory. Proceedings, 1998. XI, 657 pages. 1998.

Vol. 1467: C. Clack, K. Hammond, T. Davie (Eds.), Implementation of Functional Languages. Proceedings, 1997. X, 375 pages. 1998.

Vol. 1468: P. Husbands, J.-A. Meyer (Eds.), Evolutionary Robotics. Proceedings, 1998. VIII, 247 pages. 1998.

Vol. 1469: R. Puigjaner, N.N. Savino, B. Serra (Eds.), Computer Performance Evaluation. Proceedings, 1998. XIII, 376 pages. 1998.

Vol. 1470: D. Pritchard, J. Reeve (Eds.), Euro-Par'98. Parallel Processing. Proceedings, 1998. XXII, 1157 pages. 1998.

Vol. 1471: J. Dix, L. Moniz Pereira, T.C. Przymusinski (Eds.), Logic Programming and Knowledge Representation. Proceedings, 1997. IX, 246 pages. 1998. (Subseries LNAI).

Vol. 1473: X. Leroy, A. Ohori (Eds.), Types in Compilation. Proceedings, 1998. VIII, 299 pages. 1998.

Vol. 1474: F. Mueller, A. Bestavros (Eds.), Languages, Compilers, and Tools for Embedded Systems. Proceedings, 1998. XIV, 261 pages. 1998.

Vol. 1475: W. Litwin, T. Morzy, G. Vossen (Eds.), Advances in Databases and Information Systems. Proceedings, 1998. XIV, 369 pages. 1998.

Vol. 1476: J. Calmet, J. Plaza (Eds.), Artificial Intelligence and Symbolic Computation. Proceedings, 1998. XI, 309 pages. 1998. (Subseries LNAI).

Vol. 1477: K. Rothermel, F. Hohl (Eds.), Mobile Agents. Proceedings, 1998. VIII, 285 pages. 1998.

Vol. 1478: M. Sipper, D. Mange, A. Pérez-Uribe (Eds.), Evolvable Systems: From Biology to Hardware. Proceedings, 1998. IX, 382 pages. 1998.

Vol. 1479: J. Grundy, M. Newey (Eds.), Theorem Proving in Higher Order Logics. Proceedings, 1998. VIII, 497 pages. 1998.

Vol. 1480: F. Giunchiglia (Ed.), Artificial Intelligence: Methodology, Systems, and Applications. Proceedings, 1998. IX, 502 pages. 1998. (Subseries LNAI).

Vol. 1481: E.V. Munson, C. Nicholas, D. Wood (Eds.), Principles of Digital Document Processing. Proceedings, 1998. VII, 152 pages. 1998.

Vol. 1482: R.W. Hartenstein, A. Keevallik (Eds.), Field-Programmable Logic and Applications. Proceedings, 1998. XI, 533 pages. 1998.

Vol. 1483: T. Plagemann, V. Goebel (Eds.), Interactive Distributed Multimedia Systems and Telecommunication Services. Proceedings, 1998. XV, 326 pages. 1998.

Vol. 1484: H. Coelho (Ed.), Progress in Artificial Intelligence – IBERAMIA 98. Proceedings, 1998. XIII, 421 pages. 1998. (Subseries LNAI).

Vol. 1485: J.-J. Quisquater, Y. Deswarte, C. Meadows, D. Gollmann (Eds.), Computer Security – ESORICS 98. Proceedings, 1998. X, 377 pages. 1998.

Vol. 1486: A.P. Ravn, H. Rischel (Eds.), Formal Techniques in Real-Time and Fault-Tolerant Systems. Proceedings, 1998. VIII, 339 pages. 1998.

Vol. 1487: V. Gruhn (Ed.), Software Process Technology. Proceedings, 1998. VIII, 157 pages. 1998.

Vol. 1488: B. Smyth, P. Cunningham (Eds.), Advances in Case-Based Reasoning. Proceedings, 1998. XI, 482 pages. 1998. (Subseries LNAI).

Vol. 1490: C. Palamidessi, H. Glaser, K. Meinke (Eds.), Principles of Declarative Programming. Proceedings, 1998. XI, 497 pages. 1998.

Vol. 1493: J.P. Bowen, A. Fett, M.G. Hinchey (Eds.), ZUM '98: The Z Formal Specification Notation. Proceedings, 1998. XV, 417 pages. 1998.

Vol. 1495: T. Andreasen, H. Christiansen, H.L. Larsen (Eds.), Flexible Query Answering Systems. IX, 393 pages. 1998. (Subseries LNAI).

Vol. 1497: V. Alexandrov, J. Dongarra (Eds.), Recent Advances in Parallel Virtual Machine and Message Passing Interface. Proceedings, 1998. XII, 412 pages. 1998.

Vol. 1498: A.E. Eiben, T. Bäck, M. Schoenauer, H.-P. Schwefel (Eds.), Parallel Problem Solving from Nature – PPSN V. Proceedings, 1998. XXIII, 1041 pages. 1998.

Vol. 1499: S. Kutten (Ed.), Distributed Computing. Proceedings, 1998. XII, 419 pages. 1998.

Vol. 1501: M.M. Richter, C.H. Smith, R. Wiehagen, T. Zeugmann (Eds.), Algorithmic Learning Theory. Proceedings, 1998. XI, 439 pages. 1998. (Subseries LNAI).

Vol. 1503: G. Levi (Ed.), Static Analysis. Proceedings, 1998. IX, 383 pages. 1998.

Vol. 1504: O. Herzog, A. Günter (Eds.), KI-98: Advances in Artificial Intelligence. Proceedings, 1998. XI, 355 pages. 1998. (Subseries LNAI).

Vol. 1510: J.M. Żytkow, M. Quafafou (Eds.), Principles of Data Mining and Knowledge Discovery. Proceedings, 1998. XI, 482 pages. 1998. (Subseries LNAI).